Environmental Crime and its Victims

Perspectives within Green Criminology

Edited by

TOINE SPAPENS
Tilburg University, The Netherlands

ROB WHITE
University of Tasmania, Australia

MARIEKE KLUIN
Delft University of Technology, The Netherlands

Routledge
Taylor & Francis Group
LONDON AND NEW YORK

First published 2014 by Ashgate Publishing

Published 2016 by Routledge
2 Park Square, Milton Park, Abingdon, Oxfordshire OX14 4RN
711 Third Avenue, New York, NY 10017, USA

First issued in paperback 2016

Routledge is an imprint of the Taylor & Francis Group, an informa business

British Library Cataloguing in Publication Data
A catalogue record for this book is available from the British Library.

The Library of Congress has cataloged the printed edition as follows:
Spapens, A. C., author.
Environmental crime and its victims : perspectives within green criminology / by Toine Spapens, Rob White, and Marieke Kluin.
pages cm
Includes bibliographical references and index.
ISBN 978-1-4724-2278-1 (hardback : alk. paper)
1. Offenses against the environment. 2. Pollution – Law and legislation. 3. Environmental law, International. I. White, R. D. (Robert Douglas), 1956– author. II. Kluin, Marieke, author. III. Title.

K5278.S63 2014
364.1′45–dc23

2014008241

ISBN 13: 978-1-138-63775-7 (pbk)
ISBN 13: 978-1-4724-2278-1 (hbk)

ENVIRONMENTAL CRIME AND ITS VICTIMS

This book contains thought-provoking perspectives drawn from theory and practice on a persisting global problem: environmental crime. In addition to important insights on 'villains and victims', it provides new ideas on what should be considered an environmental crime as well as practical experiences in combatting it. Its multiple perspectives and innovative research questions make it a valuable resource for anyone interested in the topic, not just criminologists.

Christiane Gerstetter, Ecologic Institute, Germany and
EFFACE research project (www.efface.eu)

A pioneering work in the new and rapidly developing field of 'green' criminology, this book presents and explores in a well-structured, succinct and lucid manner various factors which set green crime apart from the conventional areas of criminal law and criminology. It explores the many challenges and factors not prevalent in traditional criminal law, and will be of value not only to academic criminal lawyers and criminologists but also administrators and members of the police force; including those involved in the enforcement of transnational environmental crime.

Jan Glazewski, Institute of Marine & Environmental Law,
University of Cape Town, South Africa

This book provides a state-of-the-art overview of current issues of the perpetration and victimization of environmental crime in a globalized world. From pollution, e-waste, emission fraud to wildlife crime, the book grasps the many manifestations, assesses the harms, and gives direction for the policing and prevention of environmental crime. This book takes green criminology to the next level.

Wim Huisman, VU University Amsterdam, The Netherlands

GREEN CRIMINOLOGY

Series Editors:

Michael J. Lynch, *University of South Florida, USA*
Paul B. Stretesky, *University of Colorado, Denver, USA*

Now two decades old, green criminology – the study of environmental harm, crime, law, regulation, victimization, and justice – has increasing relevance to contemporary problems at local, national, and international levels. This series comes at a time when societies and governments worldwide seek new ways to alleviate and deal with the consequences of various environmental harms as they relate to humans, non-human animals, plant species, and the ecosystem and its components. Green criminology offers a unique theoretical perspective on how human behavior causes and exacerbates environmental conditions that threaten the planet's viability. Volumes in the series will consider such topics and controversies as corporate environmental crime, the complicity of international financial institutions, state-sponsored environmental destruction, and the role of non-governmental organizations in addressing environmental harms. Titles will also examine the intersections between green criminology and other branches of criminology and other areas of law, such as human rights and national security. The series will be international in scope, investigating environmental crime in specific countries as well as comparatively and globally. In sum, by bringing together a diverse body of research on all aspects of this subject, the series will make a significant contribution to our understanding of the dynamics between the natural world and the quite imperfect human world, and will set the stage for the future study in this growing area of concern.

Other titles in this series:

Exploring Green Criminology
Toward a Green Criminological Revolution
Michael J. Lynch and Paul B. Stretesky

Animal Harm
Perspectives on Why People Harm and Kill Animals
Angus Nurse

Eco-global Crimes
Contemporary Problems and Future Challenges
Edited by Rune Ellefsen, Ragnhild Sollund and Guri Larsen

Contents

List of Figures

List of Tables

List of Contributors

Lieselot Bisschop is a part-time post-doctoral researcher in the Governing and Policing Security research group at Ghent University,[1] and Assistant Professor at the Department of Law, Police Science and Criminal Justice Administration at John Jay College of Criminal Justice, The City University of New York. Her areas of interest and expertise include environmental crime, organizational crime and environmental governance. She is also an assistant editor of the *European Journal of Policing Studies*.

Mary Clifford received her PhD in Justice Studies from Arizona State University and organized and edited *Environmental Crime: Law, Policy, and Social Responsibility* (1998) and *Environmental Crime* (2012) with Terry D. Edwards. Her research areas include environmental crime, anti-racism education, gender and sexual violence, and the criminalization process. She is currently a Full Professor in the Department of Criminal Justice Studies at St. Cloud State University, Minnesota.

Matthew Crow is Associate Professor and Chair of the Department of Criminal Justice at the University of West Florida. He earned his PhD from the College of Criminology and Criminal Justice at Florida State University. His research on criminal sentencing, police use of force, criminal justice education, offender re-entry, and fish and wildlife conservation policing has appeared in leading journals, including *Deviant Behavior*, *American Journal of Criminal Justice*, *Criminal Justice Review*, *Criminal Justice Policy Review*, *Journal of Criminal Justice*, *Journal of Criminal Justice Education*, *Organization and Environment*, *Police Quarterly*, *Policing* and *Women and Criminal Justice*. He recently co-edited (with John Ortiz Smykla) *Offender Reentry: Rethinking Criminology and Criminal Justice* (2014).

Matthew Hall graduated with a PhD from the University of Sheffield in 2007 having previously gained an MA in International Criminology. He is now Professor of Law and Criminal Justice at the University of Lincoln. His main research focus is on victimization, and in particular victims of crime within the criminal justice system. He is also interested in environmental law, policy making and criminal law.

Ellen Jagtman is Senior Assistant Professor in Safety Science at Delft University of Technology, where she earned a degree in Systems Engineering and Policy analysis and a PhD in Safety Sciences. Her work combines understanding safety implications and implementation issues in various transport domains and the public domain. She has supervised PhD students working on risk control in railways, on quantitative risk modelling for fire safety in large buildings, and on the relationship between rule violation, compliance, corporate crime and safety in the chemical industry. She served as project leader of Delft University of Technology's evaluation of the large-scale trials of citizens' warning cell broadcasts in the Netherlands. Since 2010 she has led Delft University of Technology's

1 www.gaps-ugent.be.

contribution to drawing up alarm text messages for the new Dutch emergency warning service NL-Alert.

Janine Janssen is a cultural anthropologist and criminologist with a special interest in the intersection between the study of multicultural society and green criminology. In her work, she has paid attention to cultural influences on ideas regarding the welfare and abuse of animals and the problematization of migrating processes of animals ('invasive exotics') by using vocabulary from the research and debate on migration and integration of humans towards and in Western societies. She is Head of Research of the Dutch police force's National Centre of Expertise for Honour-related Violence, and is also associated with the Department of Criminal Law and Criminology at Vrije Universiteit Amsterdam.

Melissa Jarrell is an Associate Professor of Criminal Justice at Texas A&M University–Corpus Christi. Her research interests include green criminology, environmental justice, environmental victimization, and environmental crime and the media. She has published articles in journals such as *Crime, Law and Social Change*, *Environmental Justice*, *Environmental Politics* and *Review of Policy Research*. She works closely with Citizens for Environmental Justice, a local grassroots organization founded in 2000 to address issues of poverty, pollution and injustice in Corpus Christi, Texas.

Marieke Kluin is a PhD Researcher in the Safety and Security Science Group of the Values, Technology and Innovation Department at Delft University of Technology. Her doctoral research focuses on the possible relationship between rule violation, compliance, corporate crime and safety in the Dutch chemical industry. The aim of this research is to explain compliance and rule violation in the framework of the interaction between field-level inspectors and regulatees, and to focus on the enforcement of regulation by field-level inspectors from three different inspectorates. The research includes a multi-case study analysing 15 Seveso corporations over a period of ten years, participant observations of Seveso inspections and a survey of chemical corporation employees. She has published the chapter 'Environmental Regulation in Chemical Corporations: Preliminary Results of a Case Study' in *Emerging Issues in Green Criminology: Exploring Power, Justice and Harm* (edited by D. Westerhuis, R. Walters and T. Wyatt, 2013) and co-authored (with Wim Huisman) the chapter 'Regulering van Veiligheid bij Bedrijven' in *Veiligheid: Veiligheid en Veiligheidsbeleid in Nederland* (edited by E.R. Muller, 2012). She was one of the convenors of the conference 'Environmental Crime and its Victims' (2012).

Ronald Kramer is Professor of Sociology and Director of the Criminal Justice Program at Western Michigan University in Kalamazoo, Michigan. His research specialty is state and corporate crime. His books include (with David Kauzlarich and Raymond Michalowski) *Crimes of the American Nuclear State: At Home and Abroad* (2010), (with Raymond Michalowski) *State-Corporate Crime: Wrongdoing at the Intersection of Business and Government* (2006) and (co-edited with William Chambliss and Raymond Michalowski) *State Crime in the Global Age* (2010). He has been honoured with the Teaching Excellence Award from Western Michigan University and with the Lifetime Achievement Award from the Division of Critical Criminology of the American Society of Criminology.

Michael Long is a Senior Lecturer in Social Sciences in the Department of Social Sciences and Languages at Northumbria University, Newcastle upon Tyne. His research focuses on green criminology, political economy and state-corporate crime. Some of his recent articles have appeared in *British Journal of Criminology*, *Social Psychology Quarterly*, *Journal of Agricultural and Environmental Ethics* and *Organization and Environment*, and he co-authored (with Paul Stretesky and Michael Lynch) *The Treadmill of Crime: Political Economy and Green Criminology* (2013).

Michael Lynch is Professor of Criminology and an associated faculty member in the Patel School of Global Sustainability at the University of South Florida. His research focuses on green criminology, radical criminology, racial bias in the criminal justice system, and corporate crime and its control. He recently co-authored (with Paul Stretesky and Michael Long) *The Treadmill of Crime: Political Economy and Green Criminology* (2013).

Peter Martin is Senior Research Associate in the Centre for Crime and Justice at Queensland University of Technology. He has published widely in the fields of rural sociology and agricultural science. His recent work focuses on carbon fraud and trading in greenhouse emissions.

Tara O'Connor Shelley is an Associate Professor at the Center for the Study of Crime and Justice and a faculty affiliate at the Center for Disaster and Risk Analysis in the Department of Sociology at Colorado State University. Her research focuses on issues that pertain to justice, law and society in the areas of: environmental crime and regulation; environmental justice; public opinion, crime and the environment, and police and society. She has a strong background as a mixed methods researcher with skills in qualitative and quantitative research. She is currently Co-Principal on several projects related to environmental victimization, including 'Understanding the Nature of Citizen Complaints in the Case of Oil and Gas Exploration in Colorado', 'Examining the Nature and Extent of Oil and Gas Inspections, Spills and Violations in Colorado' and 'Environmental Crime, Environmental Policy and Hydraulic Fracturing: The Role of Risk Perception and Exposure on Public Attitudes'. She has recently published articles in *Deviant Behavior*, *Social Psychological Quarterly* and *Organization and Environment*.

Joshua Ozymy is Associate Professor and Program Coordinator of Political Science at Texas A&M University–Corpus Christi. His environmental research focuses on how to reduce environmental harms through better institutional design. His work in this area has appeared in journals such as *Global Environmental Politics*, *Environmental Politics*, *Local Environment* and *Review of Policy Research*.

Antony Pemberton is a social scientist serving as Associate Professor and Director of Studies at the International Victimology Institute Tilburg. His research is a wide-ranging attempt to gain further insight into victimological perspectives on justice, and in pursuing it he draws on a variety of source disciplines, including political science, social and clinical psychology, criminology, legal philosophy and criminal law. Much of his work has a strong theoretical emphasis, but includes empirical studies as well, while maintaining a clear link with victim-oriented policy and other practical applications.

Gary Potter is Senior Lecturer in Criminology at London South Bank University. He teaches – and wrote – one of the longest-established undergraduate courses in Green Criminology in the UK and writes for the website of the International Green Criminology Working Group.[2] Even when not writing about criminological aspects of environmental problems (or environmental aspects of criminological problems) his research has a green angle, and he has published two books on cannabis cultivation: *Weed, Need and Greed: A Study of Domestic Cannabis Cultivation* (2010) and (co-edited with Tom Decorte and Martin Bouchard) *World Wide Weed: Global Trends in Cannabis Cultivation and its Control* (2011).

Toine Spapens is Professor of Environmental Crime at the Police Academy of the Netherlands and Full Professor of Criminology at Tilburg University, the Netherlands, having previously worked at an institute for policy research in the Netherlands. He specializes in research on organized crime and international police and judicial co-operation. His empirical studies include the trafficking in illicit firearms, large-scale cannabis cultivation in the Netherlands and the fight against organized crime in Amsterdam's Red Light District. His PhD thesis focused on the interaction between organized crime groups and law enforcement in ecstasy production and trafficking in the Netherlands.

Davyth Stewart is a Criminal Intelligence Officer with the Environmental Crime Security Sub-Directorate of the International Criminal Police Organization (Interpol), where he is the co-ordinator of the unit addressing illegal exploitation of natural resources, and the manager of Project LEAF (Law Enforcement Assistance for Forests), a forests and climate initiative to combat illegal logging and organized forest crime led by Interpol and the United Nations Environment Programme. He has served as a lawyer for governments, the private sector and NGOs, including working as the senior lawyer at the New South Wales Crime Commission in Sydney, Australia and the Serious Organised Crime Agency in London and Northern Ireland, investigating organized crime and tracing criminal proceeds. He has worked on environmental crime issues through various UN conventions and international environmental forums, including UN-REDD, UNFCCC and CITES. He has worked in Australia, the United Kingdom, Africa and France.

Paul Stretesky is a Professor of Criminology in the Department of Social Sciences and Languages at Northumbria University, Newcastle upon Tyne. His recent books include (with Michael Lynch) *Exploring Green Criminology: Toward a Green Criminological Revolution* (2014), (with Michael Long and Michael Lynch) *The Treadmill of Crime: Political Economy and Green Criminology* (2013), (with Ronald Burns and Michael Lynch) *Environmental Crime, Law and Justice* (2008), (with Mark Pogrebin and N. Prabha Unnithan) *Guns, Violence, and Criminal Behavior: The Offender's Perspective* (2009) and (with Michael Lynch) *Radical and Marxist Criminology* (2011). His research focuses on issues of the political economy of environmental crime and deviance. He is also engaged in community-based research for the non-profit organization Families of Homicide Victims and Missing Persons, Inc.

Coen van Gulijk is Assistant Professor with the Safety Science Group in the faculty of Technology, Policy and Management at Delft University of Technology and visiting assistant

2 www.greencriminology.org.

professor at the Safety Science Group at the University of Antwerp. He currently focuses on prevention of accidents in the chemical industry and the efficiency of security measures. The European Union and Dutch governmental organizations mainly fund his research on topics such as the future of fire brigades in the Netherlands, victims of catastrophes, patient safety and policy analyses related to safety and risk. He is the Secretary General of the European Safety and Reliability Association,[3] and also chairs the PGS 32 workgroup on the storage of explosives for civil use.[4]

Reece Walters is Professor of Criminology in the Centre for Crime and Justice Research and Assistant Dean Research in the Faculty of Law at Queensland University of Technology, Brisbane, Australia. He has published widely on crimes of the powerful and crimes against the environment. His current research focuses on crimes against the essentials of life, namely food, air and water. He is the author of Eco-Crime and Genetically Modified Food (2011) and is editor of a series on Critical Criminological Perspectives.

Rob White is Professor of Criminology at the University of Tasmania, Sandy Bay, Australia. He has written widely in the areas of criminology and youth studies, and has a particular interest in issues related to environmental harm, ecological justice and green criminology. His recent books include *Transnational Environmental Crime: Toward an Eco-global Criminology* (2011), *Climate Change from a Criminological Perspective* (2012) and *Environmental Harm: An Eco-justice Perspective* (2013), and he is also the author of *Crimes Against Nature* (2008).

Tanya Wyatt is a Senior Lecturer in Criminology at Northumbria University, Newcastle upon Tyne. Her research focuses on green crimes, such as wildlife trafficking and animal welfare, and these crimes' intersection with organized crime and terrorism. She is Principal Investigator for the UK Economic and Social Research Council-funded Green Criminology Research Seminar Series. Her latest book is *Wildlife Trafficking: A Deconstruction of the Crime, the Victims and the Offenders* (2013).

3 www.esrahomepage.org.
4 www.publicatiereeksgevaarlijkestoffen.nl.

Preface and Acknowledgements

This book is the result of the international conference 'Environmental Crime and its Victims' that took place on 17 and 18 September 2012 in Delft, the Netherlands. It was a joint effort by the Police Academy of the Netherlands, the University of Tasmania and Delft University of Technology.

The focus of this book is on environmental harms, crimes and their victims. One of the reasons why governments, the enforcement community and the public have trouble in finding the proper responses is the fact that such harms and crimes do not always produce immediately visible 'victims'. The chapters in this volume contribute to the discussion of victimization and how to deal with environmental harms and crimes from the perspectives of green criminology, sociology, law enforcement, community wellbeing, environmental activism and victimology.

As editors, we wish to thank the Police Academy of the Netherlands for its financial support which made the conference and the book possible, and Hinke Andriessen, Halise Aydin and Annelies Vanlandschoot for all their organizational support. We would also like to thank Ashgate Publishing and the editors of the Green Criminology Series, Michael J. Lynch and Paul B. Stretesky, for enthusiastically agreeing to publish this volume in the series.

Finally, it goes without saying that we are in particular very grateful towards the participants of the conference from so many countries: the United States, Australia, Belgium, the United Kingdom, Hungary, Spain, France and, of course, the Netherlands.

Toine Spapens
Rob White
Marieke Kluin

Introduction

Toine Spapens and Rob White

Environmental crime is a relatively new phenomenon. This is not because pollution that causes harm to humans, fauna and ecosystems is new, to take one example, but because we did not start to view this behaviour as criminal until after the Second World War. Of course, acts that inflict environmental damage involving the immediate death of humans or that harm economic interests were punishable before environmental laws came into effect. In the Netherlands, for example, the Water Control Boards already prohibited the dumping of waste oil into surface waters at the end of the nineteenth century because the contaminated water caused severe problems for farmers.

Today, a large and increasing number of rules and regulations encompass a broad range of behaviour in relation to the environment (Carrabine et al. 2009). The first main category of these laws relate to the pollution of the air, water and land (see, for instance, Walters 2007). Examples include dumping waste or blending it with other goods, and importing and using illicit pesticides. The second main category concerns illegal acts that cause direct harm to flora and fauna, such as illegal deforestation and the poaching of and trading in protected wildlife (see, for example, Boekhout van Solinge, 2008). Apart from national environmental laws, recent decades have also seen the development of an elaborate international legal framework to fight transnational environmental crime. Examples include the Convention on International Trade in Endangered Species of Wild Fauna and Flora (CITES), the International Convention for the Prevention of Pollution from Ships (MARPOL) and the Basel Convention on the Control of Transboundary Movements of Hazardous Wastes and Their Disposal. In addition, entities such as the European Union have drafted regulations for the prevention of environmental harm and pollution, such as the European Waste Shipment Regulation (EWSR). For many green criminologists, however, the concept of environmental crime is still too narrow because it does not include equally harmful acts to the environment that have not (yet) been criminalized. Instead, they favour the concept of environmental harm, which includes behaviour contributing to global warming and loss of biodiversity, as well as legal deforestation and extensive fishing outside territorial waters (see, for example, White 2012).

Environmental crimes do not always produce an immediate consequence, and the harm may be diffused. The complexity of victimization – in terms of time, space, impact and who or what is victimized – is one of the reasons why governments and the enforcement community have trouble in establishing suitable and effective responses.

Environmental crime and environmental harm covers a wide range of behaviour, and therefore a broad variety of 'villains and victims'. From a victimological point of view, as Antony Pemberton explains in Chapter 4, the perpetrators and victims of the same crime can overlap or be impossible to distinguish. Furthermore, victims may sometimes not be aware that they have been harmed. This is because the consequences may not become clear until after a longer period has elapsed, they may not attribute the harm to the environment in which they live, or they may not see the harmful behaviour as wrongdoing. Finally, humans may be only the secondary (or even tertiary) victims of environmental crime. The first casualty is often the environment itself, along with non-human animals living in that environment.

Several contributors to this book (for example, Ronald Kramer in Chapter 2, Mary Clifford in Chapter 3, Marieke Kluin and Ellen Jagtman in Chapter 9, and Melissa Jarrell and Joshua Ozymy in Chapter 16) emphasize the fact that the perpetrators of environmental crime are frequently large corporations, sometimes operating under the protection of the state. Environmental crimes and harms often result from negligence rather than outright malicious behaviour. The perpetrators are in many cases powerful economic actors with considerable political influence, and this may even allow them to dispute successfully whether their behaviour is criminal at all. Clearly, in order to understand and study environmental crimes and harm, we must take political and economic factors, and their historical development and resulting power relations, into account. According to some of the contributors (for example, Michael Long, Paul Stretesky and Michael Lynch in Chapter 16), attaining social and ecological justice requires a radical reordering of the economic and political systems at the heart of the global capitalist system.

The lack of easily identifiable victims and the difficulty in establishing cause and effect in terms of harm also influences responses to environmental crimes and harm. Law enforcement officers, for example, experience both difficulties in 'finding the victims' and in delivering proof. The same problem applies to communities when the members want to take action against corporations causing pollution, for example.

The book is divided into three parts. Part I, 'Examining the Crime and the Victimization Problem', explores how environmental crime and harm, and environmental victimization, have been theorized and addressed within green criminology.

In Chapter 1, Gary Potter analyses the relationship between environmental harm and the different types of crime associated with it. The starting point is a typology developed by Carrabine et al. (2009) which distinguishes primary and secondary green crimes. Primary crimes cover direct damage and destruction caused to environment and species, such as pollution, deforestation and animal abuse. Secondary or 'symbiotic' environmental crimes are those illegal activities arising out of illegal or negligent government or corporate activity, which can even include the flouting of rules set by such bodies themselves to regulate environmentally sensitive activities (Carrabine et al. 2009, p. 318). Potter argues that this second category should be expanded to also include corporate crimes relating to the avoidance or evasion of environmental regulation; the trafficking of products subject to environmental legislation; repression of oppositional groups and crimes of protest in response to enforcement of environmental protection laws.

In Chapter 2, Ronald Kramer analyses global warming as state-corporate criminality. State-corporate crime refers to serious social harms that result from the interaction of political organizations (governments) and economic ones (corporations). The failure to respond adequately, both by individual states and the international political community, defines global warming as a 'crime of omission'. Although there is no legal framework that criminalizes global warming and the environmental and social harms flowing from it, Kramer argues that it is a 'blameworthy harm' and should therefore be studied from a criminological perspective.

In Chapter 3, Mary Clifford also draws attention to the privileged position of corporations, which she too sees as an obstacle to effective environmental protection. She describes how historical developments in the USA led to the equal treatment of people and corporations, bestowing on them equal rights to be protected by the state. However, sanctions do not impact on corporations in the same way as individuals who commit crimes, because a corporation is not a tangible person. She compares the question of environmental harm to the problem of racism and oppression, and encourages further comparative study of how oppressive systems work.

The next three chapters address the question of victimization and redress.

In Chapter 4, Antony Pemberton notes that cases of environmental victimization regularly differ from the 'default' situations studied in victimology in which there is only one perpetrator, victim and event (or a small number of each of these), a clear breach of a criminal law, and readily ascertainable and immediate harm of a physical, psychological and/or financial nature. This raises questions about how the criminal justice system should deal with issues pertaining to environmental victimization.

Chapter 5 by Rob White discusses the importance of and need for specialized expertise in adjudicating matters of environmental crime. For effective problem-solving in relation to environmental crime and victimization, courts need to have the expertise to sift through complex evidence and to apply a wide range of sanctions and remedies.

As demonstrated in Chapter 6 by Matthew Hall, responses by the criminal justice system can take a number of different routes. Issues of recognition, restitution and redress can involve civil and criminal proceedings, as well as incorporating administrative and restorative justice types of approaches.

Part II, 'Characteristics of Different Types of Environmental Crime', provides detailed descriptions of particular types of offences and offenders.

It begins with Chapter 7 by Reece Walters and Peter Martin, which examines the emergence of carbon trading schemes. The trade in 'dirty air' is critically assessed from the viewpoint of how the contemporary politics of pollution serves to, in effect, legitimize carbon crime.

Chapter 8 by Coen van Gulijk examines the recent history of oil spills. By considering data over recent periods, he demonstrates the frequency and inevitability of such events, and the persistent nature of the problem. This has major implications for regulation and prevention strategies.

The nature and dynamics of regulation are examined closely in Chapter 9 by Marieke Kluin and Ellen Jagtman, which reports on a study of factories operating in the Dutch chemical industry and how regulators perform their tasks in relation to firms of specific sizes with variable compliance records, thus providing a systematic evaluation of the regulatory process in relation to polluting industries.

In Chapter 10, Lieselot Bisschop then discusses the nature and dynamics of the illegal trade in electronic waste. This chapter explores the harm related to e-waste, the scale of the problem and issues relating to the social organization of e-waste transportation and its regulation.

Chapter 11 by Matthew Crow, Tara O'Connor Shelley and Paul Stretesky shifts the attention from pollution offences to wildlife crime. This chapter provides a case study of wildlife crime in Florida, and provides descriptions of the main characteristics of offenders engaged in this particular kind of environmental crime.

Part II concludes with Chapter 12 by Janine Janssen, which considers how the debates about animal rights with regard to the ritual slaughter of animals for food have been framed in the Netherlands. She observes that the public discourse on this issue has frequently incorporated the explicit stigmatization of particular religious groups in ways that impede adequate deliberation of complex issues.

Part III, 'Combating Environmental Crime', considers responses to environmental crime and its victims. Its first two chapters address this question from a law enforcement perspective.

In Chapter 13, Toine Spapens examines the efforts of the Dutch police and the problems they experience in tackling environmental crime in the Netherlands. He explores three issues in particular that add to the complexities of environmental enforcement responses:

the lack of 'visible' victims, the relationship between administrative and law enforcement authorities, and the fact that environmental crimes are often cross-border crimes.

Addressing environmental law enforcement at the international level, in Chapter 14, Davyth Stewart describes the initiatives within Interpol to combat illegal logging. Of particular interest is the recent launch of Project LEAF (Law Enforcement Assistance for Forests) in order to enhance the capacities of member states in dealing with this type of environmental crime.

In Chapter 15, Melissa Jarrell and Joshua Ozymy give a practical example of how the local environmental justice movement developed in Corpus Christi, Texas, and describe the role of academics in empowering the community. This chapter once again underlines the difficulties victims experience in proving the causality between environmental problems and health effects, as well as the immense power gap between communities and large-scale local industries. It also demonstrates the importance of community-based and community-led social action on environmental issues.

The concluding chapters focus on the effects of two specific environmental efforts.

Chapter 16 by Michael Long, Paul Stretesky and Michael Lynch analyses the effects of state enforcement mechanisms on the overall trend in toxic releases in the USA. Through reference to the Treadmill of Production theory, they compare figures on carbon dioxide releases with information about enforcement activities. They argue that the latter have had little causal effect on toxic emissions, and that environmental regulation under existing systems of production is ultimately constrained by the imperatives of that system to expand.

Finally, Chapter 17 by Tanya Wyatt studies the extent to which the International Consortium on Combating Wildlife Crime (ICCWC) is attaining its goal of raising awareness of wildlife crime and making the problem a mainstream one within national law enforcement agencies. As part of this study, she undertook an analysis of international media as well as interviewing representatives of Interpol. She found that the ICCWC appears to be increasing awareness of wildlife crime issues within the United Nations, and that media coverage likewise seems to be increasing.

The chapters in this volume provide a diverse and provocative array of arguments, critiques and recommendations pertaining to environmental crime and its victims. Our hope is that they will stimulate further research in this area, and that they will contribute substantively to both the theoretical understanding of the issues and practical measures to address environmental crime.

References

Boekhout van Solinge, T., 2008. 'Eco-crime: the Tropical Timber Trade', in *Organized Crime: Culture, Markets and Policies*, edited by D. Siegel and H. Nelen. New York: Springer, 97–112.

Carrabine, E., Cox, P., Lee, M., Plummer, K. and South, N. 2009. *Criminology: A Sociological Introduction* (2nd edn). Oxford: Routledge.

Walters, R., 2007. 'Crime, Regulation and Radioactive Waste in the United Kingdom', in *Issues in Green Criminology: Confronting Harms against Environments, Humanity and Other Animals*, edited by P. Beirne and N. South. Portland, OR: Willan Publishing, 186–205.

White, R., 2012. 'The Foundations of Eco-global Criminology', in *Eco-global Crimes*, edited by R. Ellefsen, R. Sollund and G. Larsen. Farnham: Ashgate, 15–31.

PART I
Examining the Crime and the Victimization Problem

Chapter 1
The Criminogenic Effects of Environmental Harm: Bringing a 'Green' Perspective to Mainstream Criminology

Gary Potter

Introduction: Environmental Harm as Social Harm

Environmental problems, in particular those caused by human economic activity, are among the defining issues of the twenty-first century. For many people, damage to the environment is seen as problematic in its own right: nature has intrinsic value, and harm to nature is something to care about purely because of this. Increasingly, however, environmental harm is recognized not just as a problem for the natural world, but as a major contributory factor in a broad array of social problems: environmental harm often causes, exacerbates or otherwise contributes to social harm. From a social science perspective, it becomes clear that the social world cannot be understood in separation from the natural world.

Current sociological thinking recognizes this: human-caused environmental damage is seen as one of the major contributors to contemporary 'risk society' (Giddens 1991; Beck 1992). The concept of the risk society recognizes the way that late-modern societies are characterized by the distribution of and exposure to the 'manufactured risks' associated with industrial and post-industrial economic activity. In relation to environmental harm, we can point to the way industrial society has contributed to (among other things): the production of greenhouse gases, ozone-depleting substances and other air-, water- and land-borne pollutants; the acidification of oceans; the depletion (locally and globally) of natural resources including old-growth forests, mineral deposits, fish stocks and fresh water; the use of radioactive materials for energy production or warfare; the production and distribution of carcinogenic and other harmful chemicals; the destruction of natural habitats, and the depletion of biodiversity. Related manufactured risks include: global warming; damage to the ozone layer; increased incidences of cancers, birth defects and other health problems; desertification of once-fertile land and sea areas; food, water and other resource shortages, and unpredictable changes to local and global eco-systems and weather patterns (climate change). Specific tangible harms range from the physical (including death, injury and illness; damage to and loss of property) through the economic (loss of production and economic opportunities; increased competition for resources; costs of physical consequences of environmental victimization) to the cultural (loss of traditional ways of life; impacts of migration and urbanization). Such harms overlap with broader contemporary economic and political concerns and have a tendency to increase inequality and social conflict.

Along with other social sciences, the academic field of criminology has begun to engage with the environmental harm/social harm nexus, not least through the emergence and development of a distinct 'green criminology' in the last two decades or so. However, while green criminology has made significant contributions to the understanding of specifically 'green' crimes, with a few notable exceptions (particularly around the likely impact of climate change on crime; Agnew 2012; Hall and Farrall 2013) criminology has been slow to engage with any wider analysis of how environmental harm contributes to contemporary patterns of crime more generally.

The purpose here is to go some way to fill this gap. Primarily, this chapter serves to outline and categorize the various connections between environmental harm and crime, with a particular focus on the overlap between environmental victimization and criminality. The aim here is not so much to produce an exhaustive list of crimes that have an environmental element to their genesis as to provide a framework for understanding how environmental problems may relate to contemporary and future patterns of crime, and hence to criminology in general. Such a cataloguing exercise is useful in its own right, especially as we uncover so many more connections between environmental harm and crime than are normally considered in the literature. However, the aim here is to go further and to tentatively develop the theoretical bases to our understanding of the interplay between harms to the environment and the general problem of crime.

The argument is that an ecological perspective can make important contributions to criminological theory: broadly speaking, as we increasingly recognize that sustained environmental harm often creates social harm, and that environmental victimization often contributes to criminality, it follows that criminology should recognize environmental harm not just as crime, but as an important contributory factor in the genesis of crime. If we accept the prediction that environmental problems – and therefore related social problems – are likely to persist, and probably accelerate, as we move further into the twenty-first century, we should recognize that the links between this and crime are also likely to accelerate. This leads to the final aim of this chapter: to make the argument that a green criminology (that is, a criminology that is informed by an ecological as well as a social science) deserves to be seen as having something useful to say about the problem of crime as a whole, rather than remaining a niche area confined to focusing on the sub-category of environmental crime.

Environmental Harm as Criminogenesis

To illustrate the importance of an ecologically informed perspective to a full understanding of contemporary and future patterns of crime and criminalization, we need to consider the range of ways in which environmental harm is implicated as a direct or indirect causal factor in crime. The aim here is essentially to present a list of examples drawn from the academic literature, media reports (and some personal observations and experiences) to make the case that environmental harm *in general* contributes significantly to crime *in general*, and therefore should be of central interest to criminology. The aim is not to be definitive: there are undoubtedly more examples of the criminogenic aspects of environmental harm to be included, and much quantitative research and theoretical analysis is needed to understand the incidence and relative severity of the different types of crime and their links to different types of environmental harm. Likewise, the aim is not to produce a thorough literature review: the aim is to bring together discussion on the different ways in which crime and environmental harm are related, not to exhaustively review the literature in each example. Disclaimers aside, it is hoped that what follows is sufficient as a tentative typology that both begins to shape further academic work in this area and substantiates the claims made in the discussion and conclusions that follow.

Primary Green Crimes: The Criminalization of Environmentally Harmful Activities

Just as one of the 'causes' of crime is the labelling of certain activities as criminal in the first place (Becker 1963), one way in which environmental harm contributes to increases in crime is through the criminalization of environmentally harmful practices. Much green criminological work to date has focused on this area, and a good starting point for current purposes is to draw on one well-established typology of green crimes. Carrabine et al.'s concept of 'primary green crimes' covers 'direct … damage and destruction caused to environment and species' (Carrabine et al. 2009, p. 394), and includes 'air pollution; deforestation; species decline and animal abuse; and water pollution and resource depletion' (Carrabine et al. 2009, p. 389). The point here is that 'most (if not all) of these have been the subject of legislative efforts (if not necessarily legislative success) in recent years' (Carrabine et al. 2009, p. 389).

To illustrate how significant the criminalization of environmentally harmful activities can be, we can draw on the example of recent legislative action in the UK. The New Labour government of Tony Blair (1997–2007) was notorious for creating new crimes (that is, expanding the scope of the criminal law to cover an increasingly wide variety of behaviours). It was widely reported in the media that over its ten years in power, 3,605 new offences were created, of which 852 came from legislation originating in the Department for the Environment, Food and Rural Affairs. This was more than that instigated either by the Home Office (which we would normally associate most readily with criminal legislation[1]) or the Department for Business, Enterprise and Regulatory Reform[2] (which we might expect to be involved in corporate and financial crime). The trend is reflected elsewhere, and it has been stated that the fastest-growing area of international law is environmental law (Sands and Galizzi 2004).

The use of criminal law to restrict or regulate environmentally harmful activities is not new: Carrabine et al. (2009, p. 397) cite examples from the 1940s and 1950s, and common law rights to clean water date back to at least the sixteenth century in the UK. Often these laws are direct responses to public health concerns – the Clean Air Act 1956, for example, has its genesis in the great London fog, or 'killer smog', of 1952. As Hall and Farrall (2013) point out, the criminalization of environmentally harmful activities (both the creation of new crimes and the more rigorous enforcement of existing laws[3]) reflects public and professional attitudes about what activities should be seen and treated *as criminal* as much as the intrinsic harm related to specific activities. It follows that the more the public become aware of – and demand action on – environmentally harmful activities, the more such activities will likely be subject to criminalization. With an increase in both actual environmental problems and awareness of the extent and nature of harms stemming from them (through greater access to information via the Internet, for example), it seems likely that the criminalization of environmentally harmful activities (the creation of primary green crimes) will continue to expand.

---

1 The old Home Office has since been split into the separate departments of the Home Office and the Ministry for Justice. The latter would now be expected to take the lead in most 'traditional' crime and criminal justice legislation.

2 Since renamed the Department for Business, Innovation and Skills.

3 The record fine levied by the US government on BP over the *Deepwater Horizon* oil spill of 2010 and the crackdown on illegal gold mining in Peru discussed below are two examples of more rigorous enforcement of existing laws.

Secondary or Symbiotic Green Crimes: Crime as a Response to the Criminalization of Environmental Harms

Carrabine et al. compare primary green crimes to secondary or 'symbiotic' ones: 'crime growing out of illegal or negligent government or corporate activity, which can even include the flouting of rules set by such bodies themselves to regulate environmentally sensitive activities' (Carrabine et al. 2009, p. 318). Examples given are state violence against oppositional groups (such as the bombing of the Greenpeace ship *Rainbow Warrior* by the French secret service, resulting in the death of one crew member) and the involvement of organized crime in the transportation and dumping of hazardous waste (Carrabine et al. 2009, pp. 394–6). However, arguably this conceptualization does not go far enough in covering criminal activity that might be considered as symbiotic green crime. With some consideration, the concept of secondary green crimes can be further developed and we can identify a number of sub-categories.

Corporate Crime Relating to the Avoidance or Evasion of Environmental Regulation

Examples here might include public and private bodies engaging in illegal dumping of waste, in fraud to cover up levels of pollution produced, or in corruption to avoid the introduction or enforcement of legislation in the first place (see, for example, Pellow 2004; Ruggiero and South 2010; Walters and Martin 2012). The primary green crimes with which these examples are symbiotic involve efforts to criminalize excessive pollution and waste production.

Organized Crime Involved in Trafficking of 'Products' Subject to Environmental Legislation

Along with the example of trade in hazardous waste (see, for example, Szasz 1986; Scarpitti and Block 1987; Ruggiero 1996), we have the transportation and marketing of endangered species and their products and body parts (see, for example, Wyatt 2012; Wyatt 2013). Here, controls over dumping of hazardous waste along with bans on poaching and trade in particular species would be the related primary green crimes.

Crimes of Repression Against Oppositional Groups

Here the state or other powerful vested interests (including corporations and organized crime groups) break the law in an attempt to repress environmental campaigners or those who try to enforce the law. As well as the example of the *Rainbow Warrior* cited above, we can point to a number of examples where high-profile conservationists and environmental campaigners have been assassinated.[4] In a similar, if less extreme, vein we have the widely reported alleged misuse of police powers in the UK, for example, including the controversial technique of 'kettling' protesters (see Oreb 2013), the use of undercover police officers to infiltrate environmental campaign groups and the police exaggerating levels of violence among campaigners when policing protests. Here it is the efforts of environmental

---

4 See Day (1991); Kane (2012); Pearce (2013); 'Remembering Murdered Environmentalists', *Environmental history timeline*: http://66.147.244.135/~enviror4/people/environmental-murders/ (accessed 29 August 2013).

campaigners to prevent environmentally harmful activities, and the efforts of corporate bodies to counter such campaigns, with which these crimes are symbiotic.

Crimes of Protest in Response to Enforcement of Environmental Protection Laws

Although Carrabine et al. (2009) define secondary green crimes specifically as those committed by governments and corporations, there are also crimes committed by less powerful groups and individuals that share common characteristics with other symbiotic green crimes. Just as powerful interests break the law in attempts to avoid their activities being constrained as primary green crimes, so do other groups affected by the enforcement of laws seeking to protect the environment. An example here would be the riots in and around Puerto Maldonado in Peru in 2012. Here, the government decided to make a concerted effort to clamp down on illegal gold-mining in the region, an activity banned because of the environmental damage resulting from the leaking of mercury used in mining into local water systems poisoning fish and other creatures (including humans) as the heavy metal entered the food chain. Many local communities were economically dependent on this illegal activity; enforcing the ban left many miners unable to provide for their families. The response across the area was large-scale riots, with mining communities turning to violence (met, in turn – some observers suggest – by excessive violence from the state).[5] Other examples can be found, particularly (but not exclusively) across the developing world, where communities dependent on illegal mining, logging, poaching or drug crop cultivation violently resist law enforcement activities.

It is clear that symbiotic green crime can exist in many more forms than those suggested by Carrabine et al. (2009), and that they are not limited to (even if they are dominated by) powerful bodies such as states, corporations or organized crime groups. As such, we might propose an alternative definition according to which symbiotic green crimes are those crimes that stem from efforts to avoid the enforcement (or introduction) of legislation designating environmental harmful practices as (primary green) crime. If the criminalization of environmentally harmful activities does continue to expand, then it seems likely that there will also be a growth in these secondary crimes.

Beyond Secondary Green Crimes: Environmental Harm as a Cause of Crime

The categories of primary and secondary green crimes cover the breaking of laws designed to protect the environment, and the commission of other crimes in an attempt to avoid such laws. However, these do not cover all the ways in which environmental harm contributes to criminal activity. A further group of crimes, which we might (in the spirit of consistency) choose to label as 'tertiary' green crimes, can be identified: those committed by environmental victims or as a result of environmental victimization. Splitting these into further sub-categories, we can recognize crimes committed as a deliberate or direct response to environmental harm and crimes exacerbated by the experience of environmental victimization.

---

5 See, for example, 'Peru: Illegal Miners Die In City Gold Riots', Sky News, 15 March 2012: http://news.sky.com/story/3487/peru-illegal-miners-die-in-city-gold-riots (accessed 27 August 2013).

Crime as a Response to Environmental Harm: Protest and Direct Action

One way in which environmental harm leads to crime involves how individuals and groups respond directly to environmental victimization. Williams (1996) argues that violence in particular emerges and has a tendency to escalate in such situations, especially where the original victims have little political or economic power compared to those causing environmental problems. Victim responses can take the form of non-violent protest, but direct action as a protest tactic may incorporate damage to property or violence against people, escalating in some cases to riots and even armed resistance.

It is important to recognize that it is not just the *reactive* responses of those directly exposed to environmental victimization that may manifest as crime, but also the *proactive* responses of those who seek to prevent future exposure to environmental harm and the *sympathetic* responses of those who (reactively or proactively) respond to environmental harm inflicted on, or threatened to, others (or, for that matter, to non-humans or to ecosystems and environments). These are all related and manifest in similar forms.

Williams (1996) demonstrates how escalation of victim responses from those experiencing actual or threatened environmental victimization (reactive and proactive responses) can result in violence against property and people, including riots or armed conflict. Examples cited by Williams include Bougainville in the Solomon Islands (where local resistance to copper mining by Rio Tinto included blowing up electricity pylons which 'catalysed an independence struggle, which has transmuted into an ongoing conflict with blockades and a shoot-to-kill policy involving local people, [Rio Tinto], the Papuan militia, and the Australian government' (Spriggs 1994, cited in Williams 1996, p. 32), conflict in Ogoniland, Nigeria (where local tribal people engaged in acts of sabotage and violence in response to environmental damage caused by Shell and its oil extracting and refining activities in the region), and the violent response of the people of Tahiti to French nuclear tests in the South Pacific. In all of Williams's examples, violence from environmental victims was met with violence from the state or corporate interests.

Examples of sympathetic responses include the direct action protest tactics of radical environmental and animal rights groups. Scarce (2006) provides a particularly detailed account of some of these groups[6] and their members operating in the USA and elsewhere. Such groups engage in a range of criminal activities that have become known as 'eco-tage'. Brisman produces an extensive list of examples:

> firebombing, defacing, or slashing the tires of SUVs; vandalizing business walls and windows with glass-etching cream and spray-paint; damaging construction equipment used for housing developments or megastores; burning buildings (such as laboratories, horse corrals, and unoccupied housing developments); tree-spiking (placing spikes in trees to fend off loggers' chainsaws); 'net-ripping' (which, similar to tree-spiking, involves dumping into the ocean tons of steel I-beams welded together to form large spikes that destroy bottom-trawling nets); blocking access to forest land that would otherwise be logged; disrupting hunts or otherwise preventing recreational hunters from hunting; sabotaging research or facilities using animal-testing techniques; and liberating or removing animals from fur farms or laboratories and industries that conduct animal-based research. (Brisman 2008, pp. 754–5)

6 Including the ELF (Earth Liberation Front), ALF (Animal Liberation Front), Sea Shepherd and Earth First!

Sometimes tactics advance to more serious criminal activity, including threats of – and actual – violence against people (Scarce 2006), with some particularly extreme examples resembling terrorism (see, for example, Beckhusen 2013).

There is more to all this than victims committing crime as deliberate protest tactics or as a reaction to environmental harm. Protest behaviours that may previously be seen as non-criminal become criminalized, and activities that may rightly be seen as criminal (such as eco-tage) come to be redefined as eco-terrorism, implying that a more repressive state response is justified (Scarce 2006; Aaltola 2012; Ellefsen 2012).[7] Further, as we have seen, state responses to these activities may themselves involve criminal activity: police can act illegally, and corporate and organized crime interests have also been implicated in crimes against protesters and campaigners.

As the number, variety and severity of man-made environmental harms – and the level of awareness of these – all increase (or are seen to be increasing), we can expect more in terms of violent responses from victims and sympathizers alike. In turn, we can expect escalating severity in the responses to such protests – whether increased criminalization of protest or an increase in symbiotic green crimes of the repressive type (see also Potter 2012).

Crime as a Response to Shortage of Resources

Next we have crimes that are committed as a response to shortages of (or competition for) resources. This may include thefts and inter-personal violence committed by individuals and groups, such as the widespread food riots reported in 2008 or the looting commonly reported after natural disasters. We can also include examples of state-level crimes, including wars and internal conflicts as regimes seek to secure water, food, oil or other resources for their own populaces (see, for example, Bächler et al. 1993). We may also expect an increase in state repression (maybe in conjunction with corporate bodies), forced depatriation (that is, the removal of people from their traditional homelands) or genocide[8] as certain population groups are seen as little more than competition for scarce resources or their lands as convenient dumping grounds for hazardous waste. Examples here include the removal of the Guaraní and other Paraná river people to make way for the Yacyretá hydro-electric dam project on the border of Argentina and Paraguay (Kane 2012), or the 'environmental genocide' of Native Americans whose lands are used to dump hazardous waste or site hazardous industries (Brook 1998). It has also been argued that the genocide in Rwanda in 1994 and ongoing conflicts in the Middle East are both at least partly explained by competition over natural resources exacerbated by high population growth (and, in the Middle East, external demands for oil). In general, wherever we see a mix of increasing demand and decreasing availability of resources, we must expect more conflict.

Crime as a Product of Exposure to Environmental Harm

As well as crime and conflict as a direct response to environmental victimization, as outlined in the previous two sections, we can recognize a number of ways in which exposure to specific environmental harms has been implicated as a contributing explanatory factor in

7 Although some extreme examples are perhaps rightly called terrorism, governments have been criticized for using anti-terrorist legislation inappropriately against environmental campaigning groups.

8 Of course, some of these activities may not be defined as crime at the national level, but may involve breaches of international law or of human rights.

particular patterns of crime. The link here can be quite direct, or somewhat diffuse. Two examples are particularly notable, at least in terms of published research.

The first is the apparent direct link between extreme weather conditions (which are expected to become more common with the impact of global warming and climate change) and crime. The correlation between hot weather and violent crime has often been documented in criminological research (see, for example, Simister and Van de Vliert 2005). Elsewhere, Wacholz (2007) has demonstrated a specific link between climate change and environmental catastrophes, and violence against women. It is not simply temperature change that seems relevant here – Mares (2013), for example, related changing crime rates to fluctuations in both temperature and precipitation (also linked to climate change). A recent review article drew on 60 'rigorous' studies and sought to quantify this relationship. The authors' summary of their findings is compelling:

> We find strong causal evidence linking climatic events to human conflict across a range of spatial and temporal scales and across all major regions of the world. The magnitude of climate's influence is substantial: for each 1 standard deviation (1σ) change in climate toward warmer temperatures or more extreme rainfall, median estimates indicate that the frequency of interpersonal violence rises 4% and the frequency of intergroup conflict rises 14%. Because locations throughout the inhabited world are expected to warm 2 to 4σ by 2050, amplified rates of human conflict could represent a large and critical impact of anthropogenic climate change. (Hsiang et al. 2013)

Aside from climate change, there is a growing body of evidence linking exposure to heavy metals and other toxic substances to increased crime. One particularly extreme example, in terms of overall conclusions and the number of studies in agreement, is the argument made from a number of studies that declining crime rates seen across the developed world from the mid- to late 1990s onwards can be linked to the reduction of the use of lead in products, including petrol and paint (Nevin 2000; Nevin 2007; Stretesky and Lynch 2001; Stretesky and Lynch 2004; McCall and Land 2004; Wolpaw Reyes 2007; Marcus et al. 2010). The more general point here is that exposure to pollutants (of which lead may only be one example) may have effects on human behaviour through negative impacts on brain development. Although this idea might be criticized by some criminologists as overly positivist, it would be poor science to simply ignore the evidence. It seems likely that other pollutants – industrial and post-industrial societies produce many – may also turn out to relate to health and, in turn, social problems, including crime.

Crime Related to Changes in Economic or Cultural Conditions

There is more to the experience of environmental victimization operating as a contributory factor to crime rates than the research suggesting that the ingestion of pollutants or exposure to particular weather conditions 'causes' crime. We can also recognize that those who are the victims of environmental harm may become more likely to commit normal crimes at later points in their lives as an indirect result of changes to economic or cultural conditions. Dispossessed peoples (those who have lost their lands or traditional ways of life, as is the case for many environmental victims) often experience multiple deprivation, including physical and mental health problems, economic hardship and what Alexander (2010) calls 'poverty of the spirit' (what we might think of as individual and group-level psychological and emotional deficit caused by the sudden loss of traditional cultural practices).

Williams (1996) discusses 'victim syndrome', where environmental victims face a series of social, legal and psychological problems – including criminal victimization – after the immediate impacts of the environmental harm they have encountered. Those who are forced to migrate (whether internally or internationally) may face distrust and alienation from their new neighbours and host communities. Those tribal peoples whose traditional lands are encroached upon and whose isolation from 'Westernized' society is undermined may experience similar economic and cultural tensions. In all of these circumstances, affected populations are arguably more vulnerable not just to becoming involved in crime as offenders, but also to (further) criminal victimization. Let us consider how the experience of dispossession or displacement related to environmental harm can feed into criminality with a brief case study:

> Peruvian tribal people in the Tambopata National Reserve have increasingly been exposed to eco-tourism. While, on the one hand, eco-tourism contributes to the protection of the local environment as it provides an economic alternative to logging, mining and deforestation for agricultural purposes, it is not without its problems. With their traditional lands much reduced by deforestation, and their traditional way of life somewhat compromised by the demands of eco-tourism, lifestyles have changed considerably. Many local people do find work – in hospitality, as guides, or selling traditional goods as tourist trinkets. However, this has exposed them to a cash economy and concept of property ownership to which they are still largely unaccustomed. Reports of theft – from tourists, but also from each other have shot up where previously the concept of theft (related as it is to a concept of property) was previously unknown. Similarly, alcoholism and interpersonal violence are reportedly on the increase. (Fieldwork 2012)

Hall and Farrall (2013) discuss a number of ways in which climate change has general criminogenic consequences. These include the criminalization of environmentally harmful practices (primary crimes), increases in property and violent crimes, emerging illegal markets stemming from conflict over resources, and people trafficking and associated sex and drug trade as people desperate to migrate are taken advantage of by organized crime outfits. They make the point that while crime rates actually tend to go down in relation to immigration (citing Sampson 2008), experiences of fear of crime and certain types of victimization (such as racially or xenophobically motivated crimes) increase in countries hosting large or sudden influxes. Agnew (2012) approaches the same topic – climate change as a cause of crime – from the perspective of dominant criminological theories. He argues that climate change is likely to contribute to a range of 'criminogenic mechanisms', including increased strain, reduced control, reduced social support, altered beliefs and the fostering of values favourable to crime, fostering of traits conducive to crime, increased opportunities for crime, and increased social conflict, with the predicted likely result of increased levels of individual, group, corporate and state crime (Agnew 2012, p. 34; see especially fig. 1). The obvious limitation of both of these works is that they focus only on climate change. While this may be one of the more high-profile environmental harms facing the world, and the one with the most obvious global reach, a plethora of other environmental problems need to be faced (only some of which we have encountered earlier in this chapter). It seems reasonable that many of these will have a similar range of criminogenic effects, even if they are more limited in their geographic range.

There are some further points to be made about how environmental harm, through its impact on social, economic and cultural life, may further contribute to possible increased criminality at the population level. Alexander (2010) demonstrates how epidemic levels of addiction are particularly common among groups of peoples who have been dispossessed, citing groups such as Aboriginal Australians and Native Americans who have had their traditional lands 'stolen' and ways of life eroded. While there is some debate about whether addiction actually causes crime, the correlation between high levels of addiction and crime is well established (see, for example, Stevens 2010; Potter and Osiniagova 2012). At the very least, use of illegal drugs necessitates the crimes of drug possession and supply. Another, similar, indirect link between environmental harm and crime is also suggested by recent and ongoing research.

Psychologists have suggested a link between mental and emotional well-being and exposure to the natural world, with the converse being that as humans remove themselves from nature, they also undermine their psychological health: most recently, for example, evidence suggests that 'Happiness is greater in natural environments' (McKerron and Mourato 2013). At the same time, sociologists have begun to explore the relationship between happiness, or subjective well-being, and criminality, with a paper presented at the American Sociological Association Annual Meeting in 2011 suggesting that happier young people were less likely to be involved in criminal activity (McCarthy and Casey 2011). Putting these two together suggests that erosion of the natural world or removing people from contact with nature may lead to greater levels of unhappiness and depression, which in turn may relate to greater involvement in criminal behaviour.

Some of the points made in these last two sections will invite criticism, whether along the lines of the overstatement of positivist connections between pollutants and crime or for the vagueness of alleged connections between exposure to the natural environment and tendencies towards criminality, and there is insufficient space here to explore either side of the arguments in any depth. Nevertheless, they come together – along with other observations made – to support a broader point that is harder to ignore. It is clear that environmental victimization can and does contribute to a number of different forms of inequality, deprivation and social harm – whether related to health, economic opportunities, physical environment, political involvement or social and cultural conditions. The idea that criminality and also the experience of criminal victimization (at least as measured by criminal statistics and the workings of the criminal justice system) are related to deprivation, and inequality is, of course, a staple of both empirical research and criminological theory.

Conclusions: Towards an Ecologically Informed Criminology

There are two major lessons to draw from all of this. Firstly, it becomes clear that environmental harm is implicated, to a greater or lesser degree, in contributing to a wide range of crime – far wider than those that are usually discussed within the field of green criminology. Secondly, it also becomes clear that for a large sub-set of the crimes for which environmental harm is a contributory factor, those who we might properly see as environmental victims go on to become involved in other crime. In particular, environmental victims often seem to be at risk of participating in offending behaviour and therefore becoming labelled as 'criminals'. It seems that they are also at some risk of becoming victims of (further) crime, such as when they seek to raise their voices in protest and are then victims of state or corporate violence or, more notably, when dispossession, dislocation or deprivation make them vulnerable to 'normal' criminal victimization (see Hall and Farrall 2013).

Taking the second lesson first, there are implications here for both our understanding of environmental victimization and for broader criminological understandings of the offender/victim dichotomy. In terms of environmental victimization, we can add increased risk of further criminal victimization and increased risk of offending behaviour (and, therefore, increased risk of becoming involved in the criminal justice system) as extra problems faced by those who are exposed to environmental harm. While the overlap between environmental victimization and offending behaviour has been briefly touched on by others (Williams 1996; Hall and Farrall 2013) and is implicit in those studies that look at the relationship, for example, between lead poisoning and offending, such studies tend to focus only on one type of environmental harm. It takes consideration of *all* the ways that environmental harm may contribute to crime to arrive at the full picture: environmental victimization in general can be seen to contribute to offending behaviour.

In terms of a broader criminological understanding of the relationship between victim and offender statuses, it is well recognized that (a) populations of victims of crime and criminal offenders tend to overlap considerably (Hartless et al. 1995; Farrall and Maltby 2003), and (b) offenders are often the victims of a multitude of social harms, coming from backgrounds of multiple deprivation and social exclusion (see, for example, Social Exclusion Unit 2002; see also Hillyard et al. 2004). Environmental victimization is not just another form of deprivation and social exclusion, it tends to co-exist with, or even cause, other social harms.

This recognition that there is much overlap between environmental victimization and criminality brings us back to the first lesson, and to the major conclusion of this chapter: the idea that a 'green' perspective can be relevant to criminology as a whole, not just that part of it that focuses on 'green' crimes. Green criminology has, at least until recently, struggled to be accepted by the criminological mainstream. It has been subject to criticism, particularly by those of a realist persuasion, for focusing on subject matter that falls well beyond the central criminological concerns of those offences that contribute to the bulk of crime statistics and the workings of the criminal justice system. Among the criticisms levelled against green criminology has been that it prioritizes concern for the environment and other species over those of human society, and that in doing so it is overly political and value-laden in its aims and practice. However, it is possible – desirable, even – to recognize a green perspective in criminology not just as a political or moral perspective that cares for the environment and for non-human animals, but as an ecologically informed social science (see Potter 2013 for a discussion of the criticisms levelled at green criminology and a response to them).

The point of taking an ecologically informed approach is to recognize that the social world cannot be understood as completely separate from the natural world. Humanity depends on interaction with nature, if only because we breathe air, drink water and consume food. The world we live in is, ultimately, a single eco-system where everything interacts, even if some of these interactions appear to be quite remote. Harming the environment means affecting the weather, water and other natural systems on which society (as well as the natural world) depends. Sociology has begun to recognize this: the idea that environmental harms relate to social harms is central to the concept of the risk society as formulated by Beck (1992). Politicians and policy makers have also increasingly come to recognize this, even if there is much resistance from many within their ranks: more and more environmentally harmful practices are subject to national and international legislation and political debate, even if their failures to deal effectively with environmental problems often seem to outweigh their successes. Criminology needs to do this as well: not only are environmentally harmful activities increasingly subject to control under the criminal law (and therefore clearly within the remit of criminology), such activities (along with various social responses to them) are also implicated in contributing to a range of social harms which, in turn, are related to a range of crimes.

It is clear that the strength of the relationship between environmental harm and crime varies depending on the specific environmental issues – the links are more prominent in those places where the nexus between environmental and social harm is most proximate. This often means, for various reasons, developing rather than developed world countries, and poor rather than rich communities. In many cases it may mean rural and wilderness rather than urban areas. However, for a number of environmental harms, given their international and even global impacts, the impact is ultimately to be felt *everywhere*. As Beck says, 'smog is democratic' – ultimately we are all potential victims of environmental harm. Over time, as Agnew has argued with the example of climate change, the criminogenic effects of environmental harm will be felt in the cities of Europe and North America, not just those of the global South. For this reason, it seems clear that an ecological (or green) perspective should be central to any effort towards a thorough understanding of contemporary and future patterns of crime, and therefore central to contemporary criminology.[9]

References

Aaltola, E. 2012. 'Differing Philosophies: Criminalisation and the Stop Huntingdon Animal Cruelty Debate', in *Eco-global Crimes: Contemporary Problems and Future Challenges*, edited by R. Ellefsen, R. Sollund and G. Larsen. Farnham: Ashgate, 157–80.

Agnew, R. 2012. 'Dire Forecast: A Theoretical Model of the Impact of Climate Change on Crime', *Theoretical Criminology* 16(21), 21–42.

Alexander, B. 2010. *The Globalization of Addiction: A Study in Poverty of the Spirit*. Oxford: Oxford University Press.

Bächler, G., Böge, S., Klötzli, S. and Libiszweski, S. 1993. *The Destruction of Nature as a Cause of Conflict*. Münster: Agenda-Verlag.

Beck, U. 1992. *Risk Society: Towards a New Modernity*. London: Sage.

Becker, H. 1963. *Outsiders: Studies in the Sociology of Deviance*. New York: Free Press.

Beckhusen, R. 2013. 'In Manifesto, Mexican Eco-terrorists Declare War on Nanotechnology', *Wired*: www.wired.com/dangerroom/2013/03/mexican-ecoterrorism/ (accessed 30 August 2013).

Brisman, A. 2008. 'Crime–environment Relationships and Environmental Justice', *Seattle Journal for Social Justice* 6(2), 727–817.

Brisman, A. 2010. 'The Indiscriminate Criminalisation of Environmentally Beneficial Activities', in *Global Environmental Harm: Criminological Perspectives*, edited by R. White. Cullompton: Willan Publishing, 161–92.

9 There are other areas where crime relates to environmental harm that have not been discussed in this chapter, such as environmental blackmail and environmental terrorism (Williams 1996; Brisman 2008), drug cultivation (Del Olmo 1998) and the production of synthetic drugs (Brisman 2008), and the criminalization of environmentally beneficial practices (Brisman 2010). In these examples, environmental harm may be caused by criminals or by the processes of criminalization and criminal justice. Conversely, this chapter has focused on areas where environmental harm can be seen to be a contributory cause of crime.

Brook, D. 1998. Environmental Genocide: Native Americans and Toxic Waste', *American Journal of Economics and Sociology* 57(1), 105–13.

Carrabine, E., Cox, P., Lee, M., Plummer, K. and South, N. 2009. *Criminology: A Sociological Introduction* (2nd edn). Oxford: Routledge.

Day, D. 1991. *The Eco Wars: A Layman's Guide to the Ecology Movement*. London: Paladin.

Del Olmo, R. 1998. 'The Ecological Impact of Illicit Drug Cultivation and Crop Eradication Programmes in Latin America', *Theoretical Criminology* 2, 269–78.

Ellefsen, R. 2012. 'Green Movements as Threats to Order and Economy: Animal Activists Repressed in Austria and Beyond', in *Eco-global Crimes: Contemporary Problems and Future Challenges*, edited by R. Ellefsen, R. Sollund and G. Larsen. Farnham: Ashgate, 181–205.

Farrall, S, and Maltby, S. 2003. 'The Victimisation of Probationers', *Howard Journal of Criminal Justice* 42(1), 32–54.

Giddens, A. 1991. *The Consequences of Modernity*. Stanford, CA: Stanford University Press.

Hall, M. and Farrall, S. 2013. 'The Criminogenic Consequences of Climate Change', in *Routledge International Handbook of Green Criminology*, edited by N. South and A. Brisman. London: Routledge, 120–33.

Hartless, J., Ditton, J., Nair, G. and Phillips, S. 1995. 'More Sinned Against than Sinning: A Study of Young Teenagers' Experiences of Crime', *British Journal of Criminology* 35(1), 114–33.

Hillyard, P., Pantazis, C., Tombs, S. and Gordon, D. 2004. *Beyond Criminology: Taking Harm Seriously*. London: Pluto Press.

Hsiang, S., Burke, M. and Miguel, E. 2013. 'Quantifying the Influence of Climate on Human Conflict', *Science*: https://www.sciencemag.org/content/341/6151/1235367.abstract (accessed 30 August 2013).

Kane, S. 2012. *Where Rivers Meet the Sea: The Political Ecology of Water*. Philadelphia, PA: Temple University Press.

Lynch, M. and Stretesky, P. 2007. 'Green Criminology in the United States', in *Issues in Green Criminology: Confronting Harms Against Environments, Humanity and Other Animals*, edited by P. Beirne and N. South. Cullompton: Willan Publishing, 248–69.

Marcus, D., Fulton, J. and Clarke, E. 2010. 'Lead and Conduct Problems: A Meta-analysis', *Journal of Clinical Child and Adolescent Psychology* 39(2), 234–41.

Mares, D. 2013. 'Climate Change and Crime: Monthly Temperature and Precipitation Anomalies and Crime Rates in St. Louis, MO 1990–2009', *Crime, Law and Social Change* 59, 185–208.

McCall, P. and Land, K. 2004. 'Trends in Environmental Lead Exposure and Troubled Youth, 1960–1995: An Age-period Cohort-characteristic Analysis', *Social Science Research* 33, 339–59.

McCarthy, B. and Casey, T. 2011. 'Get Happy! Positive Emotion, Depression and Juvenile Crime', paper presented at the American Sociological Association Annual Meeting, Caesar's Palace, Las Vegas, 11 August 2011: http://citation.allacademic.com/meta/p_mla_apa_research_citation/4/9/8/4/6/p498466_index.html (accessed 30 August 2013).

McKerron, G. and Mourato, S. 2013. 'Happiness is Greater in Natural Environments', *Global Environmental Change*: www.sciencedirect.com/science/article/pii/S0959378013000575 (accessed 30 August 2013).

Mielke, H. and Zahran, S. 2012. 'The Urban Rise and Fall of Air Lead (Pb) and the Latent Surge and Retreat of Societal Violence', *Environment International* 43, 48–55.

Nevin, R. 2000. 'How Lead Exposure Relates to Temporal Changes in IQ, Violent Crime, and Unwed Pregnancy', *Environmental Research* 83(1), 1–22.
Nevin, R. 2007. 'Understanding International Crime Trends: The Legacy of Preschool Lead Exposure', *Environmental Research* 104, 315–36.
Oreb, N. 2013. 'Case Comment: The Legality of "Kettling" after Austin', *Modern Law Review* 76(4), 735–42.
Pearce, F. 2013. 'Grisly Trend: Green Activists are Facing Deadly Dangers'. *Yale Environment 360*, 19 February: http://e360.yale.edu/feature/grisly_trend_green_activists_are_facing_deadly_dangers/2620/ (accessed 29 August 2013).
Pellow, D. 2004. 'The Politics of Illegal Dumping: An Environmental Justice Framework', *Qualitative Sociology* 27(4), 511–25.
Potter, G. 2012. 'I Predict a Riot: Green Politics, Environmental Activism and Socio-ecological Despair', *Criminal Justice Matters* 90(1), 20–21.
Potter, G. 2013. 'Justifying "Green" Criminology: Values and "Taking Sides" in an Ecologically Informed Social Science', in *Values in Criminology and Community Justice*, edited by M. Cowburn, M. Duggan, A. Robinson and P. Senior. London: Policy Press, 125–41.
Potter, G. and Osiniagova, A. 2012. 'Getting "High" from Crime: Perspectives on the Drug–crime Connection', in *The Meaning of High*, edited by J. Fountain, D. Korf and M. Wouters. Pabst: Langerich, 164–89.
Ruggiero, V. 1996. *Organised and Corporate Crime in Europe: Offers That Can't Be Refused*. Aldershot: Dartmouth.
Ruggiero, V. and South, N. 2010. 'Green Criminology and Dirty Collar Crime', in *Critical Criminology* 18(4), 251–62.
Sampson, R. 2008. 'Rethinking Crime and Immigration', *Contexts* 7(1), 28–33.
Sands, P. and Galizzi, P. 2004. *Documents in International Environmental Law* (2nd edn). Cambridge: Cambridge University Press.
Scarce, R. 2006. *Eco-Warriors* (updated edn). Walnut Creek, CA: Left Coast Press.
Scarpitti, A. and Block, A. 1987. 'America's Toxic Waste Racket', in *Organized Crime in America: Concepts and Controversies*, edited by T.S. Bynum. New York: Criminal Justice Publishers, 115–28.
Simister, J. and Van de Vliert, E. 2005. 'Is There More Violence in Very Hot Weather? Tests Over Time in Pakistan and Across Countries Worldwide', *Pakistan Journal of Meteorology* 2(4), 55–70.
Social Exclusion Unit. 2002. *Reducing Re-offending by Ex-prisoners*. London: Social Exclusion Unit.
Spriggs, Matthew. 1994. 'The Failure of the Bougainville Peace Talks', *Pacific Research* 7(4), 19–23.
Stevens, A. 2010. *Drugs, Crime and Public Health: The Political Economy of Drug Policy*. London: Routledge.
Stretesky, P. and Lynch, M. 2001. 'The Relationship between Lead Exposure and Homicide', *Archives of Pediatrics and Adolescent Medicine* 155(5), 579–82.
Stretesky, P. and Lynch, M. 2004. 'The Relationship between Lead and Crime', *Journal of Health and Social Behaviour* 45(2), 214–29.
Szasz, A. 1986. 'Corporations, Organised Crime and the Disposal of Hazardous Waste: An Examination of the Making of a Criminogenic Regulatory Structure', *Criminology* 24(1), 1–27.

Wachholz, S. 2007. '"At Risk": Climate Change and its Bearing on Women's Vulnerability to Male Violence', in *Issues in Green Criminology: Confronting Harms Against Environments, Humanity and Other Animals*, edited by P. Beirne and N. South. Collumpton: Willan Publishing, 161–85.

Walters, R. and Martin, P. 2012. 'Cameron's Hot Air: Pollution, Fraud and the Politics of Carbon Emissions', *Criminal Justice Matters* 90(1), 6–7.

Williams, C. 1996. 'An Environmental Victimology', *Social Justice* 23(4), 16–40.

Wolpaw Reyes, J. 2007. *Environmental Policy as Social Policy? The Impact of Childhood Lead Exposure on Crime.* National Bureau of Economic Research Working Paper 13097: www.nber.org/papers/w13097.pdf (accessed 15 October 2013).

Wyatt, T. 2012. *Green Criminology and Wildlife Trafficking: The Illegal Fur and Falcon Trades in Russia Far East.* Saarbrücken: LAP Lambert Academic Publishing.

Wyatt, T. 2013. 'From the Cardamom Mountains of Southwest Cambodia to the Forests of the World: An Exploration of the Illegal Charcoal Trade', *International Journal of Comparative and Applied Criminal Justice* 37(1), 1–15.

Chapter 2
Climate Change: A State-corporate Crime Perspective

Ronald Kramer

Introduction

Any consideration of environmental crime and its victims should include an analysis of anthropocentric global warming and associated climate change. Outside of a nuclear war, there is no other form of environmental crime that can produce a wider range of victims. The social and environmental harms caused by climate change have been variously described as an ecological catastrophe, an existential threat and an apocalyptic event. Some scientists have even expressed a more cosmic concern. They assert that Earth, a dynamic planet rich with life, is cosmically rare and invaluable, and that the existence of intelligent life or technological civilization anywhere else in the universe is extremely doubtful. Therefore, these cosmologists argue that since climate change threatens human civilization and intelligent life on Earth, it would constitute a 'cosmic' crime (Abrams and Primack 2011; Gribbin 2011).

However one assesses the potential harm and range of victimization, a growing number of criminologists appear to agree with Rob White (2011, p. 36) that: 'present action and lack of action around climate change will most likely constitute the gravest of transnational environmental crimes.' There exists a growing body of literature analyzing global warming and climate change from a criminological perspective (South 2009; White 2009; White 2011; White 2012; Lynch and Stretesky 2010; Lynch et al. 2010; Agnew 2011a; Parenti 2011; Kramer 2012; Kramer and Michalowski 2012; Michalowski and Kramer 2013). This chapter argues that global warming can best be conceptualized as *state-corporate criminality* (Michalowski and Kramer 2006).

Although energy corporations' and state agencies' continued emission of greenhouse gases that are widely recognized by the scientific community to cause global warming could also be viewed as a criminal act, this analysis focuses on the abject political failure to act to regulate or mitigate these emissions, and the socially organized denial of climate change that shapes that failure. These extremely consequential crimes of omission by individual states and the international political community will be examined from the state-corporate crime perspective. Given the devastating effects of climate change, the chapter will briefly consider the question of how these 'blameworthy harms' (Agnew 2011b) might be brought within the boundaries of criminology. Then, after sketching out the state-corporate crime perspective, it will present a theoretical analysis of the crimes of the critical political failure to act to mitigate global warming and the socially organized denial of climate change, drawing on recent social science research concerning these questions.

Climate Change as a Criminological Issue

The emission of heat-trapping greenhouse gases (GHGs) into the atmosphere, primarily through the burning of fossil fuels, causes the Earth to warm. This global warming in turn has a number of very harmful effects on Earth's climate. Scientific research on global warming and climate change demonstrates the catastrophic nature of the harms that are being inflicted on the ecosystem (Hansen 2009; Hamilton 2010; McKibben 2010b; Dow and Downing 2011; Richardson et al. 2011; Climate Central 2012; Honisch et al. 2012)—harms that are more severe and occurring at a much faster pace than predicted in the 2007 Intergovernmental Panel on Climate Change (IPCC) Fourth Assessment Report. The environmental damage caused by global warming will in turn result in a wide range of social, economic and political harms to human communities and the social systems on which they depend (Dunn 1995; Dyer 2010; Parenti 2011; Climate Central 2012; Klare 2012).

For criminologists concerned with global warming and the environmental and social harms flowing from it, there is currently no established body of international or domestic law that offers a legal framework to bring these harms within the boundaries of criminology. There are some efforts under way to change this situation. The British lawyer Polly Higgins, for instance, has proposed that *ecocide* be recognized by the United Nations as an international crime along with genocide, crimes against humanity, war crimes, and crimes of aggression. Higgins defines ecocide as: 'The extensive destruction, damage to or loss of ecosystem(s) of a given territory, whether by human agency or by other causes, to such an extent that peaceful enjoyment by the inhabitants of that territory has been severely diminished' (Higgins 2010, p. 63). If adopted, 'ecocide' would constitute a legal definition under which global warming and climate change would become not just an environmental problem, but also an international crime. However, the likelihood that the United Nations, dominated as it is by the carbon-dependent and carbon-profiting nations of the global North, would establish ecocide as an international crime is slim.

Another effort to bring harmful greenhouse gas emissions within a legal framework is the ongoing lawsuit brought by a number of US states against the five largest US utilities in an effort to have their emissions defined as a 'public nuisance' (*businessGreen* 2011b). If successful, this suit could force the federal government to impose more stringent regulations on the fossil fuel industry (*businessGreen* 2011a). Furthermore, the US Supreme Court (2007) decision in *Massachusetts* v. *Environmental Protection Agency* that greenhouse gases fit within the Clean Air Act's definition of air pollution could eventually lead to the greater legal regulation of these gases by the Environmental Protection Agency, although the agency has been very slow to act. Despite these efforts, the emissions of carbon dioxide and other greenhouse gases are not currently defined as 'crimes' within any legal system.

Internationally, with regard to global warming there is still nothing comparable to the Montreal Protocol, which was adopted in 1987 to eliminate aerosols and other chemicals that were responsible for a growing hole in the Earth's protective ozone layer. This protocol has been successful in eliminating the hydrofluorocarbons (HFCs) that damage the ozone layer. Consequently, some policy experts have suggested that we should curb global warming by including greenhouse gases under this existing, and demonstrably successful, treaty (Broder 2010). To date, the Kyoto Protocol of 1997 is the only major international accord aimed at regulating and reducing greenhouse gas emissions. Unfortunately, this treaty has done little to reduce carbon emissions, and in its present form provides little in the way of a legal framework that criminologists can use as a juridical warrant to address anthropogenic global warming as a state-corporate crime (Michalowski and Kramer 2013).

The lack of a legal framework on which criminologists can base their study of the emission of greenhouse gases as crimes should not be seen as a barrier to this inquiry. Indeed, unless criminologists escape the juridical trap that mandates they only study what states, through their law-making systems, tell them is a crime, the social injuries caused by the most powerful actors in the contemporary world—transnational corporations and national states—will remain forever outside their reach (Michalowski and Kramer 2006; Michalowski 2010). Instead, criminologists concerned with global warming can and should utilize concepts such as *social injury/harm* (Michalowski 1985; Tift and Sullivan 2001; Hillyard et al. 2004; Pemberton 2007; Agnew 2011b) as the starting point for their inquiries. As White points out: 'A basic premise of green criminology is that we need to take environmental harm seriously, and in order to do this we need a conceptualization of harm that goes beyond conventional understandings of crime' (White 2011, p. 21). Lynch and Stretesky have also argued that green criminology should study the 'harms that directly damage the ecosystem or its parts (direct victimization of the environment), or victimize species through ecosystem damage (indirect victimization)' (Lynch and Stretesky 2010, pp. 70–71). They note that, insofar as 'scientists are continually discovering new ways in which global warming produces harm … it is important for green criminologists to stay abreast of this literature in order to address the varieties of victimization and emerging crimes and harms science identifies.' Given the catastrophic scenarios detailed in the scientific literature on climate change, a green criminology perspective would argue that criminologists should treat the grave harms and forms of victimization, both present and future, resulting from global warming and climate change as serious crimes warranting criminological analysis. As White points out: 'Climate change is arguably the most important issue, problem and trend in the world today and a key area of interest to eco-global criminology' (White 2011, p. 36).

Agnew (2011b) has recently attempted to develop an integrated definition of crime based on blameworthy harms, public condemnation and state sanctioning. But he recognizes that there exist 'unrecognized blameworthy harms' that are not condemned and sanctioned. Climate change appears to fall into this category. Agnew advocates that a 'major mission' of criminologists should be that of 'making the public and the state aware of unrecognized blameworthy harms' (Agnew 2011b, p. 43). Given the catastrophic scenarios detailed in the scientific literature on climate change, criminologists should treat the grave blameworthy harms, both present and future, resulting from global warming and climate change as serious crimes warranting criminological analysis. And part of that analysis should focus on why these blameworthy harms do indeed remain unrecognized or unacknowledged.

The Concept of State-corporate Crime

As criminologists take up the issue of climate change, Lynch et al. argue that the state-corporate crime approach 'provides a useful tool for examining' the crimes related to global warming (Lynch et al. 2010, p. 215). Likewise, in his analysis of transnational environmental crime, White also notes the importance of investigating the nation state as 'a major facilitator of harm in its own right, either on its own or in conjunction with specific sectional interests (such as particular transnational corporations)' (White 2011, p. 13).

The concept of state-corporate crime, developed by Kramer and Michalowski (1990; 2006), refers to serious social harms that result from the interaction of political and economic organizations. The idea emerged out of the recognition that some organizational crimes are the collective product of the interaction between a business corporation and a state agency engaged in a joint endeavor. The concept of state-corporate crime seeks to breach the conceptual wall between economic crimes and political crimes in order to create a new lens through which we can examine the ways illegal acts and social injuries often emerge from intersections of economic and political power. As Michalowski and Kramer have noted: 'Contemporary social scientists have largely forgotten what our 19th century counterparts knew so well. There is neither economics nor politics; there is only *political-economy*' (Michalowski and Kramer 2007, p. 201; emphasis added).

State-corporate crime has been formally defined as 'illegal or socially injurious actions that result from a mutually reinforcing interaction between (1) policies and/or practices in pursuit of the goals of one or more institutions of political governance and (2) policies and/or practices in pursuit of the goals of one or more institutions of economic production and distribution' (Michalowski and Kramer 2006, p. 15). As this definition makes clear, Michalowski and Kramer also propose to extend the scope of criminology beyond legal definitions, incorporating harmful social actions that violate neither criminal nor regulatory laws at the state level. While the concept of state-corporate crime could be applied to illegal or other socially injurious actions in societies ranging from private production systems to centrally planned political economies, most of the research to date has focused on state-corporate crimes within the private production system of modern capitalism (Michalowski and Kramer 2006). State-corporate crimes within a global capitalist political economy involve the active participation of two or more organizations, at least one of which is in the civil sector and one of which is in the state sector. The time has come to extend this framework to the study of the critical role of corporations and political states in both promoting the release of greenhouse gases and refusing to seriously address the resulting consequences of global warming and planetary climate change.

As a sensitizing concept, the term 'state-corporate crime' has three useful characteristics. First, it directs attention toward the way in which upper-world crime emerges at *organizational intersections*, in this case the intersection of institutions of accumulation and institutions of governance. In doing so, it foregrounds the ways in which many deviant organizational outcomes are not discreet acts of institutional wrongdoing, but rather the product of the relationships between different social institutions pursuing different goals and responding to different sets of pressures.

Second, it approaches the state as a nexus of *relationships* rather than a set of governmental institutional actors (Sassen 1993; Wonders and Solop 1993). This relational model directs us to examine the ways in which horizontal and vertical relationships between economic and political institutions contain powerful potentials for the production of illegal and other socially injurious actions. For example, US legislation designed to address global climate change, or more often the failure to pass legislation to address climate change, cannot be understood simply as a set of decisions taken by legislators pursuing varying political or organizational agendas. Rather, these outcomes are the product of long chains of relationships and conflicts among carbon-intensifying corporations (for example, petroleum, coal, auto and auto-related, highway construction), carbon-reducing industries (for example, alternative energy, urban mass transit), political organizations of workers and communities dependent on these various industries (for example, unions, chambers of commerce), environmental organizations, lobbying firms, banks and other nodes of finance capital with a stake in environmental policy, along with a complex stew of regulatory bodies, advisory commissions, think tanks and international governance and non-governmental organizations. It is the flows of 'information,' data, money and interpersonal linkages along these channels of power that constitutes the real operations of the US capitalist state. This relational approach provides a more nuanced understanding of the processes leading to deviant state actions than approaches that treat governments as closed systems, or locate the wrongdoing within individual decision makers operating within individual institutions.

Third, approaching the state-corporate context as a relational process directs analytic attention to the *vertical relationships* between different levels of organizational action in government and business. It asks us to be alert to three things. The first is the way particular individuals can, by their institutional movements and locations, shape flows of information, data and money through what Mills (1956) called the 'circulation of elites.' The second is the way in which standard operating procedures and cultures within institutions can facilitate or inhibit deviant organizational behavior (Vaughn 1996). And the third is the way larger-scale political economic arrangements define the particular relationship between capital and the state (for example, regulatory welfare state, neo-liberal workfare state, state capitalism and so on) and shape the opportunities and rewards for both socially harmful and socially responsible behaviors by individuals and organizations (Jessop 1991).

By examining these three levels, we can recognize that political-economic arrangements are more than technical mechanisms for determining the relationship between state and capital. They also reflect and reproduce particular ideologies not just of the relationship between capital and state, but the relationship between capital and individuals and individuals and the state.

The Failure to Mitigate GHG Emissions

In *The Politics of Climate Change*, Giddens argues that 'the state must be the prime actor' in addressing climate change (Giddens 2011, p. 94). If one accepts this premise, then a further argument can be made that the failure by individual states and the international political community (of states) to undertake any serious efforts to regulate or mitigate global warming constitutes negligent state criminality (Friedrichs 2010) or state crimes of omission (Barak 1991; Kauzlarich et al. 2003). As Friedrichs notes: 'The most serious form of negligent state criminality involves the unnecessary and premature loss of life that occurs when the government and its agents fail to act affirmatively in certain situations' (Friedrichs 2010, p. 140). Anthropogenic global warming and its attendant victimization would qualify as one of those situations.

Since global warming stems from the production of heat-trapping greenhouse gases, some have argued that the continued high levels of carbon dioxide emissions by energy corporations and by state agencies such as the US military are therefore crimes of corporate and state violence (Hansen 2009; Sanders 2009). In view of the extensive scientific evidence of the environmental and social harm resulting from emission-caused global warming described above, it would be reasonable to expect that the international political community and its member states would move immediately and aggressively to mitigate the production of greenhouse gases. Yet, to the contrary, many of the key corporate and state actors responsible for the greatest production of greenhouse gases have not only chosen to continue their current production practices, but in many cases have supported policies that will expand these emissions. Climate activist Bill McKibben argues that given the massive amount of carbon contained in the proven coal, oil and gas reserves of the fossil fuel companies (around 2,795 gigatons)—fuel that if burned would push us well past the internationally accepted limit of a 2° Celsius rise in the Earth's temperature—we need to view the fossil fuel industry as a 'rogue industry, reckless like no other force on Earth. It is Public Enemy Number one to the survival of our planetary civilization' (McKibben 2012, p. 7).

While structural and cultural forces in the global capitalist political economy shape the ongoing emission of harmful greenhouse gases by the fossil fuel industry (Foster 2009;

Lynch and Stretesky 2010; White 2011; Kramer and Michalowski 2012), it is the failure of state officials, particularly in the United States, to take effective and immediate actions to compel both the private corporate sector and other governmental institutions in the structural ensemble of the state to *reduce* these emissions that is of particularly concern here. No other industry is allowed to dump its main waste (carbon dioxide) for free into what should be considered a 'public trust' (the atmosphere) that government has a legal obligation to protect (Morris 2012). Thus, this chapter argues that the failure of the US government to drastically mitigate greenhouse gas emissions that are responsible for the criminal harms related to climate change is a state-corporate crime of omission. As Giddens has pointed out: 'At present, the U.S., the country with the greatest responsibility to develop a far-reaching climate change policy, has done nothing at all on a national level. It is almost alone among industrial states in this respect' (Giddens 2011, p. 89). And if the USA takes no action, there is little hope for any strong and effective international agreement on climate change to be negotiated.

It is not that the international political community has not attempted to address the issue of climate change at all (Michalowski and Kramer 2013). The 1992 UN Framework Convention on Climate Change is designed to limit the worldwide emission of greenhouse gases. Because industrialized nations represent the largest source of greenhouse gas emissions, the treaty established different and higher standards for these nations than for developing ones. During treaty negotiations, the USA was the only industrialized nation that refused to accept *binding* rules for the reduction of greenhouse gases, and the US delegation eventually succeeded in obtaining treaty language that made compliance with greenhouse gas reduction goals voluntary. In 1994, President Clinton reversed the previous Bush administration policy and announced that the USA would comply with the treaty goals of reducing greenhouse gas emissions to 1990 levels.

In December 1997, delegates from 170 nations met to address the issue at the third Conference of the Parties (COP) to the Framework Convention on Climate Change in Kyoto, Japan. This meeting resulted in the aforementioned Kyoto Protocol, a multilateral agreement on legally binding targets for the reduction of greenhouse gas emissions. The Kyoto Protocol mandated a 5 percent reduction of greenhouse gases by 2012, with the USA agreeing to cut emissions by 7 percent, the European Union committed to 8 percent reductions, and Japan committed to 6 percent reductions. Achieving these goals would require that the USA and other developed countries reduce pollution and consumption in key areas by as much as 30 percent (Yamin 1998). In recognition of the difficulty developing nations would have in modernizing their economies while simultaneously reducing greenhouse gases, no binding targets or timetables were set for developing nations (Leaf 2001).

The Kyoto Protocol, which included several novel legal mechanisms to facilitate compliance (Michalowski and Kramer 2013), would only become legally binding upon the USA after its ratification by the US Senate. But just prior to the Kyoto conference in 1997, the Senate indicated it would *not* ratify any climate change protocol that failed to impose legally binding standards for reduction of greenhouse gas emissions on the developing world, or that would cause serious economic harm to the USA. Facing rejection of the treaty, the Clinton administration elected not to submit the protocol to the Senate for ratification. Clinton stated that he would not do so until there was 'meaningful participation' in greenhouse gas reductions in 'key developing countries' (Leaf 2001, p. 1,219).

Due to the political gridlock on this issue, Kyoto was not ratified during the remainder of the Clinton administration, and in March 2001 the new administration of George W. Bush formally withdrew the USA from the protocol. In June 2001, the administration introduced a series of unilateral initiatives on climate change, which included funding for further research on the issue and several unilateral moves to reduce greenhouse gas emissions, such as selling cleaner-burning US technology to the developing world and voluntary energy efficiency programs for US consumers. These initiatives, however, did not include any binding targets or timetables for the reduction of US emissions and were quickly abandoned as the issue of global warming became increasingly polarized in US political discourse (Leaf 2001). The Bush administration itself played a leading role in the politicization of the climate change issue by pursuing a cooperative state-corporate strategy that 'actively attempted to refute the science of global warming and install in its place economic and environmental policies that not only ignore but deny the views of the scientific community on climate change' (Giddens 2011).

Lynch et al. (2010) have examined the politicization of global warming under the Bush administration as a form of state-corporate crime. They analyzed the coordinated intersection of state and corporate activity and interests that resulted in collusive agreements and arrangements between the fossil fuel industry and the Bush administration with regard to a number of energy and environmental policies related to global warming. They documented how corporate actors from the fossil fuel industry made their interests known to the Bush administration and how they sought to directly influence energy and environmental policies through lobbying, meetings and the drafting of proposed policy language. The Bush administration in turn adopted the proposed policies, appointed industry executives and leaders to key policy making positions within the government and attempted to muzzle or censure federal climate scientists such as NASA's James Hansen. Thus, Lynch et al. conclude that the administration was able to 'produce domestic policies that contributed to rather than impeded the progress of global warming' (Lynch et al. 2010, p. 227). Furthermore, they note that, 'Because of the immense power the U.S. wields internationally, the Bush Administration was able to forestall implementation of international treaties on global warming.'

The election of Barack Obama in 2008 caused some environmental activists and scientists to hope that there would be a change in US climate change policy. President Obama appeared to have a better grasp of the issue of global climate change and to be more committed to crafting a stronger policy to mitigate the problem than his predecessor (Derber 2010). Expectations were high for the annual UN climate conference (COP 15) held in Copenhagen during December 2009. Many hoped that Copenhagen would mark a turning point in the climate change debate. However, the conference ended in failure. A minimalist accord was negotiated at the very end that had no emissions targets or timetables. John Sauven, executive director of Greenpeace UK, invoked the language of criminality to describe the failure: 'The city of Copenhagen is a crime scene tonight, with the guilty men and women fleeing to the airport. There are no targets for carbon cuts and no agreement on a legally binding treaty' (BBC 2009, p. 3). Similarly, White contends that the failure at the Copenhagen conference was indeed a state-corporate crime, noting that, 'The abject failure of the Copenhagen talks to actually do something about carbon emissions and to address climate change issues in a substantive fashion is a striking example of the fusion of state and corporate interests to the detriment of the majority' (White 2011, p. 148).

Subsequent UN climate conferences at Cancun in 2010 (COP 16), Durban in 2011 (COP 17) and Rio de Janeiro in 2012 (Rio+20: 'The Conference on Sustainable Development') also failed to produce the strong international accord that environmental activists insist is necessary to head off climate change disaster. The last-minute deal arrived at in Durban in December 2011 does extend the Kyoto Protocol and launches negotiations on a more comprehensive and ambitious treaty regime (to take effect by 2020), but in the estimation of the Union of Concerned Scientists (2011, p. 1), 'will do little to accelerate near-term emissions reductions.' Many hoped that the Rio+20 conference, taking place in the same city twenty years after the UN Framework Convention of Climate Change had been negotiated, would assess why that treaty had been inadequate and take new legally binding steps to deal with the impending ecological catastrophe. But as the renowned environmental leader Vandana Shiva points out, 'the entire energy of the official process was focused on how to avoid any commitment. Rio+20 will be remembered for what it failed to do during a period of severe and multiple crises and not for what it achieved' (Shiva 2012, p. 1). The failure of these international conferences led some critical commentators to place the blame squarely on the corrupting relationship between corporations and states. Journalist George Monbiot argued that:

> These summits have failed for the same reason that the banks failed. Political systems that were supposed to represent everyone now return governments of millionaires, financed by and acting on behalf of billionaires. The past twenty years have been a billionaires' banquet. At the behest of corporations and the ultra-rich, governments have removed the constraining decencies-the laws and regulations-which prevent one person from destroying another. To expect governments funded and appointed by this class to protect the biosphere and defend the poor is like expecting a lion to live on gazpacho. (Monbiot 2012, p. 1)

With the failures of Copenhagen, Durban and Rio+20, the high hopes some had held for the Obama administration's ability to make a difference on the issue of climate change policy have been dashed (Hertsgaard 2011; Hertsgaard 2012). The failure of the Obama administration to successfully conclude a strong international agreement on climate change, however, must be placed within a broader political and economic context. First, President Obama took office during one of the worst economic crises in US history. The Wall Street financial crash of 2008 and the subsequent global recession, itself a monumental state-corporate crime (Scheer 2010; Barak 2012; Ferguson 2012), produced a political situation which demanded that the new administration had to first respond to the economic crisis and also severely limited its domestic political options for undertaking any new responses to climate change that might further weaken the economy in the short run. Second, and even more important, President Obama faced a Republican Party that obstructed any effort to deal with the issue of global warming in any way (Mooney 2005; Mooney 2012; Deans 2012). The administration was fully aware that any climate change treaty it submitted to the US Senate had absolutely no chance of being ratified due to unified Republican opposition.

The current Republican Party not only obstructs any action to mitigate climate change, it has also recently waged an unprecedented legislative assault on environmental regulations and safeguards of any type. After Republicans took control of the US House of Representatives in the 2010 midterm elections, they voted nearly two hundred separate times to block, delay or weaken foundational environmental laws that protect the air, water, wildlife and lands (Deans 2012). On the issue of global warming, the House voted in 2011 to repeal the EPA's authority to regulate greenhouse gas emissions, an authority that had been confirmed by the US Supreme Court (2007) in *Massachusetts* v. *Environmental Protection Agency*. Not a single Republican voted against the repeal, which then did not survive in the Senate (Deans 2012). None the less, House Republicans also voted down an amendment that simply stated that climate change is real, caused by human activities, and puts public health at risk. As Bob Deans of the Natural Resources Defense Council observed concerning these votes:

> We all have a right to our opinion. Something is badly askew, however, when the weight and consensus of the scientific world can be callously tossed aside by politicians who refuse to face facts and instead insist on blocking every reasonable attempt to begin the vital process of reducing the industrial carbon pollution that is changing our climate and threatening us all. That sorry spectacle was on vivid display in the 2011 House of Representatives. (Deans 2012, p. 16)

The corrupting influence of money in the form of corporate campaign contributions (to both major political parties) provides a partial explanation for these Congressional efforts to block climate change and other environmental actions. Lessig (2011) argues that money does indeed corrupt the legislative process and that the current campaign finance system has rendered Congress politically bankrupt. With billions of dollars of profits at stake, corporations in the fossil fuel industry have made a huge investment in lobbying efforts on Capitol Hill and used large campaign contributions to individual legislators to advance their economic interests in the Congress. According to Deans, since 1990 the oil and gas industry has contributed some $239 million in campaign contributions, and he notes: 'Most has gone to Republicans who support industry goals like limiting environmental protections, blocking measures to reduce climate change, and allowing drilling in the Alaska National Wildlife Refuge' (Deans 2012, p. 88).

Another factor responsible for this failure to mitigate climate change in the USA is the growing ideological extremism of the Republican Party. Kabaservice (2012) has documented how the current Republican Party evolved into one of the most uniformly ideological parties that has ever existed in US history. This ideological extremism has been fueled in recent years by the so-called 'Tea Party,' a right-wing populist movement. Skocpol and Williamson (2012) conclude in their analysis of this movement that grassroots activism, billionaire industrialist supporters (such as the Koch brothers, who made most of their money in hydrocarbons) and a right-wing media machine have combined to create and power the Tea Party and give it an extraordinary ability (out of all proportion to its numbers) to reshape the Republican Party and the national political discourse. As a result, they argue that the Republican Party has become an obstacle to any policies that might help the USA respond to the political and economic challenges of the day, including climate change. Two well-known scholars of Congress concur with this assessment (Mann and Ornstein 2012a; Mann and Ornstein 2012b). As they conclude in a recent study: 'The GOP [Republican Party] has become an insurgent outlier in American politics. It is ideologically extreme; scornful of compromise; unmoved by conventional understanding of facts, evidence, and science; and dismissive of its political opposition' (Mann and Ornstein 2012b, p. 1).

The Ideological Denial of Climate Change

As Michalowski points out: 'state crime arises not out of the singular actions of institutional actors or particular organizational goals, but out of the relational processes through which institutions of governance and accumulation, aided by ideological processes, ensure that individuals will embrace the goals of accumulation and governance as their own'

(Michalowski 2010, p. 26). The socially organized ideological denial of climate change illustrates this process well. A key factor in the Republican Party's political obstructionism on the issue of global warming, and in the general failure of the USA to produce any substantive domestic or international policy to mitigate greenhouse gas emissions, is the increasing politicization and polarization of the issue of climate change within US political culture. This politicization is primarily the result of the activities of a rogue fossil fuel industry and a conservative global warming denial counter-movement that deserves special examination.

Global warming denial efforts are largely carried out by conservative think tanks, such as the now infamous Heartland Institute (Ward 2012), which are funded for the most part by money from corporations in the fossil fuel industry (Gelbspan 2004; Greenpeace 2011, Jacques et al. 2008; Oreskes and Conway 2010; Powell 2011; Union of Concerned Scientists 2012a; Union of Concerned Scientists 2012b). For example, Western Fuels, a large coal cooperative, and the giant ExxonMobil oil company have each contributed millions of dollars to conservative think tanks and environmental skeptics working to deny global warming (Adams 2009; Jacques 2009; McNall 2011; Powell 2011). Oreskes and Conway (2010, p. 247) note that 'ExxonMobil's support for doubt-mongering and disinformation is disturbing but hardly surprising. What is surprising is to discover how extensive, organized, and interconnected these efforts have been, and for how long' (Oreskes and Conway 2010, p. 247).

As the Union of Concerned Scientists (2012b) has documented, corporations have a long history of corrupting science at the public's expense. The global warming denial counter-movement has taken this effort to a new level in its attempt to influence the US dialogue on climate science and policy (Union of Concerned Scientists 2012a). The denialist movement produces a large amount of ideological propaganda built around lies and deceptions masquerading as science. This corporate-friendly propaganda can be viewed as a set of what Norgaard (2011) calls 'legitimating and normalizing narratives.' These cultural narratives, which legitimate and normalize fossil fuel industry practices and cast doubt on climate science, are then disseminated through conservative think tanks, industry trade associations, right-wing opinion leaders, the Tea Party, the corporate media and by some Republican Party elected officials (Gelbspan 1998; Gelbspan 2004; McCright and Dunlap 2000; 2003; Hoggan 2009; Jacques 2009; Friel 2010; Hamilton 2010; Oreskes and Conway 2010; Powell 2011; Union of Concerned Scientists 2012a).

According to Diethelm and McKee (2009), denialist arguments (narratives) fall into the following categories: (1) conspiracy theories, (2) fake experts, (3) cherrypicking of data, (4) impossible expectations of what research can deliver and (5) misrepresentation and logical fallacies. Washington and Cook examined these arguments used by climate change denialists and concluded: 'Their goal is to convince the public and the media that there are sufficient grounds not to take the action recommended by the consensus position of mainstream science. To achieve this, the vocal minority employs rhetorical arguments that give the appearance of legitimate debate where there is none' (Washington and Cook 2011, p. 43).

The efforts to impede governmental actions that would force the fossil fuel industry to stop dumping its waste into the atmosphere have been very successful. A study of the conservative movement's impact on US climate change policy by McCright and Dunlop 'demonstrates how a powerful countermovement effectively challenged the environmental community's definition of global warming as a social problem and blocked the passage of any significant climate change policy' (McCright and Dunlop 2003, p. 348). The orchestrated denial of climate change, despite extensive scientific evidence to the contrary, is a state-corporate crime of *commission*. It is not a failure to act, but a deliberate attempt to thwart efforts to respond in an effective and just way to the emerging problems resulting from global warming. And as documented in the extensive research cited above, these efforts have indeed been extremely successful in creating doubt and re-shaping public opinion in a way that has hampered any political action on climate change in the USA.

A number of factors appear to be related to the success of this climate science disinformation and denial campaign in the US Congress. One is the crucial role the conservative think tanks, in alliance with scientific skeptics, have played in undermining the scientific consensus on global warming among the general public and specific politicians (McCright and Dunlop 2000; Powell 2011). A second factor is the influence of lobbyists from the coal, oil and gas companies who promote the denialist narratives. Lynch et al. (2010) documented the impact of these corporate lobbyists with regard to the politicization of climate change under the George W. Bush administration, and these lobbying tactics appear to be equally successful in Congress. Boeve and Smith point out that oil and gas corporations maintain an army of 786 lobbyists in Washington, DC—an army that 'is bigger than Congress itself which has only 535 members' (Boeve and Smith 2012, p. 1). A third factor is the promotion of climate change denial narratives by right-wing media such as Fox News and the Rush Limbaugh radio program. Many conservative politicians rely heavily on these 'news' sources, and are thus exposed to a constant drumbeat of climate change disinformation. In addition to the effect of right-wing media, the 'balancing norm' of the mainstream media also allows the views of denialists to be placed on a par with the views of climate scientists and thus also has an influence on the broader political culture (Powell 2011; Washington and Cook 2011).

Research shows that conservative white males, whom McCright and Dunlop (2011) call 'cool dudes,' are more likely than other adults in the USA to espouse climate change denial. This social group, of course, disproportionately occupies positions of power within the economic system and within the Republican Party. McCright and Dunlop (2011) argue that integrating insights from two separate theories can explain the link between the rejection of climate science and social and economic privilege. First, Kahan et al.'s (2007) identity protection cognition thesis argues that risk perception is shaped by cultural worldviews (hierarchical, individualistic in this case) that are shared by members of salient in-groups. Information threatening to one's cultural worldview and the beliefs associated with belonging to a particular group will be rejected to protect one's identity and the status and esteem that individuals receive from group membership. Information about climate change provides just such a threat to these conservative white males who hold hierarchical and individualistic cultural worldviews and is therefore likely to be rejected by them. In addition, Jost et al. (2008) assert that conservatives have stronger system justification tendencies, supporting maintenance of the status quo and resisting attempts to change it. System justification is associated with the denial of problems, such as climate change, that threaten system functioning. McCright and Dunlop's data provide additional empirical support for these theories, and they conclude that 'the unique views of conservative white males contribute significantly to the high level of climate change denial in the United States' (McCright and Dunlop 2011, p. 1,163). While this 'cultural cognition' approach provides important insights about the phenomenon of climate change denial, it does have its limits. As Klein astutely points out: 'The deniers are doing more than protecting their cultural worldview-they are protecting powerful interests that stand to gain from muddying the waters of the climate debate' (Klein 2011, p. 18).

Conclusion

On the podium in Philadelphia in 1939, what Edwin H. Sutherland really said in his key speech as President of the American Sociological Association—once the camouflage is removed—is that white-collar crime is wrong—indeed, that often it is despicable—and that sociologists and economists ought to pay close attention to such matters and join with him in a crusade to do something about them (Geis 1982, p. 18).

As the social science research cited above demonstrates, the ties between the fossil fuel industry and conservative think tanks that provide the denialist narratives are well documented, as are the linkages between the think tanks and the Republican Party that obstructs any attempt to deal with climate change in the USA and international political arena. The worst effects of climate change and the harms it will impose on its victims cannot be avoided unless there are drastic and rapid reductions in global greenhouse gas emissions. The energy corporations and their political and ideological supporters understand all too well that achieving these necessary reductions will require a radical reordering of the economic and political systems at the heart of the global capitalist system. This is what they are desperately fighting to avoid, and they are using every powerful tool available to them to perpetrate this catastrophic environmental state-corporate crime. A crusade, a transformative international social movement that has as its goal the drastic reduction of greenhouse gas emissions, is desperately needed. Following the lead of Sutherland, perhaps we criminologists can play a role in provoking this movement by using the conceptual language of *crime* to bring greater attention to these matters and help generate moral outrage at the destructive relationship between the fossil fuel industry and states that allows catastrophic climate change and its victimization to continue unabated.

References

Abrams, N.L. and Primack, J.R. 2011. *The New Universe and the Human Future: How a Shared Cosmology Could Transform the World*. New Haven, CT: Yale University Press.

Adams, D. 2009. 'ExxonMobil Continuing to Fund Climate Sceptic Groups, Records Show,' *The Guardian*, July 1: www.guardian.co.uk/environment/2009/jul/01/exxon-mobil-climate-change-sceptics-funding/ (accessed May 3, 2012).

Agnew, R. 2011a. 'Dire Forecast: A Theoretical Model of the Impact of Climate Change on Crime,' *Theoretical Criminology* 16, 21–42.

Agnew, R. 2011b. *Toward a Unified Criminology: Integrating Assumptions About Crime, People, and Society*. New York: New York University Press.

Barak, G. (ed.). 1991. *Crimes by the Capitalist State: An Introduction to State Criminality*. Albany, NY: State University of New York Press.

Barak, G. 2012. *Theft of a Nation: Wall Street Looting and Federal Regulatory Colluding*. Lanham, MD: Rowman and Littlefield.

BBC. 2009. 'Copenhagen Summit Battles to Save Climate Deal.' BBC News, December 19: http://news.bbc.co.uk/2/hi/science/nature/8422031.stm (accessed September 19, 2011).

Boeve, M. and Smith, B. 2012. 'Fossil-fuel Subsidies are the Real Job Killers,' *Common Dreams*, April 12: www.commondreams.org/view/2012/04/13-0 (accessed April 13, 2012).

Broder, J. 2010. 'A Novel Tactic in Climate Fight Gains Some Traction,' *The New York Times*, November 8: www.nytimes.com/2010/11/09/science/earth/09montreal.html?ref=science&src (accessed 10 March 2011).

Burbach, R., Nunez, O. and Kagarlitsky, B. 1996. *Globalization and Its Discontents: The Rise of Postmodern Socialisms*. London: Pluto Press.

businessGreen. 2011a. 'Green Groups to Sue US Government Over Atmospheric Pollution,' *businessGreen*: www.businessgreen.com/bg/news/2068121/green-sue-government-atmospheric-pollution (accessed March 6, 2014).

businessGreen. 2011b. 'US States Accuse Polluting Power Stations of "Public Nuisance,"' *businessGreen*: www.businessgreen.com/bg/news/2034401/accuse-polluting-power-stations-public nuisance (accessed October 20, 2011).

Carter, J. 1977. 'Proposed Energy Policy': www.pbs.org/wgbh/americanexperience/features/primary-resources/carter-energy/ (accessed March 21, 2012).

Climate Central. 2012. *Global Weirdness: Severe Storms, Deadly Heat Waves, Relentless Drought, Rising Seas, and the Weather of the Future*. New York: Pantheon Books.

Deans, B. 2012. *Reckless: The Political Assault on the American Environment*. Lanham, MD: Rowman & Littlefield.

Derber, C. 2010. *Greed to Green: Solving Climate Change and Remaking the Economy*. Boulder, CO: Paradigm Publishers.

Diethelm, P. and McKee, M. 2009. 'Denialism: What is It and How Should Scientists Respond?', *European Journal of Public Health* 19, 2–4.

Dow, K. and Downing, T. 2011. *The Atlas of Climate Change: Mapping the World's Greatest Challenge*, 3rd edn. Berkeley, CA: University of California Press.

Dunn, T. 1995. *Militarization of the U.S.–Mexico Border: Low Intensity Warfare Comes Home*. Austin, TX: University of Texas Press.

Dyer, G. 2010. *Climate Wars: The Fight for Survival as the World Overheats*. Oxford: Oneworld Publications.

Engelhardt, T. 2010. 'Tomgram: Bill McKibben, the Enthusiasm Gap in the White House', *TomDispatch.com*, September 16: www.tomdispatch.com/blog/175296/ (accessed May 3, 2012).

Ferguson, C. 2012. *Predator Nation: Corporate Criminals, Political Corruption, and the Hijacking of America*. New York: Crown Business.

Foster, J.B. 2009. *The Ecological Revolution: Making Peace with the Planet*. New York: Monthly Review Press.

Friedrichs, D. 2010. *Trusted Criminals: White Collar Crime in Contemporary Society*, 4th edn. Belmont, CA: Wadsworth.

Friel, H. 2010. *The Lomborg Deception: Setting the Record Straight About Global Warming*. New Haven, CT: Yale University Press.

Geis, G. 1982. 'Edwin H. Sutherland: A Biographical and Analytic Commentary,' in *White-collar and Economic Crime*, edited by P. Wickman and T. Dailey. Lexington, MA: Lexington Books, 3–21.

Gelbspan, R. 1998. *The Heat is On: The Climate Crisis, the Cover-up, the Prescription*, updated edn. Reading, MA: Perseus Books.

Gelbspan, R. 2004. *Boiling Point: How Politicians, Big Oil and Coal, Journalists, and Activists are Fueling the Climate Crisis—and What We Can Do to Avert Disaster*. New York: Basic Books.

Giddens, A. 2011. *The Politics of Climate Change*, 2nd edn. Cambridge: Polity Press.

Greenpeace. 2011. *Who's Holding Us Back? How Carbon Intensive Industry is Preventing Effective Climate Legislation*. Amsterdam: Greenpeace International.

Gribbin, J. 2011. *Alone in the Universe: Why Our Planet is Unique*. Hoboken, NJ: John Wiley & Sons.

Hamilton, C. 2010. *Requiem for a Species: Why We Resist the Truth About Climate Change*. London: Earthscan.

Hansen, J. 2009. *Storms of My Grandchildren: The Truth About the Coming Climate Catastrophe and Our Last Chance to Save Humanity*. New York: Bloomsbury.

Hertsgaard, M. 2011. 'Durban: Where the Climate Deniers-in-chief Ran the Show,' *The Nation*, December 14: www.thenation.com/article/165155/durban-where-climate-deniers-chief-ran-show (accessed February 2, 2012).

Hertsgaard, M. 2012. 'Déjà Vu at Rio+20,' *The Nation*, June 14: www.thenation.com/article/168387/deja-vu-rio20 (accessed June 14, 2012).

Higgins, P. 2010. *Eradicating Ecocide: Exposing the Corporate and Political Practices Destroying the Planet and Proposing the Laws Needed to Eradicate Ecocide*. London: Shepheard-Walwyn Publishers.

Hillyard, P., Pantazis, C., Tombs, S. and Gordon, D. (eds.). 2004. *Beyond Criminology: Taking Harm Seriously*. London: Pluto Press.

Hoggan, J. 2009. *Climate Cover-up*. Vancouver: Greystone Books.

Honisch, B. et al. 2012. 'The Geological Record of Ocean Acidification,' *Science* 335, 1,058–63.

IPCC. 2007. *Climate Change 2007: Climate Change Impacts, Adaptation, and Vulnerability*. Geneva: Intergovernmental Panel on Climate Change.

Jacques, P. 2009. *Environmental Skepticism: Ecology, Power and Public Life*. Farnham: Ashgate.

Jacques, P., Dunlap, R. and Freeman, M. 2008. 'The Organization of Denial: Conservative Think Tanks and Environmental Skepticism, *Environmental Politics* 17, 349–85.

Jessop, B. 1991. *State Theory: Putting Capitalist States in Their Place*. Philadelphia, PA: University of Pennsylvania Press.

Jost, J., Nosek, B. and Gosling, S. 2008. 'Ideology: Its Resurgence in Social, Personality, and Political Psychology,' *Perspectives on Psychological Science* 3, 126–36.

Kabaservice, G. 2012. *Rule and Ruin: The Downfall of Moderation and the Destruction of the Republican Party, from Eisenhower to the Tea Party*. New York: Oxford University Press.

Kahan, D., Braman, D., Gastil, J., Slovic, P. and Mertz, C. 2007. 'Culture and Identity-protective Cognition: Explaining the White-male Effect in Risk Perception,' *Journal of Empirical Legal Studies* 4, 465–505.

Kauzlarich, D., Mullins, C. and Matthews, R. 2003. 'A Complicity Continuum of State Crime, *Contemporary Justice Review* 6, 241–54.

Klare, M. 2012. *The Race for What's Left: The Global Scramble for the World's Last Resources*. New York: Metropolitan Books.

Klein, N. 2011. 'Capitalism vs. the Climate,' *The Nation*, November 28, 11–21.

Kramer, R. 2012. 'Public Criminology and the Responsibility to Speak in the Prophetic Voice Concerning Global Warming,' in *State Crime And Resistance*, edited by E. Stanley and J. McCulloch. London: Routledge, 41–53.

Kramer, R. and Michalowski, R. 1990. 'Toward an Integrated Theory of State-corporate Crime,' paper presented at the American Society of Criminology Meeting, Baltimore, MD, November.

Kramer, R. and Michalowski, R. 2006. 'The Original Formulation,' in *State-corporate Crime: Wrongdoing at the Intersection of Business and Government*, edited by R. Michalowski and R. Kramer. New Brunswick, NJ: Rutgers University Press, 18–26.

Kramer, R. and Michalowski, R. 2012. 'Is Global Warming a State-corporate Crime?', in *Climate Change from a Criminological Perspective*, edited by R. White. New York: Springer, 71–88.

Leaf, D. 2001. 'Managing Global Atmospheric Change: A U.S. Policy Perspective, *Human and Ecological Risk Assessment* 7, 1,211–26.

Lessig, L. 2011. *Republic, Lost: How Money Corrupts Congress—and a Plan to Stop It*. New York: Grand Central Publishing.

Lynch, M. and Stretesky, P. 2003. 'The Meaning of Green: Contrasting Criminological Perspectives,' *Theoretical Criminology* 7, 217–38.

Lynch, M. and Stretesky, P. 2010. 'Global Warming, Global Crime: A Green Criminological Perspective,' in *Global Environmental Harm: Criminological Perspectives*, edited by R. White. Cullompton: Willan Publishing, 62–84.

Lynch, M., Burns, R. and Stretesky, P. 2010. 'Global Warming and State-corporate Crime: The Politicization of Global Warming Under the Bush Administration,' *Crime, Law and Social Change*, 54, 213–39.

Mann, T. and Ornstein, N. 2012a. *It's Even Worse Than It Looks: How the American Constitutional System Collided with the New Politics of Extremism*. New York: Basic Books.

Mann, T. and Ornstein, N. 2012b. 'Let's Just Say It: The Republicans are the Problem,' *Washington Post*, April 27: www.washingtonpost.com/opinions/lets-just-say-it-the-republicans-are-the-problem/2012/04/27/gIQAxCVUlT_story.html (accessed March 6, 2014).

McCright, A. and Dunlap, R. 2000. 'Challenging Global Warming as a Social Problem: An Analysis of the Conservative Movement's Counter-claims,' *Social Problems* 47, 499–522.

McCright, A. and Dunlap, R. 2003. 'Defeating Kyoto: The Conservative Movement's Impact on U.S. Climate Change Policy,' *Social Problems* 50, 348–373.

McCright, A. and Dunlop, R. 2011. 'Cool Dudes: The Denial of Climate Change Among Conservative White Males in the United States,' *Global Environmental Change* 21, 1,163–72.

McKibben, B. 2010a. 'Copenhangover: Rallying for Next Steps,' *Mother Jones*, January 19: www.motherjones.com/politics/2010/01/copenhagen-next-steps (accessed March 15, 2012).

McKibben, B. 2010b. *Eaarth: Making Life on a Tough New Planet*. New York: Times Books.

McKibben, B. 2012. 'Global Warming's Terrifying New Math: Three Simple Numbers that Add Up to Global Catastrophe—and that Make Clear Who the Real Enemy Is,' *Rolling Stone*, August 2: www.rollingstone.com/politics/news/global-warmings-terrifying-new-math-20120719 (accessed March 6, 2014).

McNall, S. 2011. *Rapid Climate Change: Causes, Consequences, and Solutions*. New York: Routledge.

Michalowski, R. 1985. *Order, Law and Crime*. New York: Random House.

Michalowski, R. 2010. 'In Search of "State and Crime" in State Crime Studies,' in *State Crime in the Global Age*, edited by W. Chambliss, R. Michalowski and R. Kramer, Cullompton: Willan Publishing, 13–30.

Michalowski, R. and Kramer, R. 2006. *State-corporate Crime: Wrongdoing at the Intersection of Business and Government*. New Brunswick, NJ: Rutgers University Press.

Michalowski, R. and Kramer, R. 2007. 'State-corporate Crime and Criminological Inquiry, in *International Handbook of White-collar and Corporate Crime*, edited by H. Pontell and G. Geis. New York: Springer, 200–219.

Michalowski, R. and Kramer, R. 2013. 'Transnational Environmental Crime,' in *The Handbook of Transnational Crime and Justice*, 2nd edn., edited by P. Reichel and J. Albanese. Thousand Oaks, CA: Sage Publications, 189–212.

Mills, C.W. 1956. *The Power Elite*. New York: Oxford.

Monbiot, G. 2012. 'The Earth Cannot be Saved by Hope and Billionaires,' *Common Dreams*, June 19: www.commondreams.org/view/2012/06/19 (accessed June 19, 2012).

Mooney, C. 2005. *The Republican War on Science*. New York: Basic Books.

Mooney, C. 2012. *The Republican Brain: The Science of Why They Deny Science—and Reality*. Hoboken, NJ: John Wiley & Sons.

Morris, D. 2012. 'Texas Judge Rules "The Sky Belongs to Everyone,' *Common Dreams*, July 26: www.commondreams.org/view/2012/07/26-2 (accessed July 26, 2012).

Norgaard, K.M. 2011. *Living in Denial: Climate Change, Emotions, and Everyday Life*. Cambridge, MA: MIT Press.

Oreskes, N. and Conway, E. 2010. *Merchants of Doubt: How a Handful of Scientists Obscured the Truth on Issues from Tobacco to Global Warming*. New York: Bloomsbury Press.

Parenti, C. 2011. *Tropic of Chaos: Climate Change and the New Geography of Violence*. New York: Nation Books.

Pemberton, S. 2007. 'Social Harm Future(s): Exploring the Potential of the Social Harm Approach,' *Crime, Law and Social Change* 48(1–2), 27–41.

Powell, J. 2011. *The Inquisition of Climate Science*. New York: Columbia University Press.

Richardson, K., Steffan, W. and Liverman, D. 2011. *Climate Change: Global Risks, Challenges and Decisions*. New York: Cambridge University Press.

Sanders, B. 2009. *The Green Zone: The Environmental Costs of Militarism*. Oakland: AK Press.

Sassen, S. 1993. *Losing Control? Sovereignty in the Age of Globalization*. New York: Columbia University Press.

Scheer, R. 2010. *The Great American Stickup*. New York: Nation Books.

Shiva, V. 2012. 'Rio+20: An Undesirable U-turn,' *Common Dreams*, July 3: www.commondreams.org/view/2012/07/03-2 (accessed March 6, 2014).

Skocpol, T. and Williamson, V. 2012. *The Tea Party and the Remaking of Republican Conservatism*. New York: Oxford University Press.

South, N. 2009. 'Ecocide, Conflict and Climate Change: Challenges for Criminology and the Research Agenda in the 21st Century,' in *Eco-crime and Justice: Essays on Environmental Crime*, edited by K. Kangaspunta and I.H. Marshall. Turin: UNICRI, 37–53.

Tift, L. and Sullivan, D. 2001. 'A Needs-based, Social Harms Approach to Defining Crime,' in *What is Crime? Controversies Over the Nature of Crime and What to Do About It*, edited by S. Henry and M. Lanier. Lanham, MD: Rowman & Littlefield, 179–203.

Union of Concerned Scientists. 2011. 'Outcome at Durban Climate Negotiations Offers Limited Progress,' *Common Dreams*, December 13: www.commondreams.org/newswire/2011/12/13-8 (accessed March 15, 2012).

Union of Concerned Scientists. 2012a. *A Climate of Corporate Control: How Corporations Have Influenced the U.S. Dialogue on Climate Science and Policy*. Cambridge, MA: UCS Publications.

Union of Concerned Scientists. 2012b. *Heads They Win, Tails We Lose: How Corporations Corrupt Science at the Public's Expense*. Cambridge, MA: UCS Publications.

US Supreme Court. 2007. Opinion of the Court in *Massachusetts* v. *Environmental Protection Agency*, 549 US 497.

Vaughn, D. 1996. *The Challenger Launch Decision: Risky Technology, Culture and Deviance at NASA*. Chicago, IL: University of Chicago Press.

Ward, B. 2012. 'Heartland Institute Leak Exposes Strategies of Climate Attack Machine,' *Common Dreams*, February 21: www.commondreams.org/view/2012/02/21-9 (accessed February 21, 2012).

Washington, H. and Cook, J. 2011. *Climate Change Denial: Heads in the Sand*. London: Earthscan.

White, R. 2008. *Crimes Against Nature: Environmental Criminology and Ecological Justice*. Cullompton: Willan Publishing.

White, R. 2009. 'Dealing with Climate Change and Social Conflict: A Research Agenda for Eco-global Criminology, in *Eco-crime and Justice: Essays on Environmental Crime*, edited by K. Kangaspunta and I.H. Marshall. Turin: UNICRI, 14–35.

White, R. (ed.). 2010. *Global Environmental Harm: Criminological Perspectives*. Cullompton: Willan Publishing.

White, R. 2011. *Transnational Environmental Crime: Toward an Eco-global Criminology*. London: Routledge.

White, R. (ed.). 2012. *Climate Change from a Criminological Perspective*. New York: Springer.

Wonders, N. and Solop, F. 1993. 'Understanding the Emergence of Law and Public Policy: Toward a Relational Model of the State,' in *Making Law: The State, the Law and Structural Contradictions*, edited by W. Chambliss and M. Zatz. Bloomington, IN: University of Indiana Press, 204–28.

Yamin, F. 1998. 'The Kyoto Protocol: Origins, Assessment, and Future Challenges,' *Review of European Community and International Law* 7, 113–28.

Chapter 3
The Corporation as Villain and Victim: Reflections on Privilege, Complicity, Awareness, and Accountability

Mary Clifford

Introduction

In the early 1990s, the term 'environmental criminology' was most directly connected to the crime prevention through environmental design (CPTED) work of Paul and Patricia Brantingham (1981). At the time, their definition of 'environment' was seen to be a fairly significant departure from what environmental sociologists were studying. Their focus on environment was less a reference to the natural environmental and more of a social reference to conditions surrounding when and where crime occurred with the expressed intent of making efforts to reduce the convergence of conditions which made crime more likely to happen.

Some of us were using that term, arguably incorrectly (although those conversations are ongoing), but when we used the term, we knew we were focused on an entirely different set of crime questions. For those interested in environmental issues, in using the terms 'environmental crime' and 'environmental criminology' the focus was actually on how to best ask interdisciplinary and (at the time what we called) international justice questions about the role of the criminal justice and other social systems and institutions, like government and higher education, in addressing environmental issues. When people and groups within our academic circles were asking these questions about environmental accountability and harm, it became more and more clear that the traditional criminal justice models were problematic. For one reason, the focus on the adversarial nature of legal proceedings, where victims and offenders 'fight' to claim title to who is 'right' under the law did not have a means by which an ecosystem or a body of water could bring a complaint against those causing it harm.

Moving at the time into a broader study of what some were calling 'green criminology' and others were discussing as 'environmental crime' and 'environmental criminology,' we were all focused fundamentally on a similar question: How do we reflect on the obstacles between our desire to secure environmental stability within a process where one has to secure and prove access to their place in the judicial process? From this question, a host of additional questions and areas of interest are being explored all around the world in an effort to assess the issue more completely, and for some, to create ways to best assure a fair, accessible process for securing the stability of (and, in our language, 'justice' for) 'nature,' natural systems, ecosystems, and animals, including humans. The fact that the systems, institutions, and structures designed to assess justice exist in a social position of superior placement, in a place to make judgments about the environment, while at the same time enjoying the benefits of its very existence because the social systems are made possible by the life-giving systems of the natural environment is a fascinating paradox. Within this paradox lie some interesting social problems which require redress. There is a rather faulty kind of logic in place when a social system is granted the authority to make decisions which give people the ability to determine whether or not they affect these natural systems in negative ways. This must be discussed. Further, the discussion of how this social system has defined 'people' is central to uncovering the kind of flawed thinking which has allowed—or more specifically, made legal—the acceptability of this ongoing environmental harm. The idea that this kind of work was absent from traditional criminology seemed obvious to those of us captured by what was seen as an obvious need for this work in the field of criminology, and we believed it was—still believe it is—in need of deliberate focused attention. The idea that solutions to these environmental problems might come from within this same social system, a system that purports to advocate justice, seemed clearly less obvious.

The focus here is to review the structure of social systems as they have developed and evolved in the United States. Attention is directed specifically to the corporation and the legal system which defines and supports this structure in an advantaged way. While giving advantage to the corporation, this same legal system offered diminished support to the African American communities after slavery, and in fact supported the construction of neoslavery with additional legal support being offered by judicial decisions, policing agencies, and informal structures of deviance-defining. Attention is devoted to the unsustainable construction of privilege, and in the USA this comes to a large degree in the form of race, class, and gender privilege, but we will focus here on race and class. The idea is complex yet simple: in order to reach a collective capacity to address the injustice of environmental harm, we have to move beyond oppressive systems of the past which are the obstacles that stand between us and environmental protections. One of the best ways to do that is to deconstruct the dichotomous ways of seeing victim and offender as two separate and opposing people or positions, and instead to think creatively about ways to move environmental concerns out of the same systems of justice created to regulate individual behaviors. Countries referred to as 'developing nations' are taking a lead in this, and efforts to unpack the ways in which privilege and self-superiority have been developed in the United States as a guiding principle must be reconsidered to value relationship-building over corporate control and economic indicators of success.

Discussing a History of a System of Systems

The roots of the criminal justice system in the United States predate US independence as a nation. This means, of course, that the justice system was in place before the abolition of slavery, before the right to vote was extended to Americans who were not white, male property owners (albeit this happened in stages), and preceded the Industrial Revolution which led to the rise of the modern corporate state. Massive protests and social activism was intent on organizing an expansion of civil rights for people of color, and with that the rights of women and children. In its short history as a country, the USA has orchestrated the rise of the corporate state, originally an ideological structure created as a tool for economic systems, and sandwiched historically between the engines of the slave plantation and the more recent US economic expansion into the global marketplace.

The dramatic changes in these United States over the last hundred years have required parallel and in some cases dramatic social change in various social systems, including the political system, the economic system, educational systems, religious systems, and family systems, as well as the way individuals relate to and understand these systems. More recently, the technological and computer advances of the digital age have warranted even further reflection and modification to the traditional laws, social attitudes, and social practices. While critical reflection could be offered on various social systems, focused attention is given here to the corporate structure within the economic system and the role of the justice system—particularly the legal system, the judicial system, and the related enforcement systems—as an obstacle to the creation of essential and sustainable environmental protection efforts.

These biological and ecological systems overlap, of course, with the social systems humans have organized; however, it would be hard to argue with the fundamental idea that these natural systems are in fact the supporting systems upon which human systems were built and *are* sustained. Many of the systems created in the United States, using the corporate advancements made over the last hundred years as a something of a historical marker, have been built on policies and practices that go back in history even further still. Interestingly, the corporate advancements made over the last 100 years can also be used as something of an economic marker of success. Ironically, legal assessments as to the appropriate and inappropriate degrees of human interaction with ecological and biological systems act as both plaintiff and prosecutor. And yet, it only takes a bit of deliberate reflection to reach the obvious, or at least one obvious, conclusion—that the fusion of the corporation and the economic system and the justice system was purposeful and intentional. Interestingly, ironically, or intentionally, it is unquestionably undeniable that in intellectual efforts to better understand how social systems affect the environment, the fundamental nature of these natural and ecological systems as the foundation for human life is overlooked, if not ignored intentionally.

In his book *The Rules of Sociological Method* (1895), sociologist Emile Durkheim described sociology as the 'science of social institutions, their genesis, and their functioning.' The massive US expansion as a nation has created systems out of these social institutions which require management. Traditional ways of managing social harm include policies, regulations, laws, violations, enforcement practices, investigations, prosecutions, and punishments, to name a few—in fact, lots of rules. But rules and regulations drafted by humans are not necessarily the same rules and regulations that govern biological and ecological systems. And interestingly, to say that the rules and regulations in the United States were drafted by people would require a clarifying statement. The 'people' who drafted the original framework of laws to regulate society were white, male property owners of good moral character. This is an idea we will return to later.

Efforts to address or redress environmental harm seem to operate outside of both the legal or economic structures designed by 'people.' Remember how easy it is to forget that the natural environment is a foundational structure for the existence of human life. The institutions and systems of the US social environment could not exist without the ability to breathe air, eat food, and drink water. In an effort to better understand how the legal system could be used by the founders to create 'justice' in the USA, as discussed above, it appears that the foundational aspects of the laws of nature seem to again go unacknowledged. This, too, is an important point we will return to later.

Under the current criminal justice and legal system, efforts to address various specialized areas in society inevitably became specialized areas of law. Several examples of what have been identified as specialized areas of legal practice which, it has been argued, do not fit neatly into the traditional criminal justice system include family courts, probate courts, tax courts, water courts, land courts, administrative courts, small claims courts, juvenile courts, drug courts, business and commercial courts, Indian and Native American courts, domestic violence courts, and more recently environmental courts (Zimmer 2009, pp. 11–12).

In spite of their best efforts, the rules of nature do not fit neatly into the existing system of criminal justice designed to provide legal redress when a dispute arises.

When it comes to addressing environmental issues, particularly environmental harms and crimes, consider what is known:

1. Many people will knowingly purchase products harmful to the environment.
2. Many people will knowingly use controversial, potentially hazardous technologies.
3. Many people will knowingly eat foods that are genetically modified despite not fully understanding the consequences of this modification.
4. Many people will knowingly use drugs processed, marketed, and recommended by medical professionals with little understanding of either the short- or long-term consequences to the individual, as well as to the environment, as a result of toxic chemicals used in production processes.

All of us are likely in a position to say that we have participated in at least some of these processes in one way or another. Certainly, ongoing efforts to minimize risk and maximize utility are pursued by government regulatory agencies and/or by the companies themselves. And yet, meanwhile, why do smart, informed people behave in ways that they know may not be good for them?

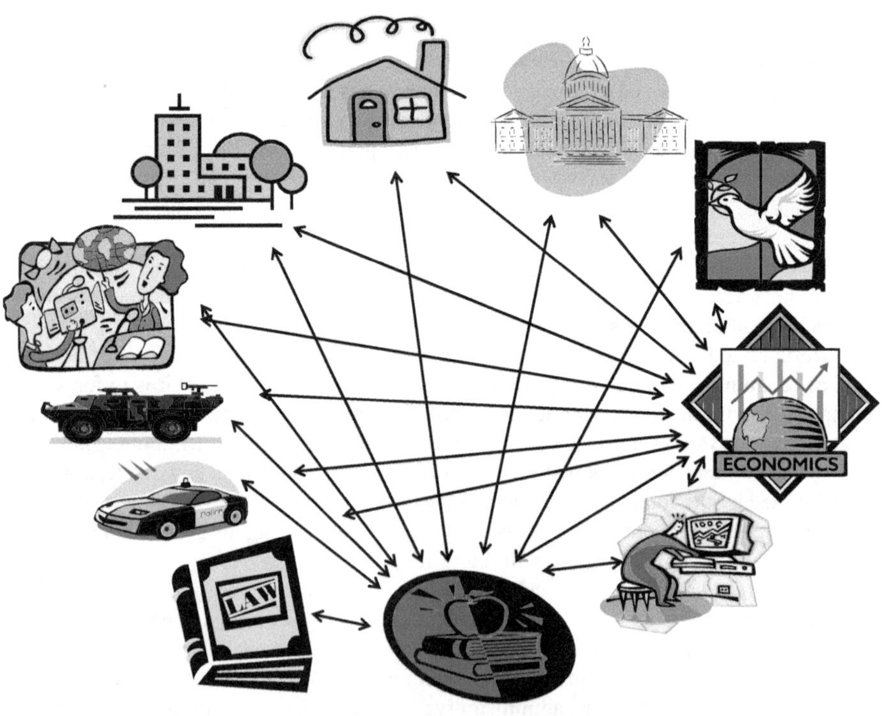

Figure 3.1 Graphic representation of social system interactions

What About Those Interesting Interactions Between People and Institutions?

Many of the regulatory and enforcement systems designed to make groups and individuals accountable to the larger society are said to be connected to and processed through the criminal justice system. Figure 3.1 was designed to highlight the fact that each of these systems has a dynamic effect as it connects with other systems which are also connecting with even more systems. The systems reflected here, although not an exhaustive list, include (beginning at the noon position as if looking at a clock) the family system, the political system, the religious system, the economic system, technological systems, educational systems, legal systems, enforcement systems, military systems, communications systems, and the systems associated with industry and corporations. Each of these systems interacts with other systems, and the dynamics of these systems become complicated quickly.

Whether focused on the systems and institutions or on the monstrous network that has been created to manage these human systems, outrage develops when systems are not accountable to people who are injured by the actions and practices of these same systems. While the categories of 'victim' and 'offender' are familiar ways to discuss harm within the current system of justice, some of the controversy becomes rhetorical when the language of 'victim' and 'offender' is also used to create sides and draw battle lines as controversies develop. Figure 3.2 represents the centrality of the justice system, where some might say, 'The capitalistic buck stops here.'

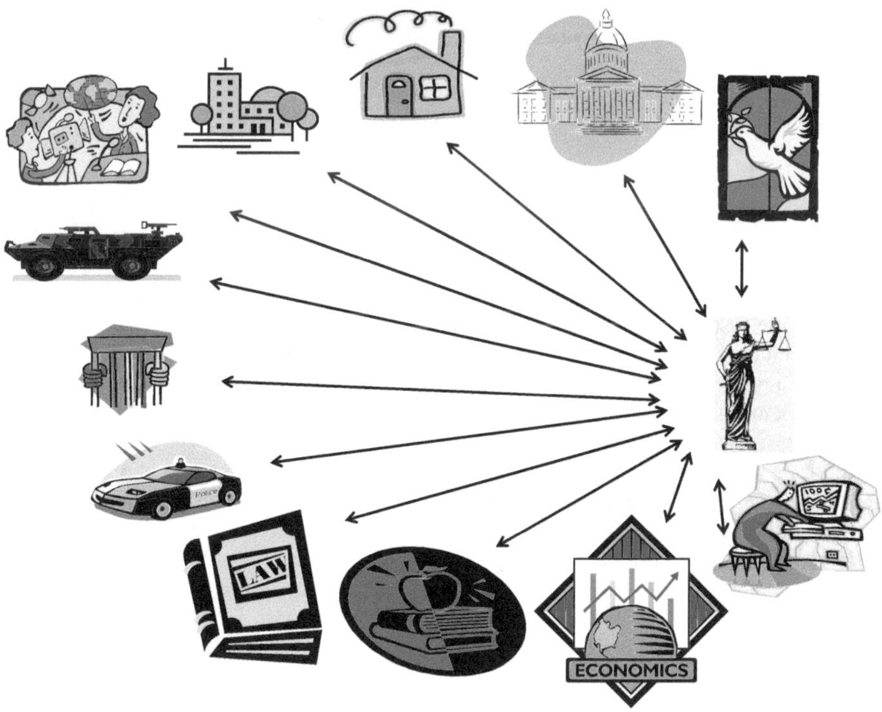

Figure 3.2 The centrality of the justice system in mediating system conflict

Figure 3.3 Social system interaction effects on the individual

When you consider the macro level social systems and the network of institutional systems created in an effort to regulate society, it is easy to think about how any individual might have difficulty navigating each of these various systems and institutional structures. At the same time, one cannot overlook the natural laws and the foundational reality of nature as the essential system upon which social systems and institutions rest. It seems to me this cannot be said enough. Figure 3.3 has been included for a little comedic effect, but it reflects a degree of truth. The burden of the complexity of the contemporary structure of social systems and institutions takes a toll.

The idea that we look to one specific system—the criminal justice system—to address, support, or refute the complaints raised by other systems is profound. Although there is much to be said about the influence these various institutions have on the criminal justice system, the focus of this chapter is on the relationship between the environment, people, corporations, and the criminal justice system.

Corporations as People ... Really? Really.

In the United States, the 2012 presidential election campaign produced a laser-like focus on the role of corporations in US life. Republican presidential nominee Mitt Romney featured strongly in nightly news reports and social media outlets after his response to an individual at a campaign rally who had challenged him about his reputation for putting corporations over people. Romney famously replied: 'Corporations are people, my friend.'[1] His comments were quickly seized upon by members of the opposing Democratic Party. US Senate candidate Elizabeth Warren, subsequently elected as Democratic Senator for Massachusetts, referred to Romney's comments in a highly publicized speech at the Democratic National Convention in the form of an introduction to President Bill Clinton. In part of her speech, she said:

> No, Governor Romney, corporations are not people. People have hearts. They have kids. They get jobs. They get sick. They cry, they dance, they live, they love and they die. And that matters. That matters because we don't run this country for corporations, we run it for people.[2]

Despite a resounding response to the ideology behind Warren's speech in local news and social media, Romney's assessment is absolutely legally and economically correct.

As has been suggested above, the criminal justice system in the United States operates from within a collection of social institutions. The 14th amendment to the US Constitution was ratified on July 9, 1868, granting citizenship to all persons born or naturalized in the United States, including former slaves. The suggestion to the court was that a corporation should be identified and legally defined as a 'person.' While the original purpose of articles of incorporation in business was to organize teams or business entities for large-scale projects, such as interstate road construction or bridges, the judges agreed. These judges, working from within the emerging legal structure of the day, took the definition of a person and applied it to property, while choosing at the same time to avoid its application to an entire race of individuals for which the 14th Amendment's Equal Protection Clause was originally drafted to serve. This point requires further explanation, and was illustrated beautifully in the award-winning film *The Corporation* (Archbar et al. 2003).

A brief history lesson reminds us that the people who were held as slaves were emancipated in the United States as a result of the 13th Amendment to the US Constitution. According to author and historian Howard Zinn, the 14th Amendment was passed to ensure equal rights were extended to freed slaves. The 14th Amendment was written to ensure that no state could deprive any person of life, liberty, or property without due process of the law—referred to more commonly as the Equal Protection Clause. In *Santa Clara County* v. *Southern Pacific Railroad*, the Chief Justice of the US Supreme Court stated that for the purposes before the court, which was an issue of taxation, corporations had the same rights as a person as outlined in the 14th Amendment.[3] Over time, the focus of this provision was redirected, however, and the court began according corporations the same rights as natural persons.

Arguably, the result was that rather than protecting newly freed slaves, the 14th Amendment was used to create the legal definition of corporate personhood. Consider, for example, that 307 cases were brought before the Court under the 14th Amendment

1 tpmtv, 'Romney: Corporations Are People, My Friend': www.youtube.com/watch?v=KlPQkd_AA6c (accessed March 6, 2014).

2 ABC News Specials, 'Elizabeth Warren's Full Speech at DNC: "Corporations Are Not People"': www.hulu.com/watch/398415 (accessed March 6, 2014).

3 NPR, 'What Is the Basis for Corporate Personhood?' John Witt interviewed by Melissa Block on *All Things Considered*, October 24, 2011: www.npr.org/2011/10/24/141663195/what-is-the-basis-for-corporate-personhood (accessed March 6, 2014).

between 1890 and 1910. Of those, 288 cases were brought by corporations and 19 by African Americans.[4] Because the legacy of forced labor and genocide in the United States is often easily overlooked or forgotten, the role of forced labor and slavery as a foundation for the contemporary structure of social institutions and the resulting social systems, which has expanded into a global system of corporate governance, is often not included in conversations about the organizing principles and values that were incorporated into these arguments before the courts.

Corporate structures which (or perhaps we should say 'who') have demonstrated (or perhaps we should say 'perpetrated') harm against workers, human health, animals, and the biosphere have been afforded the same rights, legally, as an individual. But think about this further. While the collective 'we' tend to forget that the environmental systems are the foundation upon which human and nonhuman ecological systems exists, the collective 'we' also tends to forget that the social systems of today were developed out of what some might call a massive legal, specifically judicial, set of decisions, where the law was interpreted to the benefit some and to the disadvantage of others. Since that time, in decisions on how to protect a corporation from protesters upset about wages or environmental harms, the state's obligation to protect the corporation as a person is invoked again, and the judicial structure of the adversarial system sets up one side against the other. Corporations assert the state's obligation to protect the life, liberty, and property of the corporation in the same way it was designed to protect the people. Considerable attention over time, however, suggests that the practice of treating people and corporations as equal under the law has produced disparate effects.

Lawyers, policy makers, police officers, and even environmentalists and citizens of the United States have been repeatedly exposed to exchanges between environmentalists or workers and individual rights within the adversarial nature of the justice system, within the familiar 'victim' or 'perpetrator' model, where the rights of individuals exist in opposition to decisions made by the corporation. This means we, as a collective, have been intentionally misdirected away from a life-sustaining social system which affirm human rights by laws and practices allegedly designed to ensure equal protections and equal justice in the form of life, liberty, and property. But don't forget; this social misdirection, whether intentional or unintentional, was built upon the continued misdirection away from forgotten yet essential environmental systems. Profoundly divisive along racial lines, this legal precedence produced tremendously effective advantages for private business. Slaves who had been effectively removed from their connection to the land were in short order subjected to a second set of legally sanctioned obstacles by the courts shifting their attention to legal clarifications being brought to address the newly identified corporation. The result: any movements toward racial equality were obliterated and replaced with a legally sanctioned elevation of the corporate structure over rights and privileges originally designed for humans. The court system, the central arbiter for disputes, became completely redirected as a resource for people, and instead was entangled in legal wrangling by corporations, leaving few resources to meet the needs of newly emancipated slaves and setting up an entirely new industrial path to economic advantage.

The invisibility of this state-supported corporate advantage is clearly demonstrated historically by the convict lease system which emerged largely in the South after the emancipation of the slaves was written into US law as the 13th Amendment to the Constitution. The state and private industry had significant financial interconnections.

4 Howard Zinn in *The Corporation*.

Blackmon (2008) in his book and subsequent documentary film of the same title, *Slavery By Another Name*, writes about the use of African Americans in what developed as the convict lease system (Blackmon 2008). It is important to note that many African American scholars, perhaps most notably Frederick Douglass and W.E.B. Du Bois, wrote about the convict leasing system at the time, but their efforts were largely ignored and did not make a significant transformative impact on the process of the day (Ortiz 1974; Douglass 1893).

Industry, with support from outright corrupt or decisively immoral action, was contracting with state governments, including constables, judges, and duly appointed lawmen, in what amounted to an illegal slave trade. Using or designing vague or hastily created laws and bogus convictions, African American men were arraigned on illegitimate charges, processed through kangaroo courts, and then sentenced to prison. Once in prison, the state would lease these 'inmates' to industry for a fee. Once this system was in place, states stood to make a lot of money, as did the corporate officials. For example, the state of Alabama made $14,000 in 1874, its first year of convict leasing. By 1890, revenue was $164,000 (estimated at approximately $4.1 million dollars today) (Ortiz 1974). The post-slavery convict lease system, also referred to as neoslavery, worked within the same human trafficking networks created by slavery. By all accounts, this emerging arrangement was ruthless, much more destructive to workers than the institution of slavery.

Historically, slave owners had to maintain a healthy slave class or their industry would fail. If a slave died, slave owners would incur replacement costs and decreased productivity. Under the convict lease system, with a ready supply of fresh workers and no accountability for injuries or deaths, industry expanded production. Slaves died at rates of 30–40 percent (Blackmon 2008). When additional workers were needed, corporate officials would do another sweep of the local jails. When the local jails were empty, pseudo-justice officials would do another sweep of black men in the local and surrounding communities (Blackmon 2008). Racial segregation—an inherently racist and discriminatory practice upon which these exploitive, slave labor economic systems were built—was reinforced again as standard operating procedure by the legal system in the form of Supreme Court decision, *Plessy* v. *Ferguson* in 1896.[5] Written with the expressed intent of giving recourse to slaves not accorded their legal rights as free persons, in practice the 14th Amendment was used as a tool for industry rather than as a protection for newly emancipated slaves. The priority of economic advancement over the needs of people was taking hold and expanding.

The laws and the legal system itself are increasingly under scrutiny and heavily critiqued for what critical social theorists identify as the creation of intentional bias in favor of the corporation and the corporate structure and those who benefit from the corporate structure—which, surprisingly, has disproportionately been rich, white land-owning males. Also of interest is the fact that because the corporate structure is *not* a tangible person who can be held accountable in the same way as people are held accountable, penalties and fines and the sentences imposed for infractions when they are enforced do not impact corporate offenders in the same way as individuals who commit crimes. The idea of corporate personhood was legally redesigned to be a 'get out of jail free' card. Even better still for the corporation, the corporate structure was interpreted to ensure that individuals within the corporate structure would not go to jail in the first place. The mold was cast. Individuals were vulnerable to the actions of the corporations, at the direction of the courts, while the financial support from the corporations to the state incentivized a ready-made enforcement system,

5 *Plessy* v. *Ferguson*, 163 US 537 (1896).

while at the same time insulating individuals within the corporations from legal challenges for any harmful actions taken by the corporation.

Individual Actions and Corporate Practice

The famous philosopher and political critic Noam Chomsky invites reflection on the differences between institutions, such as slavery or corporations, and individuals. He reminds us that historically it is the case that the institutions have done things that are identified as barbaric and 'inherently monstrous,' while the individuals participating in these institutions may be viewed by people as 'the nicest guys you can imagine'—churchgoing, friendly, good to their children, and even nice to their slaves.[6] But how is it possible to embody these two dramatically different personas, one well liked socially and the other responsible for atrocious acts? The writers and researchers in *The Corporation* do a daring thing. In response to this question, they interview Robert Hare, consultant to the FBI on psychopaths. Because a corporation is considered a legal person, he has been asked to assess, using personality scales, the question as to whether a corporation has a personality. Consider the following checklist assessing elements of corporations as persons:

1. callous unconcern for the feelings of others;
2. incapacity to maintain enduring relationships;
3. reckless disregard for the safety of others;
4. deceitfulness: repeated lying and conning others for profit;
5. incapacity to experience guilt;
6. failure to conform to social norms, particularly with regard to lawful behaviors.

Using criteria from the World Health Organization and the DSM-IV, Hare offered a corporation-as-person personality assessment, suggesting that the corporation is an example of the prototypical psychopath.[7] This, of course, raises significant questions about the corporation itself and the role it plays in society, as well as the role of the justice system in perpetuating the legal designation of a corporation as a person. Because conversations intended to address environmental harms are systematically structured to be taking place between groups of people with decisions being made about people who have been systematically stripped of their humanness by people who are themselves the beneficiaries of this psychopathic corporate system, I argue the following: *Any conversations intended to address environmental harms must include, at their center, discussions about how people with privilege remain complicit in either tacit or explicit approval of the unequal power distributions built into and maintained by contemporary social systems and institutions.*

As humans have moved through the world, their experiences have been dramatically different. As white humans, we must consider the simple fact that *the power structure which maintains these benefits remains 'hidden' by, to, and from the same people who benefit from these exclusive privileges.* As white people, we must acknowledge the historical advantages built into the way we were taught to see justice in the world, which is dramatically different from the way communities of color have experienced and were educated about justice, and more specifically injustice, as this psychopathic notion of 'just us' (justice) was built into

6 Noam Chomsky in *The Corporation*.

7 Robert Hare in *The Corporation*.

the system of exploitation which quickly became the US marketplace, and the maintenance of this economic marketplace was reinforced formally and informally by earthly laws, God's laws, tradition, and social convention. Any issues raised about this system were reified by white judges interpreting laws made by white politicians and enforced by white 'peace officers' to preserve the supermajority of any economic advancement for the people who write, interpret, and enforce the governing systems in place.

The Business of Policing Environmental Harms Perpetrated by Corporations

Earlier in this chapter I suggested that when slaves were removed from their land and sent away from the only place they had known as home, after the process of relocating their homes, their communities, awaiting the reconfiguration of their legal identities which had been negotiated by white people for years, and finding a way to re-establish an economically viable means of survival which was something else they walked away from in exchange for their freedom and being legally released from a lifetime of bondage, active legal efforts were afoot which (whether deliberately or unintentionally) resulted in a further stripping a sense of belonging from the newly emancipated slaves. when lawyers and business owners rejected these legally defined 'rights'—a fundamental aspects of one's humanity—by overlooking the application of these rights (again whether deliberately or unintentionally) by not seeing them as humans worthy of the kind of legal standing that took priority over the corporate interests being played out in the courts when the lawyers and business officials deliberately and meticulously applied the idea of personhood to a newly created social abstraction called a corporation.

Certainly, it is worth at least a passing mention that the process described here might sound quite a lot like the way the US government treated First Nation people, removing them from their land, and then attempting to strip them of their identity. In this case, we can reflect on the effects of the legal actions related to the 14th Amendment and its judicial interpretation, resulting in the creation of this legally defined entity, now legally recognized as a corporation, now a legally identifiable as a person with legal standing.

Interestingly, when you look at the human condition over time and you think about the perpetrators of harm, do you see those individuals who have sheltered themselves in the ideological framework of the corporation? Did the creators of this corporate legal structure which has seemed to work in drastically successful ways in securing economic stability and viability see the potential harm? Like slavery, at what point was the harm witnessed and ignored? The corporation is the economic equivalent of the educational system's ivory tower, or the political system's president and Congress, or the justice system's Supreme Court. When you ask yourself how all these people lived and worked and interacted in the multiplicity of dynamic social systems where these inequities were evidenced every day, expressed in subtle and not so subtle ways, don't you also have to ask what was the effect of seeing the harm, and then training yourself to look away? What is the effect of perpetrating harm, whether through a corporation, through the courts, or through the institution of slavery, on the people who perpetrate that harm? How is it possible that white people were capable of maintaining an invisible masque of injustice through horrific social persecution of other people, even to the death? There are lessons in the institution of slavery, which were replicated in the system of the convict lease system, which are paralleled in the growth and expansion of the corporation.

How do people go to church on Sunday morning, and then go to attend a lynching later that afternoon? Where do you go when you are raised in the belly of the corporation and the systems which support its psychopathy? How long until those systems, too, meet the psychological definition of psychopathy? Where do individuals raised in such systems go to have their humanity tested? For those of us studying the perpetration and prevention of environmental harms, perhaps reclaiming a strong sense of our humanity breaks down the socially constructed obstacles that keep us separated from our innate connection to the land. Does the corporation as an institutional structure which seems to rely on the same ideologies which were driving the institution of slavery also need to be eradicated before a reclamation of people and natural systems can be recalibrated into the values which direct the global marketplace and ensure that environmental systems are prioritized in a way which will be sustainable?

Two of Too Many Examples

Read 'Torn from the Land' (Lewan and Barclay 2001) or 'What Happened to Black Wall Street on June 1, 1921?'[8] In the first, white people took farm land that belonged to Black Americans through 'cheating, intimidation, even murder.' In the second, on June 1, 1921, Tulsa, Oklahoma was the site of an attack by a mob of white people that left over 3,000 Black Americans dead, and over 600 successful black-owned businesses were burned to the ground.[9] Several efforts to better understand the ongoing effects of the persecution of black people by white people in the United States are under way. One such effort can be found in the anti-racism education initiatives hosted by some religious communities and some higher education institutions. Anti-racism work is the academic review to organize communities into awareness of the intersections of systemic power and race.[10]

Systemic power is defined as the legitimate legal ability to access and/or control those institutions organized by the state. In relation to race, systemic power functions as though it were cubed (see the box below).

$$\mathbf{P^s = P^1 \times P^2 \times P^3}$$

P^s Systemic power.
P^1 Power over people of color; power which provides the ability of white people to control and regulate the lives of people of color.
P^2 Power which gives privilege and advantage to white people.
P^3 Power which socializes all of us into racial rules.

Source: Crossroads Antiracism Leadership Development Institute (2012), 'Defining Systemic Power' graphic. © Crossroads: www.crossroadsantiracism.org.

8 Ujamaa Network, 'What Happened to Black Wall Street on June 1, 1921?', *Bayview National Black Newspaper*, San Francisco, CA, February 9, 2011.

9 Ibid.

10 For more on the work of Crossroads, see http://crossroadsantiracism.org/ (accessed March 6, 2014).

Systemic power is the legitimate/legal ability to access and/or control those institutions sanctioned by the state. In relation to race, systemic power functions as though it were cubed. The misuse of racialized power has a cubing effect. P^1 is represented by the number 10. When you raise P to the second power, P^2, this is represented by $10 \times 10 = 100$. But the cubing effect of P to the third power, written out as $10 \times 10 \times 10$ is not 300; $P^3 = 1{,}000$.

Another way to think about the effects of a racialized structure has been to describe it as an iceberg. The most obvious effects of a racialized system are the tip of that iceberg, the part you can see, presented here as P^1. But if you know about icebergs, you know that most of an iceberg is hidden underneath the surface of the water. Just underneath the surface is the aspect of systemic power that advantages white people because of their skin color. Also referred to as white privilege, or in its extreme form white supremacy, the idea that white people are advantaged is a larger aspect of this issue, P^2, yet the way it is reflected in society often remains hidden just under the surface. Finally, the deepest, if not the largest, part of that iceberg is represented by P^3. P^3 represents racism's power to destroy us all. Just as the full scale of the obstacle of the iceberg and the potential damage it can cause remain hidden, the idea that we see ourselves not as humans but as members of a social binary based on race has a dehumanizing effect. Most of those who study and offer workshops in the field of anti-racism work highlight how these deep and hidden dangers affect both white and non-white people. The costs are a disconnection from our humanity in desensitizing, perhaps psychopathic, ways.

The Crossroads Antiracism Leadership Development Institute (2012) outlines two socialization processes, one for whites and one for people of color, that support and reinforce each other in a 'dance' that helps to maintain the race construct in society:

1. **Internalized Racial Oppression (IRO)**—a complex multi-generational socialization process that teaches people of color to believe, accept, and/or live out negative social definitions of self;
2. **Internalized Racial Superiority (IRS)**—a complex multi-generational socialization process that teaches white people to believe, accept, and/or live out superior social definitions of self.

The victim and the villain interact in an intimate dynamic where sometimes even lethal harm goes unnoticed. How is this possible? How is it possible to maintain a mindset which utterly ignores the health and wellness of self and others? I suggest that the dehumanization of 'the Other' is the foundation upon which global environmental exploitation is built. The small-scale equivalent of psychopathy in *The Corporation* is a similar dynamic which generates the kinds of desensitization that allow for the expression of harm to self and to others. In the case of slavery, and the process of emancipation and equal protection, the result is to create a racialized, segregated system of both formally and informally justifiable abuse. The idolizing of the corporate structure, the prioritization of capital expansion over everything else, produces a kind of social harm which must be rejected and upended if we are ever going to ensure environmental justice and the related environmental protections.

The intellectualizing of profits over people has been the centerpoint for an intellectual bondage many white people do not even see—a split personality where they go to church, pray for their fellow humans everywhere, go on mission trips, while at the same time attempting to obliterate any trace of their own culpability in creating 'the Other' and justifying while ignoring the harm they do as they move through the world.

Oppressor and Oppressed: The Lens Through Which We See Self and Other

Work in the environmental justice movement in the United States has been linked to race and class in various ways, perhaps most famously through Robert Bullard's *Dumping in Dixie* (1990), or from within the native community's attention to the Earth as described in *Resource Wars: Native and Environmental Struggles Against the Corporation* (Gedicks and LaDuke 1993) and various other efforts. Yet the perpetration of major injustices against large masses of people, such as native people and people of color, would not have been possible without the collusion of individuals from within, most notably, the justice system. The image of the blind Lady of Justice does not even come close to accurately reflecting the blatantly obvious influences major social systems such as corporations have on the justice system. It is time we called out the charade, because these judicial choices catastrophically change people's lives.

Many people in the USA may remember the case of Anne and Carl Braden. The Bradens offer a personal example of the social costs to white people organizing for racial equality: their efforts to work to desegregate housing resulted in death threats, bombings, and their social activism met the full weight and force of the criminal justice system. Referring back to the full effect of racism—P^3 in the Crossroads model presented above—the extent of the harm done to people of color might seem obvious. What is less obvious is the damage racism does to white people, as Anne Braden described:

> In a sense, the battle [for racial justice] is and always has been a battle for the hearts and minds of white people [in the United States]. The fight against racism is not something we're called on to help people of color with. We need to become involved as if our lives depended on it because, in truth, they do.[11]

Another aspect of the collusion of the criminal justice system, and perhaps one of the most prominent places where the ongoing distancing of harm done by the corporation is found in the criminal justice system today, is the expanding use of privatized prisons. It isn't difficult to see the connections between the racialization of this system and the convict leasing system of 150 years ago discussed above. Consider these statistics about incarceration rates from the American Civil Liberties Union (ACLU 2012):

- With only 5 percent of the world's population, the United States has 25 percent of the world's prison population.
- Nearly half of all prisoners in state prisons are locked up for nonviolent offenses.
- In 2007, US states spent more than $44 billion on incarceration and related expenses, a 127 percent increase compared to 1987. In comparison, over the same period, spending on higher education rose by 21 percent.
- The US prison population rose by a staggering 700 percent between 1970 and 2005.

But the statistics do not apply evenly across the entire US population. They also highlight the racialized aspect of these incarceration rates: 1 in every 106 white males, 1 in every 36 Hispanic males, and 1 in every 15 black males (ACLU 2012).

11 Anne Braden, "Welcome!', Anne Braden Institute for Social Justice Research, University of Louisville, KY: http://anne-braden.org/ (accessed March 6, 2014).

In her recently published *Birth of a White Nation*, history professor Jacqueline Battalora outlines how the benefits of whiteness, and related restrictions and oppressions to non-whiteness, were crafted, law by law, and how a legal system was carefully crafted using racism alongside various elements of Christian theological principles to regulate women and black people (Battalora 2013). We can see, as outlined in the presentation of the power structure outlined above, the harm done to people of color. As an increasingly aware society, we are learning a little about the effects of such a racialized past for both white people and people of color through excellent works like *The New Jim Crow* (Alexander 2010) and *Post Traumatic Slave Syndrome* (Leary 2005). We see the privilege afforded white people. But why is it so hard to see the lack of connection by white people, more specifically those individuals who have unapologetically connected themselves to the white framework which advances an exploitive corporate mindset and prioritizes this kind of exploitative mindset found in institutions such as slavery? How do they continue to justify this action to themselves, how do *we*, as white people, continue to justify this action to *ourselves*, to other people, to the natural environment being exploited while they continue in an all-out effort to advance a mindset which is unsustainable? Evidence that has always been there, but has been hidden in the minds of white people who focused instead on creating and expanding the superiority and expansive wealth of whiteness, is found again in the mindset prioritizing the advancement of the corporation. One bridge back to the priority of protecting the natural environment is through exposing the myth of an unbiased justice system, and building relationships with people—all people—and with our selves. Perhaps another way back is offered by reconsidering the adversarial system, so that instead of asserting that capital might makes right, we start moving actively toward prioritizing people, relationships, and accountability to others, even groups of others.

Under Layers of Black and White, Shades of Green

The systems of justice and the institution of slavery exist alongside seemingly intractable problems of sex trafficking, drug trafficking, and global climate change. Aspects of the system of capitalism itself could be used to illustrate what happens when the perpetrator of harm is also the creator of the system which arbitrates abuses—a system where advantage is granted with no accountability, where individual exploitation is part of doing business, where the ideas represented in the mindset that created the institution of slavery, the corporation, the informal and formal methods for preserving privilege are dependent upon the supporting systems, such as government and the criminal justice system, to lock in that advantage. The ideology is doing the damage, in the form of the people who designed slave systems, and in the form of the people who assigned individuals rights to corporations, and then went about legally enforcing the plan which allows them to be the perpetrator of harm while ignoring the harm and instead identifying and focusing on wealth accumulation as the ultimate measure of 'success.'

With these fundamentals outlined, it might not be at all surprising to note that the shift in global attitude away from such a 'First World' mindset is happening literally on the ground in so-called 'developing' countries where systems of human and environmental exploitation are being rejected outright by the people. Oscar Olivera from the Coalition in Defense of Water and Life describes how Bechtel Corporation, a US-based transnational company, moved into Bolivia and implemented laws to allow companies to repossess houses if a water bill was unpaid, removing people from their homes and giving the company the right to auction them off.[12] People were being forced to make choices between sending their children to school or going to the doctor and paying for basic services such as water. The people of Bolivia took to the streets, rallying behind the slogan 'The water is ours, damn it!' Perhaps predictably, the government used law enforcement to defend the corporation, yet failed to convince the people that water was a commodity to be bought and sold like any other good or service. Olivera says: 'People wanted water not tear gas. People wanted justice not bullets.'

Vandana Shiva, physicist, ecologist and seed activist, offers another example of global organizing around environmental issues, and is perhaps best known for her 'Occupy the Seed' movement. The mission of the Permaculture Research Institute is to work with individuals and communities worldwide to expand the knowledge and practice of integrated, sustainable agriculture using the whole-systems approach of permaculture design. This will provide solutions allowing permanent abundance by training local people to become leaders of sustainable development in their own communities and countries (International Permaculture Day 2012). These grassroots organizing teams have simply rejected the tenets of 'success' and 'productivity' as scripted and designed by the corporate mindset commonly found in the United States. Shiva has famously traveled around the world combating the activities of big business, suggesting that 15 corporations would like to control the conditions of our lives, but millions of people around the world are telling those corporations, 'not only do we not need them, but we are going to develop systems that nourish the Earth and nourish human beings.'[13] Challenging US patents held by W.R. Grace, the group focused on green revolution has repeatedly attempted to disrupt the corporate control of farming in their local communities, and working as a worldwide coalition it showed that 'the corporation was the pirate.' Confronting what it calls corrupt or illegitimate laws, attempts to regulate and control the distribution of crop seeds have been rejected by the people. They are laws that are not worth complying with. Farmers who save their own seeds and do not use pesticides are showing production yields three times larger than those who are locked into the corporate structure. 'We will violate [these laws] because saving seeds is a duty to the Earth and to future generations,' she argues. 'We have managed to create systems that are sustainable for people.'[14]

How is it that privileged people who define themselves as living in the 'First World' overlook the privilege they maintain? How is it that white people don't see the harm and violence which is required to sustain the systems of privilege they support? If harm and violence is invisible between humans, between classes, and between genders, how is it that, in particular, white people in the USA can talk about the history of the United States and 'rugged individualism,' but completely ignore the federal efforts to wipe out, eliminate, *kill* native people, or give freedom to slaves and then strip them of their lands or businesses through violence? How is it that people in the USA do not see the ways the colonial mindset infuses international policy, corporate policy, religious policy, family dynamics, even to this day? As a collective of humans on the planet, do we really not see the harm we do while we hang on to the ideology driving this collection of systems in the USA that is still tethered to the white, privileged, racist, corporate social design?

12 Oscar Olivera in *The Corporation*.

13 Vandana Shiva in *The Corporation*.

14 Ibid.

The Ideology Driving Corporate Practice Regulates More Than We Know

If we limit our thinking to the many ways socially sanctioned institutionalized harm is present throughout the structures of our racialized past, we overlook how similar dynamics of power and oppressive control are also present in many other social systems and institutions in the United States. This social ideology has reified its acceptability in many forms, which ironically, rather than making it easier to see, makes it even harder to notice. To only discuss the institution of slavery would be to ignore elements of this dynamic that have been driving the historical reverence for this ideology of oppression which led to the creation of the institution of slavery and the corporate power structure. But the ideology of oppression is driving the systems it creates, so who creates the systems? The only answer possible: Well, *we* do.

There is a question here of who do I mean when I say 'we,' of course. This is a complex issue, but a relatively simple answer might be anyone who advocates this historically documented ideology of power developed historically and described by Joe Feagin as the 'white racial frame' with various levels of abstraction, but which in general views whites as mostly superior and people of color as less socially significant (Feagin 2010). Robin DiAngelo (2011) asks the question, 'How did we learn to internalize white dominance so well?' She suggests the following:

- We live segregated lives.
- We are taught in our culture to see our experiences as objective and representative of reality.
- We are raised to value the individual and to see ourselves as individuals rather than as a part of a socialized group.
- In our dominant positions, we are almost always racially comfortable, and expect to remain so.
- We feel we should be judged by our intensions rather than the effects of our behaviors.
- We believe that if we can't feel our social power, that we don't have any.
- We think it is important not to notice race.
- We confuse not understanding with not agreeing.
- We will be the judges of whether or not racism has occurred.
- Racism has been constructed as belonging to extremists and being very bad.

Questions about the macro levels and systems beg questions about micro, or individual, levels of expression of this same ideology, manifesting perhaps in interactions between individuals as a similar form of exploitive harm. Is possible to see this same dynamic in interpersonal relational exchanges between people—real people—not just corporate personhood.

Consider child abuse, family violence, intimate partner violence, bullying in the schoolyard, human trafficking or modern slavery, and people—including children—who are exploited for sex. Not all families or relationships, of course, are places where people are subjected to forms of abuse. Although some people might idealize the characteristics of family life, even within loving, intimate, and intensely personal institutions like the family, to only see the positive aspects without acknowledging a range of positive and negative is to overlook part of the dynamic. The same could apply to religious groups, work groups, neighborhoods, or communities. If one experiences the kind of exploitive dynamic we see in larger systems, it is easy to see how such an ideology might perhaps create an expectation of harm on an individual level. From within the context of the ideas outlined here, it is not hard to see the ideology of the corporate structure present in a smaller system—in this case, a family system. Consider the corporation and the family at their best and at their worst.

At their best, both the corporation and the family do the following:

- They serve as a resource for learning and making connections into the outside world.
- They serve as an efficient way to organize goals, plan for the future, and learn (what you choose to focus on) from the past.
- They serve as a means for garnering support and collaboration to move beyond the abilities and/or limitations of any individual.
- They serves as a vehicle for learning about self and other.

At their worst, both the corporation and the family also do the following:

- They provide a structure of oppressive power.
- They provide a structure where money, or the person who makes the most money, dictates all the decisions, hopes, and aspirations of the people in the home.
- They provide a historical model where those who enjoy a self-ascribed position of power, a position which is enforced and supported by other formal (and informal) social systems, can look past the harm they do or even deny the harm they do, and end up with an attitude that people must be accountable to them, rather than having mutual accountability.
- They set the stage for an overarching expectation of exploitation in other aspects of life.

Religious systems and institutions, educational systems and institutions, economic systems and financial institutions, and other systems and institutions like the family system and the institution of marriage could all be reflected on with an eye toward the assessment of the kind of power and the way the system is intended to operate and the way it actually operates. Certainly, we all know people with families who are healthy and happy, but when you consider the statistics in the USA with regard to intimate partner violence, child sexual abuse, dating violence, and reflections of gender violence in a variety of media outlets, and the challenges posed by ecofeminists in the raising of their questions about how society treats the Earth, it is clear that the kinds of oppressive practices outlined in relation to the corporate structure are not too different from the dynamics at play in many other social systems. And interestingly, and perhaps ironically, if you ask people whether they support intimate partner violence, child sexual abuse, dating violence, and so on, right down to whether they think people should take actions they know are harmful to the natural environment, very few are going to say that they agree with these things, even when they in fact *do* them.

The Villain as the Victim and the Victim as the Villain

If it is true that the people who do the harm do not see the harm they *do*, if they minimize their actions in their own minds, or in the actions they take in response to the damage they create, whether from within the safety of the corporate structure or in a self-selected romantic relationship, do the victims of harmful events see the harm *being done* to them? What does it take for victim to become complicit in a system of oppression? Do you remember the list of what researchers have discovered about environmental harm that appeared earlier in this chapter? Here it is again for you to review in the light of the intervening discussion:

1. Many people will knowingly purchase products harmful to the environment.
2. Many people will knowingly use controversial, potentially hazardous technologies.
3. Many people will knowingly eat foods that are genetically modified despite not fully understanding the consequences of this modification.
4. Many people will knowingly use drugs processed, marketed, and recommended by medical professionals with little understanding of either the short- or long-term consequences for the individual, as well as for the environment, as a result of toxic chemicals used in production processes.

When researching environmental harms, just as society at large tends to forget how critical the underlying biological and ecological systems are to the sustenance of social life, we may also forget thc people often participate, to varying degrees, in their own harm. When this happens, the origins are thought to be deeply seeded, referred to in some places even as unconscious ideologies. In the United States, the ideology responsible for creating systems of oppression, including slavery and exploitive corporations—entities described as an excellent model for demonstrating an example of psychopathic behavior, with no heart and no soul—is pervasive. The criminal justice system has been resoundingly implicated in sustaining and perpetuating the oppressive ideological theme, using legal and judicial systems and enforced by law enforcement agents and corrections officials. The authority of the criminal justice system has been used to reinforce the existing privileged, racist, oppressive social ideologies which warranted the kinds of equal protection ratification of the 14th Amendment was intended to provide, the kinds of rights specific racialized groups were having trouble securing. We purchase the products. We use the products. And we say we have no choice. We collude in our own victimization. Consider the following formulation:

The Villain

- Slave systems required slave owners to 'see' past the slave as a human to justify barbaric treatment.
- Corporations as people see no harm; corporate officials are taught to see no harm.
- Sex offenders and other offenders often negate the harm they do or experience cognitive distortions which allow them not to 'see' what they do as harmful or offending behavior.
- Rapists do not 'see' what they do as rape.
- Batterers do not 'see' what they do as battery, but say they were provoked.
- Child abusers are 'teaching the child a lesson,' and therefore helping them, not hurting them.

The Victim

- Victims often, at least for a time, feel and perhaps are 'stuck' in the system, hopeless, and are unable to see any way out.
- Victims continue to work within dysfunctional or exploitive systems.
- Victims do not see what they do as a co-dependent relationship.
- Victims do not see how they support the abuse or abuser.

- Victims do not see how their sadness or suffering matters.
- Victims do not see themselves as adding value.

Large-scale social disagreements and outrage usually break down into two camps: the victim who is harmed and the perpetrator who does the harming. People on both sides of the argument begin the process of choosing sides, and they place themselves in a position of being forced to defend the side they are on as either 'right' or 'wrong.' This dichotomy does not serve either side well, because as was suggested above, people don't often fit neatly on one side of the debate or the other. If we are able to see people as shades of both, the focus shifts from who is 'right' or 'wrong' to how we solve the problem in front of us. To shift this way of thinking is difficult for all of us from within the United States, because we all grew up under the rather exploitive world view reflected in the ideology that drove the creation of the institution of slavery and resulted in an exploitive corporate structure and the seemingly intractable displays of harm noticeable in a variety of micro and macro level systems, and perhaps most importantly, in the way we relate to our natural environment.

How much of the corporation-as-psychopath mentality is present in the psyches of people who live and work in the systems which were created at the time of slavery and remain steeped in the exploitive ideology which made slavery and other forms of oppression possible? How long can the criminal justice system be used as both the designer and enforcer of these systems while its role in the process is described as without bias and prejudice? How much longer can the criminal justice system hold the position that these systems are fundamental and essential to American life while this system of justice simultaneously sides with the winners? Can the United States, from a position of privilege and a lack of accountability, see the wisdom in the opposing voices coming out of communities from within the emerging global economy?

Although significant questions remain, I argue here that much progress could be made toward successfully addressing environmental issues if environmental efforts are increasingly linked to anti-racism and other anti-oppression work. People in the United States are steeped in an exploitive institutional ideology which has created harmful systems that have historically also been presented as the modern cure for any problem the world is facing. The ideology driving slavery and the development of the corporate structure was presented as a fantastic organizing tool, yet the costs for the creators of that system include disconnection from their humanity and, more importantly, the Earth. Working within these oppressive and exploitive systems, we have never learned to see the truth of the harm being done to people through that exploitative thinking, or the white racial frame, and we have been taught to ignore the harm done to the perpetrators, too. As both victim and villain, we must seek out the truth of our own connection to exploitation and replace these ideologies with efforts to build relationships to people and create sustainable communities globally. Anti-racism efforts offer at least one more bridge between the harmful ideologies which promote systems of exploitation, and these ideologies must be transformed in the hearts and minds of people, including corporate 'persons.' The corporation, like the rest of us, is a human creation, both operating outside ideology and created because of it. The corporation is both victim and villain—as are we all.

Questions for Future Reflection

How can people with privilege, those raised within a white framework with a sense of entitlement who are taught overt and covert ways to use harm to their advantage, to assert their internalized superiority over others (in the USA this has most particularly been structured and directed toward people of color, but for our purposes here, this includes animals, and the natural environment) as a means for demonstrating their superiority be taught, educated, enticed, interrupted, and encouraged to expand their awareness and to unlearn privilege?

How can white people who bear the benefit of complicity and carry the afflictions of entitlement assume responsibility for reconnecting to their humanity and become educated in ways to support rather than take over and control the kinds of community building and development of human capital being demonstrated in communities of color around the world?

How can people with privilege who are taught to assert, and rewarded for asserting, their superiority over others as a means for seeing themselves as superior, as having value, expect to fully become allies in a global social movement to prevent environmental harm when history has taught us that to use harm is to make ourselves visible?

How can people with privilege be taught to see the ways they are complicit in maintaining systems that oppress others?

How much of the corporation-as-psychopath ideology is conveyed to other people and institutions, and to what degree?

How can a system of justice built up around laws and enforcement systems designed to benefit specific groups of white people, primarily men, ever be seen as just when that same system is simultaneously exploiting targeted groups and actively denying the harm or abuse present in that social system, and how can it be useful as a tool for resolving the conflicts in environmental justice work?

References

Alexander, M. 2010. *The New Jim Crow: Mass Incarceration in an Age of Colorblindness*. New York: The New Press.

American Civil Liberties Union. 2011. '[Infographic] Combatting Mass Incarceration: The Facts,' June 17: https://www.aclu.org/combating-mass-incarceration-facts-0 (accessed March 6, 2014).

Archbar, M., Abbott, J. and Bakan, J. 2003. *The Corporation Film*: www.thecorporation.com.

Battalora, J. 2013. *Birth of a White Nation: The Invention of White People and Its Relevance Today*. Houston, TX: Strategic Book Publishing & Rights Co.

Blackmon, D. 2008. *Slavery By Another Name: The Re-enslavement of Black Americans from the Civil War to World War II* (ebook). New York: Anchor Books/Random House Digital. Film: www.slaverybyanothername.com/pbs-film (accessed March 6, 2014).

Brantingham, P. and Brantingham, P. 1981. *Environmental Criminology*, Thousand Oaks, CA: Sage.

Bullard, R. 1990. *Dumping in Dixie: Race, Class and Environmental Quality*. Boulder, CO: Westview.

Crossroads Antiracism Leadership Development Institute. 2012. 'Defining Systemic Power' graphic: www.crossroadsantiracism.org.

DiAngelo, R. 2011. 'My Class Didn't Trump My Race,' in *Perspectives on Human Differences*, edited by K. Koppelman. Upper Saddle River, NJ: Pearson.

Douglass, F. 1893. 'History Is a Weapon: The Convict Lease System,' in I.B. Wells, F. Douglass, I.G. Penn, and F.L. Barnett, *The Reason Why the Colored American Is Not in the World's Columbian Exposition* (pamphlet), ch. 3. Reproduced online: www.historyisaweapon.com/defcon1/fredouconlea.html (accessed March 6, 2014).

Feagin, J. 2010. *The White Racial Frame: Centuries of Racial Framing and Counter-framing*. New York: Routledge.

Gedicks, A. and LaDuke, W. 1993. *The New Resource Wars: Native and Environmental Struggles Against Multinational Corporations*. Boston, MA: Southend Press.

International Permaculture Day. 2012. 'Vandana says "Occupy the Seed": Join the Seed Freedom Fortnight of Action, 2–16 October 2012,' *PermacultureNews.org*: http://permaculturenews.org/2012/08/20/vandana-says-occupy-the-seed-join-the-seed-freedom-fortnight-of-action-2-16-october-2012/ (accessed October 15, 2013).

Leary, J.D. 2005. *Post Traumatic Slave Syndrome: America's Legacy of Enduring Injury and Healing*. Milwaukie, OR: Uptone Press.

Lewan, T. and Barclay, D. 2001. 'Torn from the Land,' *The Authentic Voice*, December 2: www.theauthenticvoice.org/mainstories/tornfromtheland/ (accessed March 6, 2014).

Ortiz, P. 1974. 'Convict Labor in America,' *Solidarity*: www.solidarity-us.org/site/node/1974 (accessed March 6, 2014).

Zimmer, M. 2009. 'Overview of Specialized Courts,' *International Journal of Court Administration*, August 1–14: www.iaca.ws/files/LWB-SpecializedCourts.pdf (accessed October 15, 2013).

Chapter 4
Environmental Victims and Criminal Justice: Proceed with Caution

Antony Pemberton

Introduction

It is safe to say that the burgeoning field of environmental criminology (in its green rather than its geographical sense) has yet to pay much attention to those who fall victim to environmental harms and crimes. In the sixteen years since an issue of the journal *Social Justice* launched the term 'environmental victimology' (see, for example, Williams 1996), not much has happened (see Hall 2012). This lack of any sustained interest is particularly stark when contrasted with the large and growing academic attention devoted to victims of crime in general (see, for example, Hoyle 2011) and other types of misfortune, for instance large-scale disasters (Neria et al. 2009).

Part of this is undoubtedly due to the fact that much relevant research is not carried out under the flag of victimology. The fragmented nature of the field of victims' studies means that academics in the fields of traumatic stress and clinical psychology, as well as scholars in the fields of transitional justice and human rights, often embark on victimological studies without any reference to victimology, the latter being more often than not the domain of lawyers and criminologists studying victims (for this observation, see Pemberton 2010; Groenhuijsen and Pemberton 2011).

This qualification does not apply to the area which is most squarely the remit of victimologists, including myself: the development of a victimological perspective on criminal justice systems. The challenges that the peculiar features of environmental victimization—as analyzed by Williams (1996)—might pose for victims' access to, use of and experience with criminal justice have yet to be given the attention they require (Cardwell et al. 2011). This is all the more acute due to the fact that at the national, supranational and international levels policymakers and environmental justice advocates are turning to the criminal process as a solution to (some of) the problems faced by environmental victims (see, for example, Hall 2012; Hall, Chapter 6 in this volume; Jarell and Ozymy 2012; Skinnider 2011; Higgins et al. 2013). The measures taken to improve the lot of victims of violent and property crime within the penal process in many jurisdictions across the developed world (see, for example, Groenhuijsen and Letschert 2012) are taken to be an inroad to do the same for victims of environmental harm. The sense emanating from the scant literature on this subject is that the lack of (public, but also academic) interest and awareness of the urgency of improving the lot of environmental victims in this way is the main barrier to doing so. More attention to environmental victimology would as a matter of course lead to greater awareness of the criminal nature of much environmental harm and to an increased role for criminal justice in offering a solution for the problems faced by environmental crime victims.

This chapter, however, offers a decidedly more skeptical view of this development. The extent to which criminal justice may offer a solution for the problems facing environmental victims can be helpfully analyzed by contrasting the *reality* of environmental victimization and what is (or would be) involved in its *social construction* (see also Hannigan 2006; White 2008). This is informed by the understanding that social problems, even when they are real, are socially constructed (see, for example, Best 2008), and that the forces and processes involved in this social construction may cause (large) differences between the two.

In particular, this chapter will adopt the perspective that the attempts to convince the public and political actors of the reality of environmental crime and to understand those suffering the consequences as real victims of crime (Jarell and Ozymy 2012) involve processes of *framing* (Entman 1993; Entman 2007). It especially involves aligning the reality of environmental problems with a 'master' *crime* frame (see, for example, Snow and Benford 1992; Snow 2004). This process can be critically scrutinized in three interrelated ways: first, to the extent to which the realities faced by victims of environmental harm fit this frame; second, whether adopting the crime frame prioritizes certain elements or situations of environmental harm, and finally, whether the solution—(the outcome of) the criminal justice process—emphasized in the crime frame merits the faith proponents place in it. In developing these points I will also expand upon the victimological truth that victims' participation in criminal justice is a decidedly mixed blessing, meriting equal consideration to so-called secondary victimization (Laxminarayan 2012) as to the benefits of participation (Lens et al. 2013).

The chapter proceeds as follows: the following section discusses key issues in framing theory. This culminates in the understanding that social movements often advance their cause by aligning their views with a 'master' frame, attempting to gain wider support. This can be a successful strategy, but the features of the master frame in question also impose restrictions on the way the social problem in question is understood. This tension lies at the heart of the argument advanced in this chapter. The subsequent section offers a brief summary of some of the most distinctive features of environmental victimization (see also Williams 1996; Hall 2012). This sketch focuses on the ways in which the harms and wrongs visited on victims of environmental crime contrast with 'ordinary' forms of crime, and in particular on the characteristics that make identification of victims of environmental harm *as crime victims* more complex. The next section further develops the notion of crime as a master frame, and outlines its main features, including the manner in which the social problems defined as crime are connected to their remedy: the criminal justice system. The final section concludes by combining the insights of previous sections to critically assess the use of framing environmental victimization as crime.

Key Notions of Framing

In Robert Entman's influential view, framing can be seen as the 'process of culling a few elements of perceived reality and assembling a narrative that highlights connections between them to promote a particular interpretation' (Entman 1993; Entman 2004; Entman 2007). A fully formed frame of a social problem performs four functions: it offers a definition of the problem in question; it offers an analysis of its causes; it guides moral judgment, and it promotes a particular remedy to the problem. Frames serve as a tool for individuals to make sense of their own experience and to inform others about the key characteristics of a particular problem (Benford and Snow 2000). It does so by introducing or raising 'the salience or apparent importance of certain ideas, activating schemas that encourage target audiences to think, feel, and decide in a particular way' (Entman 2007). Frames are also a focal point for social movements that strive to achieve public and political acknowledgment of social problems and to improve the lot of those suffering its consequences (see, for example, Gamson 1992; Benford and Snow 2000).

The process of gaining acceptance for a particular social movement's position by a wider audience involves connecting the social movement's frame to existing frames. Establishing this connection involves frame alignment (Snow et al. 1986; Benford and Snow 2000). This usually occurs in one of four forms. In *frame bridging*, the movement reaches out to those already known to be predisposed to similar issues (for instance, one liberal cause to another), while *frame amplification* entails emphasizing core values that the movement shares with potential supporters to mobilize them into action. *Frame extension* and *frame transformation* apply to situations in which the social movement's frame is (to a degree) at odds with that of the wider audience. The former concerns expanding and adapting the movement's frame to overcome this divide, while the latter entails the more radical attempt to reshape the audience's frame—to reject their current way of viewing (the particular) reality (in question) and adopt that of the social movement instead.

An opportunity for frame alignment arises when a *master frame* is available (Snow and Benford 1992). This is a broad frame that has already been applied successfully in different contexts. Casting the social movement's objectives in line with this master frame has the dual advantage of making the reasoning behind these objectives easy to understand for potential supporters while enlisting supporters of the previous issues cast in terms of the master frame to the cause of the social movement in question.

These advantages come at price, though, because of the restrictions the master frame imposes. The social movement will have to play by the rules the master frame dictates. It is more resistant to change precisely because it has been deployed before. Moreover, the social movement only stands to profit from allegiance with the master frame if potential supporters view the social problem in question as a particular instance of the master frame. The awareness of the price that will have to be paid will lead to intra-movement disputes about 'selling out' on the movement's message and core values ('realists' versus 'idealists' or 'moderates' versus 'radicals'; Benford 1993). A particular Herculean feat is the idealist strategy of attempting to transform the master frame itself to align it with the movement's position.

Framing issues is a key component of the exercise of power in democracies (Carragee and Roefs 2004; Entman 2007). The adage that the media is not successful in telling people *what to think*, but is 'extremely successful in telling people *what to think about* (Cohen 1963) can be viewed in terms of Steve Lukes's 'third face of power' (Lukes 1974): power is largely exercised by shaping perceptions, cognitions and preferences in such a way as to secure support and acceptance of the status quo. Successful power wielding is therefore often largely a question of 'telling people what to think about' (see, for example, Entman 2007). This is familiar terrain for (critical) criminologists, who have highlighted the ways in which political interests have influenced and often distorted the definition of crime problems, even to the extent that some view the definition of crime as such as a function of power politics (for example, Hulsman 1986; Van Swaaningen 1997).

However, framing analysis does offer some fresh insights. Any move from uncovering the social construction of crime and the bias in this construction to the outright denial of its ontological reality—which is errant in any case—should proceed in full awareness that alternative conceptions of the social problems addressed by crime are also subject to processes of framing (Best 2008; see also Robinson and Darley 2007). Indeed, some of the vitriol aimed at the concept of crime is probably better understood as criticism of the way crime is framed, rather than its underlying reality. The crime frame includes behavior that should on closer inspection not be included in the concept, and excludes behavior that should. The difference between the reality of crime and the crime frame can also be viewed in terms of a number (a patterned set) of psychological or moral heuristics (see Sunstein 2003). Much of the distortion of the framing of crime is due to these heuristics, with the power bias in crime definition working through these heuristics, but also being constrained by them.

A Sketch of an Environmental Victimology

Introduction

Environmental crime and victimization encompass a wide range of phenomena and behavior (see, for example, White 2008), from climate change to illegal waste dumping, from water pollution to the abuse of animals and other non-human life (see elsewhere this volume). Exact definitions and categorizations vary (Carrabine et al. 2004). It is difficult, impossible even, to do adequate justice to this diversity within the space of this chapter. The magnitude of the problem of environmental harm—which might be the greatest danger to the future of life on this planet (see, for example, Hansen 2009; Kramer 2013)—warrants victimological attention in its own right, as do the consequences of environmental change for the geography of crime and victimization (Parenti 2011).

In a more abstract and academic sense, the relevance of an environmental *victimology* (see Williams 1996) is that cases of environmental victimization regularly differ from the 'default' situation studied in victimology: one perpetrator (or a small number), one victim (or a small number); one event (or a small number), all of which entail a clear breach of a criminal law, and result in readily ascertainable and immediate harm of a physical, psychological and/or financial nature (see, for example, Pemberton 2009). On each count, environmental victimization is different—to paraphrase a well-known Vulcan philosopher: 'It's *crime*, Jim, but not as we know it.'[1] The contrast between the experience of environmental victimization and 'ordinary' crime victimization is an important, but underdeveloped site of victimological reflection and research (Hall 2012).

The key issue addressed in this section is that these realities present a challenge to the common framing of crime and criminal victimization. Indeed, the awareness of this fact has prompted many environmental criminologists to maintain that the common view of crime and/or criminal justice is misguided (White 2008). In other words, in view of the reality and the urgency of the social problem of environmental victimization, transformation of the crime frame is in order. I will return to this issue below.

In this section I will first briefly discuss some of the familiar differential characteristics of the experience of environmental victimization: its nature as white-collar/corporate crime; the role of state actors; the overlap between victims and offenders; the large numbers of victims, including non-human victims, and the difficulties in self-definition of victims. This is followed by an examination of the difficulties that these characteristics pose for victims'

1 To be precise this is in fact a famous misquote of *Star Trek* character Spock, who never actually said the words, 'It's life Jim, but not as we know it.' Instead, the source is the 1987 hit single 'Star Trekkin,' by The Firm. I should also add that there are, of course, forms of environmental crime that do fit the mold of ordinary crime—for instance, crimes involving poisoning (see, for example, Emsley 2006).

understanding of the harmfulness and the wrongfulness of the damage that has been done to them.

Perpetration of and Victimization by Environmental Crime

White-collar/corporate crime

Although environmental crimes can be perpetrated by a wide range of offenders, they are typically linked to large transnational corporations (see White 2008), and the most harmful instances of environmental crime have become emblematic corporate and/or white-collar crimes (see also Bakan 2004). Multinational industrial conglomerates can inflict damage upon the environment well beyond the capability of any individual person.

In addition, the power wielded by these organizations can be put to use to shape the policies, legal framework and public opinion in which they operate. Environmental crime is not afforded the attention the size and scope of the problem merits at least in part because of this fact. Moreover, the combination of these organizations' considerable resources with the difficulties in establishing harm and wrongdoing (see below) allows them additional opportunities to deflect criticism relating to their environmental conduct and to reframe the problematic and/or wrongful nature of the effects their operations have on the environment. They can opt for strategies of denial/avoidance, in which any experienced harm is offset by wider gains and the veracity of wrongfulness is questioned. Where ordinary perpetrators might deny their involvement in a crime, dispute the fact that what happened constituted the requirements of the criminal law, white-collar/corporate perpetrators are more prone to dispute whether the act of which they have been accused in fact does or should constitute a crime at all. The difficulties in establishing harm and causality can draw out legal processes, which offers opportunities to divide and even blame groups of victims.

The involvement of state actors

States and state representatives are often complicit or actively involved in the commission of environmental crime (Kramer 2013). Much white-collar and corporate crime occurs under the protection of the state and/or state representatives: bending legal rules to condone or even legalize the harm done. In many instances, victims fall prey to abuse of power, rather than crime in its legal definition.

In addition, the state might not abet or be involved in the commission of environmental crime, but might fail to protect its citizens. This can be a matter of inability: failed or conflict-ridden states lack the resources to enforce protection (see, for example, Parenti 2011). Indeed, this is likely to be true of many states, especially in the developing world. The extent to which most states have the regulatory capacity and the resources to enforce any environmental legislation they have in place, particularly when this is pitted against the often powerful interests supporting the perpetration of environmental crime, often begs the question whether it is abuse of power as much as lack of sufficient state power that causes the worst problems for inhabitants of these states.

This is also related to the aspect of transnationality of environmental crime (White 2011). Combating its perpetration may only be possible in an international or supranational context, not the province of one state alone. The interests of states may differ, with one state reaping the profits of acts damaging another's environment.

Distinguishing perpetrators and victims

The perpetrators of environmental harm may be difficult to distinguish from the victims. In general, the juxtaposition of victims and perpetrators in crime is overstated (see, for example, Fattah 1991). Being a perpetrator increases the risk of becoming victimized by crime, and vice versa.

However, this lack of distinction gains new meaning in cases of environmental damage. The perpetrators and victims of the same crime can overlap or be impossible to distinguish. Many environmental risks are caused by free-rider problems: the problem of climate change is not caused by one person's emissions of carbon dioxide or methane, but by the sum of the greenhouse gases produced by the whole of humanity. The difficulties for victims in being aware of the damage that befalls them through environmental crime (see below) mean that they are often supportive of or participate in the activities that harm them.

Large numbers of victims

An obvious characteristic of environmental victimization is the multitude of victims that often suffer the consequences (Williams 1996). Even relatively minor cases of pollution might cause harm to hundreds of victims, while climate change endangers all life on our planet (Hansen 2009). Moreover, although the damages may befall a specific group at a particular time, environmental victimization is often characterized by a good measure of spatial and temporal diversity.

Environmental victimization often does not follow geographical divisions: much environmental crime is transnational (White 2011). The impact of environmental harm originating in one area of the globe can impact the lives and livelihoods of people living elsewhere—in fact, all over the world. Externalizing the negative environmental impact means activities profiting one jurisdiction can cause great damage elsewhere.

The processes of environmental victimization mean that exposure to the same environmental hazard, and the unfolding of its etiology, can take place over a long timescale (White 2008). The illegal dumping of hazardous waste can be a source of contamination for years or even decades. The health effects of exposure can take additional years to materialize.

Self-definition of victims

Many victims will not self-define as such: they may not be aware that they have been harmed, while if they are aware, they may often attribute the harm to other causes and/or may not consider the experienced harm to constitute wrongdoing (see below). The latter is particularly true in those cases where exposure to the environmental harm was—at least to a degree—voluntary, for instance due to the victims' own occupation or lifestyle.

The intergenerational dimension of environmental victimization—with some of the most devastating consequences reserved for future generations—means that a prominent group of victims cannot self-define due to the fact they have not been born yet, or even because the environmental damage will prevent their existence (Williams 1996).

Non-humans and the environment

Humans are mostly only the secondary (or even tertiary) victims of environmental crime. The first casualties are the environment itself and/or non-human animals living in the environment (White 2008). This magnitude of harm largely outweighs any consequences experienced by humans, while other living creatures lack many of the possibilities available to humans to accommodate and adapt to environmental harm.

Environmental criminologists stress the importance of including non-human animals and the environment as direct victims themselves, rather than merely a function of the (physical or material) harm done to humans (White 2008). The notions of ecological and species justice reflect the understanding that humans are but one component of the biosphere and/or one species among many. The environment is worth protecting in its own right, and it is questionable on what grounds humans can claim a privileged position *vis-à-vis* other living entities on our planet.

Establishing Environmental Victimization

Establishing harm

A typical definition of victims of crime, contained in the EU Directive establishing minimum standards on the rights, support and protection of victims of crime of October 25, 2012, is: 'a natural person who has suffered harm, including physical, mental or emotional harm or economic loss which was directly caused by a criminal offence.'[2] Suffering harm is therefore a requisite component of victimization by crime. As a rule, victims are aware of the harm experienced. Indeed, they can offer a unique, albeit subjective, account of what this harm entails, although the veracity of the victims' accounts of the extent of harm may be called into question in a criminal trial (Pemberton 2014).

A relevant issue in cases of environmental victimization is victims' lack of awareness of the harm done to them or lack of requisite skills to connect the symptoms of the harm caused with its cause (Williams 1996; Skinnider 2011; Hall 2012). Expert (medical) opinion may be needed to establish that any harm has occurred, while establishing its etiology is an even more difficult matter. Chemical, radiological or biological contamination often eludes human senses, so that the victim is unaware of the experience when it occurs (Hyams et al. 2002). The consequences often become clear after a longer period, and even when this is so, the symptoms may not be restricted to one source.

Indeed, uncovering the fact that any attributable harm has occurred may not be a matter of directly assessing a clear causal chain, but instead of establishing anomalies in the distribution of ailments across populations (Williams 1996). Exposure to a harmful substance raises the risk of the development of disease or fatality, rather than identifying an isolated cause; assessing harm and wrongdoing proceeds through statistical inference.

The extent to which the distributive pattern of harm is recognized as wrongdoing can also be due to its link to other (social) injustices. A certain amount of pollution is unavoidable, and so is random variation in the distribution of pollution. However, this changes when variation correlates with race or wealth. Studies of environmental damage in the United States have shown environmental damage disproportionately afflicting minorities or the poor (Stretesky and Lynch 1999).

The difficulties in establishing a causal chain from the harmful behavior to the harm itself and forecast harm in the future make these connections uncertain. This uncertainty in turn provides a basis for *wishful thinking*, in which the current and future consequences are brought into line with the (often short-term) benefits of actions damaging the environment (Gifford 2011). This is also connected to the way people react to messages suggesting their

2 The Directive subsequently also explicitly includes family members of a person whose death was directly caused by a criminal offense and who have suffered harm as a result of that person's death. This addition was largely motivated to ensure that co-victims of homicide would also fall under the remit of the Directive, a matter that was often subject to discussion without this specific mention.

own complicity. Seeing the difficulty in adjusting one's own behavior and the sense of guilt that would accompany these messages if they were to be accepted to be true, people are prone to *guilty bias* (Ditto et al. 2009). This means that they are likely to view the problem in question in a way that assuages their feelings of guilt. Denying that any harm has occurred serves this purpose.

Establishing wrongdoing

The aforementioned EU definition of victims of crime suggests that establishing harm in itself is not sufficient to warrant the label 'victim of crime': for most legal purposes, it has to be directly caused by a criminal offense. A recurring issue in the environmental criminological literature is that this definition rules out much environmental crime when it is not recognized by criminal law. As Kramer (2013) recently emphasized in this respect: 'unless criminologists escape the juridical trap that mandates they only study that which states, through their law-making systems, tell them is a crime, the social injuries caused by the most powerful actors in the contemporary world, transnational corporations and national states, will remain forever outside their reach.' This fact, coupled with the acknowledgement that many other forms of non-criminal harm are considerably more damaging than crime, has led some authors to advocate a social harm-based approach, *zemiology*, to replace criminology.[3]

However, without delving too deeply into this subject, any all-out replacement of crime by harm risks losing sight of a key component of crime and the experience of criminal victimization. Robert Agnew's recent definition of crime as 'blameworthy harms' (Agnew 2011) appears to be an appropriate middle ground between the legalistic and zemiological approaches. It stops short of blindly following the criminal law, but successfully incorporates the key emotional and cognitive elements in the conception of crime which distinguish it from other harms. From a victimological perspective, it is relevant that the experience of victimization by crime can only be fully understood by recognizing its moral significance, its wrongfulness (see, for example, Pemberton 2014). As Antony Duff has helpfully summarized: 'the wrong done to the victim of rape, or wounding, or burglary, is in part constituted by, but also part constitutes the harm that she suffers: to understand such harm, we must understand it is a criminal harm- as a harm that consists in being wrongfully injured' (Duff 2003, p. 47).

The relevance here is that a number of social psychological heuristics converge (see, for example, Cushman et al. 2006; Markowitz and Shariff 2012) on the understanding that the characteristics of environmental victimization will reduce the extent to which experienced harm will be viewed as morally wrong. Some of the heuristics involved in downplaying the harm involved in environmental damage reoccur here: wishful thinking supplies a sense that no damage is done and therefore no wrong has occurred, while guilty bias contributes to a denial of the wrongfulness or (at least) one's own wrongdoing. In addition, I will briefly discuss the intent principle, the action principle, the contact principle, ingroup–outgroup heuristics and the identifiable victim/offender effect.

3 Hillyard (2006) proposes that we 'need an approach which not only focuses on crime harms but also a whole range of other harms including the harmful activities of national and local states, corporations and institutions upon people's lives, whether in respect of the lack of wholesome food, inadequate housing or heating, low income, exposure to various forms of danger and violations of basic human rights.'

The harm in environmental victimization is often not *intended* by the offenders, whose actions are often better characterized as reckless and negligent (see O'Hear 2004). They may not be in a position to foresee and/or control the outcome.[4] Even when the latter is true, the environmental harm is largely a by-product of their intended goal—or indeed, a negative external effect—rather than its main purpose (Markowitz and Shariff 2012). As has been demonstrated by research into the well-known trolley problem (Foot 1967), harm that is the goal of an action is considered to be worse than when it is an (inevitable) by-product of an action (see, for example, Hauser 2006).

Environmental crime is often characterized by the offender's omissions: the offender does not follow guidelines and regulations or does not take the precautions necessary to avoid contaminating others.[5] This can be connected to *the action principle*, also known as *omission bias* (Sunstein 1993). It reflects the intuitive understanding that the wrongful consequences of an action are morally worse than the same consequence of omitting to act.[6]

The action principle and the intent principle are not only visible in widely shared intuitions, but can also be defended with reference to philosophical and legal standards. This does not apply (equally) to most of the other heuristics: *in-group bias* may even be antithetical to this. However, even though our recent history has seen a distinct widening of our moral circle (Singer 1981), including all of humanity and non-humans as well, it remains true that our sense of moral obligation toward the outer limits of this circle—those with whom we experience a greater geographical, cultural, temporal or biological difference—is considerably weaker than to our next of kin (Brewer 1999). In other words, when the going gets tough and meeting our moral obligations becomes costly, the moral circle contracts and the interests of our own in-group become our main or our only moral concern.

The *contact principle* concerns the understanding that using physical contact to cause harm to a victim is morally worse than causing equivalent harm to a victim without using physical contact (Cushman et al. 2006), while *identifiable victim and offender effects* denote the greater willingness to save the lives of identified victims or punish identifiable offenders compared to the same number of lives of unidentified or statistical victims and offenders (Jenni and Loewenstein 1997; Small and Loewenstein 2005). Environmental harm often lacks both contact and identifiable victims and offenders. These phenomena share characteristics with the notion that establishing the wrongfulness of environmental harm involves abstract, effortful, cognitive processes (Weber 2006). This contrasts with the visceral, immediate, emotional responses elicited by other forms of criminal wrongdoing. Understanding that certain behavior amounts to criminal wrongdoing—like other forms of moral judgment—normally precedes any effortful cognitive work (Haidt 2001). Environmental harm of this more abstract kind may therefore be understood to be similar to crime, but not *feel* like it.

Finally, the struggle to convince the public of the inconvenient truth of the magnitude of environmental damage means that the environmental movement often adopts a *Pandora's box* scenario (Nisbet and Scheufele 2009), involving a multitude of near-imminent catastrophes for which humanity is to blame either through action or inaction. This message

4 For this reason, most definitions of the crime of ecocide define it is a crime of strict liability (see, for example, Higgins et al. 2013).

5 Carrabine et al. (2004) call this secondary or symbiotic green crime.

6 I should note here that Sunstein (1993) has cogently argued that this does not mean that this distinction applies equally—if at all—to governmental action. In defining the state's reaction to environmental harm, it does not carry the same weight as it does in individual matters: *omitting to act* involves the same sort of choice as *choosing to act*.

is in line with scientific evidence, although it sometimes emphasizes the risks beyond what most scientists would find defensible. Nevertheless, it offers opponents inroads to provide a reassuring counter-message that in part plays on wishful thinking and guilty bias (Weber and Stern 2011). For the current analysis, the most important point is that the experience of dread and unknown risk (Slovic 1987) that accompanies the Pandora's box scenario sits uneasily with viewing behavior as crime—an issue that is misunderstood or neglected in most criminological literature. I will return to this below, but the key difference is the predominantly fearful reaction to dread/unknown risk compared to the predominantly angry reaction to crime (see Ditton et al. 1999; Lerner and Keltner 2001; Litvak et al. 2010), which in turn gives rise to different appraisal and action tendencies (see Skitka et al. 2006).

Summing Up

This section has repeated what is probably well known to many readers of this volume: perpetration of environmental crime is often transnational in nature, may involve corporations and/or states whose resources may be put to use to prevent environmental harm (let alone crime) from being perceived as such, and may be committed by the same people who are eventually harmed. The multitude of victims often do not self-define as such: this may be impossible when it comes to future generations or non-human victims, but even humans alive today may lack awareness of what is happening to them and/or deny that their harm is wrongful in nature.

The processes involved in environmental victimization are considerably more complex than those in 'ordinary' crime. This makes it more difficult to understand that harm has occurred. Even those (eventually) suffering the consequences are often motivated to downplay negative effects and/or attribute them to other sources—a line of thinking supported by the powerful vested interests profiting from perpetration of environmental crime.

When the harm in environmental victimization becomes apparent, there are many psychological barriers to experiencing it as *wrongful*. There is a good deal of difficulty in establishing the culpable intent of perpetrators of environmental harm, who are often (seen to be) reckless and/or negligent rather than malicious. The complexity of the causal chain—including the lack of contact between victims and perpetrators and the statistical nature of much of the harm and wrongdoing involved—makes understanding the wrongfulness of many environmental crimes a cognitive exercise, rather than the visceral experience it is for 'ordinary' forms of crime.

The difficulties in establishing the occurrence of harm and wrongdoing leave environmental crime vulnerable to trade-offs that are highly taboo in the case of 'ordinary' crime (for the notion of a taboo trade off, see Fiske and Tetlock 1997). To put it bluntly: it is difficult to envisage a defense of murder and rape that would consider the profits made or jobs created by the process of murdering or raping as a counterargument. If anything, that would make the wrongdoing worse. Nevertheless, this is often exactly what happens in cases of environmental harm: the damage done to victims is downplayed and offset against the gains for others, including the perpetrators themselves (Bakan 2004). It also suggests that recognition of environmental crime as such will be a function of the extent to which it can be linked to other forms of wrongdoing—for instance, racism or organized crime—rather than of its intrinsic qualities as *blameworthy harm* in itself, including the magnitude of the damage inflicted upon its victims. I will return to this issue in the final section.

Framing Victimization by Crime

Defining New Victims and New Crimes

In his book *Random Violence: The Way We Talk About New Victims and New Crimes*, Joel Best (1999) analyzes the patterned way in which new victims and new crimes are framed in public discourse by news outlets and advocacy organizations. According to Best, this pattern is visible irrespective of the evidence base, and it applies in similar fashion to reports concerning victims of stalking or of alien abduction. The similarities across situations are evidence of the 'crime' master frame to which they are connected (see the similarities to the processes described in Snow 2004). The pattern consists of the following elements:

- **Victimization is widespread and consequential**—The case for attention to a group of victims is made first by reference to the extent of suffering. This applies to the number of victims, which are either large are at least larger than most people would think (see the following point), but especially to the impact of individual instances of victimization.
- **Victimization often goes unrecognized; awareness of victimization should be improved**—The widespread and consequential nature of the problem contrasts with a lack of recognition for those bearing the brunt of it. A key issue in victim advocacy is raising awareness of the size and impact of the problem, which includes teaching victims and others to recognize their own victimization.[7] Coupled with this is the perception that victims' justified claims will be doubted, and that this doubt is a source of further anguish for victims, covered by the term *secondary victimization*. Raising awareness should then contribute to the extent to which claims are respected.
- **There are qualms about the label 'victim'**—A recurrent point of discussion is the term used to describe those suffering victimization. The connotations of the word 'victim' are often a bone of contention, for instance because of the connotations of helplessness associated with victimhood. Other terms, for instance 'survivor,' maybe more appropriate. It might also be due to the importance of separating one's self from the victim group: the term 'victim' is reserved for those who are either deceased or still in relationships where violence is a regular feature. It might also be that the term 'victim' is not specific enough: Best notes that the focus is most often on one particular type of victimization.[8]
- **The relationship between victims and victimizers is straightforward and unambiguous**—The roles of victims and victimizers in the definition of new victims is clear-cut: victimizers intentionally exploit the victims for their own gain, while the victims are blameless for what happened.

---

7 A particularly problematic example of this phenomenon was the recovered memories debacle of the end of the 1980s and beginning of the 1990s, in which thousands of individuals, mostly women, were coaxed into believing they were suffering from repressed memories of past sexual abuse by their own therapists (see, for example, Loftus 1997).

8 It is of interest to note that although the groups represent victims, deal with similar issues and propose similar solutions, they rarely refer to other victim groups or are even aware of them.

These characteristics offer both an exposition of the considerable magnitude and urgency of the problem while simultaneously offering reasons why it has gone unnoticed until now, and for the effectiveness of paying closer attention to the problem in establishing magnitude and urgency. They also serve to pre-empt objections about the importance of the problem: not only is doubt and skepticism misguided, it also exacerbates the problem.

The latter point—the straightforward and unambiguous relationship between victims and victimizers—is the key to fully understanding the social problem in question as crime. Crime is an exceptionally powerful frame. The fact that crime is *wrong*, not merely *bad*, elevates the moral stakes involved. This demonstrates the power of framing a social problem as crime. Once the hurdle of defining something as a crime has been cleared, the master crime frame does the rest. As noted above, for crime to be understood as such, the notion of wrongdoing is a necessary element (Duff 2003; Agnew 2011). Once something is successfully defined as a crime, it is evident that it is a social problem: crime is problematic in and of itself, but it is also a matter of public concern. In Duff's terms: crime is a wrong, and indeed a public wrong—not in the sense that it is a wrong against the public rather than the victim—but that it transgresses the values by which the political community defines itself as a law-governed polity (Duff 2003, p. 48; see also Duff 2001).

This criterion is also pivotal in the frame analysis, as it supplies the problem definition, the causal analysis of the frame, the moral judgment and—as I will argue below—the remedy. Constraints of space here do not allow for a full analysis of the consequences. Instead, the remainder of this chapter focuses on three issues that will supply further ammunition to question the utility of the crime master frame for environmental victimization. The following points will be developed:

- the form of the stereotypical victim–victimizer dyad can vary, as long as it maintains the unambiguous relationship between victim and victimizer;
- the media portrayal of the master crime frame largely serves other purposes than the communication of risk and danger;
- the master crime frame by necessity involves a central position for the criminal justice system in the provision of the remedy, even in situations where its effectiveness—in particular for victims of crime—is suspect.

Framing Victims and Offenders: Stereotypical Descriptions

For many readers, the notion of the straightforward and unambiguous relationship between victims and victimizers will trigger recall of Nils Christie's (1986) description of the 'ideal victim.' Briefly, Christie described the ideal victim along the following lines (see also Dignan 2005): the victim is weak in relation to the offender—the 'ideal victim' is likely to be either female, sick, very old or very young (or a combination of these); the victim is, if not acting virtuously, then at least going about their legitimate, ordinary everyday business; the victim is blameless for what happened; the victim is unrelated to and does not know the 'stranger' who has committed the offense, and the offender is unambiguously big and bad. And indeed, Christie's 'little old lady' and her victimizer fit the mold well.

However, as I have argued elsewhere (Pemberton 2009; Pemberton 2012) Christie's stereotype, for all its rhetorical value, needs further scrutiny. First of all, his framing of the stereotype suggests the view of the victim as the prime mover in the definition of the victim–offender dyad: a point which also frequently resounds in societal analyses of penal developments (see, for example, Boutellier 2002). The societal emphasis on idealized victims abets the reduction of compassion for the offender and increases 'populist punitiveness' (Roberts et al. 2003). Instead, both social psychological research (for instance, Small and Loewenstein 2007; Van Prooijen 2010) and analysis of legal decision making (Bandes and Blumenthal 2012; Sundby 2003) suggest that by and large the reaction to the offender comes first; where our views of offenders change, so do our views of victims of crime. In my view this is well captured in the comparison of Christie's ideal victim with Roy Baumeister's 'Myth of Pure Evil,' which includes the following characteristics: the offender intentionally inflicted severe harm on the victim; this harm was primarily motivated by the wish to harm the victim, merely for the pleasure of doing so; the harm was not inflicted for instrumental reasons, nor was it used reluctantly; evil and evil offenders are so by nature, and this nature has a permanent quality; the harm is committed by the other, the stranger, or even the enemy, and the victim is innocent and good (Baumeister 1997). Although Baumeister's stereotype is obviously similar to Christies', in Baumeister's conception the focus in the victim–victimizer dyad is on the latter rather than the former.

Second, the stereotype described by the ideal victim is not the only one that suits the purpose of framing: others are possible, as long as they offer the same straightforward and unambiguous moral and causal analysis of crime and victimization (see, for example, Pemberton 2009). Of particular note is the stereotype employed by the violence against women movement, which was initially pitted against the ideal victim stereotype, and in particular its depiction of the victim and victimizer as strangers to each other. Instead, here the dyad is a combination of a *survivor*—a woman who has experienced repetitive violence at the hands of a man—*an intimate terrorist* (Johnson 1995) whose violence serves control and patriarchy (see, for example, Hoyle 2007). Due to the prolonged nature of this victimization, the consequences are often severe, even if the individual instances of violence are not (see, for example, Campbell 2002). The solution to these problems lies in changing the offender's misogyny, his beliefs about appropriate sex roles (see also the Duluth model of Pence and Paymar 1993).

The fact that the frame becomes the calling card for a particular social movement contributes to the vigorous defense of the stereotypical dyad, including its causal and moral components. The issue of intimate partner violence offers particular evidence of this: even in academic circles, considerable effort is expended in maintaining the straightforward and unambiguous link, instead of entertaining the probably accurate notion that the same or similar phenomena may be attributed to different causes (see the clash between feminist and family violence researchers: for instance, Dobash and Dobash 2004; Dutton 2006; Felson 2002; Johnson 1995; and see Johnson 2006 for a rejoinder). Findings that shed doubt on this threaten the strength of the frame, which is all the more true when these findings are embedded in a rival frame (see Entman 2007). For the current analysis, this suggests that environmental crime—to be successfully recognized as such—needs a stereotypical and straightforward victim–victimizer dyad of its own.

Framing and the Moral Workout

The clarity of the moral judgment within the frame is the key element of the public attraction to crime narratives. It is no news that media attention to crime is vastly disproportionate to its magnitude as a social problem (see, for example, Reiner 2002). Part of its attraction might be due to distortions in perception, with people displaying a tendency to overestimate the occurrence of various types of crime (see, for example, Slovic 1987; Tversky and Kahneman 1974) and the political and media manipulation and amplification of these distortions (see Cohen 1972).

Nevertheless, the notion that the interest in crime can be explained in this manner incorporates the dubious assumption that people are interested in learning about crime primarily or solely as a means to more accurately assess their own risk of criminal victimization. This notion, although widespread, does not stand up to much scrutiny. For one thing, people in fact have a fairly accurate sense of their own risk; distortions apply to the trajectory and magnitude of crime in general (Van Dijk and Vollaard 2012). Moreover, this type of explanation mistakes crime as being a risk similar to a public health hazard: it overlooks crime's defining characteristic as *a public wrong*.

In contrast to the utilitarian perspective, Jack Katz noted over 25 years ago that 'the public do not appear to read crime news in a naïve search about the empirical truth about crime' (Katz 1987, p. 60). The explanation Katz provided is too often overlooked in the discussion of framing of crime and victimization, while it is particularly relevant to the current topic. Katz observed that crime reporting refrains from displaying exceptional cases. To be sure, there is a large overrepresentation of the most severe crimes, with homicide at the pinnacle (see, for example, Reiner 2002). The point is that the content, typecasting and plot of the narratives all follow a constant pattern that varies little from day to day, from one place to the next, from one situation to another. The sense in which crime news is *news* differs from other news: it is a newest version of the same, familiar, scripted tale, instead of new information or a new tale. The function, then, of crime news is that it provides a good base for a *moral workout*. As Katz summarized:

> Crime is in today's newspaper, not because it contradicts the beliefs readers had yesterday, but because readers seek opportunities to shape up moral attitudes they will have to use today. Like vitamins useful in a body only for a day, like physical exercise whose value comes from its recurrent practice, crime news is experienced as interesting by its readers because of its place in a daily moral routine. (Katz 1987)

The stark 'evil versus good' narratives in crime news do not serve to challenge people's moral values, but allow them to exercise moral dilemmas of a lesser magnitude they encounter on a daily basis. This applies to 'new' crimes with their 'new' criminals and victims as well: although the heightened attention to these new crimes can be attributed to their newness, the plots of the accompanying stories serve as variants on the tried-and-tested crime news that went before them.

Crucially, the ways newspaper readers process and the ways the media end up portraying severe cases of crime entail focusing our emotional energy on confirming, not challenging, the accuracy of our existing view of the world. Our values are confirmed, and so is our connection to others who share these values.[9] In this way, the moral workout also serves to boost our self-esteem, and adds to this experience by demarcating a line between us (the readers of crime news) and them/the others (the criminals), showing *our* moral superiority to *them* (see also Ranulf 1938). In Nietzsche's somewhat hyperbolic, but still accurate assessment, it incorporates the 'exalted sensation of being allowed to despise and mistreat someone as "beneath him"' (Nietzsche 1887 [1966]).

The emotional experience of reading crime news is most often a form of anger, moral outrage (Darley and Pittman 2003), which in turn is connected with a sense of certainty and individual control, optimism and carelessness in thought (Litvak et al. 2010), magnifying the

---

9 In doing so, reading crime news fulfills the basic psychological need to belong and the need for certainty (see Heine et al. 2006).

straightforward and unambiguous nature of the typical crime news scenario. The experience of moral outrage also influences the perception of the causal structure of the problem, and thereby its solution. It precedes and underlies the judgment that another individual was to blame for the problem (Alicke 2000), and that (part of) the solution lies in punishing this individual for the conduct (Darley and Pittman 2003; Feigenson and Park 2006). This initial emotional assessment is then strengthened by further thoughts about the matter: in moral judgment, cognition is mostly tasked with providing adequate reasons for the initial assessment, rather than critically scrutinizing it.[10]

Crime news is at odds with the message of environmental harm on a number of levels. The key point is that understanding crime reporting as a form of risk communication fails to do justice to its primarily *moral* nature, both in depiction and consumption.

Criminal Justice as a Remedy

The crime frame comes equipped with its own solution: the criminal justice system. It is probably no news that this remedy has many faults: from a poor coverage rate through bias in its administration to a large discrepancy between its stated aims of retribution and prevention and its actual outcomes (see, for example, Van Dijk 2007; Wacquant 2009; Tonry 2011).

This is all the more true for forms of crime appear less intrinsically suited to the structure of criminal justice. A relevant example is that of international crimes—genocide, crimes against humanity and war crimes (see, for example, Groenhuijsen and Pemberton 2011)—as the characteristics of these crimes share certain similarities with environmental crime.[11] A number of additional dilemmas include: establishing individual guilt for crimes committed as a collective and/ or in the name of a collective (see, for example, Drumbl 2005; Levinson 2003); the wealth of evidence of collective evil, coupled with a lack of proof of individual wrongdoing (Osiel 2005); the uncertain line between culpable and inculpable parties (Osiel 2005), including the role of bystanders (Fletcher 2005), the difficulty of finding a remedy suitable to the enormity of the crimes committed (Pemberton and Letschert 2012), and coupled with the previous points, the diminished likelihood of achieving goals of criminal justice such as retribution and general or special prevention (Aukerman 2002). In practice, moreover, these shortcomings have been exacerbated by problems of selectivity, insufficient proportionality and lengthy procedures (Drumbl 2007). It is noteworthy that these features have not led to a modest posture for international criminal justice. Instead, it is accompanied by a triumphant and aspirational rhetoric of 'ending impunity' and 'delivering safety and justice on a global scale,' even in academic debate (Drumbl 2007).

Something similar is visible in the recent enthusiasm of advocates for the possibilities of criminal justice processes to significantly contribute to the immaterial and material benefits of victims of crime (see Weinstein 2011; Pemberton and Letschert 2012). To be sure, some progress has been made from Judith Herman's assessment that 'if one set out intentionally to design a system for provoking symptoms of posttraumatic stress disorder, it might look very much like a court of law' (Herman 1992). However, this progress is still far removed from warranting the complete volte-face toward the expectation that (criminal) justice

10 As Jonathan Haidt (2001) noted, it is a lawyer defending a client, rather than a judge reviewing the evidence.

11 These include multitudes of victims and perpetrators, complex processes of perpetration over a protracted period, state involvement.

processes might serve the will-o'-the-wisp of *closure* (Weinstein 2011), with participation in criminal processes and its outcome offering victims the cathartic experience necessary to 'move on with their lives' (Fletcher 2005). Similar observations can be made concerning the criminal justice system as an avenue for victims to receive material compensation. Most victims who apply for compensation in the criminal justice process do not receive it, while those that do, do not receive it in full (Strang 2002). The coverage rate of criminal injuries compensation schemes is normally only a fraction of those eligible for an award (Miers 2007). Moreover, the lengthy nature of the procedures implies that those most acutely in need of compensation run a real risk of receiving it when it is (much) too late, which is particularly true when compensation is needed to cover health care costs. Criminal justice would only serve as an expensive and time-consuming impediment to doing what is both necessary and urgent (Pemberton et al. 2014).

Indeed, any expectation that criminal justice procedures can serve all or even most victims' interests is increasingly suspect: a wide divide separates the flurry of *legislative* activity from the piecemeal gains in improving the position of victims in the criminal justice system *in practice* (Pemberton and Groenhuijsen 2012). This is not to say that some measure of justice is unachievable for victims of crime, or that no benefit is to be expected from reorienting criminal justice toward inclusion of victims of crime. Instead, it means that these benefits will be small, conditional and easily missed in the expectation of grand, cathartic consequences.

Again, the gap between rhetoric and possibilities is widest in international criminal justice. Criminal justice is poorly suited to accommodating hundreds or thousands of victims. Erecting barriers for access to international criminal justice has therefore been a necessity (Groenhuijsen and Pemberton 2011), even though this has resulted in adding the insult of the international community's (apparent) denial of victim status to the injuries of many victims.

International criminal justice institutions focus our attention on establishing the blame of individual perpetrators (Drumbl 2007). The complexities of international crimes make this a long and arduous process with a high failure rate. Making compensation or reparations to victims conditional on the outcome of this process means it will be a long wait, but also contingent on the coincidence of the case meeting the burden of proof for an individual perpetrator. The extent to which this can be ascertained has no relation to the damages the victims have sustained, and is irrelevant to their suffering.

There is something telling about the ease with which the cause of justice is invoked in the 'international community' spending $50 million on each case against suspects of international crimes (as is the case in the International Criminal Court or the International Criminal Tribunal for Rwanda (Drumbl 2007), while funding to ameliorate the suffering of their tens of thousands of victims is permanently in short supply. Elsewhere (Pemberton and Letschert 2012), Rianne Letschert and I have argued that any legal-philosophical justification for this acts as a cover for a considerably less palatable but nevertheless basically human motivation. The horrors of international crime form obvious and severe instances of injustice, which is at loggerheads with people's need to believe in a just world (Lerner 1980; Hafer and Begue 2005). One element of the daily moral workout consists of looking down upon others, but another is that crime does not pay: eventually, bad things happen to bad people. Separating perpetrators from others, the victims included, helps this process no end. Viewed through the justice motive, punishing the offender has large advantages over 'restoring' the victim (see, for example, Pemberton 2012). Our justice-related distress at a murder is easily reconciled with the outrage at the murderer;

not so much with sympathy for the victim's family, from whom we would rather distance ourselves (Hafer and Begue 2005). Our need for closure in respect to this distress might be quenched by the cathartic act of sentencing the murderer and his or her subsequent removal to prison; it is instead contradicted by viewing the enduring pain and the often lifelong recovery process of the victim's family. The much-maligned concept of closure is better understood as being that of the person observing victims, not of the victims of themselves

Criminal justice is a necessary remedy for the social problem of crime, but that does not mean it is a very good one. In the case of international crimes, it serves as a lightning rod that offers a relatively straightforward release for the distress we feel at viewing these sites of injustice that can only be described in terms of their enormity. There is a real danger of international criminal justice being akin to a moral hazard: our relatively recent sense of obligation in crimes committed elsewhere on the globe is converted into a righteous search for and sentencing of 'hostis hominis generis,' rather than caring for their victims. My worry is that this is a likely scenario for environmental crime as well. At the very least it begs the question whether successfully making the public aware of the criminal reality of much environmental harm will not merely result in channeling resources in a search for someone to blame, rather than in increased attention on the prevention of environmental victimization and the care of its victims.

Conclusion

There is no doubt in my mind that most readers of this volume will readily understand that much of the environmental harm visited on our planet is criminal in nature. Neither do I doubt that they would be right in thinking this to be true. Nevertheless, environmental harm has a number of intrinsic qualities that obstruct understanding it as crime. By the time I have finished this paragraph, another species will have become extinct, but I am still more prone to see my neighbor mistreating his dog as a crime.[12] The difficulties in viewing environmental crime as *crime* are in part a function of the power of those who stand to gain from its perpetration, however the *third face of power* is not the only or even the main reason for this difficulty. My neighbor's dog is known to me, as is my neighbor; likewise, the harm and wrongdoing in his hitting and kicking the dog are visible and emotionally apparent: the differences with the case of the extinct species are obvious. Much optimism about reshaping the way we view this situation and crime in general is unfounded, particularly if appeals to reason are the main vehicle to achieve this end. The evidence base of the primacy of emotion and intuition in moral judgment grows larger every day. Although it is true that the 'emotional dog can learn new tricks' (Haidt 2004), it still wags the 'rational tail' (Haidt 2001).

But on the other hand, this does not rule out the possibility that awareness of the criminal nature of (at least some) environmental harm will increase, perhaps in similar vein to the process surrounding violence within the family. A key issue, then, is that this will involve the framing of environmental crime in the victimizer–victim dyad that is part and parcel of crime. The 'poster boy' of environmental crime will involve the straightforward and morally unambiguous situations—for instance, those connected to other forms of wrongdoing, like racism or organized crime—rather than the situations which are more complex and/or involve victims who are partly to blame for their own victimization.

---

12 This is hypothetical: my neighbor does not own a dog.

This is reinforced by the understanding that the environmental harm most readily seen as crime will be amenable to the moral workout people receive from crime news. This moral workout involves feelings of anger, control and blame, which seems at odds with the messages of anxiety and fear connected to the most dangerous forms of environmental harm. If there ever was a 'dread risk,' this is it: because of the magnitude of the problem, but also because of the unclear and complicated processes by which it endangers us all. Coming to grips with the processes involved in the scenario of the Earth following the course of Venus—whose barren landscape appears to be caused by greenhouse gases' positive feedback loops—may be a straightforward matter for a NASA scientist like James Hansen, but is unlikely to be so for large swaths of the population. Finding ways to communicate this danger in a manner that leads to a substantial change in behavior, instead of fueling the resistance, is a challenge that is in dire need of further examination (see Markowitz and Shariff 2012). It is, however, hard to see how the necessarily dumbed-down message inherent to crime news is conducive to this purpose. More generally, I hope that the discussion of Katz's moral workout in this chapter will reignite scrutiny of the view that crime is experienced as *a risk* to which the main reaction is *fear*, rather than *a wrong* to which the main reaction is *anger*.

Finally, I do not share some of my colleagues' optimism about the extent to which criminal justice can offer a solution to the suffering of environmental victims. In my view, and notwithstanding the progress that has been made over recent decades, the victimological evidence suggests that the criminal justice system is still best viewed as something of a necessary evil and a minor boon. If experience in international criminal justice is anything to go by, emphasis will be directed toward blaming and punishing a small number of perpetrators, rather than assuaging victims' suffering. Given the complexity of environmental crime—including the difficulties of establishing intent and the causal chain toward victims' suffering—many deserving victims will be waiting a long time in vain for the criminal justice process to run its course and offer them any reparation. And those are the cases that go to trial: the odds are that the real extent of environmental crime will be at least of the magnitude of 'ordinary' crime.

The master crime frame and criminal justice march to the beat of their own drum. This chapter has attempted to question whether the plight of victims of environmental harm is in time with this rhythm. Meeting the challenge of developing a fully fledged environmental victimology will be pivotal in providing an answer.

References

Agnew, R. 2011. *Toward a Unified Criminology: Integrating Assumptions About Crime, People and Society*. New York: New York University Press.

Alicke, M.D. 2000. 'Culpable Control and the Psychology of Blame,' *Psychological Bulletin* 126, 556–74.

Aukerman, M.J. 2002. 'Extraordinary Evil, Ordinary Crime: A Framework for Understanding Transitional Justice,' *Harvard Human Rights Journal* 15, 39–98.

Bakan, J. 2004. *The Corporation: The Pathological Pursuit of Profit and Power*. London: Constable.

Bandes, S.A. and Blumenthal, J.A. 2012. 'Emotion and the Law,' *Annual Review of Law and Social Science* 8, 161–81.

Baumeister, R.F. 1997. *Evil: Inside Human Violence and Cruelty*. New York: Henry Holt.

Benford, R.D. 1993. 'Frame Disputes Within the Nuclear Disarmament Movement,' *Social Forces* 71, 677–701

Benford, R.D and Snow, D.A. 2000. 'Framing Process and Social Movements: An Overview and Assessment,' *Annual Review of Sociology* 26, 611–39.

Best, J. 1999. *Random Violence: How We Talk About New Crimes and New Victims*. Berkeley, CA: University of California Press.

Best, J. 2008. *Social Problems*. London and New York: Norton.

Boutellier, H. 2002. *The Safety Utopia: Contemporary Discontent and Desire as to Crime and Punishment*. Houten: Springer.

Brewer, M. 1999. 'The Psychology of Prejudice: Ingroup Love or Outgroup Hate?', *Journal of Social Issues* 55, 429–44.

Campbell, J.C. 2002. 'Health Consequences of Intimate Partner Violence,' *Lancet* 359(9,314), 1,331–6.

Cardwell, P.J. French, D. and Hall, M. 2011. 'Tackling Environmental Crime in the European Union: The Case of the Missing Victim?', *Environmental Law and Management* 23(3), 113–21.

Carrabine, E., Iganski, P. Lee, M. Plummer, K. and South, N. 2004. *Criminology: A Sociological Introduction*. London: Routledge.

Carragee, K.M. and Roefs, W. 2004. 'The Neglect of Power in Recent Framing Research,' *Journal of Communication* 542, 214–33.

Christie, N. 1986. 'The Ideal Victim,' in *From Crime Policy to Victim Policy*, edited by E. Fattah. Basingstoke: Macmillan, 17–30.

Cohen, B. 1963. *The Press and Foreign Policy*. Princeton, NJ: Princeton University Press.

Cohen, S. 1972. *Folk Devils and Moral Panics*. London: Paladin.

Cushman, F., Young, L. and Hauser, M. 2006. 'The Role of Conscious Reasoning in Moral Judgement: Testing Three Principles of Harm,' *Psychological Science* 1,712, 1,082–9.

Darley, J.M. and Pittman, T.S. 2003. 'The Psychology of Compensatory and Retributive Justice,' *Personality and Social Psychology Review* 7, 324–36.

Dignan, J. 2005. *Understanding Victims and Restorative Justice*. Maidenhead: Open University Press.

Ditto, P.H., Pizarro, D.A. and Tannenbaum, D. 2009. 'Motivated Moral Reasoning,' *Psychology of Learning and Motivation* 50, 307–38.

Ditton, J., Bannister, J., Gilchrist, E. and Farrall, S. 1999. 'Afraid or Angry? Recalibrating the "Fear" of Crime,' *International Review of Victimology* 6, 83–99.

Dobash, R.P. and Dobash, R.E. 2004. 'Women's Violence to Men in Intimate Relationships: Working on a Puzzle,' *British Journal of Criminology* 44, 324–49.

Drumbl, M.A. 2005. 'Collective Violence and Individual Punishment: The Criminality of Mass Atrocity,' *Northwestern University Law Review* 99, 539–610.

Drumbl, M.A. 2007. *Atrocity, Punishment and International Law*. Cambridge: Cambridge University Press.

Duff, R.A. 2001. *Punishment, Communication and Community*. Oxford: Oxford University Press.

Duff, R.A. 2003. 'Restoration and Retribution,' in *Restorative and Criminal Justice: Competing or Reconcilable Paradigms?*, edited by A. von Hirsch, J.V. Roberts, A. Bottoms, K. Roach and M. Schiff. Oxford: Hart Publishing, 43–59.

Dutton, D.A. 2006. *Rethinking Domestic Violence*. Toronto: UBC Press.

Emsley, J. 2006. *Elements of Murder: A History of Poison*. Oxford: Oxford University Press.

Entman, R.M. 1993. 'Framing: Toward Clarification of a Fractured Paradigm,' *Journal of Communication* 434, 51–8.

Entman, R.M. 2004. *Projections of Power: Framing News, Public Opinion, and U.S. Foreign Policy*. Chicago, IL: University of Chicago Press.

Entman, R.M. 2007. 'Framing Bias: Media Distribution in the Distribution of Power,' *Journal of Communication* 571, 163–73.

Fattah, E. 1991. *Understanding Criminal Victimization*. New York: Prentice-Hall.

Feigenson, N. and Park, J. 2006. 'Emotions and Attributions of Legal Responsibility of blame: A Research Review,' *Law and Human Behavior* 30, 143–61.

Felson, R.B. 2002. *Violence and Gender Reexamined*. Washington, DC: American Psychological Association.

Fiske, A.P and Tetlock, P. 1997. 'Taboo Trade-offs: Reactions to Transgressions that Transgress the Spheres of Justice,' *Political Psychology* 182, 255–97.

Fletcher, L.E. 2005. 'From Indifference to Engagement: Bystanders and International Criminal Justice,' *Michigan Journal of International Law* 26, 1,013–62.

Foot, P. 1967. 'The Problem of Abortion and the Doctrine of Double Effect,' *Oxford Review* 5, 5–15.

Gamson, W.A. 1992. *Talking Politics*. New York: Cambridge University Press

Gifford, R. 2011 'The Dragons of Inaction: Psychological Barriers that Limit Climate Change Mitigation and Adaptation,' *American Psychologist*, 66, 290–302.

Groenhuijsen, M.S. and Letschert, R.M., eds. 2012. *Compilation of International Victims' Rights Instruments*, 2nd revised edn. Nijmegen: Wolf Publishing.

Groenhuijsen, M.S. and Pemberton, A. 2011. 'Genocide, War Crimes and Crimes Against Humanity: A Victimological Perspective,' in *Victimological Approaches to International Crimes: Africa*, edited by R.M. Letschert, R. Haveman, A. de Brouwer and A. Pemberton. Antwerp: Intersentia, 9–34.

Hafer, C.L. and Begue, L. 2005. 'Experimental Research on Just-world Theory: Problems, Developments and Future Challenges,' *Psychological Bulletin* 1,311, 128–67.

Haidt, J. 2001. 'The Emotional Dog and its Rational Tail,' *Psychological Review* 98, 814–34.

Haidt, J. 2003. 'The Emotional Dog Does Learn New Tricks: A Reply to Pizarro and Bloom,' *Psychological Review* 100, 197–8.

Hall, M. 2012. 'Environmental Victims: Challenges for Criminology and Victimology in the 21st Century,' *Journal of Criminal Justice and Security* 134, 371–91.

Hannigan, J. 2006. *Environmental Sociology*, 2nd edn. London: Routledge.

Hansen, J. 2009. *Storms of My Grandchildren: The Truth About the Coming Climate Catastrophe and Our Last Chance to Save Humanity*. New York: Bloomsbury.

Hauser, M. 2006. *Moral Minds: How Nature Designed our Universal Sense of Right and Wrong*. New York: Ecco.

Heine, S.J., Proulx, T. and Vohs, K.D. 2006. 'The Meaning Maintenance Model: On the Coherence of Social Motivations,' *Personality and Social Psychology Review* 10(2), 88–110.

Herman, J.L. 1992. *Trauma and Recovery*. New York: Basic Books.

Herman, J.L. 2003. 'The Mental Health of Crime Victims: Impact of Legal Intervention,' *Journal of Traumatic Stress* 162, 159–66.

Higgins, P., Short, D. and South, N. 2013. 'Protecting the Planet: Proposal for a Law of Ecocide,' *Crime, Law and Social Change* 59, 251–66.

Hillyard, P. 2006. Criminal Obsessions: Crime Isn't the Only Harm,' *Criminal Justice Matters* 62, 26–46.

Hoyle, C. 2007. 'Feminism, Victimology and Domestic Violence,' in *Handbook of Victims and Victimology*, edited by S. Walklate. Cullompton: Willan Publishing.

Hoyle, C. 2011. 'Victims, the Criminal Process and Restorative Justice,' in *Oxford Handbook of Criminology*, 5th edn., edited by M. Maguire, R. Morgan and R. Reiner. Oxford: Oxford University Press, 398–425.

Hulsman, L.H.C. 1986. 'Critical Criminology and the Concept of Crime,' *Crime, Law and Social Change* 101, 63–80.

Hyams, K.C., Murphy, F.M. and Wessely, S. 2002. 'Responding to Chemical, Biological, or Nuclear Terrorism: The Indirect and Long-term Health Effects May Present the Greatest Challenge,' *Journal of Health Politics, Policy, and Law* 27, 273–91.

Jarell, M.L. and Ozymy, J. 2012. 'Real Crime, Real Victims: Environmental Crime Victims and the Crime Victims' Rights Act (CVRA),' *Crime Law and Social Change* 58, 373–89.

Jenni, K.E. and Loewenstein, G. 1997. 'Explaining the Identifiable Victim Effect,' *Journal Of Risk and Uncertainty* 14, 235–57.

Johnson, M.P. 1995. 'Patriarchal Terrorism and Common Couple Violence: Two Forms of Violence Against Women,' *Journal of Marriage and the Family* 57, 283–94.

Johnson, M.P. 2006. 'Conflict and Control: Gender Symmetry and Asymmetry in Domestic Violence,' Violence against Women 12(11), 1,003–18.

Katz, J. 1987. 'What Makes Crime News?', *Media, Culture and Society* 9, 144–75.

Kramer, R. 2013. 'Carbon in the Atmosphere and Power in America: Climate Change as State-corporate Crime,' *Journal of Crime and Justice* 362, 153–70.

Laxminarayan, M.S. 2012. *The Heterogeneity of Crime Victims: Variations in Procedural and Outcome Preferences*. Nijmegen: Wolf Legal Publishers.

Lens, K.M.E., Pemberton, A. and Bogaerts, S. 2013. 'Heterogeneity in Victim Participation: A New Perspective on Delivering a Victim Impact Statement,' *European Journal of Criminology* 10(4), 479–95.

Lerner, J. and Keltner, D. 2001. 'Fear, Anger, and Risk,' *Journal of Personality and Social Psychology* 81, 146–59.

Lerner, M.J. 1980. *The Belief in a Just World: A Fundamental Delusion*. New York: Plenum Press.

Letschert, R.M. and Van Boven, T. 2011. 'Providing Reparation in Situations of Mass Victimization: Key Challenges Involved,' in *Victimological Approaches to International Crimes: Africa*, edited by R.M. Letschert, R. Haveman, A. de Brouwer and A. Pemberton. Antwerp: Intersentia, 153–84.

Levinson, D.J. 2003. 'Collective Sanctions,' *Stanford Law Review* 56, 345–428.

Litvak, P.M., Lerner, J.S., Tiedens, L.S. and Shonk, K. 2010. 'Fuel in the Fire: How Anger Impacts Judgement and Decision Making,' in *International Handbook of Anger: Constituent and Concomitant Biological, Psychological, and Social Processes*, edited by M. Potegal, G. Stemmler and S. Spielberger. Dordrecht: Springer, 287–311.

Loftus, E.F. 1997. 'Creating False Memories,' *Scientific American* 277, 50–55.

Lukes, S. 1974. *Power: A Radical View*. London: Macmillan.

Markowitz, E.M. and Shariff, A.F. 2012. 'Climate Change and Moral Judgement,' *Nature Climate Change* 2, 243–7.

Miers, D. 2007. 'Looking Beyond Great Britain: The Development of Criminal Injuries Compensation,' in *Handbook of Victims and Victimology*, edited by S. Walklate. Cullompton: Willan Publishing, 337–62.

Neria, Y., Galea, S. and Norris, F.H. 2009. *Mental Health and Disasters*. Cambridge: Cambridge University Press.

Nietzsche, F. 1887 [1966]. *On the Genealogy of Morals*, translated by W. Kaufmann and R.J. Hollingdale. New York: Random House.

Nisbet, M.C. and Scheufele, D.A. 2009. 'What's Next for Science, Communication? Promising Directions and Lingering Distractions,' *American Journal of Botany* 96, 1,767–78.

O'Hear, M. 2004. 'Sentencing the Green-collar Offender: Punishment, Culpability, and Environmental Crime,' *Journal of Criminal Law and Criminology* 951, 133–276.

Osiel, M. 2005. 'The Banality of Good: Aligning Incentives Against Mass Atrocity,' *Columbia Law Review* 105, 1,751–861.

Parenti, C. 2011. *Tropic of Chaos: Climate Change and the New Geography of Violence*. New York: Nation Books.

Pemberton, A. 2009. 'Victim Movements: From Varying Needs to Diversified Criminal Justice Agendas,' *Acta Criminologica* 22, 1–23.

Pemberton, A. 2010. *The Cross-over: An Interdisciplinary Approach to the Study of Victims of Crime*. Apeldoorn and Antwerp: Maklu.

Pemberton, A. 2012. 'Just-world Victimology,' in *Victimology and Human Security: New Horizons, Proceedings of the 13th Symposium of the World Society of Victimology*, edited by H. Morosawa, J. Dussich and G. Kirchhoff. Nijmegen: Wolf Legal Publishers, 45–69.

Pemberton, A. 2014. 'Respect, Empathy, Wrongfulness: Key Distinctions in a Theory of Victims' Rights,' in *Routledge International Handbook of Victimology*, edited by I. Vanfraechem, A. Pemberton and F. Ndahinda. Oxford. Routledge, forthcoming.

Pemberton, A. and Groenhuijsen, M.S. 2012. 'Developing Victims' Rights Within the European Union: Past, Present, Future,' in *Victimology and Human Security: New Horizons, Proceedings of the 13th Symposium of the World Society of Victimology*, edited by H. Morosawa, J. Dussich and G. Kirchhoff. Nijmegen: Wolf Legal Publishers, 535–59.

Pemberton, A. and Letschert, R.M. 2012. 'Global Justice and Global Criminal Laws: The Importance of Nyaya in the quest for Justice after International Crimes,' *Tilburg Law Review* 17(2), 296–303.

Pemberton, A., Letschert, R.M., De Brouwer, A.M. and Haveman, R.H. 2014. 'Coherence in International Crimes: A Victimological Perspective.' Forthcoming.

Pence, E., and Paymar, M. 1993. *Education Groups for Men Who Batter: The Duluth Model*. New York: Springer.

Ranulf, S. 1938. *Moral Indignation and Middle Class Psychology*. New York: Schocken.

Reiner, R. 2002. Media Made Criminality: The Representation of Crime in the Mass Media,' in *The Oxford Handbook of Criminology*, edited by M. Maguire, R. Morgan and R. Reiner. Oxford: Oxford University Press.

Roberts, J., Stalans, L., Indemaur, D. and Hough, M. 2003. *Penal Populism and Public Opinion: Lessons from Five Countries*. New York: Oxford University Press.

Robinson, P.H. and Darley, J.M. 2007. 'Intuitions of Justice: Implications for Criminal Law and Criminal Policy,' *Southern California Law Review* 81, 1–68.

Shapland, J., Wilmore, J. and Duff, P. 1985. *Victims in the Criminal Justice System*. Aldershot: Gower.

Singer, P. 1981. *The Expanding Circle*. Oxford: Clarendon Press.

Skinnider, E. 2011. *Victims of Environmental Crime: Mapping the Issues*. Vancouver: International Centre for Criminal Law Reform and Criminal Justice Policy.

Skitka, L.J., Bauman, C.W., Aramovich, N.P. and Scott-Morgan, G. 2006. 'Confrontational and Preventative Policy Responses to Terrorism: Anger Wants a Fight and Fear Wants "Them" to Go Away,' *Basic and Applied Psychology* 284, 375–84.

Slovic, P. 1987. 'Perception of Risk,' *Science* 236, 280–85.

Small, D.A. and Loewenstein, G. 2005. 'The Devil You Know: The Effects of Identifiability on Punishment,' *Journal of Behavioral Decision Making* 185, 311–18.

Snow, D.A. 2004. 'Framing Processes, Ideology, and Discursive Fields,' in *The Blackwell Companion to Social Movements*, edited by D. Snow, S. Soule and H. Kriesi. Oxford: Blackwell, 380–412.

Snow, D.A. and Benford, R.D. 1992. 'Master Frames and Cycles of Protest,' in *Frontiers in Social Movement Theory*, edited by A.D. Morris and C.M. Mueller. New Haven, CT: Yale University Press, 133–55.

Snow D.A, Rochford, E.B., Worden S.K. and Benford, R.D. 1986. 'Frame Alignment Processes, Micromobilization, and Movement Participation,' *American Sociological Review* 51, 464–81.

Strang, H. 2002. *Repair or Revenge: Victims and Restorative Justice*. Oxford: Clarendon Press.

Stretesky, P. and Lynch, M. 1999. 'Corporate Environmental Violence and Racism,' *Crime, Law and Social Change* 30, 163–84.

Sundby, S. 2003. 'The Capital Jury and Empathy: The Problem of Worthy and Unworthy Victims,' *Cornell Law Review* 88, 343–79.

Sunstein, C.R. 1993. *The Partial Constitution*. Cambridge, MA: Harvard University Press.

Sunstein, C.R. 2003. 'Moral Framing and Moral Heuristics,' *Minnesota Law Review* 88, 1,556–97.

Tonry, M. 2011. *Retributivism Has a Past: Has it a Future?* Oxford: Oxford University Press.

Tversky, A. and Kahneman, D. 1974. 'Judgment under Uncertainty, Heuristics and Biases,' *Science* 185, 1,124–31.

Van Dijk, J.J.M. 2007. *World of Crime*. Thousand Oaks, CA: Sage.

Van Dijk, J.J.M. and Vollaard, B. 2012. 'Self Limiting Crime Waves,' in *The International Crime Drop: New Directions in Research*, edited by J. van Dijk, A. Tseloni and G. Farrell. Basingstoke: Palgrave Macmillan, 250–67.

Van Prooijen, J.W. 2010. 'Retributive Versus Compensatory Justice: Observers' Preference for Punishing in Response to Criminal Offenses,' *European Journal of Social Psychology* 40, 72–85.

Van Swaaningen, R. 1997. *Critical Criminology: Visions from Europe*. Thousand Oaks, CA: Sage.

Wacquant, L. 2009. *Punishing the Poor: The Neoliberal Government of Social Insecurity*. Durham: Duke University Press.

Weber, E. 2006. 'Experience-based and Description-based Perceptions of Long-term Risk: Why Global Warming Does Not Scare Us Yet,' *Climatic Change* 77, 103–20.

Weber, E.U. and Stern, P.C. 2011. 'Public Understanding of Climate Change in the United States,' *American Psychologist* 664, 315–28.

Weinstein, H.M. 2011. 'Editorial. The Myth of Closure: The Illusion of Reconciliation. Final Thoughts on Five Years as Co-editor in Chief,' *International Journal of Transitional Justice* 5, 1–10.

Wemmers, J.A. 1996. *Victims in the Criminal Justice System*. The Hague: WODC/Kugler.

White, R. 2008. *Crimes Against Nature: Environmental Criminology and Ecological Justice*. Cullompton: Willan Publishing.

White, R. 2011. *Transnational Environmental Crime: Toward an Eco-global Criminology*. London: Routledge.
Williams, C. 1996. 'An Environmental Victimology,' *Social Justice* 234, 16–40.

Chapter 5
Eco-justice and Problem-solving Approaches to Environmental Crime and Victimisation

Rob White

Introduction

Environmental crime involves transgressions against humans, specific eco-systems and animals. Not all environmental harm is seen as criminal, however. Moreover, even when harm has been criminalised, sanctions and remedies have tended to be inadequate and insufficient. How justice is played out in practice is vital to the morale and effectiveness of environmental law enforcers and regulators. Lots of hard investigative work can go into gathering evidence and building cases against polluters, illegal fishers, transporters of toxic waste and so on. New technologies and new collaborations between police and non-police agencies may be required, as well as extensive use of resources, time and energy (see White 2011a; White 2011b; White 2012).

However, what happens when cases get to court? Here the immediate concerns are which courts the cases are heard in (for example, magistrates/lower courts or superior courts), what kind of court (for example, generalist or specialist) and the penalties imposed on offenders (for example, fines or action orders) and remedies to the harm caused (for example, remediation). For environmental law enforcement personnel, a crucial issue is the effect of perceptions that magistrates or judges do not provide adequate orders in relation to the nature of the offences. This is especially so when people spend a large amount of work in compiling their cases. Court decisions can have a profound effect on the morale and work activities of enforcement officers and environmental social movement activists alike, especially in new areas of interest such as that of environmental law enforcement.

The valuing of environmental harm is essential if this crime is to garner the resources needed to fight it. Central to this process are the decisions made in and by the court. Typically, until recently, the usual pattern of judicial decision-making was marked by the following features:

- Environmental crime is not viewed as a 'real' crime.
- Environmental crimes are devolved to lower courts
- There is poor judicial knowledge about environmental crimes.
- There are few case precedents due to low prosecution rates.
- A low 'value' is placed on environmental crimes and harms.
- There are few well-trained personnel on the ground.
-

This chapter addresses the following issues:

1. What kind of court is best suited to dealing with environmental crime?
2. Which approaches to justice are most appropriate to this project?

As the central fulcrum upon which 'justice' hinges, the dynamics and nature of the court have a major bearing on what occurs prior to a case and what happens after a case has been officially processed. The mission of the court is ostensibly to achieve a just outcome. We will therefore begin with concepts of justice.

Environmental Crime and Justice

The overall aim of criminal law is to prevent certain kinds of behaviour regarded as harmful or potentially harmful. But the purposes of criminal law vary, and involve a constant weighing up of moral wrongness, individual autonomy and community welfare (Findlay et al., 1994). What falls within the ambit of criminal law (and what does not) is the outcome of a social process that is ongoing and inherently political, since it embodies basic principles and visions of the kind of society in which people prefer to live.

A primary task of criminal law is to stipulate the degree of seriousness of criminal conduct. This involves assessing such factors as the physical impact of the conduct on the victim, psychological trauma, the monetary value of property crimes and so forth. Social scientists who study crime argue that it is 'harm' that needs to be measured and assessed, but in doing so, the study of crime must go beyond existing legal definitions and criteria (Hillyard et al. 2004; Hillyard and Tombs 2007; Matthews and Kauzlarich 2007). This is so for several reasons.

Firstly, wrongdoing is perpetrated by states themselves, yet it is nation-states that define what is criminal, corrupt or unjust. There is therefore a need for the development of criteria and definitions of crime that are not restricted to specific states' laws, but are more universal in nature (for example, that appeal to 'human rights' or 'environmental rights' or 'animal rights'). Secondly, harms perpetrated by powerful groups and organisations, such as transnational corporations, are frequently dealt with by the state as civil rather than criminal matters. This reflects the capacity of the powerful to shape laws in ways that do not criminalise their activities, even when they are ecologically disastrous. Thirdly, there are extra-legal concepts and factors that need to be studied if we are to fully capture the nature of environmental harm, and this requires a different way of framing the issues. An ecology-based analysis of activity will provide quite a different picture of 'harm' than an economics-based analysis. What is defined as criminal harm, and the measure of the seriousness of that harm, are contingent upon the social interests bound up with the definitional process (White 2013).

Within a green criminology perspective, there are three broad conceptualisations of harm (see Figure 5.1). Each of these is construed in relation to particular notions of rights and justice: with variable focus on humans, environments and animals. Justice within an eco-justice perspective is initially framed in terms of the subject or victim that is liable to be harmed.

Figure 5.1 An eco-justice perspective – three approaches to justice, rights and harms

ENVIRONMENTAL JUSTICE AND HUMAN RIGHTS

Focus: Environmental rights as an extension of human or social rights in order to enhance the quality of human life.

Concepts: *Intergenerational responsibility* – The present generation is responsible for ensuring environmental equity for future generations.

Environmental justice – Everyone has the right to a healthy environment, and there ought to be environmental equity for present generations.

Emphasis: Environmental harm is constructed in relation to human-centred notions of value and use.

ECOLOGICAL JUSTICE AND ECOLOGICAL CITIZENSHIP

Focus: Human beings are merely one component of complex ecosystems that should be preserved for their own sake via the notion of the rights of the environment.

Concepts: *Ecological citizenship* – humans are responsible for the preservation and conservation of nature.

Ecological justice – concerning the quality of the biosphere and rights of non-human species.

Emphasis: Environmental harm is constructed in relation to notions of ecological harm and destructive techniques of human intervention.

SPECIES JUSTICE AND ANIMAL RIGHTS

Focus: Non-human animals have rights based upon utilitarian notions (maximising pleasure and minimising pain), inherent value (right to respectful treatment) and an ethic of responsible caring.

Concepts: *Anti-speciesism and animal rights* – addressing the discriminatory treatments of animals as Other.

Animal welfare – dealing with issues of animal abuse and suffering, and the nurturing of respectful relationships.

Emphasis: Environmental harm is constructed in relation to the place of non-human animals within environments and their intrinsic right not to suffer abuse, whether this be one-on-one harm, institutionalised harm or harm arising from human actions that affect climates and environments on a global scale.

Source: Adapted from White 2008; see also White 2013.

In practice, however, justice is usually articulated and understood as a balance between several interlinked elements. Schlosberg (2007) identifies the key categories or dimensions of justice as including distribution, recognition, participation and capability. The notion of justice as fairness is associated with questions of *distribution*. Justice, according to this conception, defines how we distribute various rights, goods and liberties, and how we define and regulate social and economic equality and inequality. What matters are the rules of distributive justice and how these are constructed. The rules may be procedure-based, such as providing equal opportunities for everyone to attain valued goods, or they may be oriented towards consequentialist and substantive conceptions of justice that ensure equal outcomes. Arguments occur concerning what the principles governing those proposed distributions should be (for example, need, desert, entitlement). Such principles are deemed to be relevant to both humans and non-humans, particularly in the context of extending the notion of rights to environments and particular animals.

Recognition refers to the equal dignity accorded to all, as well as the politics of difference where everyone is recognised for their particular distinctiveness. Schlosberg observed that 'A lack of recognition in the social and political realms demonstrated by various forms of insults, degradation and devaluation at both the individual and cultural level inflicts damage to oppressed individuals and communities in the political and cultural realms' (Schlosberg 2007, p. 14). Derogatory language used in relation to animals provides one illustration of subordinated and disrespected identity as this applies to the non-human (see Beirne 2009). Here it is argued that contemporary practices of cultural domination are such that the rights, interests and needs of eco-systems and animals are rendered invisible in ordinary life, and accordingly fewer legal, social and economic resources are devoted to acknowledging, supporting and respecting the non-human.

The need for *participation* is also defined as an important component of justice. Participation generally refers to a person's membership and engagement in the wider community, and is supported by the institutionalisation of democratic and participatory decision-making procedures. As applied to the non-human world, participation basically involves human advocacy, where the voice of animals or trees or eco-systems is 'heard' via the human third party. Humans can thus speak 'on behalf of' that and those which cannot participate directly for themselves in human affairs that affect them.

Capability is important to justice as well. This refers to the ability to achieve valuable functionings within the context of one's essential character and setting. For humans, capabilities are about a person's opportunities to do and to be what they choose in the context of a given society. Wellbeing is about 'doings' (activities) and 'beings' (states of existence), and enhancing capability means concentrating on the opportunity to be able to have combinations of functionings and for the person to be free to make use of this opportunity or choose not to (Schlosberg 2007). Translated into an eco-justice context, capability means that each thing should be able to flourish as the thing it is. It is argued, for example, that 'Every component of the Earth Community has three rights: the right to be, the right to habitat, and the right to fulfil its role in the ever renewing processes of the Earth Community' (Berry, quoted in Cullinan 2003). What this actually means in practice is difficult to determine, however, since nature is by definition complex, uncertain, interconnected and ever-changing. Capabilities (as possibilities) are therefore changing, open-ended, dynamic and subject to ongoing deliberation.

In the context of the doing of justice, we still need to pinpoint those principles of justice that will most likely lead to desired outcomes. The notion of maximising dominion or positive liberty is a useful starting point in this regard. Furthermore, there is the matter of establishing an institutional basis for action. This involves implementing strategies that embody the justice principles identified above. Here it is suggested that repairing harm and restoration are practical ways in which justice can be done at a concrete level (see White 2013).

Dealing with environmental crime in ways that best approximate the principles and practices of justice outlined above requires that we examine the structure and processes of courts. In doing so, the objective is to identify those characteristics and qualities that best match the justice mission. We thus move from abstract philosophy to discussion of what happens in the courtroom and the sanctioning process.

Specialist and Problem-solving Approaches to Environmental Crime

Environmental crime has typically been assigned low value by magistrates and judges, as reflected objectively in sentencing outcomes (sentencing patterns over time in relation to various environmental offences) (see de Prez 2000a; de Prez 2000b; White 2011b). These kinds of issues are being addressed in various ways, most of which involve in one form or another specialist knowledge or the establishment of specialist courts.

The notion of 'special expertise' in dealing with environmental harms and crimes does not refer solely to the establishment of specific and separate environmental courts as such. Such developments are not always needed or desirable, particularly in jurisdictions which have experienced the recent consolidation of a wide range of criminal matters (including environmental) into generalist courts (as opposed to the development of crime-specific and client-specific specialist tribunals, courts and agencies). What *is* vital, however, is the development and growth of specific expertise with regard to environmental matters, incorporating elements pertaining to valuation of the harm, degrees of seriousness, extent and nature of victimisation, and remedies suited to the nature of the crime and its perpetrator(s). Analysis of instances where such expertise has been institutionalised within criminal justice – as in the case of specialist environmental courts – can none the less provide insight into the types of expertise and dynamic understandings now being required in this area of law.

Interpol, for example, provides information to support the work of prosecutors of environmental crimes, while in England a substantial tool kit has been prepared to guide magistrates in assessing the seriousness of environmental offences, determining sentencing criteria for environmental offences, and working through specific types of cases (Interpol Pollution Crime Working Group 2007; Magistrates' Association 2009). The work of ecological economics is also essential in this regard. This kind of analysis provides multiple criteria for evaluating the value of natural resources, wilderness, animals, fish and other species (see Orr 1991; Richardson and Loomis 2009). In the context of courts, both economic and non-market valuation is a vital part of deliberation over the nature of harm and potential damage claims against perpetrators (Duffield 1997).

From a legal perspective, the value of environmental harm is linked to the seriousness of environmental offences. Assessing the seriousness of environmental offences usually involves criteria such as the immediate and direct impact of the environmental crime; its wider effects in environmental, social and economic terms; human fatality, injury or ill health; the health of flora and fauna, and the offence pattern, especially for serial offenders (see Magistrates' Association 2009).

The concept of environmental harm is built into various statutes and guidelines pertaining to environmental crime and justice. In general, distinctions are made on the basis of seriousness, material environmental harm and level of nuisance. In commenting on Australian environmental laws, Bricknell points out that:

> There is some variation in how harm is defined but 'serious' and 'material' environmental harms are basically distinguished by the intensity and extent of the environmental impact and the actual or potential loss of (or damage to) property. The harm incurred is referenced to a predetermined monetary threshold and further differentiated as to the willfulness or intentional nature of the act. (Bricknell 2011, p. 13)

Research into US legal systems has demonstrated that environmental criminal statutes and environmental sentencing guidelines represent two very different ways of defining and assessing the harm addressed by environmental crimes (Mandiberg 2009). Federal environmental crimes contained in legislation such as the Clean Water Act, Clean Air Act and Resource Conservation and Recovery Act tend to utilise criminal provisions mainly to punish failure to abide by these regulatory systems. The point of each regulatory system is to manage contact between a pollutant and the air, water or soil, not to prevent it. The net result is that the focus is not on environmental harm as such, but rather on unacceptable (or significant) environmental harm – as measured by predetermined technical and administrative thresholds.

In contrast, US federal environmental crime sentencing guidelines focus more on matters of actual harm rather than risk reduction concerns. There is evidence here of the importance of graduated punishments based on the seriousness of the harm being addressed, and support for increased punishment for violators who actually harm the environment. Interestingly, in both sets of legal instruments there is little formal definition of 'environmental harm', and the lack of clarity gives rise to different interpretations of what this might refer to. There are also difficulties with conceptualisations of 'seriousness' and 'causality' (see Mandiberg 2009).

Greater consistency in approach and outcome can be achieved by specialist agencies that deal with environmental crimes, harms and issues on a regular basis. It is notable, therefore, that today there are over 350 environmental courts and tribunals (ECTs) authorised in some forty countries, and the number is growing (Pring and Pring 2009). In part, the growth in the number of ECTs has mirrored the increasing importance of environmental matters in international forums and law. The impetus of specialist judicial forums stems from continual pressures worldwide for effective resolution of environmental conflicts, coupled with expanding recognition of the need for procedural and substantive justice *vis-à-vis* environmental matters.

For instance, the 1992 United Nations Conference on Environment and Development adopted a series of principles. Principle 10 of the Rio Declaration, in mandatory terms, specifies that 'Effective access to judicial and administrative proceedings, including redress and remedy, shall be provided' by states in environmental matters. Pring and Pring explain that effective 'access to justice' can be seen in:

> three basic stages – at the beginning, middle and end of the adjudication process: (1) access to get to and through the ECT door; (2) access within the ECT to proceedings which are fair, efficient, and affordable, and (3) access to enforcement tools and remedies that can carry out the ECT's decision and provide measurable outcomes for preventing or remedying environmental harm. (Pring and Pring 2009, p. xiii)

The building blocks for an effective environmental court or tribunal include the mobilisation of scientific and technical expertise and the competence of judges and decision-makers.

With regard to the latter, the establishment of courts with special expertise in environmental matters provides an institutional setting within which judicial training can find most purchase. The United Nations Environment Programme (2007), for example, has put resources into judicial training on environmental law. These documents are underpinned by the idea that we need to take environmental crime seriously, and to do so we need sanctions that reflect the seriousness of the crime. However, a defined environment court reaffirms and concretises the importance of these ideas. It does so by providing a ready forum for the development of specialist expertise aided by the availability of technical experts within the court itself (see Preston 2011a; Westerhuis 2013; Walters and Westerhuis 2013). Moreover, such courts and tribunals provide a ready platform for the further extension of environmental jurisprudence and coherent sanctioning processes.

The multiple demands placed upon specific environmental protection agencies by different sections of government, business and community, and the varied tasks they are required to juggle (for example, compliance, education, enforcement), may lead to a dilution of their enforcement capacities and activities in both the national sphere and the international arena. The expense of fighting cases in higher courts is itself a deterrent for agencies that are cash-strapped yet have to assume the legal costs associated with prosecution. Special environmental courts and tribunals offer the hope of lower costs and an array of alternative dispute-resolution procedures (Pring and Pring 2009). Accordingly, the establishment of such agencies may well have a positive ripple effect throughout the environmental law enforcement and prosecution landscape.

It may well be that an International Environment Court (or equivalent) with requisite United Nations support is required as well (see Higgins 2012; but also see Hinde 2003). This is especially so if we are to deal adequately with environmental matters such as those pertaining to the international spaces of our oceans (for example, pollution, concentrations of plastic, illegal fishing, transference of toxic materials). Such a court could draw together transboundary expertise from the various environmental law enforcement networks to assess environmental crimes and harms that have international or global consequences.

Legal activists and green criminologists also argue that the law itself must be radically altered, and that action should be directed to crime prevention regardless of the existing laws that allow environmental harms to continue. With respect to the first course of action, for example, there is growing momentum behind the idea of embedding the crime of ecocide as one of the five 'crimes against humanity' (see Higgins 2010; Higgins 2012).

In addition to proposed legal developments, a range of penalty types, approaches and mechanisms have emerged in relation to environmental sanctions. These fall broadly into the categories of civil, administrative and criminal justice responses (see White 2010). The sanctioning process for environmental offences presently covers a broad range of strategies, with new possibilities on the horizon. Bell and McGillivray (2008), for instance, mention the use of cumulative penalties, as in the case of points systems in motoring offences, so that a penalty infringement notice does not become 'routine' or permit wealthy operators the 'right' to pollute. The more often you cause harm, the greater the penalty each time. Ensuring that the enforcement hammer is brought down hard enough on violators is also seen by Eastern African judges as essential to counter the idea that low fines are merely the cost of doing business (Mwebaza 2010). The United Nations Environment Programme's Global Judges Programme includes reference to the imposition of deterrent fines based upon 'economic benefit of noncompliance'. This takes into account the value to the violator of deferred compliance – that is, the money that should have been spent on environmental improvements that was presumably invested elsewhere, earning a rate of return on an annual basis (United Nations Environment Programme 2007). Financial sanctions with bite are at least on the agenda, if not yet fully realised in practice.

Meanwhile, the recent trend in countries like Australia towards alternative sentencing options reflects both the difficulties of prosecution, especially in relation to corporations, and a shift in thinking away from the offender towards addressing the nature of the offence (see Walters and Westerhuis 2013). For instance, the range of sentencing options available across Australia, while they vary from jurisdiction to jurisdiction, includes an increasing number and type of orders (Preston 2007):

- orders for restoration and prevention;
- orders for payment of costs, expenses and compensation;
- orders to pay investigation costs;
- monetary benefits penalty orders;
- publication orders;
- environmental service orders;
- environmental audit orders;
- payment into environmental trusts or for other purposes;
- orders to attend training;
- orders to establish training course;
- orders to provide financial assurance.

How this burgeoning range of sentencing options translates into particular sentencing outcomes warrants ongoing and close scrutiny. Importantly, it also points us in the direction of *problem-solving*, rather than punishment per se, as a key objective of courts dealing with environmental harm (Walters and Westerhuis 2013). The rationales for such a move are indicated in Figure 5.2.

Figure 5.2 The need for problem-solving methods

Definitions: contradictory principles, illegal acts that are normally condoned, potential harms and risks
Expertise: technical, traditional knowledge, ecological, environmental jurisprudence
Complexity: issues, trends, internationalisation
Dealing with multiple parties: multiple agencies, victims, communities
Specificity: tailored solutions to the problem and to the offender

For instance, the application of suitable sanctions for particular offences and offenders demands sensitivity to, and flexibility based upon, the social and economic context of the perpetrators of environmental crime. This is not simply a matter of tailoring sanctions to suit the offender, as in the case of small versus large firms that commit acts of environmental crime. Rather, it is to also recognise that different classes or categories of environmental 'criminal' will respond quite differently to the sanctioning process. The wildlife poacher who acts as an individual, but one located within a particular cultural setting that legitimises wildlife theft (such as abalone poaching), sees and acts in the world differently to the organised crime syndicate stealing animals from the wild for global markets. Each type of offender and each sort of offence demands a nuanced and carefully weighed response that best contributes to forestalling environmental harms in the future. Again, this is best achieved when courts adopt a problem-solving rather than solely punishment-oriented regime. Databases such as the one being maintained by the New South Wales Law and Environment Court (Preston and Donnelly 2008a; Preston and Donnelly 2008b) provide a valuable resource for researchers interested in analysing how well this approach to dealing with environmental harms and crimes is working out in practice for different groups (for example, individuals, small to medium-sized companies, large corporations).

The power of companies and elite individuals to resist prosecution or avoid criminal proceedings is an issue. There are clear social differences in the ability of the powerful, in relation to the less powerful, to protect and defend their interests. This is evident in how the powerful are able to manipulate rules of evidence, frustrate investigatory processes, confuse notions of accountability and forestall potential prosecution by ostensibly abiding by and complying with record-keeping procedures (Gunningham et al. 1995; Hughes 2004). The expense of legal remedies in dealing with environmental harm is further complicated by the ways in which companies contest the domains of contractual and legal responsibility, and by the notions of 'privileged information' as a means to restrict access to essential evidence (White 2010).

Related to the question of dealing with different offenders is the matter of combining different strategies of intervention and enforcement. For example, some jurisdictions now employ what is called an 'environmental enforcement sweep' to deal with instances where a community faces multiple environmental burdens. This involves using administrative, civil and criminal enforcement tools in tandem to address the problems in a comprehensive fashion (Dighe and Pettus 2011). Typically, this kind of intervention model will deal with a variety of violations of different environment laws. Having a dedicated environment court, one capable of dealing with multiple agencies dealing collectively with particular investigations and prosecutions, leads to less fragmentation at the prosecution and implementation stages, a more holistic understanding of events and issues, and a more coherent adjudication process.

A problem-solving court must not only deal with competing and overlapping legal principles, and ecological, social and economic objectives. It must not only deal with a highly variable offender list, involving individual persons, communities and corporations. It must also consider the question of 'victimisation' and the ways in which victimhood is construed within the domains of environmental law and ecological realities. For example, research undertaken in the United States has shown that the penalties relating to hazardous waste sites in areas with large white populations are higher than those with minority or indigenous populations. Furthermore, there is less environmental enforcement relating to facilities in communities with higher minority and low-income populations (Pinderhughes 1996; Lynch et al. 2004; Konisky 2009). Criminal justice needs to be applied equitably and fairly if social justice is to be the outcome. Here, key considerations pertain to repairing the harm, acknowledging and compensating victims, rehabilitating specific biospheres and ensuring the survival of particular plant and animal species. Considerable expertise is a must if any or all of this is to be achieved.

A problem-solving court has the potential to expand the boundaries of 'good practice' in resolving conflicts over environmental matters. As part of this, it provides an opportunity to develop further the specific area of environmental jurisprudence. This is evident in New South Wales, for example, where the Land and Environment Court has concretely addressed a number of intersecting 'justice' considerations (Preston 2011a, pp. 30–31):

1. **Substantive justice** – the court has been a leader in developing jurisprudence in relation to principles of ecologically sustainable development (principle of integration, precautionary principle, inter- and intra-generational equity, conservation of biological diversity and ecological integrity and internationalisation of external, environmental costs including the polluter pays principle), environmental impact assessment, public trust, sentencing for environmental crime.

2. **Procedural justice** – access to justice, including removal of barriers to public interest litigation in relation to standing, interlocutory injunctions, security for costs, laches and costs.
3. **Distributive justice** – inter- and intra-generational equity, and the polluter pays principle, balancing public and private rights and responsibilities.
4. **Restorative justice** – victim–offender mediation and the polluter pays principle for environmental crime.
5. **Therapeutic justice** – adopting court practices and procedures to improve the welfare of litigants, including improving accessibility.

Institutionalisation of specialist expertise thus reinforces and embellishes the further development of innovative practice and practical implementation of the law in relation to what have often formerly been simply abstract declarations of principle and emergent rights with little applied substance.

Weighing up diverse information, conflicting principles and appropriate responses demands a sophisticated court able to sift through complex evidence and which can be confident in its application of sanctions and remedies. In other words, there is a need for specialist environmental courts (or at the very least, generalist courts with specialist expertise in environmental matters).

An environmental court is better able to address the pressing, pervasive and pernicious environmental problems that confront society (such as global warming and loss of biodiversity). New institutions and creative attitudes are required to address these problems. Specialisation enables use of special knowledge and expertise in both the process and the substance of resolution of these problems. Rationalisation enlarges the remedies available (Preston 2011a, p. 29).

These specialist courts, in turn, must be based upon problem-solving models of intervention, especially given the nature of the tasks at hand. The particular contours, resources and capacities of such courts will vary greatly depending upon the national context (Pring and Pring 2009). Their presence, however, allows the possibility of global networking and collaborations that can bolster the fight against environmental crime in the most effective and creative ways.

One emergent aspect of environmental courts as specialist problem-solving courts is the increasing attention being paid to the notion of 'restorative justice' as applied to this area of jurisprudence (Preston 2011b; Besthorn 2012). The restorative justice perspective is informed by concepts such as those of harm reparation, social restoration, community harmony and problem-solving. A retributive system of justice is essentially punitive in nature, with the key focus on using punishment as a means to deter future crime and to provide 'just deserts' for any harm committed. A restorative approach is concerned with promoting harmonious relationships by means of restitution, reparation and reconciliation involving offenders, victims and the wider community (White et al. 2012). A restorative justice approach seems to be ideally suited to dealing with environmental crimes in so far as they hold out the promise that things will be done to rehabilitate or repair the harms that have occurred.

There are other issues and constraints as well. The prosecution and sentencing of environmental crime really only finds purchase within particular jurisdictions and national contexts. The problem, however, is that frequently the key actors involved in such crimes are global entities, able to take advantage of different systems of regulation and legal compliance (Braithwaite and Drahos 2000). If a global company, for example, is bound by rules in one country but not in another, its behaviour is likely to differ in each setting and across jurisdictions (see, for example, Hughes 2004).

Harm is not necessarily the same as victimisation, especially if the latter is interpreted as applying strictly to humans. For example, environmental victimisation has been defined as specific forms of harm which are caused by acts (such as the dumping of toxic waste) or omissions (such as failure to provide safe drinking water) leading to the presence or absence of environmental agents (for example, poisons, nutrients) which are associated with *human* injury (see Williams 1996). Management of these forms of victimisation is generally retrospective (after the fact), and involves a variety of legal and social responses (Hall 2013). Importantly, the central actor in this definition is humans (not non-human animals or ecosystems). Much the same can be said of re-conceptualisations of environmental rights as 'human rights', in that the selfsame concept is premised upon notions of humanity.

None the less, the law does allow for a modicum of protection for the non-human as well as the human. This is reflected in legislation pertaining to endangered species (for example, particular animals such as tigers) and to conservation more generally (for example, in the form of national parks). Harm is central to these forms of social regulation as well, but whether 'harm to the environment' is of consequence *unless* it is measured with reference to human values (for example, economic, aesthetic, cultural) is of ongoing concern with regard to legal decision-making (see Lin 2006). In essence, natural objects (such as trees and forests) lack legal rights (and agency or volition), and so must rely upon humans to bring actions to protect them. Some argue that the inherent interests of 'natural objects' ought to be protected through legal actions by the objects themselves, with humans serving as their guardians or trustees (Stone 1972; Lin 2006).

Preston describes how future generations or non-human biota may be considered victims:

> Environmental harm may require remediation over generations and hence the burden and the cost of remediation is transferred to future generations. Remediation of contaminated land and restoration of habitat of species, populations and ecological communities are examples of intergenerational burdens passed from the present generation to future generations. Where intergenerational inequity is caused by the commission of an environmental offence, the victims include future generations....The biosphere and non-human biota have intrinsic value independent of their utilitarian or instrumental value for humans. When harmed by environmental crime, the biosphere and non-human biota also are victims. The harm is able to be assessed from an ecological perspective; it need not be anthropocentric. (Preston 2011b, p. 143)

Identification of victims is only part of the process, however. The voice of the victim needs to be heard as well as part of justice proceedings.

From the point of view of green criminology, this provides an opening for the extension of justice across the human, environment and animal domains. Environmental harm can be distinguished on the basis of *whom or what precisely is being harmed or victimised.* As indicated in Figure 5.1, there are three broad theoretical tendencies within green criminology that frame how specific writers view the nature of environmental issues, including harm and responses to harm. These approaches present different dimensions of injustice which are relevant to an overarching eco-justice perspective. Each approach is concerned with particular conceptions of rights and different types of harmful transgression. To date, most judicial and legal attention has been devoted to humans as environmental victims.

However, the definition of 'victim' is evolving and expanding. Public interest law, for example, has been utilised to give standing to human representatives of non-human entities such as rivers and trees. For instance, a river was represented at a restorative justice conference in New Zealand by the chairperson of the Waikato River Enhancement Society (Preston 2011b, p. 144, footnote 53). In increasing number of cases there are 'surrogate victims' who are recognised as representing the community affected (including harms to particular biotic groups and abiotic environs) for the purpose of the restorative process. Public trust and public interest law have been used to establish future generations as victims of environmental crime (Preston 2011b; Mehta 2009), the victims including human as well as the environment and non-human biota, for which surrogate victims (such as parents or non-governmental organisations) have provided representation. Who speaks for whom or what is nevertheless still controversial, especially when it comes to natural objects such as trees, rivers and specific ecosystems. The subject raises important and fascinating issues regarding the criteria by which judgments about environmental victimisation are to be made, and the kind of ecological and zoological expertise required to adequately be a surrogate victim for the non-human.

Conclusion

The complexities and harms associated with environmental crime demand responses that are themselves flexible and multi-dimensional. From the point of view of jurisprudence and the operation of the court, specialist environmental courts that operate on the basis of problem-solving methods are the most likely to succeed in achieving the mission of eco-justice. At the very least, specialist expertise and knowledge is required to adjudicate and respond to cases involving environmental victims.

Translating the work of such specialist courts into action will require careful consideration of specific legal issues (for example, conceptions of ecocide, applications of the precautionary principle) as well as sociological analysis of how best to deal with different kinds of offenders (for example, working-class, corporate). There are also issues relating to how victims and victimhood are to be conceptualised and represented within the court, and how compensation, remediation, rehabilitation and restoration – for victims – is to be accomplished. There is much work yet to be done.

References

Beirne, P. 2009. Confronting Animal Abuse: Law, Criminology and Human–animal Relationships. New York: Rowman & Littlefield.

Bell, S. and McGillivray, D. 2008. *Environmental Law*, 7th edn. London: Oxford University Press.

Besthorn, F.H. 2004. 'Restorative Justice in Environmental Restoration – the Twin Pillars of a Just Global Environmental Policy: Hearing the Voice of the Victim', *Journal of Societal and Social Policy* 3(2), 33–48.

Besthorn, F.H. 2012. 'Speaking Earth: Environmental Restoration and Restorative Justice', in *Restorative Justice Today: Practical Applications*, edited by K. Wormer and Walker. Los Angeles, CA: Sage, 240–53.

Braithwaite, J. and Drahos, P. 2000. *Global Business Regulation*. Cambridge: Cambridge University Press.

Brickey, K. 2008. *Environmental Crime: Law, Policy, Prosecution*. New York: Aspen Publishers.

Bricknell, S. 2011. *Environmental Crime in Australia*. AIC Reports Research and Public Policy Series 109. Canberra: Australian Institute of Criminology.

Cullinan, C. 2003. *Wild Law: A Manifesto for Earth Justice*. London: Green Books in association with The Gaia Foundation.

Dighe, K. and Pettus, L. 2011. 'Environmental Justice in the Context of Environmental Crime', *United States Attorneys' Bulletin* 59(4), 3–14.

Duffield, J. 1997. 'Nonmarket Valuation and the Courts: The Case of the Exxon Valdez', *Contemporary Economic Policy* 15(4), 98–110.

Findlay, M., Odgers, S. and Yeo, S. 1994. *Australian Criminal Justice*. Melbourne: Oxford University Press.

Gunningham, N., Norberry, J. and McKillop, S., eds. 1995. *Environmental Crime: Proceedings of a Conference Held 1–3 September 1993, Hobart*. Canberra: Australian Institute of Criminology.

Hall, M. 2013. *Victims of Environmental Harm: Rights, Recognition and Redress Under National and International Law*. London: Routledge.

Higgins, P. 2010. *Eradicating Ecocide: Laws and Governance to Prevent the Destruction of Our Planet*. London: Shepheard-Walwyn.

Higgins, P. 2012. *Earth is Our Business: Changing the Rules of the Game*. London: Shepheard-Walwyn.

Hillyard, P. and Tombs, S. 2007. 'From "Crime" to Social Harm?', *Crime, Law and Social Change* 48, 9–25.

Hillyard, P., Pantazis, C., Tombs, S. and Gordon, D., eds. 2004. *Beyond Criminology? Taking Harm Seriously*. London: Pluto Press.

Hinde, S. 2003. 'The International Environmental Court: Its Broad Jurisdiction as a Possible Fatal Flaw', *Hofstra Law Review* 32, 727–57.

Hughes, S.D. 2004. 'The Current Status of Environmental Performance Reporting', *National Environmental Law Review* 4, 41–58.

Interpol Pollution Crime Working Group 2007. *Arguments for Prosecutors of Environmental Crimes*, Advocacy Memorandum, 5 June. Lyon: Interpol.

Konisky, D. 2009. 'The Limited Effects of Federal Environmental Justice Policy on State Enforcement', *Policy Studies Journal* 37(3), 475–96.

Lin, A. 2006. 'The Unifying Role of Harm in Environmental Law', *Wisconsin Law Review* 3, 898–985.

Lynch, M., Stretesky, P. and Burns, R. 2004. 'Determinants of Environmental Law Violation Fines Against Petroleum Refineries: Race, Ethnicity, Income, and Aggregation Effects', *Society and Natural Resources* 17(4), 343–57.

Magistrates' Association. 2009. *Costing the Earth: Guidance for Sentencers*. London: Magistrates' Association.

Mandiberg, S. 2009. 'Locating the Environmental Harm in Environmental Crimes', *Utah Law Review* 4, 1,177–222.

Matthews, R. and Kauzlarich, D. 2007. 'State Crimes and State Harms: A Tale of Two Definitional Frameworks', *Crime, Law and Social Change* 48, 43–55.

Mehta, M. 2009. *In the Public Interest: Landmark Judgement and Orders of the Supreme Court of India on Environment and Human Rights*, vols 1–3. New Delhi: Prakriti Publications.

Mwebaza, R. 2010. *Annual Regional Conference of Judges on Environmental Security in Eastern Africa: Summary of Presentations*. Pretoria: Institute for Security Studies.

Orr, D. 1991. 'The Economics of Conservation', *Conservation Biology* 5(4), 439–41.

Pinderhughes, R. 1996. 'The Impact of Race on Environmental Quality: An Empirical and Theoretical Discussion', *Sociological Perspectives* 39(2), 231–48.

Preston, B. 2007. 'Principled Sentencing for Environmental Offences, Part 2: Sentencing Considerations and Options', *Criminal Law Journal* 31, 142.

Preston, B. 2011a. 'Operating an Environment Court: The Experience of the Land and Environment Court of New South Wales and 12 Benefits of Judicial Specialisation in Environmental Law', keynote address, *Renewing Environmental Law: A Conference for Public Interest Environmental Law Practitioners*, University of Victoria Environmental Law Centre, West Coast Environmental Law and Ecojustice Canada, 3–4 February, Vancouver.

Preston, B. 2011b. 'The Use of Restorative Justice for Environmental Crime', *Criminal Law Journal* 35, 136–45.

Preston, B. and Donnelly, H. 2008a. *Achieving Consistency and Transparency in Sentencing for Environmental Offences*. Monograph 32, June 2008. Sydney: Judicial Commission of New South Wales.

Preston, B. and Donnelly, H. 2008b. 'The Establishment of an Environmental Crime Sentencing Database in New South Wales', *Criminal Law Journal* 32, 214–38.

Prez, de P. 2000a. 'Beyond Judicial Sanctions: The Negative Impact of Conviction for Environmental Offences', *Environmental Law Review* 2, 11–22.

Prez, de P. 2000b. 'Excuses, Excuses: The Ritual Trivialisation of Environmental Prosecutions', *Journal of Environmental Law* 12(1), 65–78.

Pring, G. and Pring, C. 2009. *Greening Justice: Creating and Improving Environmental Courts and Tribunals*. Washington, DC: The Access Initiative.

Richardson, L. and Loomis, J. 2009. 'The Total Economic Value of Threatened, Endangered and Rare Species: An Updated Meta-analysis', *Ecological Economics* 68(5), 1,535–48.

Schlosberg, D. 2007. *Defining Environmental Justice: Theories, Movements, and Nature*. Oxford: Oxford University Press.

Stone, C. 1972. 'Should Trees Have Standing? Toward Legal Rights for Natural Objects', *Southern California Law Review* 45, 450–87.

United Nations Environment Programme. 2007. *Judicial Training Modules on Environmental Law: Application of Environmental Law by National Courts and Tribunals*. Nairobi: United Nations Environment Programme.

Walters, R. and Westerhuis, D. 2013. 'Green Crime and the Role of Environmental Courts', *Crime Law and Social Change* 59, 279–90.

Westerhuis, D. 2013. 'A Harm Analysis of Environmental Crime', in *Emerging Issues in Green Criminology: Exploring Power Justice and Harm*, edited by R. Walters, D.S. Westerhuis and T. Wyatt. Basingstoke: Palgrave Macmillan, 197–217.

White, R. 2010 'Prosecution and Sentencing in Relation to Environmental Crime: Recent Socio-legal Developments', *Crime, Law and Social Change* 53(4), 365–81.

White, R. 2011a. 'Environmental Law Enforcement: The Importance of Global Networks and Collaborative Practices', *Australasian Policing: A Journal of Professional Practice and Research* 3(1), 2–16.

White, R. 2011b. *Transnational Environmental Crime: Toward an Eco-global Criminology*. London: Routledge.

White, R. 2012. 'NGO Engagement in Environmental Law Enforcement: Critical Reflections', *Australasian Policing: A Journal of Professional Practice and Research* 4(1), 7–11.

White, R. 2013. *Environmental Harm: An Eco-justice Perspective*. Bristol: Policy Press.

White, R. Haines, F. and Asquith, N. 2012. *Crime and Criminology*. Melbourne: Oxford University Press.

Williams, C. 1996. 'An Environmental Victimology', *Social Justice* 23(4), 16–40.

Chapter 6
Victims of Environmental Crime: Routes for Recognition, Restitution and Redress

Matthew Hall

Whilst Green Criminology as a subject area has continued to development since at least the early 1990s, there has been a surprising lack of engagement within this literature with environmental victimisation or the victims of environmental harm. As I have written elsewhere (Hall 2013), this may be partly based on the assumption that environmental crime (or wider notions of environmental harm) is largely victimless, or at best, such victimisation is relatively equally shared amongst the population of a given area, country or the world as a whole. More recent studies have begun to unpick such assumptions. For example, there is now growing evidence to the effect that the impacts of environmental crime (like most other forms of crime) in fact fall disproportionately on the weak, the marginalised and the powerless at a national and international level. Furthermore, the impacts of environmental crime are becoming increasingly understood and are now known to be multi-faceted and complex, including health-related (Tombs and Whyte 2010), social (Wheatley 1997), economic (Stern 2007), cultural (see Lee 2011 for a practical example) and security (Ullman 1983) impacts. It has also been noted that environmental victimisation may be criminogenic (Hall and Farrall 2012), with clear implications for wider criminology. Nevertheless, few writers have approached the question of environmental victimisation holistically, and indeed most writing on the subject tends to highlight particular case studies, be they Canadian aboriginal people affected by oil exploitation (Wheatley 1997), the Ogoniland people of Nigeria (UNEP 2011), again affected by decades of oil drilling in the Nigerian Delta, or those still suffering effects from the Bhopal Gas Plant leak of 1983 (Groombridge 1991).

This chapter endeavours to take an alternative route, by examining the different avenues of compensation and restitution available to victims of environmental harm, drawing insights from more established areas of victimological theory and research, as well as legal insights. In so doing, this chapter will offer a combined critical appraisal of the relative merits of each process from the victims' perspective. For the purpose of this chapter, the term 'compensation' will generally be used to refer to monies paid to victims of environmental harm by states: in other words, from public funds. This will be contrasted with 'restitution', which will normally come from perpetrators of environmental harm (whether individuals or corporations). I will refer to both terms collectively as 'redress'. It should be noted that in the wider literature, all these terms can be used loosely and interchangeably, and in markedly different ways to their use here. Arguably, it is precisely these kinds of conceptual uncertainties that have contributed to a situation where the questions noted above have not been subject to detailed analysis.

What Do Environmental Victims Want? What Do They Need?

In his seminal works on the growth of victim policies in Canada and England and Wales, Paul Rock (1986 and 1990, respectively) makes the important point that many such policies (especially relating to state compensation schemes) were implemented with little or no actual consultation with victims of crime themselves. Whilst research into the needs and expectations of such 'traditional' victims of crime has gathered considerable pace over the last twenty years (see Shapland and Hall 2007), at present we are faced with an almost total lack of empirical research investigating the needs of victims of environmental crime, and what such victims might actually want from a criminal justice (or other) process (Williams 1996). In the modern context, with the focus now on so-called evidence-based policy-making (see Lawrence 2006), this lack of direct consultation with environmental victims is concerning. This situation also makes it impossible to draw definitive conclusions concerning the utility of different avenues of recognition, compensation and redress for victims of environmental crime, and all the arguments presented in this chapter are made with due regard to this important caveat.

The lack of empirical evidence outlined above means we are at present forced to rely on more theoretical discussions to anticipate what victims of environmental crime might need and how they might respond to various forms of intervention and/or support. To this end, one key finding presented by a number of victimologists is that victims of more traditional crimes may value more than simply the instrumental outcomes of a justice process. For example, the analysis of Bradford (2011) of the national victimisation survey for England and Wales, the British Crime Survey, found that victims of crime express greater trust and confidence in the criminal justice system when they feel a representative of that system has listened to their concerns (and may take action in relation to them). This finding was unrelated to the outcomes of specific cases. Such findings lend support to theories of procedural justice, which hold that those members of the public who have contact with the criminal justice system judge the system through their perceptions of how fairly it takes decisions and how it treats them (with respect, sensitivity and dignity scoring highly) rather than in terms of instrumental outcomes (Tyler 1990). Indeed, even if victims do receive some form of (court-based) compensation, Shapland (1990), having interviewed victims directly on this issue, concluded that rather than being overly concerned with the amount ordered, many victims placed greater value on the feeling that, through ordering an offender to pay them compensation, their pain and suffering was being duly recognised by the judge. As Miers (1980) put it, this provides a vindication of their 'victim status'. In other words, victims of traditional crime appear to value the cathartic benefits of what they see as a vindication by the justice system over the instrumental benefit of compensation, or even knowing the offender has been punished.

Of course, it would be quite wrong to assume that those affected by environmental crime will necessarily respond to their victimisation in similar ways to victims of other, more heavily researched, crimes. That said, Lee (2009) has emphasised the importance of following a holistic, welfare approach to environmental harms, rather than concentrating purely on financial compensation or restitution. Instead, Lee places significant weight on the provision of long-term, tailored support and restoration packages in individual communities, as opposed to the provision of simple blanket compensation mechanisms. Given that 'different localities inherit different cultural norms and characteristics' (Lee 2009, p. 29), Lee also emphasises the vital role of local government in developing/facilitating the delivery of such packages.

Another important question is whether, whatever form support for victims of environmental harm takes, such schemes should focus on the short-term needs of individuals affected by environmental harm, or the longer-term needs of the community as a whole, along with the needs of future generations of potential (cultural, economic and physical) victims.

Indeed, a further indication that at least some victims of environmental degradation need much more than simple monetary recompense can be found in a telling case study by Wheatley (1997) concerning the cultural impacts on Canadian aboriginal peoples following mercury poisoning of their traditional lands and food/water supplies: 'Even after compensation was paid social problems persisted, especially in Whitedog, where solvents are smuggled into the community and 4 suicides were reported in the spring of 1995' (Wheatley 1997, p. 78).

The importance of non-monetary restitution is further supported by the more established victimological literature, which consistently holds that payments from offenders themselves carry greater symbolic value for victims of crime than monies allocated from taxation (Shapland 1990). Malsch (1999) has also emphasised the importance of 'immaterial damages' for victims of crime, and the complexities inherent in addressing these in the criminal justice context. The recognition of such damage by a criminal court (and by offenders) may be especially significant to environmental victims given the often hidden or indirect nature of their suffering. Of course, given the absence of empirical evidence, we presently have no idea whether victims of environmental harm value symbolic gestures more than, less than or equally to other types of victims.

In sum, although we lack direct evidence, if we apply what we do know based on both theory and empirical evidence from more established victimological literature, it can be seen that the simple payment of money to individuals harmed by environmentally destructive activities (whether labelled 'crimes' or not) is likely to constitute at best a broad-brush means of addressing the impacts of such activities, and at worst may fall far short of full redress, assuming such redress is even possible (see Malsch 1999). The remainder of this chapter will examine a number of potential mechanisms for providing such redress in order to evaluate how they measure up to these rather difficult criteria.

The Civil Route

A significant question arising early in any debate about environmentally destructive activities is to what extent the criminal law needs to be involved at all. For present purposes, the question therefore becomes: Are those affected by such destructive activities properly thought of as victims of environmental crime, or rather being subject to some wider notion of environmental harm? Given the stilted development of environmental criminal laws in many jurisdictions (see Redgwell 2010), civil law suits in fact represent the more 'traditional' mechanism by which such victims might acquire restitution payments (damages) from polluters whose actions have led them to suffer harm, and it chiefly for this reason I have elected to examine this area first in this chapter. The extended pedigree of such legal arguments in the civil courts is actually surprisingly long, as demonstrated by McEldowney and McEldowney (2011). They describe how, in nineteenth-century England, 'The law of nuisance came to encompass the amenity value of land, which included things affixed to the land such as trees and crops' (McEldowney and McEldowney 2011, p. 8).

Despite such historical examples, however, the tone of recent literature has become increasingly disparaging of so-called 'toxic torts' (Goldberg and Zipersky 2011) as a means of adequately compensating environmental victims, although Lin (2005) recognises that tortious remedies do bring at least two advantages over (in this case) administrative compensation systems. The first is that public agencies, which administer such schemes, may be more vulnerable to regulatory capture than the judiciary or the executive.

Secondly, it is argued, remedies in tort are based on fuller information about the impacts of alleged environmental harm compared with most administrative systems. The same advantage may naturally also accrue to criminal proceedings. Of course, claims in tort are not the only civil remedies available. In some jurisdictions, the state has legislated for specific causes of civil action in cases of environmental pollution. One example from Canada is the Alberta Environmental Protection and Enhancement Act 2000, which creates a civil cause of action for any victims suffering loss or damage as a result of conduct constituting an offence for which the defendant was convicted under the Act.

The above notwithstanding, civil actions also present considerable difficulties for environmental victims, Skinnider (2011) summarises these in the following terms: 'Limitations for such remedies include where the perpetrator is not in the same jurisdiction as the victim; where the perpetrator is not readily identifiable; evidentiary burden of proof; and costs of litigation' (Skinnider 2011, p. 74).

As such, although naturally requiring a lower standard of proof than criminal penalties, tort action must still establish culpability on the part of specified respondents – which, given the nature of polluting activity, is likely to be problematic in many cases.

Perhaps the most significant problem faced by environmental victims seeking to claim civil damages is that civil cases cost considerable amounts of money, for which, in most jurisdictions, there is no public funding. This means the cost of such actions must be borne by victims or victims' groups (Castle 1996). This is a very important limitation of the civil model, not least because, as noted above, environmental harm seems to fall disproportionately on those with limited financial means.

One potential solution to this dilemma is the use of class action processes, allowing large groups of victims to sue polluters collectively (Johnson 2004). Nevertheless, class actions have also been criticised from the perspective of environmental harm, principally because 'these legal rules were not designed with environmental actions specifically in mind and have been noted to be notoriously difficult to get certified in environmental cases' (Skinnider 2011, p. 75).

For now, pursuing civil damages is often the 'default' position many victims of environmental harms with the funds or sufficient backing must take to acquire compensation (or rather 'damages') in many jurisdictions. Given the growing evidence concerning the circumstances of those disproportionately affected by environmental harm, it is clear that civil litigation cannot remain the primary means of pursuing such claims as our understanding of the scope and impact of environmental harms increases. Examples such as the economically impoverished and displaced peoples of the Nigeran Delta (UNEP 2011) and those affected by the Bhopal Gas Plant leak (Groombridge 1991) are testament to the failure of civil law suits to adequately compensate these peoples many years after the events (Van Tassel 2011). Nor is it necessarily the case that a civil standard of proof makes such cases significantly easier to prove. At the same time, the degree of compensation available will be heavily dictated by judicial attitudes and, whilst the same may apply to restitution paid as part of criminal sentencing, civil litigation may lack many of the symbolic recognitions offered by a criminal conviction.

The Criminal Route

If the civil courts seem unable to provide a mechanism for redress for environmental victims, then we might ask what criminal justice systems can offer. Of course, not long ago the proposition that criminal justice could facilitate positive outcomes for victims themselves would have seemed somewhat contrived, but in the context of growing recognition of the role of victims within the process seen across jurisdictions (Hall 2010), the absence of such victims from environmental prosecutions is becoming noteworthy. The most likely method of achieving this in the criminal context seems to be the granting of court-based restitution orders imposed as part of the sentence against environmental offenders. Not only might such a route provide some financial redress, arguably it would also have important symbolic impact. The latter point has been acknowledged by the European Commission (2001), which has argued that imposing criminal sanctions in environmental cases 'demonstrates a social disapproval of qualitatively different nature compared to administrative sanctions or a compensation mechanism under civil law' (European Commission 2001, p. 238). The overall effect, it is suggested, is to increase condemnation of such acts and raise awareness about their dangerousness and the social harms they engender.

Criminal penalties, and in particular criminal-based restitution, have also on occasion proven a strategically beneficial option for the recovery of monies from environmental offenders. As such, following the 1989 Exxon oil spill off the coast of Alaska, the US federal government sought recovery of natural resource damages to Prince William Sound by filing criminal charges under the Migratory Bird Treaty Act and the Refuse Act (Richardson 2010, p. 4). Whilst the relevant legislation in the USA imposed significant limitations on the amount that could be claimed from polluters under civil law, both these crimes carried penalties that would require restitution to injured parties. In this case, the injured party was deemed to be the United States, for damage to its natural environment. The outcome was that Exxon pleaded guilty and a settlement was reached through negotiation with the government that involved significant financial payments to the USA.

The Exxon case provides an interesting and significant example concerning the use of criminal law to facilitate redress in cases of environmental harm. Nevertheless, from the victims' perspective, it is important to appreciate that this was a case where a state assumed the role of victim. Of course, the ensuing clean-up operation paid for from the settlement naturally befitted actual individuals affected by the disasters (and their descendants), but this was achieved only via the state effectively acquiring their conflict with the company: the very act of states 'stealing' conflicts from victims famously criticised by Christie (1977). Notably, Richardson doubts the utility of criminal law to settle the restitution claims of individual victims directly, and the remainder of this section will serve to test this hypothesis.

Restitution as Part of Sentencing for Environmental Crimes

In recent years, many countries have looked to offenders to provide monetary restitution to victims of crime: either directly though the imposition of court-based orders or through the establishment of victims' funds maintained by offender surcharges and fine payments (Whitehead and Block 2003; Canadian Department of Justice 2012). Such a move is well supported by the established literature, which, as noted above, consistently holds that payments from offenders carry greater symbolic value for victims of crime than monies allocated from taxation. The importance of the symbolic benefit to victims of receiving money directly from offenders is often used to counteract the observation that individual offenders often cannot afford to pay much if any restitution (in monetary terms), and therefore the sums involved cannot be said to compensate the victim for the harm suffered in a financial sense (Newburn 1988; Nagin and Waldfogel 1998). Of course, herein lies one of the primary distinctions between 'ordinary' offenders who commit traditional crimes and environmental offenders, which might well be large corporations. Such corporations will often be in a position to afford much more in the way of financial restitution. We might speculate that such concrete (not merely symbolic) restitution could be of greater importance to victims and communities affected by serious economic impacts or impacts on their livelihoods as a result of environmental crime, although again, to do so risks wrongly presuming what victims want.

What we do know, at least in England and Wales, is that court-based restitution for environmental crimes has not been widely utilised. On this point, the House of Commons Environmental Audit Committee (2004) received evidence from the Environmental Industries Commission suggesting that provisions available for the criminal courts to order an offender to remedy any environmental harm[1] caused were under-used and widely misunderstood. Bell and McGillivray (2008) argue that the explanation for this under-utilisation of compensation orders in environmental cases mainly stems from the existence of many statutory powers of clean-up and cost recovery available to regulatory agencies in defined situations. In addition, the authors argue, under Section 131 of the Power of Courts (Sentencing) Act, compensation orders are restricted to a maximum of £5,000 – a sum that may often be insufficient to fully restore victims or their environment to their previous state, if indeed any sum of money can achieve this. A further problem in some jurisdictions, notably Canada, is that restitution orders are sometimes restricted to certain proscribed offences which do not include environmental crime (see Canadian Department of Justice 2012).

Of course, the fact that the sums involved may be insufficient to restore victims to the state they were in prior to an environmental crime is in keeping with the notion that the purpose of restitution is largely symbolic. Elsewhere, the situation is less clear-cut. For example, in the South African criminal justice system, 'restitution' is defined as the return or repair of property by the offender 'in order to restore you [the victim] to the position you were in prior to the commission of the offence' (South African Department of Justice and Constitutional Development 2008, pp. 13–15). This was also the rationale given for the introduction of restitution orders in the Netherlands in the Terwee Act 1995 (Wemmers 1996). Such an unfettered version of restitution orders, if applied against large, rich corporations responsible for environmental harm, has the potential to be a very powerful mechanism for environmental victims – including large groups of victims – both in terms of the amount of money available and the symbolic benefit of being recognised as criminally harmed. Skinnider (2011, p. 55) has commented on the difficulty of applying restitution orders in cases of 'mass' or 'community' environmental victimisation, although he also suggests a number of solutions revolving around restoring the natural environment shared by such communities. The difficulty with Skinnider's approach, however, is that it lacks direct recognition of individual victims or their suffering, and does nothing to assist such victims with costs incurred (health costs, insurance costs, repair costs and so on).

A more fundamental difficulty with relying on such restitution orders is that achieving criminal convictions in such cases in the first place is very difficult. Not only is the question of causation difficult to resolve, underlying issues concerning the cultural willingness of prosecutors to pursue such cases remain. Even assuming a conviction is achieved for the original crime, ascribing that crime to the full ambit of possible impacts would be almost impossible (and costly for any criminal justice system). As such, O'Hear (2004) has rightly highlighted how

1 Through 'compensation orders' issued under the Power of Courts (Sentencing) Act 2000.

one of the key difficulties in applying the social harms perspective within criminal justice more broadly is that of establishing culpability for wide-ranging and diverse impacts.

Such difficulties seem to reflect broader problems criminal justice systems face when confronted with environmental offenders and environmental victims. In particular, the concept of mass victimisation is still difficult for many justice systems to assimilate. Furthermore, it has been suggested that initial low take-up rates of restitution orders for any crime in a number of jurisdictions have been largely based on cultural reticence within the judiciary to use them (see Newburn 1988; Moxon et al. 1992). On this point, matters are improving (see Ashworth 2010), but it seems clear that culturally, criminal justice systems still have some way to go before restitution orders are routinely used in environmental cases, even though, ironically, corporate environmental offenders may be in a stronger position to pay financially meaningful sums to large groups of victims.

The Administrative Route

In the majority of Western jurisdictions, it is possible for victims of some crimes to receive monetary compensation from the state, paid out of public funds. In most cases, however, the particulars of these schemes restrict the availability of compensation to those who have suffered physical injury as a result of violent crime (see Hall 2010). Consequently, environmental victimisation will almost always fall beyond the remit of such existing mechanisms.

O'Hear (2004) has argued that, more broadly, administrative compensation systems for environmental damage have numerous advantages over both civil and criminal court procedures. His main argument is that such schemes can operate under a more comprehensive set of pre-defined rules. Lin (2005) advocates the benefits of such schemes' use of standardised schedules of damages, although a criticism of these is that whilst they offer greater certainty, they also allow for very little adaptation of the rules to specific situations. Given the range of environmental harms, and the general gaps in our knowledge on this issue, an over-rigid system may not serve some victims of environmental harm particularly well.

Farber (2007) has argued that the problem of establishing full (or even partial) causation in cases of environmental crime can be avoided by offering victims what he calls 'proportional recovery' under an administrative system that compensates victims in proportion to the established chance that harm was caused to them by a given environmental incident. In cases where different groups of victims have different chances of becoming subject to environmental harm, O'Hear (2004) also advocates such a 'risk-based approach'. This again avoids the difficulty of proving causation in the criminal (or indeed, the civil) courts. That said, whilst a lower threshold of causation is one of the benefits of applying administrative compensation schemes to environmental harm, if the system becomes too open, it will not be perceived as fair by those who must fund it. This is important, because such (largely industrial) actors are also likely to have the economic and political sway to lobby against such a system. This is exactly what befell a system initiated in Japan in the early 1980s. Under this system, industry levies were used to fund compensation payments to those developing certain respiratory health problems in highly polluted areas. However, the corporations were unwilling to accept levies to pay compensation for harms they themselves (individually) had not been shown to have caused, and through political pressure the system was abandoned in 1988 (Lin 2005).

For Lin (2005), the advantages of administrative compensation systems over civil courts are clear. He argues that administrative systems typically employ specialised or expert decision-makers who can conduct their own studies and consider a broad range of information. He also suggests that administrative systems can provide more continuous oversight and distribute compensation more fairly amongst a class of victims, whilst also being more politically accountable than the judiciary. Lin's notion of a risk-based administrative compensation system for victims of environmental harm is encouraging, although he does place considerable faith in the ability of modern science to assess risk accurately.[2] However, this may be over-generous given the continuous development in knowledge of environmentally induced harms along with the still considerable gaps in that knowledge (Cross 1989).

A recent high-profile administrative compensation system related specifically to environmental victimisation is the $20 billion fund constituted through talks between BP and the US government following the 2010 *Deepwater Horizon* oil spill in the Gulf of Mexico. Unlike the state-funded criminal schemes discussed previously, this fund is financed by BP. The fund is administered by an 'Independent Claims Facility' that, controversially, is managed by an employee of BP (2010). Consequently, this is perhaps better thought of as an administrative restitution scheme which can pay monies to businesses, state departments and, significantly for present purposes, individuals demonstrating 'legitimate claims including natural resource damages and state and local response costs' (BP 2010). Given the worldwide interest in the case, it might be speculated that the speed with which the US and BP brokered the deal may reflect the kind of political underpinnings to the scheme predicted by Elias (1983) and Harland (1978). The continued high degree of controversy and interest in the workings of the scheme by the US media in particular has maintained the disaster as a political issue. Whilst overall the scheme is a positive step in the direction of addressing the needs of environmental victims more broadly, some commentators have used it to exemplify the disparity between the treatment of environmental victims in particularly newsworthy cases compared to provisions for such victims more broadly at the national and international level. Indeed, even within the United States it is notable that when the Comprehensive Environmental Response, Compensation, and Liability Act (CERCLA)[3] was passed by congress in 1980, proposed provisions relating to the compensation of individual victims of environmental damage were removed at the last minute to ensure its passage (Bronston 1983). Returning to the *Deepwater Horizon* example, Van Tassell argues:

> The Gulf of Mexico oil spill and British Petroleum's quick efforts to pay for clean-up and compensation for victims may lead many people to falsely conclude that national and international laws operate effectively to make the polluter pay for harm. In truth, clean-up and compensation is rarely accomplished so efficiently, and laws operate to insulate polluters when they disaster occurs in poorer countries. (Van Tassell 2011, n.p.)

The criticism, therefore, is that whilst highly visible, relatively lucrative compensation schemes are available for major one-off polluting events in developed jurisdictions (with the ability to put pressure on multinational corporations), this does little to address the more general absence of such compensation or restitution mechanisms internationally for more endemic,

2 Although he does present considerable evidence in favour of this hypothesis.

3 The purpose of the Act (often known as 'Superfund') is to compel polluters to clean up and restore environmental damage caused by spills and leaks of hazardous contaminants.

but perhaps less media-friendly, examples of environmental victimisation. This disparity also reflects the inequality of impact of environmental harm between rich and poor nations.

Overall, administrative compensation systems have much to recommend them, both from the perspective of victims of environmental harm and from the perspective of those running and financing them. The evidence does point to such systems being more efficient and less time-consuming than their court-based equivalents (Farber 2007). Furthermore, the removal of the need to prove causation to either the criminal or civil standard should in theory facilitate more pay-outs. The key difficulty with administrative compensation systems is that it is difficult to see how they could be rolled out to meet the full range of environmental victimisations. In reality, such schemes appear to be largely ad hoc, or focused on very specific forms of environmental harm. There also seems to be a connection between the formation of these schemes and the mediatisation and politicisation of high-profile pollution catastrophes, and these are far more prevalent in developed, rich jurisdictions than in less-developed, poor ones. Consequently, whilst they seem particularly suited to one-off disasters, it is more difficult to advocate their use as the primary means of compensating victims of environmental crime when so many of these victims would be excluded. As such, there appears to be a need to retain court-based compensation for more 'everyday' events, or where victimisation is less clear-cut.

The Restorative Route

This section will briefly consider the possibility of applying burgeoning restorative solutions to the issue of environmental victims seeking restitution or compensation. Information concerning the application of restorative processes to environmental harm is scant, although the growing evidence of its uses for victims of other crimes makes this an area worthy of detailed research. Generally speaking, pilot restorative justice schemes for adult offenders, in England and Wales and elsewhere, seem to confirm that when victims of more traditional crimes do become involved in restorative processes they draw benefits from doing so, as does the restorative enterprise itself (Shapland et al. 2011).

What does exist is a small but growing literature on what has been variously termed 'environmental mediation' and 'environmental alternative dispute resolution' (ADR) (Edwards 1985). These terms are variously defined, although one concise definition is provided by Amy: 'environmental mediation is a process in which representatives of environmental groups, business groups and government agencies sit down together with a neutral mediator to negotiate a binding solution to a particular environmental dispute' (Amy 1983, p. 1).

Of course, this definition excludes environmental victims directly, which is quite telling in an article devoted to the issue of environment degradation. In fact, victims themselves feature relatively little in this literature, with many more of the discussions revolving around the role of 'environmentalists' or 'environmental groups'. The extent to which such groups represent real victims of environmental harm is a moot point. Furthermore, one of the few studies to examine environmental ADR empirically, as well as to discuss the position of the victims directly (Matsumoto 2011), suggests that when environmental victims engage representation, or group together in an effort to increase bargaining power, this in fact complicates the process to the extent of prolonging it.

Generally speaking, the key advantages of mediation or alternative dispute resolution in environmental cases are said to be considerably lower costs and shorter timescales compared to civil or criminal justice resolutions (Mernitz 1980), although very little detailed empirical evaluation has been undertaken to test these claims. One expectation is that of Sipe (2007), who argues via quantitative analysis that environmental mediation does produce a statistically significant increase in settlement rates compared to civil law actions, but no difference in compliance rates with these agreements. Again, it is notable that Sipe's analysis does not mention victims of environmental harm.

Much of the literature concerning environmental mediation is US-based, which is a limitation given that it is under-developed nations and their people who tend to fall victim to environmental harm (see Mendelsohn et al. 2006; Spencer et al. 2011). Nevertheless, in one of the first test cases, representatives of the University of Washington's Environmental Mediation Project were appointed by the Governor of Washington State to serve as mediators in a dispute among environmentalists, farmers, developers and public officials over the damming of the Snoqualmie River. According to Shmueli and Kaufman (2006), 'the resulting agreement illustrated one of mediation's main assets – its capacity to generate creative solutions that satisfy the interests of all parties involved' (Shmueli and Kaufman 2006, p. 17). Certainly, the adaptability of mediation and other restorative options is a big plus, especially given the long-standing criticism of mainstream victimology, that policies aimed at victims tend to assume specific victim characteristics and needs. Furthermore, Matsumoto (2011) notes that mediation is a fitting solution for a situation in which, as in many environmental pollution disputes, 'the polluter and its victims are located near each other and will remain in place and maintain an on-going relationship after their dispute is resolved' (Matsumoto 2011, p. 660).

Positive features notwithstanding, environmental mediation also brings difficulties, not the least of which is the fact that 'those who have the time and resources to participate in a mediation process are not necessarily representative of the interest groups affected by the decisions issuing from this process' (Shmueli and Kaufman 2006, p. 21). This might be especially true given the economic and social standing of many victims of environmental harm. Amy (1983) has discussed the opinion expressed in some quarters of environmentalism that mediation in fact panders to the benefit of big industry and the polluters themselves. Thus, Amy contends, most environmental mediation actually takes place in a context of palatable political bias, power imbalance and the illusion of voluntariness. Dryzek and Hunter (1987) have suggested that in the aftermath of the Indian Bhopal disaster, Union Carbide was in fact very keen to engage in mediation rather than going down more legalistic routes. Whilst Amy (1983) is generally more hopeful for the overall benefit of mediation in these cases than the worst of these concerns suggests, he still injects a note of caution into his conclusion: 'As a rule, it would benefit environmentalists to have a healthy suspicion of mediation, especially when the offer to mediate comes from their opponents' (Amy 1983, p. 19).

Of course, this is a rather pessimistic interpretation of the motives of corporations wishing to enter into environmental mediation. An alternative suggestion is that mediation and alternative dispute resolution is the usual manner in which corporations resolve conflicts with each other, thus it may be the route with which they are most familiar.[4]

Overall, the cause of environmental mediation is at present severely held back by a lack of basic empirical data concerning the nature of the settlements, the processes used and the effectiveness/enforcement of these agreements. Without such information, it is very difficult

4 My thanks to Professor Joanna Shapland of the University of Sheffield for this alternative interpretation.

to test many of the claims being made. It is also problematic that the majority of information we have comes only from developed countries, which, as noted previously, do not bear the brunt of environmental victimisation. Even within these countries, environmental victims will tend to be especially marginalised groups. The concern, then, is that such groups lack the political or social power to meaningfully influence a mediation exercise when on the other side of the table one has large multinational corporations, and perhaps their own state. In such instances, it is suggested that such victims may well need the guarantees and protections (and the enforcement power) of formalised justice systems (whether criminal or civil). There is also a further complication, in that the literature that exists on environmental mediation, when it mentions victims' difficulties at all, fails to consider the possibility of multiple groups of victims with competing interests sitting around the table. That said, a recent ecocide mock-trial experiment staged in the Supreme Court of the United Kingdom has indicated the suitability of restorative justice as means of sentencing offenders for environmental crime (Rivers 2012).

Discussion

Environmental crime and environmental harm, despite their historical pedigree, are novel problems behind which scientific and sociological knowledge is still lagging. It is perhaps for this reason above all others that none of the systems discussed above seem well adapted to offering redress mechanisms for environmental victims. Indeed, this is an observation that can apply at both the national and international levels. Whilst space is lacking here to examine developments at the international level with regard to compensation and restitution for victims of environmental harm (and the environment itself), developments such as the 1989 Basel Convention on the Control of Transboundary Movements of Hazardous Wastes and their Disposal (specifically, its Protocol on Liability and Compensation for Damage Resulting from Transboundary Movements of Hazardous Wastes and their Disposal) and the 1998 UNECE ('Aarhus') Convention on Access to Information, Public Participation in Decision-Making and Access to Justice in Environmental Matters seem to confirm that whilst states are willing to express aspirations or make rhetorical moves in this area, it is rarely the case that such aspirations are transposed into something more concrete (and costly), as demonstrated (to give one example) by the low take-up of the Basel Protocol (see Hall 2013).

One of the clearest messages emerging from this discussion is that civil law, and especially tort law, in itself is insufficient to achieve the purposes of restitution in many environmental cases, even if such 'purposes' are narrowly understood as basic financial compensation or restitution for physical injuries and/or illness. Put simply, the average profile of a victim of environmental harm does not tally with those who are able to mount long-term, expensive lawsuits against large multinational companies or the state itself. This is especially true if civil courts in some jurisdictions continue to resist class actions in environmental cases.

Beyond a move away from reliance on civil mechanisms, however, the debate over how best to offer redress to these victims becomes more complex. Certainly, any system of redress must address conflicting tensions between offering tailored solutions that work in particular (perhaps unique) circumstances whilst at the same time conveying a sense of certainty, fairness and consistency between cases. In this sense, an administrative-based system utilising a standard schedule of payments seems appealing, because such schemes can be devised to deal with a wider range of 'environmental harms' than the criminal justice system. Thus far, however, such schemes as have been constituted for the purpose of offering compensation or restitution to environmental victims have been restricted to very specific events, very specific countries and very specific forms of harm. There is also, as we have seen, a real concern that such schemes are often constituted for reasons of political expediency, and as such, the fear is that victims once again are being used to achieve political gain, as reported by Rock (1990).

In addition, if payment for such schemes is to come from broad-brush levies on polluting companies, with little demonstrable culpability for specific instances of environmental victimisation, then the overall fairness of the system is brought into doubt. Given that large corporations have such influence over what does and does not succeed in this regulatory sphere (see Dal Bó 2006), this lack of perceived fairness is a genuine threat to the long-term sustainability of such a system. That said, it is noteworthy that corporations who cause environmental pollution have learned to internalise and accept a variety of increasing costs to their business practices as our understanding of environmental degradation has increased. As such, what is required is a shift in cultural attitudes towards the acceptance of such costs as a normal part of doing business in this area.

At this stage, we might conclude that the practical realities of this complex problem seem to lean towards the use of administrative systems. Nevertheless, it is also suggested that criminal law has a very important part to play here, both for its ability to sanction actual polluters in a fair and consistent manner and also in its ability to compel them to pay restitution directly to victims, which, in keeping with the victimological literature, seems desirable. In fact, it could be argued that since we are often talking about rich, multinational corporations, in many instances the benefit to victims of going to the criminal courts might also be financial, as the companies are likely to have much greater funds than administrative schemes to pay restitution orders. Such funds might contribute significantly to remedying the damaged environment as well as individuals' suffering. The development of restitution orders so far shows that this is possible, although at present most systems are restrictive, with a demonstrable lack of will amongst judges and legislators to implement this kind of criminal restitution.

Conclusions

Perhaps the most significant conclusion to be drawn from this review of redress mechanisms for victims of environmental harm is that at present there is a real division between the 'haves' and the 'have nots'. Those 'fortunate' enough to be subject to media-friendly, publicly sympathetic, geographically and temporally contained environmental victimisation within a developed country have been given access to generous administrative compensation, and even criminal-based restitution and/or mediation. Those resident in poorer countries, or in poorer communities where environmental degradation is viewed as necessary for the national interest, have found themselves lacking such official channels, and are often not in a financial or social position to embark upon their own civil claims. It is possible that international law has a role to play in addressing this inequality (see Murphy 2000), but as noted above, at present there are few international instruments with any genuine force which incorporate environmental victimisation.

Ultimately, I submit that, with the possible exception of civil claims, all of the mechanisms discussed in this chapter have potential to assist victims of environmental crime/harm more fully in obtaining redress. In fact, the problem is often one of cultural resistance and extending such schemes beyond their traditional ambits. I submit that this is another important reason to include the criminal law, if only to affirm that such harm is real, costly (in many divergent ways), and something to which lawmakers, legal practitioners and judges must direct their full attention. I argue that little more progress will be made in unravelling the complexities inherent in this proposition without detailed research asking victims themselves what they want or need from any form of redress provisions. Indeed, it will be noted that no evidence is presented above concerning how victims would even communicate the full impact of the harm they have suffered to either a criminal or administrative system. Presumably, this could be achieved by some form of victim impact statement, although there is no discussion in the literature of any such statements being used in these cases. I hope the discussion presented in this chapter will provide a useful starting point for thinking about redress in these cases, but at present it remains incomplete and begs a number of important questions that can only be answered in the light of further empirical research.

References

Amy, D. 1983. 'The Politics of Environmental Mediation', *Ecology Law Quarterly* 11(1), 1–19.

Ashworth, A. 2010. *Sentencing and Criminal Justice*, 5th edn. Cambridge: Cambridge University Press.

Bell, S. and McGillivray, D. 2008. *Environmental Law*, 7th edn. Oxford: Oxford University Press.

BP. 2010. 'BP Establishes $20 Billion Claims Fund for Deepwater Horizon Spill and Outlines Dividend Decisions', press release, 16 June 2010: www.bp.com/en/global/corporate/press/press-releases/bp-establishes-20-billion-claims-fund-for-deepwater-horizon-spill-and-outlines-dividend-decisions.html (accessed 6 March 2014).

Bradford, B. 2011. 'Voice, Neutrality and Respect: Use of Victim Support Services, Procedural Fairness and Confidence in the Criminal Justice System', *Criminology and Criminal Justice* 11(4), 345–66.

Bronston, D.E. 1983. 'Compensating Victims of Hazardous Substance Pollution in the United States and Japan: A Comparative Analysis', *Fordham International Law Journal* 7(3), 501–34.

Canadian Department of Justice. 2012. 'Victim Surcharge, Restitution Orders and Compensation': http://canada.justice.gc.ca/eng/rp-pr/cj-jp/victim/restit-dedom/index.html (accessed 6 March 2014).

Castle, P. 1996. *Study of Civil Liability Systems for Remedying Environmental Damage*. London: CMS Cameron McKenna.

Christie, N. 1977. 'Conflicts as Property', *British Journal of Criminology* 17, 1–15.

Cross, Frank. 1989. *Environmentally Induced Cancer and the Law: Risks, Regulation, and Victim Compensation*. Santa Barbara, CA: Greenwood Press.

Dal Bó, E. 2006. 'Regulatory Capture: A Review', *Oxford Review of Economic Policy* 22(2), 203–25.

Dryzek, J. and Hunter, S. 1987. 'Environmental Mediation for International Problems', *International Studies Quarterly* 31(1), 87–102.

Edwards, H.T. 1985. 'Alternative Dispute Resolution: Panacea or Anathema?', *Harvard Law Review* 99, 668–84.

Elias, R. 1983. *Victims of the System: Crime Victims and Compensation in American Politics and Criminal Justice*. New Brunswick, NJ: Transaction.

European Commission. 2001. 'Proposal for a Directive of the European Parliament and of the Council on the Protection of the Environment through Criminal Law', *Official Journal* 180, E 26/06/2001:0238–0243.

Farber, D. 2007. 'Compensation for Victims of Climate Change', *University of Pennsylvania Law Review* 155, 1,605–56.

Goldberg, J. and Zipersky, B. 2011. 'Civil Recourse Revisited', *Florida State University Law Review* 39, 341–71.

Groombridge, N. 1991. 'Corporate Crime: An Environmental View': www.academia.edu/698661/Corporate_Crime_-_an_Environmental_View (accessed 6 March 2014).

Hall, M. 2010. *Victims and Policy Making: A Comparative Approach*. Cullompton: Willan Publishing.

Hall, M. 2013. *Victims of Environmental Harm: Rights, Recognition and Redress Under National and International Law*. Oxford: Routledge.

Hall, M. and Farrall, S. 2012. 'The Criminogenic Consequences of Climate Change: Blurring the Boundaries between Offenders and Victims', in *International Handbook of Green Criminology*, edited by N. South and A. Brisman. Abingdon: Routledge, 120–33.

Harland, A.T. 1978. 'Compensating the Victim of Crime', *Criminal Law Bulletin* 14, 203–24.

House of Commons Environmental Audit Committee. 2004. *Environmental Crime and the Courts: Sixth Report of Session 03–04*. London: The Stationery Office.

Johnson, K. 2004. 'International Human Rights Class Actions: New Frontiers for Group Litigation', *Michigan State Law Review*, 3, 643.

Lawrence, R. 2006. 'Research Dissemination: Activity Bringing the Research and Policy Worlds Together', *Evidence and Policy* 2, 373–84.

Lee, T. 2009. *A Welfare Approach to Mitigating Environmental Injustice: Exploring Needs of Pollution Victims*: www.welfareacademy.org/pubs/international/epckdi/2.pdf (accessed 6 March 2014).

Lee, T. 2011. 'Gulf Shrimp Season Begins in Louisiana Under Oil-black Cloud', *Huffington Post*, 22 August: www.huffingtonpost.com/2011/08/22/start-of-louisianas-shrim_n_933472.html?ir=Greenandncid=edlinkusaolp00000008 (accessed 6 March 2014).

Lin, A.C. 2005. 'Beyond Tort: Compensating Victims of Environmental Toxic Injury', *Southern California Law Review* 78, 1,439–528.

Malsch, M. 1999. 'Victims' Wishes for Compensation: The Immaterial Aspect', *Journal of Criminal Justice* 27, 239–47.

Matsumoto, S. 2011. 'A Duration Analysis of Environmental Alternative Dispute Resolution in Japan', *Ecological Economics* 70, 659–66.

McEldowney, J. and McEldowney, S. 2011. 'Science and Environmental Law: Collaboration across the Double Helix', *Environmental Law Review* 13(3), 169–97.

Mendelsohn, R., Dinar, A. and Williams, L. 2006. 'The Distributional Impact of Climate Change on Rich and Poor Countries', *Environment and Development Economics*, 11, 159–78.

Mernitz, S. 1980. *Mediation of Environmental Disputes*, New York: Praeger.

Miers, D. 1980. 'Victim Compensation as a Labelling Process', *Victimology* 5, 3–16.

Moxon, D., Martin, J. and Hedderman, C. 1992. *Developments in the Use of Compensation Orders in Magistrates' Courts Since October 1988*. Home Office Research Study 126. London: Home Office.

Murphy, S. 2000, 'Does the World Need an International Environmental Court?', *George Washington Journal of International Law and Economics* 32, 333–49.

Nagin, D. and Waldfogel, J. 1998. 'The Effect of Conviction on Income Through the Life Cycle', *International Review of Law and Economics* 18(1), 25–40.

Newburn, T. 1988. *The Use and Enforcement of Compensation Orders in Magistrates' Courts*. Home Office Research Study 102. London: Home Office.

O'Hear, M. 2004. 'Sentencing the Green-collar Offender: Punishment, Culpability, and Environmental Crime', *Journal of Criminal Law and Criminology* 95(1), 133–276.

Redgwell, C. 2010. 'International Environmental Law', in *International Law*, 3rd edn, edited by M. Evans. Oxford: Oxford University Press, 687–721.

Richardson, N. 2010. *Deepwater Horizon and the Patchwork of Oil Spill Liability Law*: www.rff.org/RFF/Documents/RFF-BCK-Richardson-OilLiability_update.pdf (accessed 6 March 2014).

Rivers, L. 2012. 'Shareholder Return: A "Nuremberg Defence"? Ecocide and Restorative Justice', *Environmental Law and Management* 24(1), 17–19.

Rock, P. 1986. *A View from the Shadows: The Ministry of the Solicitor General of Canada and the Making of the Justice for Victims of Crime Initiative*. Oxford: Clarendon Press.

Rock, P. 1990. *Helping Victims of Crime: The Home Office and the Rise of Victim Support in England and Wales*. Oxford: Oxford University Press.

Shapland, J. 1990. 'Bringing Victims in from the Cold: Victims' Role in Criminal Justice', in *Criminal Justice Reform: Looking to the Future*, edited by J. Jackson and K. Quinn. Belfast: Queens University, 1–10.

Shapland, J. and Hall, M. 2007. 'What Do We Know about the Effect of Crime on Victims?', *International Review of Victimology* 14, 175–217.

Shapland, J., Robinson, G. and Sorsby, A. 2011. *Restorative Justice in Practice*. London: Routledge.

Shmueli, D. and Kaufman, S. 2006. *Environmental Mediation*. Center for Environmental Policy Studies Series no. 24. Jerusalem: Center for Environmental Studies.

Sipe, N. 2007. 'An Empirical Analysis of Environmental Mediation', *Journal of the American Planning Association* 64(2), 275–85.

Skinnider, E. 2011. *Victims of Environmental Crime: Mapping the Issues*, Vancouver: International Centre for Criminal Law Reform and Criminal Justice Policy.

South African Department of Justice and Constitutional Development. 2008. *Service Charter for Victims of Crime in South Africa*. Pretoria: Department of Justice and Constitutional Development.

Spencer, M., Garratt, A., Hockman, E., Bryant, B. and Kohn-Wood, L. 2011. 'Environmental Justice and the Well-being of Poor Children of Color', *Communities, Neighborhoods and Health* 1(3), 219–33.

Stern, N. 2007. *The Economics of Climate Change: The Stern Review*. Cambridge: Cambridge University Press.

Tombs, S. and Whyte, D. 2010. 'Crime, Harm and Corporate Power', in *Crime: Local and Global*, edited by J. Muncie, D. Talbot and R. Walters. Cullompton: Willan Publishing, 137–72.

Tyler, T. 1990. *Why People Obey the Law*. New Haven, CT: Yale University Press.

Ullman, R.H. 1983. 'Redefining Security', *International Security* 8(1), 129–53.

United Nations Environment Programme (UNEP). 2011. 'UNEP Ogoniland Oil Assessment Reveals Extent of Environmental Contamination and Threats to Human Health', 4 August: www.unep.org/newscentre/default.aspx?ArticleID=8827&DocumentID=2649 (accessed 6 March 2014).

Van Tassell, K. 2011. 'Compensating Victims of Environmental Disasters', 18 January: http://lawprofessors.typepad.com/healthlawprof_blog/2011/01/compensating-victims-of-environmental-disasters.html (accessed 6 March 2014).

Wemmers, J. 1996. *Victims in the Criminal Justice System*. Amsterdam: Kugler Publications.

Wheatley, M.A. 1997. 'Social and Cultural Impacts of Mercury Pollution on Aboriginal Peoples in Canada', *Water, Air and Soil Pollution* 97(1–2), 85–90.

Whitehead, R. and Block, W. 2003. 'Taking the Assets of Criminals to Compensate Victims of Violence: A Legal and Philosophical Approach', *Journal of Law and Society* 5, 229–53.

Williams, C. 1996. An Environmental Victimology', *Social Science* 23(1), 16–40; reprinted in White, R. 2009. *Environmental Crime: A Reader*. Cullompton: Willan Publishing, 200–222.

PART II
Characteristics of Different Types of Environmental Crime

Chapter 7
Trade in 'Dirty Air': Carbon Crime and the Politics of Pollution

Reece Walters and Peter Martin

> Carbon trading fraudsters may have accounted for up to 90% of all market activity in some European countries, with criminals pocketing billions, mainly in Britain, France, Spain, Denmark and Holland, according to Europol and the European law enforcement agency. (Mason 2009)

> Carbon offset projects often result in land grabs, local environmental and social conflicts, as well as the repression of local communities and movements. The CDM approval process for projects allows little space for the voices of Indigenous Peoples and local communities – in fact, no project has ever been rejected on the grounds of rights violations, despite these being widespread. (Carbon Trade Watch 2013)

Introduction

As the world's globalised economies continue to release records levels of carbon dioxide, new markets and opportunities are created for criminal enterprises through government initiatives to reduce emissions. As the opening quotations suggest, emerging criminal activities in carbon fraud are widespread and lucrative, with devastating effects on indigenous populations. There have been numerous international efforts to reduce carbon emissions, none more widespread than the Kyoto Protocol through carbon taxes and sinks, and renewable or 'cleaner', where 'carbon is now tracked and traced like any other commodity' (UN Framework Convention on Climate Change 1997). In essence, pollution has now become item for global trade. It is not a trade in poisonous gases, but a financial exchange of 'property-like rights', where the big polluters (those that emit more than 25,000 tonnes of carbon per year) can trade in carbon certificates which grant a right to emit. As is often the case, new markets provide new criminal opportunities, and this chapter explores the political economy of carbon and the ways in which trading schemes have provided new opportunities for fraud and tax evasion.

Kyoto and Carbon Offsetting

The process of carbon offsetting and trading gives states and corporations legal permission to release emissions into the atmosphere, with one carbon credit equalling one tonne of carbon dioxide. Carbon markets aim to internalise the costs of greenhouse gas (GHG) pollution within firms. As such, they provide a price signal to firms that encourages minimisation of GHG emissions or a displacement of emission savings through offsets, for example by purchasing emission savings in other firms. Markets can only occur when objects are *commensurable*, so that exchange values are known and trusted. GHG instruments are remarkable to the extent that they represent no value as a tangible commodity, but instead serve as a *permit* or more accurately, as a means of settling a *liability* created through GHG emissions (Mackenzie 2009, p. 448). In creating this synthetic commodity, a multiplicity of projects and technologies in action must be made commensurate. Given this process, plus the intangibility of the instrument and the political basis for its value, issues of compliance, regulation and the potential for fraud are significant concerns (Drew and Drew 2010).

The Kyoto Protocol established upper limits or 'emission caps' for all 170 signatory countries. Large polluting nations, such as China and the USA, however, have refused to agree to mandatory caps, while the UK is widely reported to exceed its projected carbon emission target (Harvey 2011). Moreover, polluting countries can participate in reforestation initiatives or the creation of 'carbon sinks' as a contribution to reducing emissions. The process is a trade-oriented form of control based on 'supply and demand' (Labatt and White 2009). It was intended that rapidly developing and high-polluting countries such as China and India would need support, while other industrialised countries would need incentives in a global effort to reduce greenhouse gases. Countries now purchase carbon credits up to their maximum emission cap. Should an annual emission allowance not be met, then credits may be sold on the international market in what has become known as the global carbon trading industry. The number of consultants and traders offering advice in 'carbon finance', 'carbon accounting' and 'carbon investment' has increased substantially in recent years (*The European Business Review* 2010).

In the Kyoto system, many offset credits are sourced from projects in developing countries through the Clean Development Mechanism (CDM). This dependence of emitters on carbon reduction or avoidance in the poorer and developing world has been heavily criticised as a form of 'carbon colonisation' that provides opportunities for carbon fraud and corruption (Bachram 2004). In the EU emission trading scheme (ETS), a certain proportion of credits (6 per cent in Phase 3) from the CDM can contribute to emission liabilities of entities. However, significant offset credit projects have also developed in high-emitting countries such as the USA and Australia, and both domestic and international credits serve the increasing voluntary market. In general, all offset credits can be purchased in the voluntary markets, but only specifically accredited credits, such as those regulated by the CDM or other national or international accreditations systems (such as the Australian Carbon Farming Initiative), can be traded in the compliance markets (Kyoto, the European ETS and proposed markets such as the Australian ETS and Californian ETS). In the voluntary markets, purchases are commonly from entities that wish to demonstrate corporate responsibility and attract business by improving their image as 'environmentally friendly' and enhancing their branding (Peters-Stanley and Hamilton 2012). Key buyers are major airlines and financial institutions, but there are a myriad of smaller buyers, including event organisers, community groups and individuals. For most purchasers, offset credits are purchased and then 'retired' – removed from the carbon registers. Entities may also purchase carbon credits for investment purposes – for example, betting on future higher carbon prices and eventual resale – or as a pre-compliance measure to enable lower cost compliance by buying eligible credits early. These developments in the international trading and offsetting of carbon have occurred at some pace over the past six years, without due consideration for regulatory and enforcement practices. As a result, and perhaps unsurprisingly, international headlines such as 'Interpol Warns of Carbon Fraud' (Packham 2009) and 'Fraud Mastermind Cheated Taxpayers of 39 Million Pounds in just 69 Days' (Allen 2012) have provided wake-up calls for governments and industries focused on the benefits of trade rather than the opportunities of criminal entities. The emergence of carbon fraud rhetoric has provided necessary political reflection on the perils and prospects of the market's role in solving the market's problems.

Bribery, Theft and Environmental Harm

The Kyoto Protocol established 'offsetting carbon emissions' through the financing of emission reduction projects or 'carbon sinks' in other parts of the globe. The Protocol is a baseline-and-trade market where richer countries are expected to meet their emission targets through three mechanisms: first, by purchasing credits from other developed countries which have reduced emissions; second, via the Joint Implementation (JI) mechanism, which allows purchasing project-based offset credits from other countries with binding targets, and third, through the CDM, which that allows purchasing of project offset credits from developing countries that have no binding emission targets (Hepburn 2007: 379). Credits from offset projects are also utilised in the voluntary market. Emitting entities can purchase credits from carbon brokers to partially or fully offset their GHG emissions. The voluntary market is largely unregulated by the state, and while regarded initially as the 'wild west' of carbon markets, it has led to increasing self-regulation and higher standards of accreditation and certification (Hamilton et al. 2008, p. 53). That said, accusations of bribery have been levelled in Liberia involving a large carbon credits deal (Global Witness 2011). In Papua New Guinea and Peru, accusations have been made that private developers and NGOs have been swarming the tropical forests to encourage indigenous leaders to sign away their rights to the forest. In these instances, it has been reported that Peruvian indigenous peoples, for example, have been pressured to sign agreements they could not read in acts described as 'carbon piracy' (Vidal 2011). Moreover, serious accusations were made of PNG officials producing fake carbon credit certificates as a prop for explaining carbon credit deals to local leaders (Wilkinson and Cubby 2009).

An Australia-based carbon broker, Shift2Neutral, has been accused of distributing fake carbon offset credits and providing no evidence of having successfully negotiated the project with local indigenous peoples (Cubby 2011). The Carbon News Forum reported:

> Alarm bells about Shift2Neutral have recently been rung by the Tribal Coalition of Mindanao who in late November 2010 report that a 17 month old $500 million Tricom Caraga Memorandum of Understanding between Shift2Neutral and Indigenous tribes of Caraga has been dissolved. The tribal people believe that they have been conned. This follows on from reports dated 6 October 2010 that a recently signed Shift2Neutral agreement in Congo was illegal. (Carbon News Forum 2011)

Accusations of illegality in offset projects have mainly involved tropical forest contexts in developing countries. Here, the structural conditions for fraud and corruption mean that projects may be more risky and that the establishment of 'carbon credit' forests could occur through deception or bribery. Such conditions include geographical remoteness, weak governance and official corruption, low levels of economic development and uncertainty over land ownership (Contreras-Hermosilla 2002). The uncertainty over land tenure provides particularly lucrative opportunities for criminal entities. It is estimated that throughout the world, over two billion customary landowners are not recognised by national laws (Wily 2008). Such conditions, which often occur in countries exploited by illegal loggers, exist in those nations where the newly accredited UN Reducing Emissions from Deforestation and Forest Degradation (REDD+) programme will take place. This programme produces carbon credits for forest sink conservation and development, and expects to supply funds of US$17–33 billion every year – much of which will be destined for forest-rich developing countries. The programme is not just project-based, but intends to compensate governments, communities, companies and individuals in developing countries that undertake to reduce emissions loss from forests. The huge sums of money involved and the structural conditions in these countries have led to great concern among NGOs about potential fraud, corruption and bribery (Global Witness 2011).

Fraud in Carbon Markets

Fraud is notoriously difficult to define at law (Buell 2011). There are various questions of 'authenticity', 'legitimacy', acceptability' and 'imposture' that are relevant to legal notions of misrepresentation and dishonesty that underpin regulatory authorities' decisions to pursue prosecution. Such decisions have been exacerbated in the case of carbon. The carbon market poses complex conceptual questions about the nature of carbon as a tradable item. If carbon is a commodity, then it should be subject to VAT like all other tradable properties. But is it personal or real property? Most legal jurisdictions have not provided case law decisions on carbon; it is generally referred to as a 'property-like right'. This lack of legal definition and clarity has ramifications for both regulation and cross-national trading

The media have widely reported the risk of carbon fraud in both the allowance markets for example, the European ETS) and the offset credit market. Lohmann (2010) has stated that 'uncovering carbon market scandals is now a minor journalistic industry'. Large accounting firms are informing their clients and releasing scoping documents such as Deloitte's *Carbon Credit Fraud: The White Collar Crime of the Future* (Deloitte 2009) and, more recently, 'Carbon Credit Fraud – an Update' (Deloitte 2011). Moreover, tradable carbon allowances rely upon polluting industries' honesty in disclosing emissions. Emissions reporting has regularly been identified by accountants as a carbon fraud risk (see Deloitte 2009, p. 3; Lindquist and Goldberg 2010, p. 63). Regulatory and policing authorities in the EU do not have the resources to conduct the necessary proactive inspections to ensure compliance. In addition, fraud potentially exists through exaggerated or falsified estimations of carbon benefits from the proposed projects. Barr (2011, p. 335), drawing on earlier work by Ross (2001), also makes the point that powerful state actors could find it financially rewarding to over-report emissions for brief periods.

As is often the case with the identification of new forms of green crime, resistance and protest groups have provided the initial impetus for subsequent criminal justice concern (Walters 2012). The most sustained critiques of carbon credit fraud risk have come from NGOs such as Transparency International (2011), Global Witness in its report *Forest Carbon, Cash & Crime* (2011), and Greenpeace USA's *Carbon Scam* (2009). The Corner House has maintained a sustained critique of carbon trading over the last decade (The Corner House 2001; Gilbertson and Reyes 2009), including some mention of criminal fraud (Gilbertson and Reyes 2009, p. 73) and corruption (Gilbertson and Reyes 2009, p. 63). These reports challenge the authenticity of carbon credit schemes, particularly in REDD subnational projects (such as the UN's Reducing Emissions from Deforestation and Forest Degradation project), and warn of the risks of criminal engagement in these schemes. Most of these reports identify risks rather than actual cases, although a number of anecdotes have been reported, and in the case of *Carbon Scam*, Greenpeace USA analysed in detail the Noel Kempff Climate Action Project in Bolivia and identified major shortcomings in the net emissions savings and 'avoided deforestation' (Greenpeace USA 2009, pp. 9–13). There has been significant fraud in the EU ETS compliance market through VAT scams (carousel fraud) and Internet 'phishing'. In addition, there have been isolated instances of suspected fraud in the brokering of carbon offset credits in the voluntary market – a market into which investment scammers have moved (Walters and Martin 2012).

In September 2012, seven individuals were prosecuted in the UK charged with VAT fraud from trading EU carbon allowances. They were involved in complex 'carousel trades' which utilised the VAT-free export of securities within the EU and sold them on with VAT included in the sale, but without paying VAT to the government. This instance of VAT 'skimming' netted £38 million in 69 days, and reports further suggest that this type of fraud has cost the EU countries around €3 billion (Allen 2012). Four of the defendants were acquitted, but three were found guilty and sentenced up to fifteen years' imprisonment (*R.* v. *Singh* 2012, cited in Walters and Martin 2013).

This case resulted in the UK government making carbon transactions exempt from VAT (Harries 2012). Using the EU ETS registries, Internet fraudsters have also sent emails to companies that directed them to websites where they were asked to enter their identification numbers and passwords. These were used to sell on emission allowances. This scam, known as 'phishing', was reported to have costs the companies millions of euros.

There are also a number of studies (Barr 2011; Brown 2010; Drew and Drew 2010) that point to vulnerabilities concerning verification and validation in the CDM process – the largest offset scheme. Attention to deficits in the CDM process was heightened in 2006 when spot checks by UN inspectors found significant irregularities in work by three prominent verifiers (Schneider 2007, p. 24). In 2009, UN inspectors suspended the largest verifier, SGS UK, because of poor-quality documentation and lack of adequate qualifications among their staff. The process of verification is integral to safeguarding against fraud. However, the offset verification industry is very price-competitive, with revenue per project declining and verifiers highly dependent on the project developers (Brown 2010). As project developers try to cut costs, they search for the verifiers with the lowest fees rather than considering the issue of verification quality an important factor. Further, oversight of verifiers by CDM is limited by insufficient resources (Schneider 2007). Concerns have also been expressed regarding firms providing consulting advice to project developers while also acting as verifiers for the same projects (Bachram 2004, p. 5).

Human Rights Abuses

The absence of compliance trading systems in many countries and the growing social awareness of the impact of climate change has created a growing market for the *voluntary* carbon offset market.

There is significant differentiation among carbon offset products, and price is very much related to the perceived quality of the projects, such as the incorporation of sustainable development criteria, benefits for local people and their environment and being relatively free from fraud risk. This has led to high-priced specialist 'boutique' carbon markets driven by buyers from developed countries in times of excess credits and/or buyers wanting to improve their public image through projects that promote strong environmental and social benefits (Bumpus 2011, p. 623). An important aspect of ensuring quality is purchasing from registries that ensure transparency, reducing the risk of double counting of credits. Furthermore, certification by reputable verification standards, such as the Voluntary Gold Standard (VGS), promotes a positive image to the purchaser and reduces the risks of funding mismanaged or fraudulent projects.

Of considerable concern is the creation of carbon offset projects in regions afflicted by conflict and human rights abuses. For example, the Bajo Aguán Valley in Honduras witnessed the murder of 23 farmers between January 2010 and March 2011 over rights to land (Council of Hemispheric Affairs 2013). More than 3,500 peasant farmers have been petitioning for land rights for agricultural purposes since the coup d'état on 28 July 2009. Independent international human rights inspectors have observed that government officials in collaboration with private security firms have systematically oppressed local and indigenous peoples and orchestrated executions to prevent further protests, stating:

> The government has converted the area of these agrarian conflicts in Bajo Aguán into a war zone: low-flying military helicopters and planes, armed commandos passing menacingly through defenceless villages during the days after the coup; and the peasants of the region's organized movement suffer kidnappings, torture and murders. Human rights violations are growing as the peasants' claims increase. (APRODEV et al. 2011, p. 16)

Peasant farmers were attempting to reclaim land from Groupo Dinant, a large corporation that had converted disputed land into palm oil plantations that the Honduran government registered as a carbon offsets for European polluters (Nelson 2011). This issue has raised ethical and moral issues concerning carbon offsetting in countries with reported human rights violations and the extent to which the commercialisation of carbon serves to exacerbate the plight of those abused.

Investment Scams

The *modus operandi* in these scams is 'cold calling', either through email or by telephone. In 2011, the Australian Transaction Reports and Analysis Centre (AUSTRAC) reported a fake carbon credits investment scheme that cost investors AU$3.5 million (AUSTRAC 2011, pp. 28–9). The victims of the scheme were mostly small business investors and self-funded retirees who were interested in ethical investments. Telemarketers made unsolicited calls and discussed environmental concerns with the aim of drawing them into the investment scam. If interested, investors would be contacted by a representative of a Japanese-based investment scam business who would offer them the opportunity to invest in overseas carbon credits. Those who took up the offer would be asked to transfer money to accounts in Taiwan and China. A professional website had been constructed to allow victims to view their investment certificates. AUSTRAC's attention to the scam was initiated by two very large follow-up transfers. Victims subsequently reported that they had no access to their certificates and they could not be liquidated.

Similar investment scams have been found in countries with high-visibility compliance and voluntary carbon emissions trading schemes. The high public awareness of the monetisation of carbon seems to lead to opportunities for scammers to attract 'investment' money. The Financial Services Authority in the UK has recently alerted the public about a host of fraudulent carbon investment schemes offered to investors by salespeople, emails, telephone, post or even by word of mouth (Financial Services Authority 2012).

Green Criminology and Greenhouse Gas Emissions

Scholars committed to the green criminological enterprise are wedded to a project that pursues social justice and advances human and animal rights (South and Brisman 2013). Criminological analyses of climate change (White 2012; South 2012) and air pollution (Halsey 2013; Walters 2012a) have identified the ways in which state corporate power advances trade and fiscal policies. Such works inevitably involve an examination combining the concepts of harm, power and justice – most notably, the ways power is mobilised to justify a market model of capitalism with unjust and harmful consequences for the environment and the world's most vulnerable peoples.

Elsewhere, we have explored notions of violence and atmospheric justice (Walters and Martin 2013). Rather than constructing air pollution as solely an act of environmental harm, it is useful to conceptualise the deliberate and intentional release of GHGs with its widespread social and environmental consequences as an act of eco-violence. Of course, the development of 'structural' and 'symbolic' violence has existed through discourses in peace and conflict studies for some time (see Galtung 1974). These analyses have provided innovative insights in examining governmental or regime violence and individual oppressions. The advent of debates around institutional racism and sexism created a new landscape for critiquing the state apparatuses of law and social control.

Carbon markets as extension of neoliberal governance and the commodification of nature provide similar avenues to explore structural violence. For some, carbon crime is symptomatic of wider systemic properties of carbon marketisation that are inherently corruptible (Lohmann 2010) and fraudulent (Bachram 2004). Others, however, argue that 'marketisation' of carbon is a political project itself and can be shaped by social concern for its negative consequences (MacKenzie 2009). The critical philosopher Slavoj Žižek expands upon earlier notions of structure and agency and refers to 'systemic violence' or 'the often catastrophic consequences of the smooth functioning of our economic and political systems' (Žižek 2009, p. 1). The production of air pollution and the creation of devastating greenhouse gas emissions has become normalised within the 'smooth' and productive operating of contemporary trade and democracy. Yet, as Žižek notes, these institutionalised systems of trade and capital accumulation have a very real and violent edge, resulting in widespread death and damage. As a result, when observing the world's natural disasters – the tragedies of drought, famine, disease and war – Žižek reminds us that 'we should always take a self-reflexive turn and ask ourselves how we ourselves are implicated in it' (Walters 2012b).

Conclusion

Carbon trading and offsetting are premised on a market model that prioritises economic prosperity and industrial development. The harms associated with production are a secondary consideration to emission reduction targets embroiled in the global politics of trade.

This chapter concludes that carbon fraud, investment scams, fake offsets, fabrication of carbon certificates, bribery of government officials and the exploitation of and violence towards indigenous and poor peoples in developing countries point to a capitalist enterprise that is having devastating social, political and environmental impacts.

The trade in 'dirty air' is a market-led model to provide solutions to market problems. It has unfolded, like so many trade-centred initiatives, without due consideration for social and environmental justice. As green criminologists, we must continue to place such topics on the international political and intellectual agenda. Green criminology reserves a special and significant place in this regard, to identify environmental injustice and harm when they appear as progress.

References

Allen, E. 2012. 'Fraud Mastermind Cheated Taxpayers of 39 Million Pounds in Just 69 Days', *Daily Mail*, 10 December: www.dailymail.co.uk/news/article-2161520/Fraud-mastermind-cheated-taxpayer-39million-just-69-DAYS-spent-money-1million-home-Rolls-Royce-jailed-15-years.html (accessed 6 March 2014).

Association of World Council of Churches Related Development Organisations (APRODEV) et al. 2011. *Honduras: Human Rights Violations in Bajo Aguán – International Fact Finding Mission Report*, July: www.aprodev.eu/files/Central_America/201107_honduras%20ffm%20report%20bajo%20aguan.pdf (accessed 6 March 2014).

AUSTRAC. 2011. *AUSTRAC Typologies and Case Studies Report 2011*. West Chatswood, NSW: Australian Transaction Reports and Analysis Centre.

Bachram, H. 2004. 'Climate Fraud and Carbon Colonialism: The New Trade in Greenhouse Gases', *Capitalism Nature Socialism* 15, 1–16.

Barr, C. 2011. 'Governance Risks for REDD+', in *Global Corruption Report: International Climate Change*, edited by Transparency International. London: Earthscan, 6.3.

Brown, M. 2010. 'Limiting Corrupt Incentives in a Global REDD Regime', *Ecology Law Quarterly* 37, 237–67.

Buell, S.W. 2011. 'What is Securities Fraud?', *Duke Law Journal* 61, 511–81.

Bumpus, A. 2011. 'The Matter of Carbon: Understanding the Materiality of tCO_2e in Carbon Offsets', *Antipode* 43(3), 612–38.

Carbon News Forum. 2011. 'Summary of Brett Goldsworthy Shift2neutral Con Man': http://shift2nothing.com/2011/04/summary-of-brett-goldsworthy-shift2neutral-con-men/ (accessed 6 March 2014).

Carbon Trade Watch. 2013. 'Carbon Offsets': www.carbontradewatch.org/issues/carbon-offsets.html (accessed 6 March 2014).

Contreras-Hermosilla, A. 2002. *Law Compliance in the Forestry Sector: An Overview*. Washington, DC: The International Bank for Reconstruction and Development/The World Bank.

Council of Hemispheric Affairs. 2013. 'Honduran Death Squads Murder Peasants in the Bajo Aguán Valley: Reflections on the Bird Report': www.coha.org/21693/ (accessed 6 March 2014).

Cubby, B. 2011. 'Revealed: Scandal of Carbon Credit Firm, *Sydney Morning Herald*, 8 April 2011: www.smh.com.au/environment/revealed-scandal-of-carbon-credit-firm-20110407-1d6a4.html (accessed 6 March 2014).

Deloitte. 2009. *Carbon Credit Fraud: The White Collar Crime of the Future*, November: https://www.deloitte.com/assets/Dcom-Australia/Local%20Assets/Documents/Services/Forensic/Carbon_credit_fraud.pdf (accessed 6 March 2014).

Deloitte. 2011. 'Carbon Credit Fraud – an Update', Deloitte Forensic Foresight: www.deloitte.com/view/en_AU/au/insights/ca42b7c6ab0e1310VgnVCM1000001a56f00aRCRD.htm (accessed 6 March 2014).

Drew, J.M. and Drew, M.E. 2010. 'Establishing Additionality: Fraud Vulnerabilities in the Clean Development Mechanism', *Accounting Research Journal* 23(3), 243–53.

Financial Services Authority. 2012. 'Carbon Credit Trading': www.fsa.gov.uk/consumerinformation/scamsandswindles/investment_scams/carbon_credit (accessed 27 October 2013).

Galtung, J. 1974. *Peace, Violence and Imperialism*. Oslo: Dreyer, Gilbertson, T. and Reyes, O. 2009. *Carbon Trading: How it Works and Why it Fails*. Uppsala: Dag Hammarskjöld Foundation.

Gilbertson, T. and Reyes, O. 2009. *Carbon Trading: How It Works and Why It Fails*. Uppsala: Dag Hammarskjöld Foundation.

Global Witness. 2011. *Forest Carbon, Cash & Crime: The Risk of Criminal Engagement in REDD+*, September. London: Global Witness.

Greenpeace USA. 2009. *Carbon Scam: Noel Kempff Climate Action Project and the Push for Sub-national Forest Offsets*, 15 October: www.greenpeace.org/usa/en/media-center/reports/carbon-scam-noel-kempff-clima/ (accessed 6 March 2014).

Halsey, M. 2013. 'Defining Pollution Down: Forestry, Climate Change and the Dark Figure of Carbon Emissions', in *Criminological and Legal Consequences of Climate Change*, edited by S. Farrall, T. Ahmed and D. French. Oxford: Hart Publishing, 169–92.

Hamilton, J., Sjardin, M., Marcello, T. and Xu, G. 2008 *Forging a Frontier: State of the voluntary Carbon Markets 2008*: www.ecosystemmarketplace.com/documents/cms_documents/2008_StateofVoluntaryCarbonMarket2.pdf (accessed 27 October 2013).

Harries, M. 2012. 'Fraud and Financial Crime': www.carmelitechambers.co.uk/members/mark-harries/expertise/fraud-and-financial-crime-mark-harries (accessed 6 March 2014).

Harvey, F. 2011. 'Coalition on Course to Miss Carbon Emissions Targets, Says CBI', *The Guardian*, 8 June.

Hepburn, C. 2007. 'Carbon Trading: A Review of the Kyoto Mechanisms', *Annual Review of Environmental Resources* 32, 375–93.

Labatt, S. and White, R. 2009. *Carbon Finance: The Financial Implications of Climate Change*. Toronto: Wiley.

Lindquist, C.S. and Goldberg, S.R. 2010. 'Cap-and-trade: Accounting Fraud and Other Problems', *Journal of Corporate Accounting and Finance*, May/June, 61–4.

Lohmann, L. 2010. 'Regulation as Corruption in the Carbon Offset Markets', in *Upsetting the Offset: The Political Economy of Carbon Markets*, edited by S. Bohm and S. Dabhi. London: Zed Books, 175–91.

MacKenzie, D. 2009. 'Making Things the Same: Gases, Emission Rights and the Politics of Carbon Markets', *Accounting, Organizations and Society* 34, 440–55.

Mason, R. 2009. 'Copenhagen Climate: Carbon Trading Fraudsters Pocket €5bn', *The Telegraph*, 10 December: www.telegraph.co.uk/earth/copenhagen-climate-change-confe/6778003/Copenhagen-climate-summit-Carbon-trading-fraudsters-in-Europe-pocket-5bn.html (accessed 6 March 2014).

Nelson, A. 2011. 'EU Carbon Credits Scheme Tarnished by Alleged Murders in Honduras', *The Guardian*, 3 October: www.guardian.co.uk/environment/2011/oct/03/eu-carbon-credits-murders-honduras (accessed 6 March 2014).

Packham, B. 2009. 'Interpol Warns of Carbon Fraud', *Adelaide Now*, 11 June: www.adelaidenow.com.au/news/interpol-warns-of-carbon-fraud/story-e6freo8c-1225733540371 (accessed 26 October 2013).

Peters-Stanley, M. and Hamilton, K. 2012. *Developing Dimension: State of the Voluntary Carbon Markets*. Washington and New York: Ecosystem Marketplace and Bloomberg New Energy Finance.

Ross, M. 2001. *Timber Booms and Institutional Breakdowns in South East Asia*. Cambridge: Cambridge University Press.

Schneider, L. 2007. *Is the CDM Fulfilling its Environmental and Sustainable Development Objectives? An Evaluation of the CDM and Options for Improvement. Report Prepared for WWF*. Berlin: Institute for Applied Ecology.

South, N. 2012. 'Climate Change, Environmental (in)Security', in *Criminological and Legal Consequences of Climate Change*, edited by S. Farrell, T. Ahmed, T. and D. French. Oxford: Hart Publishing, 97–112.

South, N. and Brisman, A. 2013. 'Critical Green Criminology: Environmental Rights and Crimes of Exploitation', in *New Directions in Crime and Deviance*, edited by S. Winlow and R. Atkinson. London: Routledge, 99–111.

The Corner House. 2001. *Democracy or Carbocracy? Intellectual Corruption and the Future of the Climate Debate*. Corner House Briefing 24: www.thecornerhouse.org.uk/resource/democracy-or-carbocracy (accessed 6 March 2014).

The European Business Review. 2010. 'Noble Carbon Credits: Emissions Trading is a Comparatively New Market', *The European Business Review*: www.europeanbusinessreview.com/?p=331 (accessed 6 March 2014).

Transparency International. 2011. *Global Corruption Report: International Climate Change*. London: Earthscan.

UN Framework Convention on Climate Change. 1997. *Kyoto Protocol*: http://unfccc.int/kyoto_protocol/items/2830.php (accessed 6 March 2014).

Vidal, J. 2011. 'Peruvian Amazon Could Become Global Centre of "Carbon Piracy": Report', *The Guardian*, 30 November: www.guardian.co.uk/environment/2011/nov/30/peruvian-amazon-carbon-piracy?INTCMP=ILCNETTXT3487 (accessed 6 March 2014).

Walters, R. 2012a. 'Air Crimes and Atmospheric Justice, in *Routledge International Handbook of Green Criminology*, edited by N. South and A. Brisman. Abingdon: Routledge, 134–49.

Walters, R. 2012b. 'Dirty Collar Crime and the Environment', in *Proceedings of Crime, Justice and Social Democracy: An International Conference*, 2nd edn. Brisbane: Queensland University of Technology, 103–12.

Walters, R. and Martin, P. 2012. *Risks of Carbon Fraud*. Brisbane: Centre for Crime and Justice Research.

Walters, R. and Martin, P. 2013. 'Crime and the Commodification of Carbon', in *Emerging Issues in Green Criminology: Exploring Power, Justice and Harm*, edited by R. Walters, D. Westerhuis and T. Wyatt. London: Palgrave, 46–70.

White, R. 2012. 'Climate Change and Paradoxical Harm', in *Criminological and Legal Consequences of Climate Change*, edited by S. Farrell, T. Ahmed and D. French. Oxford: Hart Publishing, 63–78.

Wilkinson, M. and Cubby, B. 2009. 'Carbon Scandal Snares Australian', *The Age*, 4 September: www.theage.com.au/business/carbon-scandal-snares-australian-20090903-f9yy.html (accessed 26 October 2013).

Wily, L. 2008. *Whose Land is It? Commons and Conflict States: Why the Ownership of the Commons Matters in Making and Keeping Peace*. Washington, DC: The Rights and Resources Initiative.
Žižek, S. 2009. *Violence: Six Sideways Reflections*. London: Profile Books.

Chapter 8
Oil Spills: A Persistent Problem

Coen van Gulijk

This has not only been the largest oil spill in our history, it has also been the most technologically complex. (President Barack Obama at the US Coast Guard Panama City district office, Panama City, Florida, August 14, 2010)

Introduction

The *Deepwater Horizon* catastrophe has had a great impact on the environment and public opinion about the risks of oil production. The future of oil production is now widely debated in scientific and non-scientific arenas. The catastrophe was so significant that the President of the United States, Barack Obama, was personally involved. He was not satisfied with the accident report issued by BP on September 8, 2010 (BP 2010). He appointed a seven-member commission to investigate the disaster independently. Its report states that safety and environmental integrity must be improved, standards for ultra-deepwater drilling and drilling need to be raised, and special attention is required for drilling in Arctic ecosystems. Unfortunately, the report is limited to analysis of the disaster and the organizations directly involved in it. Although the report mentions an earlier disaster (*Exxon Valdez*), it provides no analysis of oil spills as a recurring problem.

Greenpeace has been particularly active in the debate about arctic oil drilling through its 'Save the Arctic' campaign. Its main concern is the fragility of the Arctic and the fact that an oil spill of any size would have disastrous consequences. That discussion was aggravated on December 31, 2012, when the *Kulluk* ran aground off Sitkalidak Island in the Gulf of Alaska. Yet Greenpeace, too, only refers to the *Exxon Valdez* oil spill for a comparison, and fails to mention the recurrence of oil spills.

Clearly, the debate about safe oil production and the prevention of spills is an important one, but without much historic awareness, it is not easy to gauge the seriousness of the problem. This chapter adds to the discussion by analyzing a set of oil spill reports to answer a relatively simple question: How often do large oil spills occur, and what can we learn from them?

This chapter does not aim to demonstrate a relation between oil spills and crime, nor to stigmatize oil spills as crimes. Instead, it focuses on facts that were available in the public domain (at least in the period up to the writing of this chapter), analyzes them with a straightforward mathematical technique and draws conclusions based on that analysis. The analysis focuses on demonstrating the recurrence of oil spills, thereby unveiling just how persistent large oil spills are. For readers who are interested in the relationship between oil spills and crime, and oil spills as evidence for criminal behavior in corporations, Steffy (2011) presents an interesting insight.

Crime or no crime, the consequences of accidents in high-risk industries have a large societal impact. In 1984, Perrow described six high-risk industries in his groundbreaking book *Normal Accidents: Living with High Risk Technologies*. These high-risk industries include nuclear power, petrochemical plants, aircraft and airways, marine transport, earthbound systems (dams, quakes, mines, and lakes), and what he calls 'exotics' (space, weapons, and DNA). Nearly thirty years later, the topics Perrow addressed are easily associated with accidents that have shaken the world: the Fukushima nuclear accident in 2011, the explosion at the BP Texas refinery in 2005, the airplane crash at Lockerbie in 1988, the *Exxon Valdez* oil spill in 1989, the Tsunami in Indonesia in 2004, and the *Challenger* launch disaster in 1986. The number of publications on these incidents is overwhelming.

Typically, BP-type accidents cause large-scale marine and land oil spills. These accidental spills cause problems in many ways. They may lead to substantial environmental damage, huge financial damages, loss of human life, loss of livelihood, and court cases that last for decades. To my knowledge, oil-producing countries and corporations do not intentionally blow up their factories, sink oil tankers, or cut pipelines to create spills, though some form of organizational shortcoming often comes to light. Ironically, however, one intentional oil spill is also the largest known to humanity: the oil spill in the aftermath of the Gulf War in 1991. It resulted in a spill of a staggering 9,000,000 barrels of oil following the intentional destruction of oil wells in Kuwait (NOAA 1992).

The prevention of accidents is a difficult problem. The topic has attracted attention from various scientific disciplines, such as safety science, risk modeling, reliability engineering, social sciences, and psychology. These disciplines have developed many tools and methods to prevent accidents or reduce their impact, with layers of protection analysis (LOPA) being a prime example (Dowell et al. 2001). Other instructive sources are *Lee's Loss Prevention in the Process Industries* (Mannan 2005) and *Process Systems Risk Management* (Cameron and Raman 2005). Of course, the application of such tools and methods cannot completely prevent the occurrence of accidents and oil spills, as will be demonstrated in this chapter.

This is all despite the fact that in oil and gas production, very serious attention is devoted to accident prevention.

This chapter is a prelude to further research on oil spills. It begins with a simple analysis of a limited set of data. The National Oceanic and Atmospheric Administration (NOAA), which is closely involved in cleaning up oil spills in the United States, compiled the dataset. The database contains information on oil spills and the production of documents registering oil spills roughly for the period of the Clinton administration. Even with this limited set of data, it is clear that oil spills are a recurring problem. This helps to put discussions of the *Deepwater Horizon* catastrophe into historical perspective.

Theory

The Risk Approach to Oil Spills

The analysis of oil spills presented here adopts a risk approach. It assesses the probability of an oil spill and its consequences by means of a graphical method.

Here we will use the definition of risk developed by Kaplan and Garrick (1981). They argued that a risk analysis should involve three elements:

1. the occurrence of accident scenarios related to a particular hazard;
2. the probability of their occurrence;
3. the extent of the damage in cases when they do occur.

The first element, the occurrence of accident scenarios in risk problems, implies the presence of an accident path or scenario for a given hazard or problem to materialize. If a specific scenario has not materialized before, there must be a credible and non-negligible theoretical scenario. For instance, for a flooding to occur, a surplus amount of water is required in a body of water in the vicinity of the area under consideration. If there is no conceivable scenario available, or if it is highly unlikely to occur, it should not be taken into consideration. Note that more than one scenario can lead to damages. Flooding could take place because water levels are much higher than expected, because dams have been weakened, because rivers have changed course, or because sluices are broken. All probabilities must be included in the risk analysis. Understandably, it will be difficult to ensure that the analysis includes every possible scenario. This is defined as *epistemic uncertainty*.

The second element of the definition is the probability of a scenario materializing. In the case of a dam breach, this calculation could include dam strength assessments, inspections, historic analysis, or probability estimation methods. This usually results in an estimate of a probability per year [year^{-1}]. However, this probabilistic approach is not without problems; essentially, this estimate remains uncertain. This uncertainty is usually defined as *aleatory uncertainty*.

The third element, the extent of the damage a scenario may cause, is similar to the probability of a scenario, and scientists may use various methods to assess the damage. Typically, however, historic information is an important starting point. In addition, various mathematical modeling methods exist, which are generally deterministic, maintaining that starting with precisely determined parameters will result in non-random outcomes. Such assessments will lead to parametric uncertainty and algorithmic uncertainty—in other words, *modeling uncertainty*. When the probabilities of accidents are low (say below 0.01 [year^{-1}]) the following equation summarizes the three elements:

$$R_s = \sum_{i=1}^{S} (P_i \cdot C_i)$$

where R_s is the risk of a particular type (for example, the risk of an oil spill), S is the number of credible scenarios (that must be described), i indicates a specific scenario; P_i is the probability of scenario i materializing (this is typically given as probability per year [year^{-1}]), and C_i is the extent of the damages of scenario i.

The damage can be expressed in various units, such as human lives lost [-], financial cost [$], or the extent of environmental damage [m^2 affected]. Note that the formula dictates that the probability of occurrence and the extent of the damage are multiplied. The outcome of this calculation is therefore a *damage expectation value*: the expected amount of damage per year, or the annual costs of the risk per year. This expectation value can be expressed as [death/year] or [$/year], depending on the units that are used for assessing the extent of damages. For present purposes, the damages are expressed as barrels of oil spilt [bbl].

In this chapter, the F–N curve gives a graphic depiction of the risks described above. It shows both the probability of an oil spill happening per year and the extent of the damage in barrels of oil spilt. Because the data reflect historic occurrences, there is no need to consider credible scenarios: they have already materialized.

NOAA Reports as Sources of Data

This analysis uses two types of documents: historic analysis and annual reports. The historic analysis will be referred to as Case Histories (NOAA 1992). The annual reports will be referred to as Response Reports. The Response Reports derive from eight annual reports called *Oil and Hazardous Materials Response Reports* (NOAA 1994; NOAA 1995a; NOAA 1995b; NOAA 1996; NOAA 1998; NOAA 1999; NOAA 2001). Both data sources were produced by NOAA, or in association with it. The reports cover the period 1967–99—nearly 32 years in total—and describe 323 oil spills.

The empirical data is limited for several reasons. Firstly, NOAA was responsible for drawing up these reports, so there is a high level of consistency within the individual reports as well as between them. The fact that the NOAA used a specific set of criteria for the inclusion of the spills partly explains this consistency. The following criteria were applied for inclusion in the Case Histories (NOAA 1992):

- spills exceeding 100,000 bbl internationally, or
- spills exceeding 10,000 bbl in US waters, or
- spill involving the use of dispersants, or
- spills involving bioremediation, or
- spills involving severe environmental impacts (more than 500 birds killed, more than 100 mammals killed, smothering of over a mile of intertidal zone, closure of fisheries, and so on).

A spill exceeding 10,000 barrels (not necessarily oil) is classed as a major incident. To give the reader an idea of the scale of such a spill: one barrel [bbl] equals about 159 liters of oil. A sizable US road tanker carries about 250 barrels, so a 10,000-barrel spill is no small event; a ruptured storage tank or fuel tank of a marine vessel may cause a spill on this scale.

The authors of the Response Reports state that they use the same format as in the Case Histories, but they actually describe every event in which NOAA assisted, so the reports also include many smaller spills. Thus, two F–N curves are presented below, based on the assumption that the Case Histories and the Response Reports themselves provide consistent datasets. For the Case Histories, this assumption is reasonable because a fixed set of criteria was used. The Response Reports are also assumed to be consistent because a limited group of NOAA experts provided assistance and also performed a specific task. Moreover, the fact that the reporting took place within the jurisdiction of a single nation, the United States, contributes to the consistency of the data. For an F–N curve to render a useful result, a consistent set of data is important, as well as a sufficient number of incidents, and the NOAA data meet these criteria.

A case report in the annual reports and in the Case Histories comprises the following information (NOAA 1994):

- a list of headers that summarizes the spill name, location, product, size, use of dispersants, bioremediation, and in-situ burning, along with other special interests, the shoreline types affected, and keywords;
- a brief incident summary, including weather conditions and a description of the overall spill response;
- a description of the behavior of the spilled material, including movement, evaporation, mousse formation, and dispersion;
- a discussion of countermeasures and mitigation;
- a description of other special interest issues, such as communication problems, unusual hazards encountered, and large losses of organisms;
- a list of references that document the response operations.

This list of elements typically results in a description of two to four pages per incident.

The NOAA reports describe the extent of the damage in detail. The resources that are considered to be at risk are the following (NOAA 1994):

- **Habitats**—67 shoreline types are mentioned, including eelgrass beds, submerged aquatic vegetation (SAV), kelp, coral reefs, and worm beds.
- **Marine mammals**—These include whales, dolphins, sea lions, seals, sea otters, manatees, walruses, polar bears, population concentration areas, haulouts, migration routes, and seasonal use areas.
- **Terrestrial mammals**—these include mustelids, rodents, deer, bears, population concentration areas, and intertidal feeding areas.
- **Birds**—These include diving coastal birds, waterfowl, alcids, petrels, fulmars, shorebirds, wading birds, gulls, terns, raptors, rookeries, foraging areas, wintering areas, migration stopover areas, wintering concentration areas, nesting beaches, migratory routes, and critical forage areas.
- **Fish**—These include anadromous fish, beach spawners, kelp spawners, nursery areas, reef fish (including fish using hard-bottom habitats), spawning streams, spawning beaches, estuarine fish, and demersal fish.
- **Mollusks**—These include oysters, mussels, clams, scallops, abalone, conch, whelk, squid, octopus, seedbeds, leased beds, abundant beds, harvest areas, and high-concentration sites.
- **Crustaceans**—These include shrimp, crabs, lobster, nursery areas, and high-concentration sites.
- **Reptiles**—These include sea turtles, alligators, nesting beaches, and high-concentration areas.
- **Recreational areas**—These include beaches, marinas, boat ramps, diving areas, high-use recreational boating areas, high-use recreational fishing areas, and state parks.
- **Management areas**—These include marine sanctuaries, national parks, refuges, wildlife preserves, and reserves.
- **Resource extraction**—This includes subsistence, officially designated harvest sites, commercial fisheries, power plant water intakes, drinking water intakes, industrial water intakes, intertidal and subtidal mining leases, fish/shrimp/bivalve/plant aquaculture sites, and log storage areas.
- **Cultural**—This includes archaeological sites and Native American lands.

This list makes it clear that representing oil spills by an F–N curve which only records the size in bbl obscures detailed information about the observable environmental damage. Obviously, the location of the oil spill determines the extent of the environmental damage. NOAA classifies spill products as follows (NOAA 1994):

- **Type 1**—Very Light Oils (jet fuels, gasoline);
- **Type 2**—Light Oils (diesel, no. 2 fuel oil, light crudes);
- **Type 3**—Medium Oils (most crude oils);
- **Type 4**—Heavy Oils (heavy crude oils, no. 6 fuel oil, bunker C oil);
- **Type 5**—Hazardous Material.

In order to ensure that our empirical study only includes oil spills, the dataset is restricted to types 1–4. Some of the oils are refined oils produced in an industrial refining process, such as diesel, jet fuel, and bunker oil. Others are crude oils: unprocessed products from a well. Note that these too fall into different types. The reason for this is that the NOAA bases its classification on how the fluid behaves in the environment, not on its origin.

NOAA Data in Risk Analysis

As described above, the construction of the F–N curve as a representation of risk (R_s) requires two elements: the probability of the occurrence of an oil spill and the extent of the damage. For the F–N curve, we can only use strictly quantifiable information. This data is included in the NOAA reports, and was extracted as follows.

With the use of historic data, which is the case here, the probability of spills (P_i) is equated with the frequency of spills. This frequency is not actually in the case descriptions. Instead, it is derived from the recorded dates of oil spills. That makes the recorded date of the spill a quantified data point for this analysis. Note that the recorded date is typically the first day on which the event took place. It is quite possible for an oil spill to be an event that unfolds over the course of several days, thereby increasing the length of the event as well as the volume of oil spilt. Sometimes the origin of a discovered spill is unknown, in which case the date of the discovery is recorded. This implies that the recorded date of the spill is not an exact data point. However, since we are analyzing here a period of years, the influence of these variations is small, if not negligible.

The case descriptions include the extent of the damage (C_i) in terms of an estimated amount of oil spilt, either in barrels or in US gallons (1 bbl equals 42 US gallons). This quantified data is used in the F–N curve in conjunction with the spill date. However, the estimated amount of oil gives only a limited indication of the observable environmental damage.

Calculations of the size of a spill may rely on objective information, such as the amount of oil in a tank during a rupture. In some cases, however, the reference points are not clear, for example because the source of the spill is unknown, so estimates of the size of the spill depend purely on the expertise of the NOAA assessor. It is difficult to gauge how accurate these estimates have been. We may assume that the NOAA personnel at the time were well trained and their estimates are therefore relatively accurate, but there is no way of proving that. At this point, we can only accept the figures as correct while acknowledging that uncertainties remain. Table 8.2 in the Appendix to this chapter presents the data used to construct the F–N curve from the NOAA Case Histories.

Method of Analysis

Plotting an F–N Curve

An F–N curve is a form of a frequency distribution plot. The method for plotting it is similar to a log-probability graph, but presented in a different way: the axes are inverted (probability is on the y-axis), and the probability axis is not inverted to represent a normal distribution, but is presented as a log-scale.[1] The procedure for constructing the F–N curve from the historical data in the NOAA reports is as follows:

1 Readers can find further information on the presentation of statistical data in handbooks such as Devore (1999), which was used for this chapter.

1. Data points are extracted from the case descriptions. A data point consists of the date of a spill and its size in barrels of oil [bbl]. The name of the spill is included in the database for reference purposes only.
2. The total time span for the series is determined by subtracting the lowest spill date from the highest spill date. This yields the total time span in years [year].
3. The complete list of spills is sorted according to the size of the spill.
4. The spills are ranked as follows: the largest spill is allocated the lowest rank of 1; the second largest spill is allocated following rank number, 2, and so on until the smallest spill in the collection.
5. The rank numbers are divided by the total time span calculated in step 2. This yields the spill frequency per year [year^{-1}].
6. The figure is plotted in a scatter plot where the spill size in barrels [bbl] is on the x-axis and the frequency [year^{-1}] is on the y-axis; usually, a log-log scale is used for deriving this figure.

The result is the F–N curve for historical data. Figures 8.1 and 8.2 below show the results of this exercise.

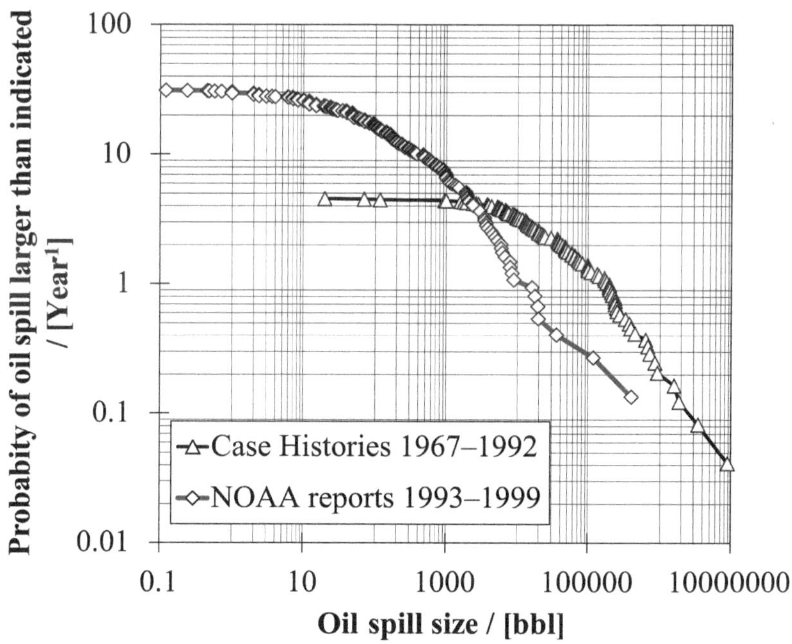

Figure 8.1 **F–N curves for oil spills based on NOAA Case Histories and NOAA Response Reports**

Results

Figures 8.1 and 8.2 present the frequency distribution of oil spills within a given time span. A data point represents the probability of a spill larger than B, where B represents the size of the spill in barrels [bbl].

Direct Interpretation of the Results

Figure 8.1 shows two curves: one for the Case Histories, and one for all of the Response Reports. As mentioned above, the Case Histories span a period of 24.4 years (1967–91), and the Response Reports cover a period of 7.4 years (1992–9). The graph reflects the difference in the reference periods.

Based on the Case Histories, the largest spill occurs with a frequency of 0.041 [year^{-1}]. When we use data from the Response Reports, the frequency is 0.134 [year^{-1}]. These figures are the inverse of the exact number of years available in the dataset. The two data points also represent the upper limit of sensible frequency estimates, implying that a spill larger than 9,000,000 [bbl] or 406,000 [bbl] occurs less frequently than 0.041 [year^{-1}] (once every 24.4 years) or once in 0.134 [year^{-1}] (once in 7.44 years), respectively.

The number of data points in the curve is important for the data point representing the smallest spill. The case histories show that the probability of a spill larger than 20 barrels occurring is 4.51 per year: in other words, on average, 4.51 oil spills happen per year. The median spill (spill 55 in the case histories) records a spill of 33,032 barrels with a frequency of 2.25 per year. This indicates that the probability of having a spill larger than 30,032 [bbl] is 2.25 per year.

The Response Reports include only spills of 10,000 barrels or more, and here the probability is 0.11 [bbl] and the frequency is 31 [year^{-1}]. When we add more data points, the frequency for the smallest spills increases.

The Size of the Deepwater Horizon *Spill*

How the *Deepwater Horizon* spill relates to the data presented here is an interesting question. It was a continuous spill of over three months' duration, and estimates of its size vary from 1,000 to 50,000 barrels per day (BP 2010). Here, we will use the final estimate of 4,900,000 barrels of oil as recorded in the report to the President on the *Deepwater Horizon* spill (Graham et. al. 2011).

A direct comparison of the historic data and the *Deepwater Horizon* spill makes clear that the size of the latter was smaller than the spill in the Arabian Gulf, which amounted to 9,000,000 [bbl], and larger than the second largest spill of 3,522,400 [bbl]. The fact that the Arabian Gulf was an intentional result of war sets it somewhat apart from accidental spills, but it is incorporated in the database and therefore treated the same as other spills. Even if the spill resulted from war, it is unclear whether the violators knew just how serious the damage would become beforehand; also, in the case of the *Deepwater Horizon* spill, was that not also tainted by severe neglect? So the frequencies of occurrence of the largest and second largest spills are 0.082 [year^{-1}] and 0.041 [year^{-1}], respectively. The comparison with historical data suggests that an oil spill the size of the *Deepwater Horizon* one occurs with a frequency of 0.041–0.082 [year^{-1}]. This would indicate that an oil spill of that size, somewhere on the globe, could occur every 12.2–24.4 years.

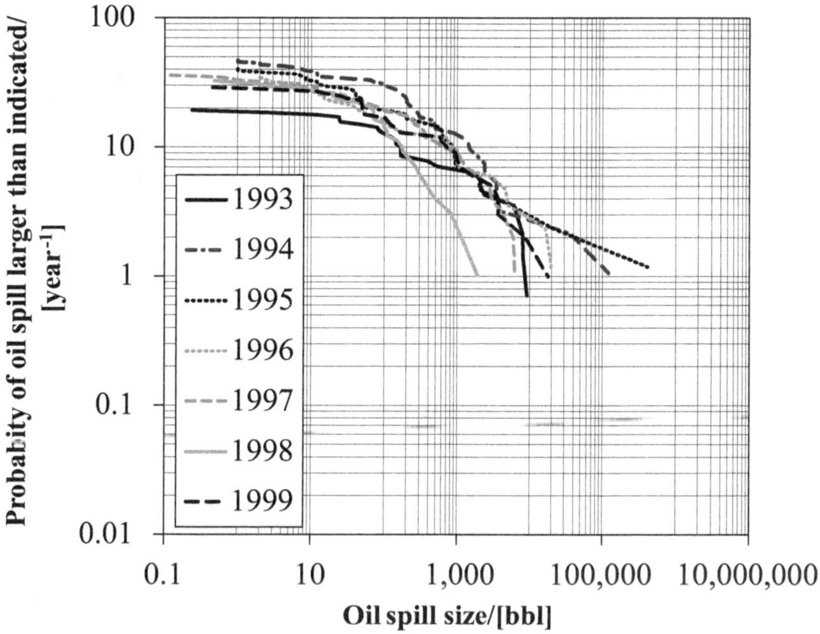

Figure 8.2 Individual F–N curves for NOAA Response Reports 1993–99

However, to increase the accuracy of the estimate, it is better to consider a number of spills. When we look at spills that are larger than 1,000,000 barrels of oil, four of these are reported in the Case Histories: the Arabian Gulf spill, the *Ixtoc I* spill (Bahia de Camheche), the Nowruz oil field, and the sinking of the *Amoco Cadiz*. The frequency of occurrence of spills larger than 1,000,000 [bbl] is 0.16–0.21 [year^{-1}]. Clearly, super-spills are not unheard of; they are actually not exceedingly rare.

Now consider Figure 8.2, which represents the data points for the individual NOAA Response Reports, broken down by reporting year.

Logically, the frequency of the largest spill does not exceed 1 [year^{-1}] because the reporting period is one year. The F–N curves show variations from year to year. In 1994, the number of spills is large (the small leak data point has a high frequency), and in 1995 the largest spill occurs (the large leak data point is the largest). Table 8.1 gives some characteristics data for the F–N curve.

Table 8.1 Characteristics of F–N curves per NOAA reporting year

NOAA reporting year	No. of oil spills/[year^{-1}]	Largest spill/[bbl]
1993	27	9,100
1994	44	119,000
1995	34	406,000
1996	29	19,643
1997	36	6,250
1998	32	1,904
1999	29	17,857

Like Figure 8.2, Table 8.1 shows that there is no obvious trend in the data: the number of oil spills varies per year, and does not show a significant decrease or increase. The same holds true for the size of the spills, which varies even more than then number of reported spills. Based on the data from the Response Reports, we can conclude that oil spills are recurring and hard to predict.

Spill Types

Having conducted a general assessment of the frequency of oil spills, it is useful to examine the data to determine the types of spill. We will base this exercise on the Case Histories, since the size of the *Deepwater Horizon* spill falls within their spill size range. The Case Histories distinguish seven origins of oil spills:

1. tank vessels
2. non-tank vessels
3. barges
4. facilities
5. pipelines
6. platforms
7. unknown.

Tank vessels are sea-going oil tankers that can carry loads in excess of two million barrels of oil. Non-tank vessels are defined as sea-going vessels that do not carry oil as cargo. Barges are river-going tankers or river going non-tankers. Facilities are land-based production or storage facilities. Pipelines are oil pipelines. Platforms are sea-based production facilities. The category 'unknown' refers to spills whose origin has not been determined. However, there is only one unknown oil spill of 119 barrels recorded in the Case Histories. Figure 8.3 shows the oil spill sizes categorized by their origin.

Every marker indicates a spill and its size, and the line indicates the range of oil spills in a given group. The outcomes show that tank vessels make up more than 50 percent of all recorded oil spills. The size of these spills varies from under 100 barrels up to 1,619,048 barrels with the sinking of the very large crude oil carrier *Amoco Cadiz*. Note that the *Exxon Valdez* spill is only a mid-size incident, with 204,500 barrels of oil spilt (the frequency is 0.70 [year^{-1}]—just over once a year).

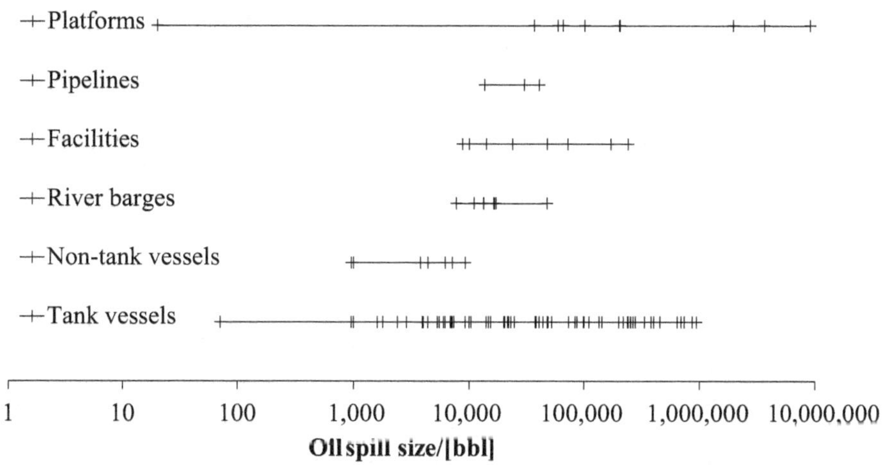

Figure 8.3 Oil spill sizes categorized by origin

The size of the spills from tank vessels depends on the severity of the damage to the ship and how the incident was responded to. Non-tanker ships create much smaller spills because they only carry bunker fuel for propulsion. The Case Histories show that spills larger than 10,000 barrels do not occur with these ships. Inland ships also tend to give rise to smaller spills; as a rule they carry much less oil, but the environmental damage is usually significant because of the confined water channels. Facilities and pipelines cause relatively big spills of up to about 250,000 barrels. Production platforms caused three out of four super-spills of over 1,000,000 barrels. In fact, the only facilities that can produce spills of such magnitude are active wells and supertankers that lose all their cargo. In the 24 years covered by the Case Histories, this is reported four times, which yields a frequency of a little over 0.2 [$year^{-1}$]. This equals one spill of over 1,000,000 barrels occurring somewhere on the globe every five years.

Discussion

Although this chapter provides an indication of the recurrence of oil spills and the probability of super-spills occurring, it is difficult to be precise. All three types of uncertainty are present: epistemic, aleatory, and modeling uncertainty. Firstly, a historic analysis published in 1991, covering the period 1967–91, underlies the estimate for the occurrence of an incident such as the *Deepwater Horizon* spill. It is possible that prevention and control of oil spills have improved since this period. Despite the fact that the data obtained from the Response Reports do not suggest structural improvements until 1999, this does not allow us to conclude that nothing significant has been achieved since then. The extrapolation of the historic data for comparison with modern-day information introduces modeling uncertainties that cannot be evaluated with the current dataset. Without further analysis, it is equally impossible to indicate whether spill frequencies have increased or decreased.

This analysis has focused primarily on the frequency of *large* oil spills. Fortunately, large spills are more easily recovered in a historic analysis, and more difficult to hide from reporting systems. This suggests that the frequency estimates for large spills are less sensitive to variations in the data. For instance, when the number of spills in a given period increases, this does not affect the data point for the largest spill (except when a larger oil spill goes undiscovered). Lengthening of the analysis period, say by one year, increases the number of recorded spills and the probability of large spills being detected, so again, this should not substantially affect the recorded frequency for *large* spills. Aleatory uncertainty is therefore less of a problem in the case of large spills than it is for small spills.

Another complication is the differences between the two datasets: the Case Histories were selected according to a specific set of criteria, but the Response Reports simply report actions and advice given by NOAA after oil spills occurred. The latter mostly concern relatively small spills in the USA, and only occasionally a large spill elsewhere in the world. This is why we computed two F–N curves in Figure 8.1. Strictly speaking, however, the evidence for the findings presented here is based on two different datasets. This modeling uncertainty will be dealt with by dividing the conclusion into two parts.

In theory, the F–N curve can only be exact when it incorporates *all* spills within a given period and when the number of spills included is relatively large. In practice, it is very hard to find data that meet these requirements. Reporting systems are known to suffer from under-reporting, and historic analyses may overlook spills (even large ones). As demonstrated above, the analysis period and the number of spills recorded in that period influence the estimates of spill frequencies. Furthermore, historic analyses are not subject to epistemic uncertainty because all spills have indeed materialized. However, the Response Reports do not address certain spills—for example, those of tarballs and waxes, which are oil products, but do not fit the definition used in the reports. This choice introduces epistemic uncertainty.

The uncertainties described above suggest that direct interpretation of the results requires caution. Unfortunately, the uncertainties can only be reduced through an extended search for all oil spills that have ever occurred. In theory, this would yield a better dataset, but of course this would extend the scope of the analysis presented here, and must be reserved for future research.

Conclusions

Because of the uncertainties in the data, it is only possible draw cautious conclusions. The analysis of NOAA Case History reports and Response Reports shows that:

1. Oil spills are recurring events that are difficult to predict.
2. Oil spills on the scale of the *Deepwater Horizon* incident are not particularly rare.

Historic analysis suggests that spills larger than 1,000,000 barrels of oil occur with a frequency of about once every five years.

This chapter is a prelude to further research into oil spills. It was driven by the following research question: How often do oil spills occur, and what can we learn from them? Since finding out everything about *all oil spills ever* would be a huge task, this chapter focused on publicly available and relatively coherent datasets: NOAA Case Histories and Response Reports that cover a period of about 32 years.

The assessment method is risk-based, which frees the analysis of discussions about crime or criminal behavior during the course of an oil spill. The question of whether an oil spill was a criminal act was beyond the scope of this chapter. It used an F–N curve to present the damage caused by oil spills. This type of presentation obscures much of the observable environmental damage, but highlights how often large oil spills have occurred and what spill frequencies may be expected.

Despite drawbacks resulting from the use of a limited historic dataset, it is clear that in the past oil spills have not been excessively rare events. The Case Histories, which report spills from all over the globe, show that an oil spill the size of the *Exxon Valdez* (204,500 [bbl]) occurred with a frequency of 0.70 [year^{-1}], and that super-spills of 1,000,000 barrels or more had a frequency of about 0.2 [year^{-1}]. The risk of a spill comparable to that of the *Deepwater Horizon* lies in the range 12.2–24.4 [year^{-1}].

The Response Reports show that there were no clear trends in the occurrence of oil spills. No reduction in size or frequency was measured over the seven-year period up to 1999. At least during that period there is no evidence of systematic improvement in the prevention of oil spills. However, the data do not allow us to draw conclusions for the period after 1999, although the *Deepwater Horizon* incident shows that large oil spills still happen.

In conclusion, although a direct comparison between historic spill data and the *Deepwater Horizon* spill is not straightforward, it was demonstrated that the occurrence of a spill of such magnitude is not particularly rare. Similar-sized leaks have occurred earlier, and we cannot assume that they will not happen again. Oil spills are indeed a persistent problem.

References

BP. 2010. *Deepwater Horizon Accident Investigation Report*: www.bp.com/liveassets/bp_internet/globalbp/globalbp_uk_english/incident_response/STAGING/local_assets/downloads_pdfs/Deepwater_Horizon_Accident_Investigation_Report.pdf (accessed March 6, 2014).

Cameron, I. and Raman, R. 2005. *Process Systems Risk Management*. Amsterdam: Elsevier Science Publishing.

Devore, J.L. 1999. *Probability and Statistics for Engineering and the Sciences*. Pacific Grove, NY: Duxbury.

Dowel, A.M., Bridges, W.G., Gollin, M., Greenfield, W.A., Poulson, J.M., and Turetski, W. 2001. *Layers of Protection Analysis*. New York: American Institute of Chemical Engineers.

Graham, B., Reilly, W.K., Beinecke, F., Boesch, D.F., Garcia G.D., Murray, C.A., and Ulmer, F. 2011. *Deep Water: The Gulf Oil Disaster and the Future of Offshore Drilling. Report to the President*, Washington, DC: National Commission on the BP Deepwater Horizon Oil Spill and Offshore Drilling: www.gpo.gov/fdsys/pkg/GPO-OILCOMMISSION/pdf/GPO-OILCOMMISSION.pdf (accessed March 6, 2014).

Kaplan, S. and Garrick, B.J. 1981. 'On the Quantitative Definition of Risk', *Risk Analysis* 1, 11–27.

Mannan S. 2005. *Lee's Loss Prevention in the Process Industries*, 3rd edn. Amsterdam: Elsevier Butterworth Heinemann.

NOAA. 1992. *Oil Spill Case Histories*. Seattle, WA: NOAA Hazardous Materials Response and Assessment Division.

NOAA. 1994. *Oil and Hazardous Materials Response Reports October 1992–September 1993*. Seattle, WA: NOAA Hazardous Materials Response and Assessment Division.
NOAA. 1995a. *Oil and Hazardous Materials Response Reports October 1993–September 1994*. Seattle, WA: NOAA Hazardous Materials Response and Assessment Division.
NOAA. 1995b. *Oil and Hazardous Materials Response Reports October 1994–September 1995*. Seattle, WA: NOAA Hazardous Materials and Response and Assessment Division.
NOAA. 1996. *Oil and Hazardous Materials Response Reports October 1995–September 1996*. Seattle, WA: NOAA Hazardous Materials Response and Assessment Division.
NOAA. 1998. *Oil and Hazardous Materials Response Reports October 1996–September 1997*. Seattle, WA: NOAA Hazardous Materials Response and Assessment Division.
NOAA. 1999. *Oil and Hazardous Materials Response Reports October 1997–September 1998*. Seattle, WA: NOAA Hazardous Materials Response and Assessment Division.
NOAA. 2001. *Oil and Hazardous Materials Response Reports October, 2001*. Seattle, WA: NOAA Hazardous Materials Response and Assessment Division.
Perrow, C. 1984. *Normal Accidents: Living with High Risk Technologies*. New York: Basic Books.
Steffy, L.C. 2011. *Drowning in Oil*. New York: McGraw-Hill.

Appendix

Table 8.2 Data used to construct the F–N curve

Spill size [bbl]	Case # [-]	Name	Date
20	81	Seal Beach well blowout	10/31/90
71	30	E-24	11/22/85
119	104	Whideby Island	12/21/84
952	45	*Howard Star*	10/5/78
1000	72	Rockaway Fuel Oil	7/31/78
1604	55	MCN-5	1/31/88
1786	22	Buckeye Pipeline	3/30/90
1932	20	*Bouchard #65*	1/9/77
2380	88	*Tamano*	7/22/72
2660	29	*Corinthos*	1/31/75
2857	78	*Seaspeed Arabia*	6/30/79
3774	16	*Bahia Paradiso*	1/28/91
3925	58	Mobiloil	3/19/84
4000	42	*Hamilton Trader*	4/30/69
4400	74	*Sarako Harvest*	2/13/91
5300	68	*Patmos*	3/21/85
5500	59	*Nestucca*	12/23/88
5690	10	ARCO Anchorage	12/21/85
5959	87	STC-101	2/2/76
6190	73	*Ryuyo Maru #2*	11/8/79
6873	107	*World Prodigy*	6/23/89
7000	39	*Globik Sun*	8/15/75
7143	91	*Tenyo Maru*	7/22/91

Spill size [bbl]	Case # [-]	Name	Date
7310	70	*Presidente Rivera*	6/24/89
7350	1	*Al Rewdatain*	10/29/77
7679	109	Z-102	12/9/75
8700	83	Shell Oil complex	4/23/85
9200	66	*Pac Baroness*	9/21/87
9458	5	*American Trader*	2/7/90
10000	4	Amerada Hess Oil	9/20/89
10000	17	*Bayou Kafousche*	3/9/73
10000	34	Ethel H (II)	2/4/77
10357	40	*Grand Eagle*	9/28/85
11000	69	*Peck Slip*	12/19/78
11900	3	*Amazon Venture*	12/4/86
13212	100	V884	4/2/83
13300	102	*Vista Bella*	3/6/91
13500	35	Exxon Bayway Refinery	1/2/90
14000	63	*Olympic Alliance*	11/12/75
14000	105	*Witwater*	12/13/68
14070	99	VL Water and Power	9/18/89
14720	18	*Betelgeuze*	1/8/79
15350	60	*Nord Pacific*	7/13/88
16300	82	SFI 41	11/24/85
16476	7	APEX 4317	7/28/90
17055	93	Texas	3/7/86
18149	28	*Concho*	1/19/81
20000	25	Chevron Hawaii	9/1/79
20000	50	*Jupiter*	9/16/90
20000	64	*Olympic Glory*	1/28/81
20400	65	*Oregon Standard*	1/18/71
21990	27	*Christos Bitas*	10/12/78
23000	33	Esso Puerto Rico	9/3/88
23810	13	Ashland Petroleum Co.	1/2/88
24780	67	*Pacific Glory*	10/23/70
30000	75	*Sanshena*	12/17/76
36650	95	*Trinimar Marine*	8/8/73
37579	110	*Zoe Colocotronis*	3/18/73
37700	38	*General Colomironis*	3/7/68
38500	71	*Puerto Rican*	10/31/84
40476	54	Lakehead Pipeline	3/3/91
40900	24	*Cabo Pilar*	10/8/87
43900	53	*Kurdistan*	3/15/79
47619	41	Hackensack Estuary	5/26/85
47620	97	UMTB 283	12/26/88
48000	85	*Sivand*	9/28/83
48875	79	*Sea Spirit*	8/6/80
52500	32	*Eleni V*	5/6/78
58640	84	Shell platform 26	12/1/70

Table 8.2 Data used to construct the F–N curve *continued*

Spill size [bbl]	Case # [-]	Name	Date
58640	108	YUMII/*Zapoteca*	10/10/87
65000	2	*Alverna*	7/30/84
65000	26	Chevron Pass Block 41	2/10/70
72000	96	US Strategic Petroleum	9/21/78
73600	21	*Brazilian Marine*	1/9/78
77000	12	*Arrow*	2/4/70
83200	62	*Ocean Eagle*	3/3/68
98955	89	*Tanio*	3/7/80
100000	43	*Hasbah 6*	10/2/80
100000	56	*Mega Borg*	6/8/90
100000	76	*Sata Barbara* well	1/28/69
109950	90	*Tarik ibn Ziyad*	3/26/75
135000	52	*Kirki*	7/21/91
142857	44	*Haven*	4/11/91
170000	77	Schulkill River spill	6/22/72
175000	9	*Aragon*	12/29/89
183000	11	*Argo Merchant*	12/15/76
200000	37	*Funiwa 5*	1/17/80
200000	103	*Velfra*	2/27/71
202381	31	Ekofisk Bravo oil field	4/22/77
213692	19	*Borag*	2/5/77
219000	101	*Venoil*	12/16/77
237600	47	*Irene's Challenge*	1/17/77
240000	92	Texaco storage tank	4/27/86
240500	36	*Exxon Valdez*	3/24/89
252429	15	*Athenian Venture*	4/22/88
254761	23	*Burmak Agate*	11/1/79
279000	86	*St. Peter*	2/5/76
334043	106	*World Glory*	6/13/68
379000	14	*Assimi*	1/7/83
398019	57	*Metula*	8/9/74
452400	51	*Khark S*	12/19/89
637500	49	*Jacob Maersk*	1/29/75
687785	46	*Independer*	11/15/79
733000	98	*Urquoila*	5/12/76
860000	94	*Torrey Canyon*	3/18/67
937000	80	*Sea Star*	12/19/72
1619048	6	*Amoco Cadiz*/APEX 3417	3/16/78
1904762	61	Nowruz oil field	2/4/83
3522400	48	*Ixtoc I*	6/3/79
9000000	8	Arabian Gulf	1/19/91

Chapter 9
A Decade of Violations in the Dutch Chemical Industry

Marieke Kluin and Ellen Jagtman

Introduction

This chapter presents the results of a trend analysis of four Dutch chemical corporations. The results are part of a larger study of 15 corporations in the Rotterdam-Rijnmond area in the west of the Netherlands. The analysis draws upon all registered violations of occupational health and safety as well as environmental regulations during 1999–2011 for each corporation. It shows the sanctioning practices of the Dutch Occupational Health and Safety Agency (OHSA) and Environmental Protection Agency (EPA) over the same time frame.

Criminological research has consistently discovered a positive correlation between past and future criminal behaviour (Nagin and Farrington 1992; Paternoster and Nagin 1991). One of the most persistent findings is that people who commit a crime at one point are more likely to commit non-compliance behaviour at a later point than non-offenders. Results of longitudinal studies of organizational crime demonstrate that most offenders are recidivists, but that only a small group of corporations is responsible for a considerable amount of the crimes committed (Clinard and Yeager 1980; Sutherland 1983; Simpson et al. 2007; Simpson and Schell 2009). Simpson and Schell (2009) conclude that it is uncertain whether these observed relationships reflect general patterns, or simply particular violations in particular periods. The results of the present study show that violations of corporations are overarching and not specifically related to just one corporation. In this chapter, we address the following research questions:

- What are the enforcement practices in the Netherlands with regard to a number of corporations that are subject to the Seveso regulations?
- Is there a relationship between prior violations and future violations when analysing the registered violations?

To answer these questions, we will focus on Dutch-based corporations. These fall under the scope of the Seveso II Directive: EU legislation that deals specifically with the control of major accidents involving dangerous substances. The Seveso legislation also aims to limit the consequences of such accidents for humans and for the environment. This research involved the most densely populated area of the Netherlands, Rotterdam-Rijnmond. It is a heavily industrialized area with large chemical plants, refineries, waste disposal corporations and residential areas, containing the largest concentration of Seveso corporations (140) in the Netherlands. Although the chemical corporations studied here are based in the Netherlands, most of them act internationally and produce, store and transport dangerous goods throughout Europe.

Gibbs and Simpson (2009) conclude that accurate measurement of corporate environmental crime is important for a number of reasons. To begin with, better insight into environmental crime rates could assist enforcement officials in the allocation of their resources. Second, it can increase our understanding of corporate environmental crime.[1] Third, it can provide insights into whether a lack of environmental performance is the result of opportunistic behaviour or of some criminogenic element within the corporation. Fourth, comparing the environmental crime rates of a number of corporations is a consistent method for classifying environmental performance because differences in corporation size are incorporated into the crime rate. In addition to this, theoretical descriptions and typologies of environmental crime are virtually non-existent, and accurate measurement can contribute to their development.

We will begin this chapter with some background on methodology and data, along with information on the EPA, the OHSA and Seveso and its databases, and their limitations. Next, we will describe the overall picture of violations and enforcement actions of 15 corporations. After that, we will discuss the sample and classification of the corporations. The remainder of the chapter consists of descriptions of the most striking violations among the corporations – all severe enforcement actions, involving large numbers of violations and recidivism. The study of four chemical corporations is based upon all registered violations and enforcement actions, and participant observations of situations relating to violations during Seveso inspections.

Methodology and Data

As will become clear in the next section, environmental data is complex and problematic. For example, for our purposes it was important to conduct research on corporate environmental violations involving smaller corporations in order to have a regional focus and to include corporations in the same industry. Moreover, the present study goes beyond registered violations and includes interactions between field-level inspectors and corporations.

Corporate offending herein is measured using all violations collected from the databases and archives of the Regional Environmental Protection Agency, the Occupational Health and Safety Agency and a shared database, especially for Seveso violations. All registered violations and enforcement activities resulting from occupational health and safety and environmental regulations were studied in relation to a period of more than ten years (1999–2011). The exact available data per corporation differ for several reasons. First, not all corporations in the sample have been in existence since 1999, the beginning of our time frame. Second, the databases were under development in earlier years, which is described in more detail in the next section. Third, Dutch corporations were obliged to submit their first Safety Report in February 2001 (Van Steen et al. 2001), therefore some corporations were not subjected to Seveso inspections prior to 2001. Data before 2001 covered Seveso pilot projects and results of other inspections obligated by Dutch law. Another source of information has been used in addition to the databases: participant observations of violations during Seveso inspections. Observations of Seveso inspections were carried out during 2009–12. Descriptions and limitations of the databases are provided in the following sections.

1 Consistent with Sutherland (1961), Braithwaite (1984) and Simpson et al (2007) we define corporate crime as a violation of any legislative requirement (regulatory, civil or criminal). We use the terms 'violation' and 'crime' interchangeably.

The Regional Environmental Protection Agency and a Description of the MIRR Database[2]

The DCMR Environmental Protection Agency is the Dutch regional environmental agency of the local and regional authorities operating in Rotterdam-Rijnmond, which includes the harbour of Rotterdam. The DCMR was founded in 1972 in order to improve environmental protection in this region, which is an industrialized area containing refineries, waste incinerators, several waste dumping sites, many large chemical plants, metallurgy and food processing plants and about 19,500 smaller companies. The tasks of the DCMR include regulation of the industries, monitoring performance, and assisting the authorities in developing suitable environmental policies. This study uses violation data collected from the 'Milieu Informatie Systeem Regio Rijnmond' (MIRR) database. The DCMR uses MIRR as an online system to monitor enforcement and compliance. Before 2001, the DCMR used a different database (Meuwissen 2004), from which the data was transferred to MIRR. The database contains enforcement and sanctioning data. MIRR captures a wider range of non-compliance behaviour than prosecution data, but still underestimates non-compliance. As mentioned above, the data for earlier years are probably less complete. Another well-known limitation is under-reporting of crime due to undetected or unsanctioned violations. It does, however, register informal enforcement actions, such as warning letters and phone calls. Other entries consist of assessments of reports handed in by the corporations, and incident and project results. Some of the incidents are categorized as exceptional. A corporation is obligated to try to control the consequences of its operations. In addition, corporations must report such incidents ('Ongewoon voorval', Dutch Environmental Management Act, Art. 17.1). Inspection data is also registered in the MIRR database. Such data result from visual inspections (for example, to determine whether an exhaust hood is installed) and from reviewing procedures, interviewing personnel and inspecting installations. Limitations are present in the inspection data as well, because violations can only be detected if an inspection is conducted. Inspection results may provide an indicator of actual crime, to the extent that the EPA can decide effectively whether a corporation has broken the law. Inspection data could be misinterpreted if corporations were only inspected for reasons such as size. Under the Seveso II Directive, all Seveso-related inspections of upper-tier corporations are conducted annually. In addition, limitations can occur when budgetary issues restrict the number of inspectors or inspections, for example. As Gibbs and Simpson (2009) conclude, visual observations still neglect non-compliance activities that go unnoticed by regulatory enforcement agencies. Besides this, inspectors may choose to exclude violations from the official inspection report when, for example, a corporation remedies the problem during the inspection. As Bentham (1789 [1996]) noted, punishment is unnecessary when other kinds of control or interventions are successful. The database includes predefined categories to specify the legal framework which we used to specify environmental violations – for example, violations related to soil (Soil Protection Act), and air, noise, registration, reporting and safety violations (all of these are covered by the Dutch Environmental Management Act).

The Occupational Health and Safety Agency and the I-net Description Database[3]

The Occupational Health and Safety Agency was established on 1 March 1890, when inspectors Struve, Kuijper and Van Loben Sels began their activities in three Dutch districts

2 In Dutch: DCMR Milieudienst Rijnmond.

3 In Dutch: Inspectie Sociale Zaken en Werkgelegenheid.

(Breda, Zwolle and Haarlem). Nowadays, the OHSA is part of the Ministry of Social Affairs and Employment, and is responsible for detecting fraud, exploitation and organized crime within the chain of work and income (labour exploitation, human trafficking and large-scale social security fraud). It supervises compliance with regulations concerning illegal employment and minimum wages, and offers insight into the effectiveness of the system of work and income. In addition, the OHSA collects complaints, tip-offs and reports about industrial accidents. Employers are obliged to immediately report industrial accidents that result in hospital admission, permanent injury or death. The OHSA established a specific department to administer the Seveso rules and regulations in April 2003, the Department of Major Hazard Control. This department also supervises implementation of the Seveso II Directive in the Netherlands, including compliance with regulations regarding working conditions and the prevention of major hazards involving dangerous substances. The present study uses violation data collected from the I-net (Inspectie Net) database. This online database has been used by the OHSA to track enforcement and compliance since 2005. Before then, the OHSA relied on the GISAI (Gemeenschappelijk Informatie Systeem Arbeids Inspectie) database, introduced in 1998, and its data were transferred to I-net after the introduction of the new system.

The I-net reports concerning chemical corporations relate to accidents, complaints, programmed inspections, unannounced inspections and follow-up inspections. Since this database only contains these specific items, it comprises fewer reports per corporation than the MIRR database. The same limitations as mentioned for the MIRR database apply to the I-net database: it only lists violations the enforcement agencies have detected and sanctioned. I-net does not make use of predefined classes for the legal framework, which is different from the database used by the DCMR, but does specify the reasons for OHSA involvement. The database is useful for this study because it provides additional information which supplements the official OHSA reaction – for example, on a corporation's behaviour – and gives more insight into the interactions between corporations and inspectors.

Seveso and the GIR Description Database

As indicated above, the current implementation of the Seveso II Directive has existed in the Netherlands since 1999. This study focuses on enforcement practice during the period 1999–2011. Seveso enforcement actions aim to remedy violations in the hope that corporations will meet the legal requirements which are enforced separately by each of the inspection agencies.

In the Netherlands, an important principle underlying the implementation of the Seveso Directive is the integration of legislation in the fields of occupational health and safety, external safety and disaster management. Therefore, the various inspection agencies employ a joint inspection method. The results of these joint inspections are registered in a database called GIR (Gemeenschappelijke Inspectieruimte BRZO) that has existed since 2007 and serves as an online joint working space for the various authorities involved in the Seveso inspections. For the purpose of this study, most of the Seveso inspection results dating from before 2007 could be obtained from reports registered in the MIRR and I-net databases. However, some of the Seveso reports pre-dating 2007 could not be traced, resulting in gaps in the data.

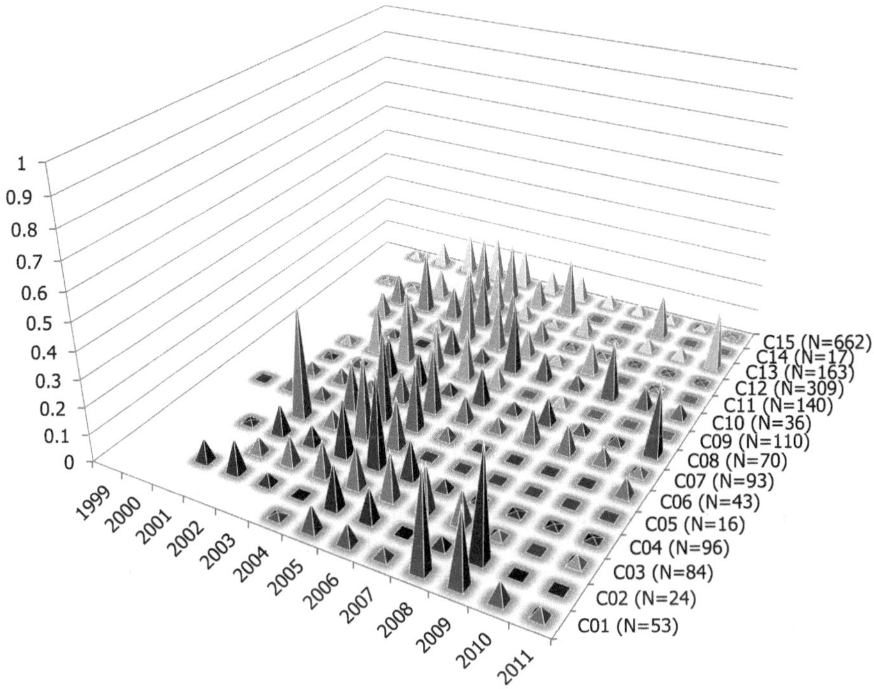

Figure 9.1 Overview of EPA violations of all 15 corporations

The Overall Picture of Violations and Enforcement Actions

The EPA and OHSA have registered a total of 2,215 violations for the 15 corporations (C01–C15) studied during 1999–2011. Of these, 1,916 were environmental violations and 299 were occupational health and safety violations. Figure 9.1 shows the EPA-registered violations for each corporation per year, while Figure 9.2 below shows the OHSA violations.

As explained earlier in this chapter, the MIRR database was under development from 1999 until 2001. This explains the empty cells for corporations in the earlier years in Figure 9.1. The outcomes show that the number of environmental violations per company varies considerably, from 16 instances for C05 to 662 for C15. Among all the 15 corporations, C15 is responsible for one third of the total number of rule violations. C12 comes second with 309 violations, which accounts for a further 16 per cent of all recorded environmental violations. The other corporations contribute 1–8 per cent to the total.

Almost three-quarters of the total number of environmental violations registered in the MIRR database took place during 2002–6. The following five years (2007–11) account for a fifth of the total number.

Apart from C12 and C15, six other corporations committed 75 per cent or more of their recorded violations during 2002–6, and less than 20 per cent during 2007–11. The number of violations of C03, C07 and C13 was also higher during 2002–6 than in the second time frame, 2007–11. However, the share over the last five years dropped less for these three corporations (37 per cent up to 42 per cent of their total number of environmental violations). C02, C08 and C10 had about the same number of violations in both periods. C01 shows a different result, because here 81 per cent of the environmental rule violations were found during 2007–11. However, we may consider this company to be an outlier because it was not subjected to Seveso inspections before 2008. Although most corporations had the largest share of environmental violations before 2007, patterns over the years differ. For example C08 and C13 show a peak in 2011. The patterns of four corporations – C02, C05, C07 and C11 – are discussed in detail in the case study below.

The picture for occupational health and safety violations (see Figure 9.2) differs from the environmental violations discussed above. The total number of violations per corporation varies from 4 (C10) to 59 (C09). As explained above, the EPA's remit covers a larger range of violations than the OHSA's, therefore it is not surprising that the number of OHSA violations is lower than the number of EPA violations. C09, C12 and C11 were responsible for 19, 17 and 13 per cent of the total number of violations, respectively; 48 per cent of the violations registered in the I-net database concern the period 2002–6, while 44 per cent relate to 2007–11. Compared to the environmental violations mentioned above, the number of occupational health and safety violations did not decrease. Again, the patterns for the 15 corporations differ considerably. Over 80 per cent of C03's violations occurred before 2002, and three-quarters or more of the violations committed by C05, C10 and C15 took place during 2002–6. All C01's violations occurred during 2007–11, and 65 per cent of C08's. When compared to the statistics on environmental violations, more corporations show years without any OHSA violations.

During the years covered by the present study, the Regional Environmental Protection Agency and the Occupational Health and Safety Agency were responsible for a total of 808 enforcement actions; 569 of these followed environmental violations, and 239 were related to occupational health and safety violations. The environmental violations resulted in fewer cases of enforcement activities than the occupational health and safety violations. Figure 9.3 shows that EPA enforcement actions made up 13–63 per cent of the number of EPA-registered violations, whereas for the OHSA, the enforcement actions accounted for 45–100 per cent of the number of registered violations. The exact cause for this is unknown, and is beyond the scope of this study.

A Case Study of Four Companies Based on Hawkins's Classification

We selected a sample of 15 corporations as part of a larger case study to explain compliance and rule violation in the framework of the interaction between field-level inspectors and regulatees. After the data analysis was completed, we discovered that it was possible to categorize the corporations in line with the classification of Hawkins (1984).

Hawkins stated that corporations' compliance with rules and regulations can range from good to bad, with organizational crime at one extreme. Hawkins developed the following four categories (Hawkins 1984, pp. 110–18):

1. **Socially responsible** – These corporations generally obey the rules when subject to regular inspection and are not subjected to severe enforcement actions such as issuing summonses. They are generally viewed as helpful and responsive to enforcement activities.

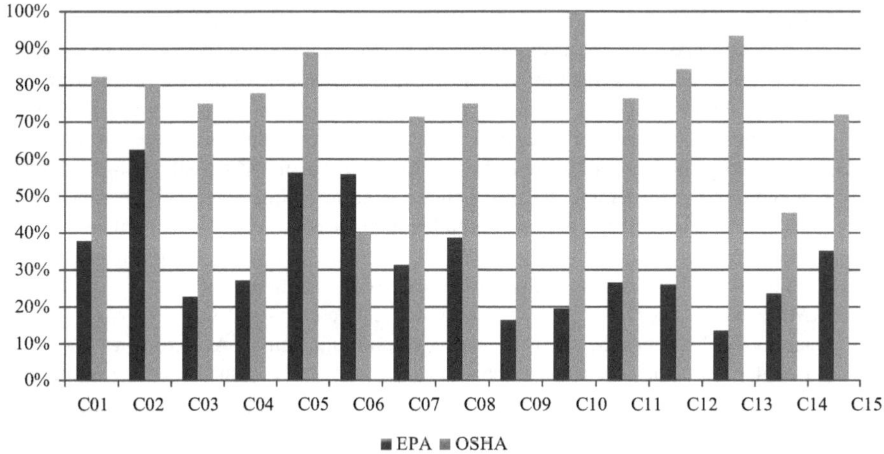

Figure 9.2 Overview of OHSA violations of all 15 corporations

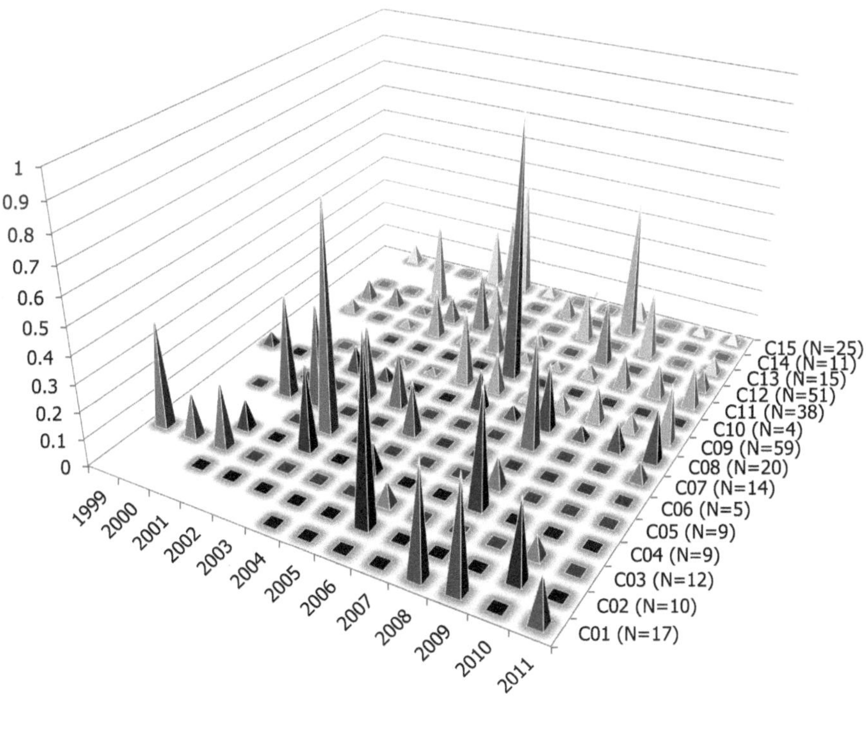

Figure 9.3 Enforcement actions as a proportion of violations per corporation

2. **Unfortunate** – Such corporations find it difficult to completely comply with inspection agencies' requests owing to technical inability or economic incapacity. Inspection agencies recognize that these companies do not possess sufficient technical knowledge and economic resources, so moral inferences about willingness to comply are not drawn here, in contrast with the two remaining categories.
3. **Careless** – These corporations can be seen as ignorant or irresponsible. Some of them find it difficult to adapt to new rules and regulations, while others fail to maintain an acceptable standard due to sloppy management, incompetence or inadequate internal sanctions. Kagan and Scholz (1984) refer to this category as 'organizationally incompetent', and blame many violations on organizational failures.
4. **Malicious** – These are corporations which deliberately try to avoid costs or reject authority. They can be seen as purposive and calculating. According to Hawkins (1984, p. 113), they are capable of both isolated and persistent instances of misconduct.

C02: An Unfortunate Corporation

Characteristics

C02 transports, stores and handles containers of hazardous substances. It is a medium-sized corporation established more than fifty years ago, with less than 250 employees, and also has establishments in other European countries. It is obliged to have a major accident prevention policy and a safety management system in place under the auspices of the Seveso II Directive (lower tier).

Violations and enforcement actions

During the period 1999–2011, C02 was responsible for a total of 24 violations of environmental rules and regulations, and a total of 10 occupational health and safety violations (see Figure 9.4).

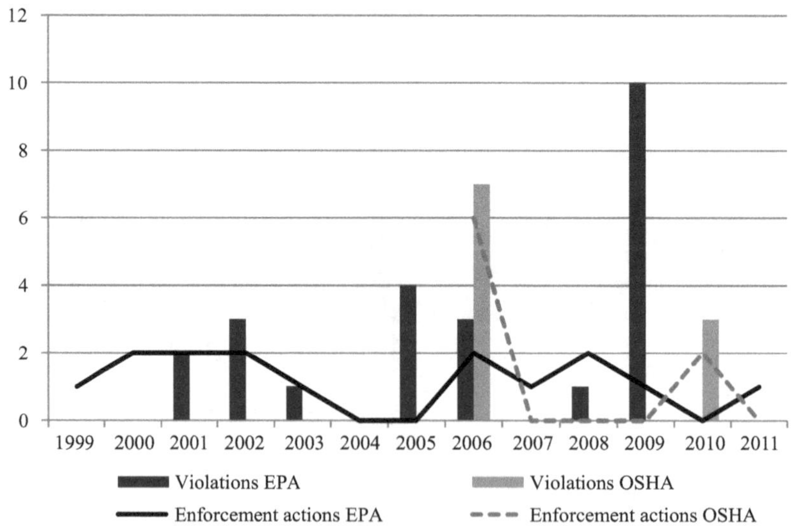

Figure 9.4 Overview of C02's violations

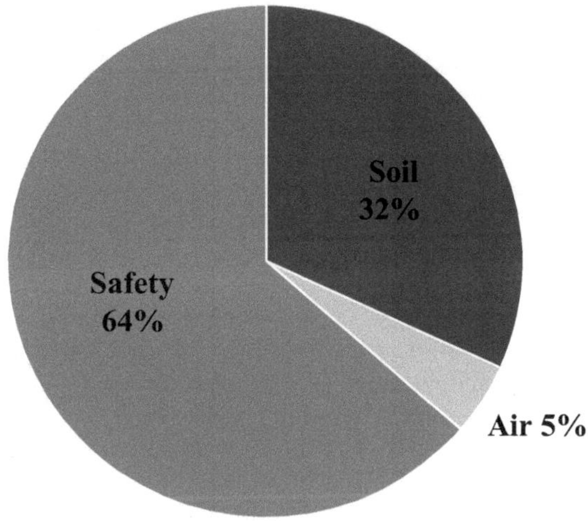

Figure 9.5 Classification of C02's environmental violations

Further analysis reveals that the majority of the environmental violations were related to safety issues (64 per cent), as can be seen in Figure 9.5. These concerned problems with fire equipment, failure to keep an up-to-date journal of hazardous goods, and dangerous storage of gas cylinders. One third of all environmental violations were related to soil issues (for example, soil protection measures or research obligations). During an environmental inspection in 2003, inspectors observed violations of regulations regarding the storage and registration of dangerous substances. One month later, an environmental inspector determined that the company had solved the observed problems. An inspection related to the introduction of the Environmental Management Act in 2009 explains the high number (10) of environmental violations during that year. The corporation was confronted with 15 enforcement actions (63 per cent) because of these environmental violations, all of which resulted in enforcement notices.

The OHSA database contains no information on C02 prior to 2006, after which all registered OHSA violations were related to Seveso rules and regulations that are described in the next section. They resulted in eight enforcement notices (80 per cent).

Registered Seveso violations and inspections

C02 has been included in the Seveso registration programme since 2002. During the first inspection in that year, inspectors identified multiple environmental violations, and the authorities subsequently allowed the corporation three months to take action to comply with the Seveso rules and regulations. The MIRR and I-net databases do not indicate whether Seveso inspections were conducted in 2004 and 2005. The inspection in 2006 was an initial one in which inspectors from all three agencies scrutinised all the safety management system elements. They detected 17 violations, of which six were related to OHSA violations. The environmental inspector identified seven other violations, and the local authorities identified four. These included an inadequate major accident prevention policy, an emergency plan that was not based on hazard and risk identification, and insufficient maintenance by the company to ensure that the premises were not accessible by unauthorized persons. As a result of follow-up activities carried out by the OHSA and EPA inspectors separately, these violations were resolved. Three environmental inspectors, two of whom were in training, carried out the 2008 Seveso inspection. They identified five violations, and the environmental inspector took enforcement action on all of these. In his enforcement notice, the inspector observed that C02 had not shown any progress in complying with the Seveso Directive since 2006. During a follow-up inspection, a violation relating to auditing remained unresolved. However, C02 did demonstrate a working method instead – a procedure which convinced the environmental inspector to grant approval. The 2009 inspection observed that C02 had made progress by appointing a permanent health and safety, quality and the environment co-ordinator, and hiring external consultants. It was felt that C02 was now more aware of the risks related to the handling of hazardous substances. Despite these improvements, the inspection team (an environmental inspector and a fire department inspector) still noted three violations, including a failure to keep a record of near-miss incidents.

The 2010 inspection was observed for the purposes of the present study. It began with the observation that no enforcement actions had been taken since the previous inspection, for reasons unclear to the environmental inspector. C02 pointed out that despite this, it had continued with its improvements. In 2010, representatives of all the inspection agencies carried out a comprehensive inspection which was prepared at a meeting in January of that year which the present authors attended. The inspection did not reveal any violations of environmental legislation, but did identify two aspects that required further improvement. With regard to corporation specifics, operational management and employees, the inspectors noticed two violations which fell under the competence of the OHSA inspector. The Dutch administrative law specifies that the competent authority must convey a formal announcement of any enforcement notice, including a description of the intended demands. The person or legal entity addressed then has the opportunity to submit views regarding the proposed requirements. In this case, C02 put forward sufficiently solid arguments to the OHSA for the authority to amend its demands. However, the OHSA did continue with two enforcement notices (observed in March 2010).

The subsequent Seveso inspection by an environmental inspector and a fire department inspector in 2011 was also observed, during which C02 demonstrated the projects and improvements it had implemented since 2010. C02 also presented a structured list of all the points for improvement it had complied with, and the inspection report concluded that C02's projects had resulted in substantial improvements. Nevertheless, the inspectors established that three violations of environmental legislation had occurred.

Conclusions

C02 ranks among the five corporations with the lowest number of violations observed in the database, and it was not subjected to severe enforcement actions following these violations. From the data, we can conclude that in earlier years C02 experienced technical problems which made it difficult to comply with its legal requirements. This improved when new personnel were hired and the corporation invested in changes in the workplace and extended its personnel's knowledge on process safety and the risks of major hazards. We therefore consider C02 to be an unfortunate corporation.

C05: A Socially Responsible Corporation

Characteristics

C05 has processed aromatic hydrocarbons for more than fifty years. It is a medium-sized corporation, part of a multinational organization with offices worldwide, that employs fewer than 250 workers. The Seveso II Directive (upper tier) stipulates that C05 is obliged to implement a major accident prevention policy, a safety management system and a safety report.

Violations and enforcement actions

C05 had a total of 16 violations of environmental regulations and nine violations of occupational health and safety rules during 1999–2011 (see Figure 9.6).

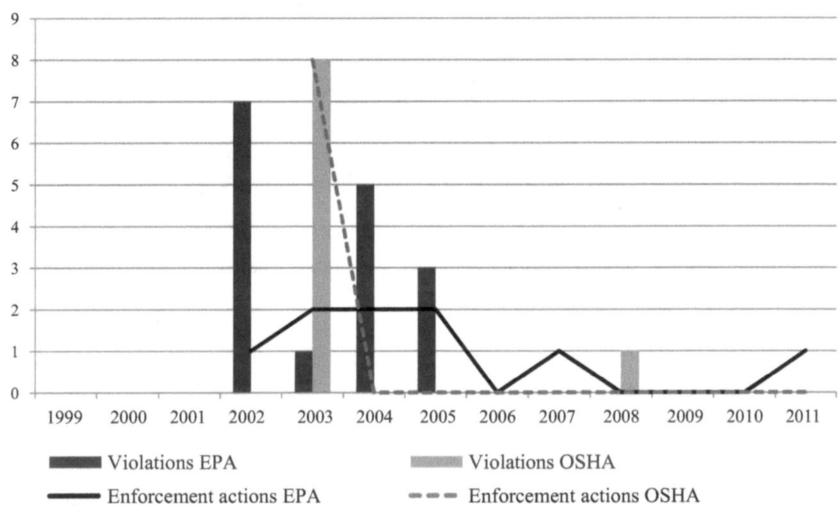

Figure 9.6 Overview of C05's violations

Figure 9.6 shows there were six environmental violations in 2002 – a high number – including leaks, soil pollution and a fire. In 2003, the OHSA also detected a relatively large number of violations of health and safety issues under the Working Conditions Act.

Figure 9.7 shows that C05 has the same percentages for general, air and safety-related violations. Most of these violations were related to the incidents mentioned above, resulting in nine EPA enforcement notices (56 per cent). In the same period, the OHSA noted a total of nine violations that resulted in eight enforcement notices (89 per cent). One of these violations was related to a maintenance shutdown which C05 was obligated to report, but failed to do so. The OHSA inspector did not continue with enforcement measures since he trusted that the corporation would not let it happen again. This is another example of the inspectors' discretion, and is mentioned in the report of the violation in the OHSA database as additional information. One of the enforcement actions consisted of a warning letter concerning working conditions. The OHSA received a complaint from one of the

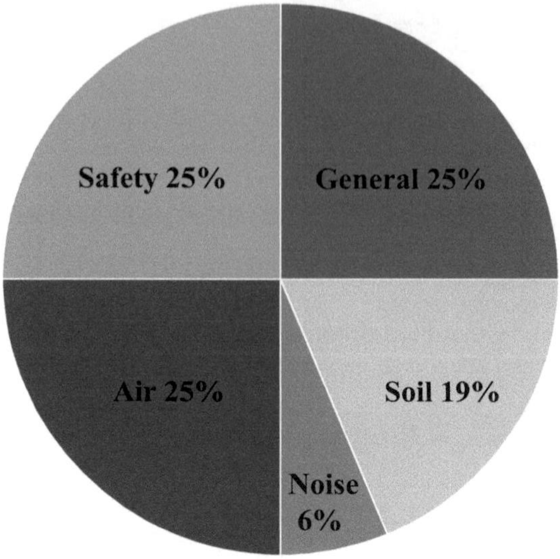

Figure 9.7 Classification of C05's environmental violations

employees in relation to working hours. OHSA inspectors investigated the complaint, but C05 proved that it had complied with the Working Conditions Act.

Registered Seveso violations and inspections

The databases mentioned Seveso inspections in 2001 and 2002, but both reports were unavailable. The first available report is from 2004, concerning a visit by inspectors from the three enforcement agencies. Although the inspection team identified points of interest, they did not detect any violations. The next available reports are for the 2007 and 2009 inspections, again involving inspectors from all three enforcement agencies, both of which identified points of interest, but did not detect any violations.

The following Seveso inspection in 2011 was observed for the present study. During it, the inspectors noticed pipelines which were not supported and were therefore waving around. C05 immediately investigated which kind of pipes these were and whether they contained product. They did, and C05 resolved the problem within the duration of the inspection. According to the inspectors, C05 showed a proactive attitude, therefore it was not classified as a violation. The inspectors took into account that C05 immediately took adequate action and that this was the only issue identified during the inspection, though they did question the adequacy of C05's own inspection procedures (observed in February 2011). This is another example of inspectors' discretion: although the final report states that problems were found, C05 adopted a proactive attitude to resolve them, so the inspectors decided not to classify them as violations (observed in February 2011; personal communication 2012).

An overview of all Seveso inspections showed that C05 was inspected every two years. This is a deviation from the norm, since C05 is an upper-tier corporation according to the Seveso rules and regulations, and therefore should be inspected annually. An OHSA inspector provided an explanation of this schedule: due to a constant lack of capacity and a new model of regulatory enforcement, it was not possible to undertake the requisite number of inspections, so the total number of inspection days for two years was combined into one inspection (personal communication 2012).

Conclusions

C05 had the lowest number of environmental violations of all the corporations, also ranking second best in the larger study concerning OHSA violations. This is even more remarkable if we take into account that it is an upper-tier, medium-sized corporation. C05 was not subject to severe enforcement actions for any of these violations. Until 2011, C05 had only one violation, and only one enforcement action after 2005. A closer look at all the Seveso inspection results suggests that C05 is a law-abiding and proactive corporation, and it is viewed as helpful and responsive to the inspection agencies' enforcement actions. Therefore, we conclude that C05 is a socially responsible corporation.

Corporation C07: A Malicious Corporation

Characteristics

C07 has been a producer of silicones, epoxy and coating resins for more than ten years. A large business with more than 250 employees, classified by the Seveso II Directive as an upper-tier corporation, it is part of a multinational organization which has offices worldwide.

Violations and enforcement actions

C07 had a total of 93 violations of environmental rules and regulations and 14 occupational health and safety violations during 1999–2011 (see Figure 9.8). With the exception of three violations, all the OHSA violations relate to Seveso rules and regulations, as described below.

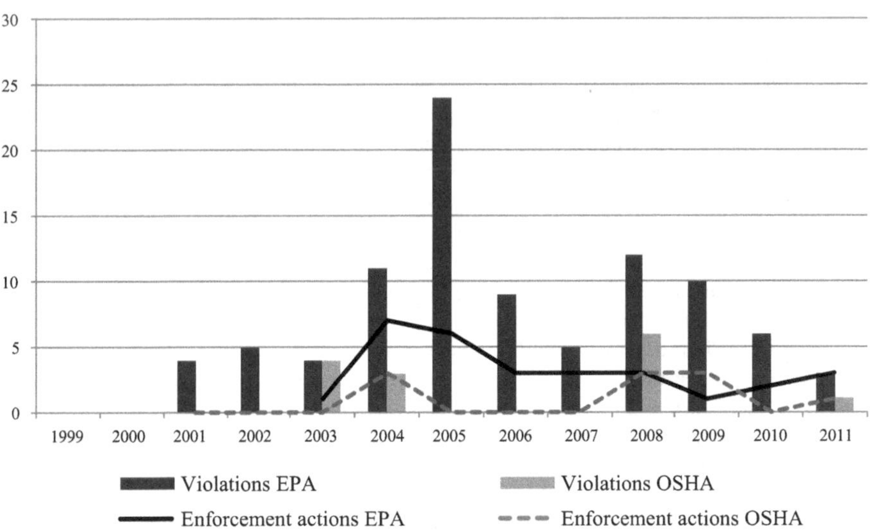

Figure 9.8 Overview of C07's violations

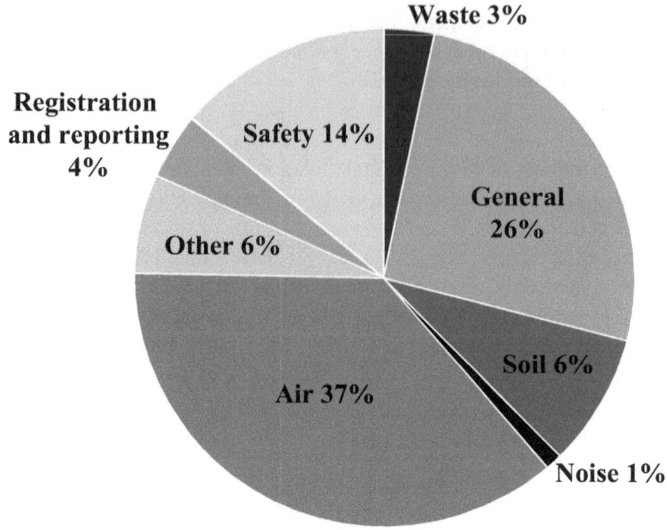

Figure 9.9 Classification of C07's environmental violations

A programmed inspection of dangerous goods storage sheds at C07 in 2004 was performed by an environmental inspector and a fire department inspector. They noted several violations, including a crack in the floor, for all of which C07 received enforcement notices. During a follow-up inspection, an environmental inspector observed that C07 had improved the situation, but points of concern still existed. In 2004, another worrying issue was that the corporation was falling behind on inspections of certain equipment, which resulted in the issuing of another enforcement notice. The vast majority of C07's environmental violations (37 per cent) relate to air quality issues (see Figure 9.9).

C07 was subject to a total of 29 enforcement actions (31 per cent), all for environmental violations. One example of an air-related problem in 2005 was when an EPA inspector detected a striking smell while driving home, and the EPA inspector subsequently discovered that C07 was responsible for it. The report mentioned that there had been a number of other similar complaints about odours emanating from C07 over the previous five years, but the data do not indicate any enforcement actions relating to air complaints in 2005 or earlier. Other incidents during this period included leaks, burst pipes and power failure (2005), some of which incidents were examined by the OHSA. One industrial accident resulted in three occupational health and safety violations. After the announcement of the enforcement notice, C07 filed an argument and the OHSA inspectors decided to extend the term for compliance to three months. The corporation was subject to a total of 10 enforcement actions (71 per cent), all of them for OHSA violations (14).

During an inspection in 2006, an environmental inspector reviewed C07's compliance measurement system. A violation was observed, and C07 received an enforcement notice allowing it six months to resolve the issue. Follow-up inspections were carried out in 2007 and 2008. After the 2008 inspection, the EPA decided to send a letter notifying C07 of legal action to settle this problem and the possibility of the imposition of a penalty payment. In 2008, another problem was reported relating to C07's emissions, which C07 investigated at the request of the EPA. C07 and environmental officers discussed the problems on several occasions. It turned out that a key process parameter had exceeded a limit. The EPA therefore judged this to be a serious violation and announced legal action. In 2009, the EPA held two programmed inspections, both of which identified violations. The violations in 2010 and 2011 related to Seveso rules and regulations, as described below.

Registered Seveso violations and inspections

An OHSA enforcement notice indicated that a Seveso inspection had taken place in 2001, as a result of which the OHSA inspector proceeded with enforcement in relation to three violations. Other results of this inspection are not traceable. The 2003 Seveso inspection identified three OHSA violations. Again, EPA data are missing, although the OHSA report indicated that an environmental inspector was present. The 2006 inspection found two violations, both of which were mentioned in the inspection report, and C07 agreed to take remedial action of one of the violations. The inspection report stated that due to this timely response, the inspectors had decided not to proceed with enforcement actions. The following inspection in 2008 identified two OHSA violations and one violation under the Fire Services Act, all of which resulted in enforcement notices.

The 2010 inspection reviewed, safety management system element D (operational control). Interviews with two employees of C07 showed that one could only hesitantly answer questions that were important since they concerned critical events. According to the inspectors, the employee should have been able to respond to these questions reflexively, especially since the interviewee had been working at C07 for a time. They stated in the 2010 inspection report that they did not proceed with enforcement measures since there was insufficient evidence that this was common among the employees, but highlighted it as a point of interest. The dangerous goods storage sheds mentioned above were a focus of this inspection as well. The inspection team concluded that they doubted whether they still met the required level of protection in accordance with all the rules and regulations. No recent assessment was available for C07, and the last one dated from 2003. As described above, environmental inspectors had already established multiple violations, C07 had been subject to enforcement measures in 2004, and at least one follow-up inspection had been carried out. In 2010, the inspectors judged structural conditions to be bad, and the EPA issued an enforcement notice that gave C07 one month to design a working method to address all three environmental violations. The inspectors presented their overall view of this inspection, and in relation to the vast number of minor issues that had emerged and the many points that required action, questioned whether C07 had failed to come to grips with the problems ('Het glipt toch niet door jullie handen?').

The next inspection of 2011 was observed for the present study. During the inspection of C07's premises, OHSA inspectors detected a loose earth wire in an explosives storage area, and suspended work at the location as a precaution. A vehicle was also found in the same area, which was also a violation. The inspection team decided to inspect the dangerous goods storage sheds again, in view of non-compliance with the outcomes of previous inspections. C07 presented the results of a research report by an external corporation and pointed out that all the action points were included in a preventive maintenance programme. During the walk-around, the inspectors observed improvements and took photographs, checking how control room operations were dealing with emergency situations. Although they did not identify any violations in that specific area, the inspection did find two OHSA violations and two environmental violations (observed in April 2011). One inspector made the following observations after the April 2011 inspection: 'These people know exactly how to manipulate things during inspections, giving the impression of safe production, and also know how to keep management satisfied.' 'The person is as slippery as an eel.' An EPA enforcement notice EPA gave C07 four months to resolve the problems, and an inspector observed during a follow-up inspection that C07 had worked hard to address the issues, but although it had made a lot of improvements, not all the issues had been dealt with. C07 promised the environmental inspector that the improvement programme would be completed before December 2011, and the EPA agreed to this. The environmental inspector stated in his report that the situation would be checked again in the next Seveso inspection.

Conclusions

C07 was subjected to severe enforcement actions for several environmental violations. Issues concerning emissions were observed over a number of years before C07 took action. Air and noise issues take a lot of time to investigate, and the sources can be difficult to pinpoint. Although such problems indicate unsafe and non-compliant behaviour, most of them do not lead to enforcement actions. Environmental violations relating to C07's dangerous goods storage sheds were reported in a number of inspection reports. Both these are examples of repeated violations concerning the same topics where remedial action failed to reach an acceptable standard. Some reports stated that C07 was falling behind with maintenance issues. From the viewpoint of environmental rules and regulations, we conclude that C07 is a malicious corporation, although it did not rank among the worst violating corporations in the larger study. Studying all the research material, it looks like this corporation is calculating and avoiding costs wherever possible. This is not reflected in the OHSA violations, which mainly consisted of Seveso violations that were addressed with lenient measures.

Corporation C11: A Careless Corporation

Characteristics

C11 is a refinery that has existed for more than 50 years. A large corporation with more than 250 employees, it is part of a multinational organization which has offices worldwide. Under the auspices of the Seveso II Directive, it is obliged to have in place a major accident prevention policy, a safety management system and a safety report (upper tier).

Violations and enforcement actions

C11 had a total of 140 violations of environmental rules and regulations during 1999–2011 (see Figure 9.10). The OHSA noted a total of 38 occupational health and safety violations during the same period.

In 2000, OHSA inspectors investigated an industrial accident at C11. They established that the corporation had violated the rules, and this resulted in the imposition of a civil penalty. Another industrial accident resulted in the issuing of an occupational health and safety warning letter in 2003. A programmed OHSA inspection in 2003 identified other violations. The large number of environmental violations in 2004 related to soil issues, fire, complaints regarding noise and air pollution and a number of other incidents.

The largest category of C11's environmental violations related to soil (30 per cent; see Figure 9.11). The corporation was subjected to a total of 37 enforcement actions (26 per cent), all for environmental violations. Reports indicated that C11 had to deal with spills, soil pollution and decontamination. Since there were a large number of soil-related violations, C11 and the Environmental Protection Agency developed an approach to deal with these issues.

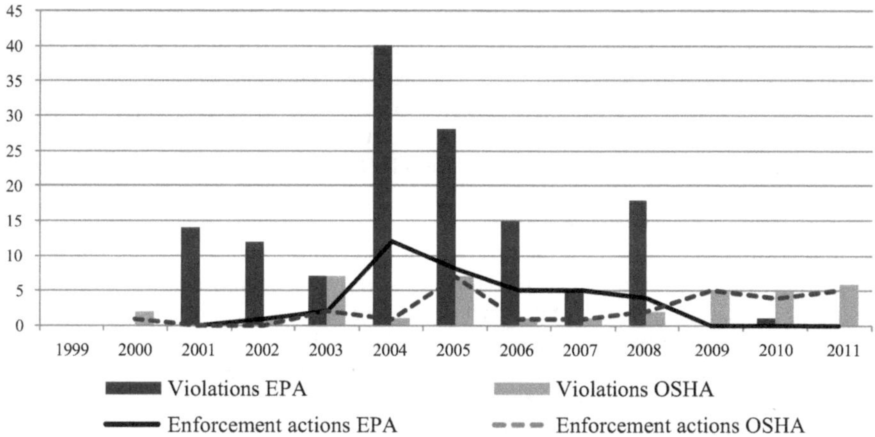

Figure 9.10 Overview of C11's violations

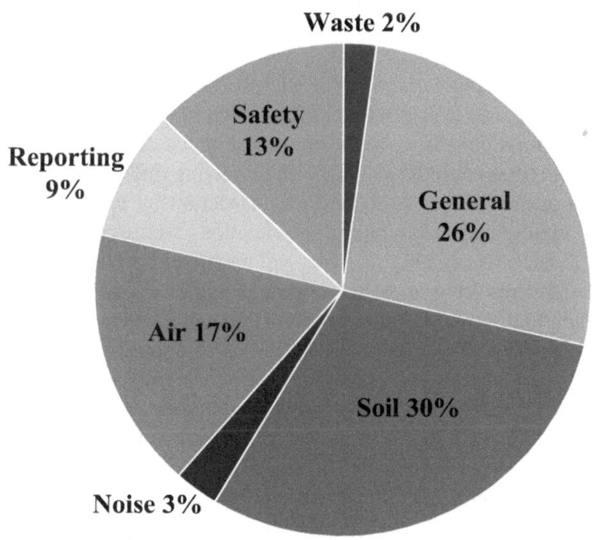

Figure 9.11 Classification of C11's environmental violations

Violations in 2005 were related to soil issues, leakage and, in common with other corporations, power failure in the area. Several installations at the corporation had incidents such as fire and higher than permitted emissions due to this power failure. A fire in 2006 was investigated by OHSA inspectors, resulting in a summons. Incidents during this period included explosion, leaks, problems relating to soil, emissions and the escape of gas. Programmed inspections, leaks and the assessment of reports by the EPA explain the number of violations in 2008. An OHSA inspection of an industrial accident in 2008 resulted in the imposition of a civil penalty. Another occupational accident that was investigated resulted in the shutting down of part of an installation and the issuing of a summons – both severe enforcement measures. An OHSA inspection in 2009 under the Work Permits Foreign Nationals Act resulted in a large civil fine. The corporation was subjected to a total of 29 enforcement actions (76 per cent), all of them for OHSA violations. Other occupational health and safety violations related to the Seveso II Directive and will be explained below.

Seveso registered violations and inspections

In 2001, inspectors from the EPA, OHSA and the fire department took part in an initial Seveso inspection in order to conduct an exploratory assessment of the safety management system. Points of interest were found, but it is unclear whether sanctions were imposed. MIRR and I-net do not show any Seveso inspections until 2004. It is possible that inspections were performed, but not registered. An enforcement notice provided information on the 2004 Seveso inspection conducted by an environmental inspector and a fire department inspector that identified four environmental violations and action points. In 2005, OHSA inspectors investigated a major accident in the context of the Seveso rules and regulations. According to the summons, C11 had not taken suitable measures to prevent a major accident and to limit the human consequences. An inspection report of 2007 indicated that all inspection agencies were in attendance. It identified one environmental and OHSA violation when inspectors detected that weather vanes were either not working properly or had not been installed. The 2008 inspection involved inspectors from all the agencies. One environmental violation was detected, along with points of interest. The 2009 inspection report described an odd situation during the closing of the inspection when the results of the inspection were shared with the corporation. The corporation indicated that different impressions of safety and environmental issues could be gained by interviewing different personnel. During this meeting, the inspectors decided to extend the inspection by two days. Although points of interest were highlighted in the report, no violations were found. In 2009, the OHSA investigated an industrial accident. It determined there had been a violation of the Seveso rules and regulations, resulting in the issuing of a summons. Two violations and points of interest concerning high-pressure equipment and the identification of instrumentation were reported as a result of the 2010 inspection. Both were sanctioned via an enforcement notice by the OHSA inspector. Another Seveso-related inspection took place in 2010, specifically designed to deal with part of C11 which used a contractor for specific tasks in its own process. This resulted in the identification of action points, but no violations were detected. All the inspection agencies participated in the inspection of 2011. Again, although the report identified action points, no violations were found.

The 2012 inspection was observed for the present study. Two environmental inspectors (on different days) and an inspector from the fire department were present. The OHSA inspector was not present, which was, in our opinion, remiss of this inspection agency given the context of recent incidents in the Dutch chemical industry and the size of the corporation. During the walk around the specific units selected for this inspection, inspectors identified that there was corrosion on the outside of some large storage tanks, their brackets that were not well maintained, and some of them had large holes in their undersides. C11 told the inspectors that none of these shortcomings were critical. Because the EPA inspection involved two different inspectors and was only brief, not all aspects regarding the integrity of the storage tanks were inspected. This was another serious deficiency in this inspection. More time should have been devoted to a thorough inspection of this issue given that the inspectors had indications that it was a continuing matter of concern.

The inspection identified one environmental violation regarding fire extinguishers (observed in September 2012).

Conclusions

The total number of environmental violations (140) and occupational health and safety violations (38) mean that C11 ranked among the five worst violators in the larger study. In both areas, C11 was subjected to severe enforcement actions such as the issuing of summonses or the imposition of civil fines. Although violations in general decreased after 2008, we conclude that C11 is a careless corporation. In our opinion, it is not purposive or calculating, but is probably finding it difficult to adapt to new ways and has continued to behave as it has always done.

Discussion and Conclusions

Our main goal in this chapter was to examine the Seveso II enforcement practices in the Netherlands. The analysis provides insights into the registered violations for four chemical corporations and the resulting sanctioning practices of the EPA and OHSA during 1999–2011. The document analysis showed that some corporations could have a series of violations relating to one issue over a prolonged period, and therefore had a higher chance of future violations. An illustrative example concerns C07's violations relating to air issues and emissions, both lasting for several years. Compliance enforcement is best practised through a continuing relationship, and although inspectors may have to deal with different corporations, they need to deal with them over a longer period. Similar to findings in previous research on compliance (Hawkins 1984; Hutter 1989), the use of formal legal sanctions against the four corporations is regarded as a last resort.

We can conclude that some of the inspectors' approaches are effective – for example, in the case of C02, where progress was made to address concerns by the subsequent hiring of qualified personnel and following up on points of action identified by the inspection agencies. Inspections are much more than an isolated event, since they are part of a broader picture of interactions between inspection agencies and corporations. For example, programmes of work were negotiated during inspections. Deterrence is another important aspect of the inspection regime. The visible presence of inspectors assessing installations in great detail – for example, climbing onto large storage tanks to inspect fire extinguishing and prevention systems – demonstrated to the corporations enforcement in action. Inspectors based their decisions during inspections and in their reports not only on the severity of the violations of rules and regulations, but also on the corporation's past behaviour and its reactions to previous contacts, but we wonder whether inspectors always have a clear view of the corporation's inspection history. The duration of the inspections also varied, which could have an influence on the detection of violations. It was expected that the higher the number of inspections, and the higher the number of inspectors, the more intense an inspection would be. This proved to be correct, since the number of inspection topics was lower when the inspection itself was less exhaustive, resulting in less intensive inspections such as were observed at C02 (compared to the previous inspection which was also observed for the present study), C11 (compared to the previous inspection report) and other corporations in the larger study.

Another element of regulation is the sanctioning approach we encountered in the reports or documents and observed during the inspections. Do inspectors immediately impose a sanction when they determine there has been a violation, or do they leave some room to negotiate, for example giving more time to resolve the situation? We came across both approaches. At some corporations, violations were resolved during the duration of the inspection and were not recorded in the inspection report, but in other cases where violations were similarly resolved, they were mentioned in the report. From safety science point of view, we could say that these violations or non-compliant behaviours can be considered weak signals, and possible indications of future unsafe situations or even incidents. It would be better to include all such situations in the inspection reports so that future inspectors can be aware of a corporation's history and focus on recurring issues. If not reported, such concerns may be overlooked when a similar violation is identified in a future inspection. We found examples of this, such as a violation that occurred in 2005 being observed again in 2010, where the inspector was not aware of the earlier violation. We also noted a difference between small and large corporations. Smaller corporations may not be able to remedy issues during an inspection due to their size, while larger corporations have more employees or more inspection days available to resolve them. This can result in skewed crime rates. Inspection agencies should be more conscious of their own data on corporations in order to be able to recognize recidivism and prior violations, and incorporate this information into future sanctioning or enforcement practices.

This research has focused on a heavily industrialized area with a major concentration of Seveso corporations in the most densely populated part of the Netherlands. This region is not necessary representative of the country as a whole, so our observations could result in a biased image of Dutch inspectors and corporations. Enforcement styles can be restricted to a particular region, a certain industry or a particular nation (Kelman 1984; Shover et al. 1984), and different enforcement strategies may work better in some industries than others. However, the potential lack of information on corporations' inspection histories is likely to a problem in other regions as well. Inspection agencies' data are biased by capacity, priorities and past incidents that influence inspectors and regulators. Therefore, data triangulation is a necessity in this kind of research. However, even with the use of data triangulation, we cannot present a complete image of prior offending and therefore an accurate measurement of the crime rate. Nevertheless, participant observation did clarify the picture by allowing greater insights into the inspection process, and especially the nature of the interactions between regulators and corporations.

References

Bentham, J. 1789 [1996]. 'An Introduction to the Principles of Morals and Legislation', in *The Collected Works of Jeremy Bentham*, edited by J.H. Burns and H.L. Hart. Oxford: Clarendon Press.

Braithwaite, J. 1984. *Corporate Crime in the Pharmaceutical Industry*. London: Routledge and Kegan Paul.

Bureau Bartels. 2012. *Onderzoek Vergelijkbaarheid Inspectieruimte*. Amersfoort: Bureau Bartels.

Clinard, M.B. and Yeager, P.C. 1980. *Corporate Crime*. New York: The Free Press.

Gibbs, C. and Simpson, S. 2009. 'Measuring Corporate Environmental Crime Rates: Progress and Problems', *Crime, Law and Social Change* 51(1), 87–107.

Hawkins, K. 1984. *Environment and Enforcement: Regulation and the Social Definition*. Oxford: Clarendon Press.

Hutter, B.M. 1989. 'Variations in Regulatory Enforcement Styles', *Law and Policy* 11(2), 153–74.

Kagan, R.A. and Scholz, J.T. 1984. 'The Criminology of the Corporation and Regulatory Enforcement Strategies', in *Enforcing Regulation*, edited by K. Hawkins and J.M. Thomas. Boston, MA: Kluwer-Nijhoff, 67–95.

Kelman, S. 1984. 'Enforcement of Occupational Safety and Health Regulations', in *Enforcing Regulation*, edited by K. Hawkins and J.M. Thomas. Boston, MA: Kluwer-Nijhoff, 97–120.

Meuwissen, M.W.A. 2004. *Evaluatie en Herontwerp van de DCMR Incidentendatabase met Behulp van PRISMA* (master's thesis, University of Technology Eindhoven, the Netherlands): http://repository.tue.nl/578015 (accessed 6 March 2014).

Nagin, D.S. and Farrington, D.P. 1992. 'The Stability of Criminal Potential from Childhood to Adulthood', *Criminology* 30(2), 235–60.

Paternoster, R. and Nagin, D.S. 1991. 'On the Relationship of Past to Future Participation in Delinquency', *Criminology* 29(2), 163–89.

Shover, N., Lynxwiler, J., Groce, S. and Clelland, D. 1984. 'Regional Variation in Regulatory Law Enforcement: The Surface Mining Control and Reclamation Act', in *Enforcing Regulation*, edited by K. Hawkins and J.M. Thomas. Boston, MA: Kluwer-Nijhoff, 121–46.

Simpson, S. and Schell, N. 2009. 'Persistent Heterogeneity or State Dependence? An Analysis of Occupational Safety and Health Act Violations', in *The Criminology of White-collar Crime*, edited by S. Simpson and D. Weisburd. New York: Springer, 63–78.

Simpson, S.S., Garner, J. and Gibbs, C. 2007. *Why Do Corporations Obey Environmental Law? Assessing Punitive and Cooperative Strategies of Corporate Crime Control*. Washington, DC: US Department of Justice.

Sutherland, E.H. 1961. *White Collar Crime*. New York: Holt, Rhinehart and Winston

Sutherland, E.H. 1983. *White Collar Crime*. New Haven, CT: Yale University Press.

Van Steen, J., Terstegge, T. and Hoogstede, V. 2001. 'Implementing Seveso II in the Netherlands: Operational Experiences in the Rotterdam-Rijnmond Region'. Paper presented to Microrisk, Crete: www.microkat.gr/microrisk2001/paper_VanSteen.htm (accessed 6 March 2014).

Chapter 10
Illegal E-waste Transports: Exploring their Harmfulness, Scale, Social Organization and Governance

Lieselot Bisschop

Introduction

The transport of discarded – non-functioning or outdated – laptops, televisions sets, fridges and other electronics from industrialized to developing countries has become common practice in the last few decades. Labelled 'second-hand goods', they are transported to developing regions such as West Africa. Indeed, a significant proportion of these transports actually feeds into the second-hand electronics market. However, other shipments never make it to the second-hand market and are dismantled for recovery of their secondary raw materials. This procedure, however, happens in precarious circumstances. This has been illustrated in recent years by several documentaries[1] filmed at dump sites in West Africa and South East Asia, in an attempt to raise awareness about illegal transports and consequent dumping of e-waste.[2] Illegal trade in hazardous waste has also been labelled a major environmental crime. It has been criminalized by the adoption of international and European legislative frameworks that regulate waste transport.[3] Broadly defined, however, environmental crime refers to harms affecting humans, environments and animals regardless of their legality (Beirne and South 2007). Inherently linked to global flows of capital, goods and people, illegal e-waste trade is an example of transnational environmental crime (Beirne and South 2007; White 2011).

Criminology has been relatively silent about (transnational) environmental crime for many years (Halsey 2004; South 1998a; White 2003). However, recent decades have witnessed an increased interest in the topic (Gibbs et al. 2010a; Gibbs at al. 2010b; Bisschop 2011; Stretesky and Lynch 2009; Van Erp and Huisman 2010; White 2011). This fits within a broader critical development in criminology which looks beyond strict definitions of crime to include legally ambiguous behaviours that cause social harm (Hillyard et al. 2004). This chapter builds upon earlier publications about this topic that have addressed issues of white-collar crime associated with the global e-waste trade (Gibbs et al. 2010b). Empirical investigations, however, remain rare – a gap which this study aims

1 For instance, the documentaries *Terra Blight* (Jellyfish Smack Productions, 2012), *E-wasteland* (David Fedele, 2012), *Exporting Harm: The High-tech Trashing of Asia* (Basel Action Network, 2013) and *Ghana: Digital Dumping Ground* (PBS, 2009).

2 E-waste is waste from electronic and electrical equipment, such as television sets, refrigerators, computers, mp3 players and batteries.

3 Basel Convention on the Control of Transboundary Movements of Hazardous Wastes and their Disposal (1992), Basel Convention Ban Amendment (1995), Montreal Protocol on Ozone-depleting Substances (1989); Bamako Convention (1998), OECD Decision C(2001)107/Final on Control of Cross-border Movements of Waste Destined for Recovery Operations; European Waste Shipment Regulation (EC) No. 1013/2006.

to help fill. The analysis focuses in particular on the European context, because this region is considered a forerunner in environmental policy and legislation (Vig and Faure 2004). This chapter draws on the findings of the author's PhD research on the governance of transnational environmental crime.[4] First, it will briefly address the methodology, then it will continue by presenting a discussion of the harmful effects of e-waste trafficking, the scale of the problem, and the social organization and governance of the illegal trade in e-waste, ending with brief concluding remarks.

Method

This chapter draws on the findings of a study of the illegal trade in e-waste passing through the port of Antwerp (Belgium) destined for Ghana, including document analysis, interviews and observation. The documents include governmental sources, research reports, corporate documents, and reports by NGOs and the media. A total of 56 semi-structured interviews were conducted with representatives of government agencies,[5] corporations[6] and NGO and media representatives.[7] The interviewees worked within the Belgian research setting of the port of Antwerp or in other EU countries as potential countries of origin of the trade in e-waste, whereas others lived and worked in Ghana as a country of destination. The empirical research also included observations of crucial sites. In Ghana, it concerned the port of Tema, the e-goods markets, informal recycling, and refurbishing firms in the cities of Tema and Accra, and the Agbogbloshie (a suburb of Accra) dump site. The field visits in Belgium took place in the port of Antwerp.

In Harm's Way

The harmful effect of environmental crimes can be seen in their impact on the quality of water, soil and air, on the survival of (endangered) species, and in contributing to climate change (Stretesky and Lynch 2009; Walters 2007). Identifying all levels and types of impact of harm is not straightforward, because it requires reflection on transferences across space and time (Goodey 2005). The following section intends to illustrate the dimensions of harm and the diversity of victims related specifically to the illegal e-waste trade.

As mentioned above, a significant proportion of the electronic and electrical equipment (EEE) transported to developing countries is dismantled to reclaim secondary raw

4 This chapter is a summary of findings previously published in L. Bisschop, 'Is it All Going to Waste? Illegal Transports of E-waste in a European Trade Hub', *Crime, Law and Social Change* 58(3) (2012): 221–49; L. Bisschop, 'Go with the E-waste Flows: The Governance Reality of Illegal Transports of E-waste in a European Trade Hub', in *Organized Crime by Hindsight: Corruption and Crisis in Enforcement*, edited by P. Van Duyne and J. Spencer, Nijmegen: Wolf Legal Publishers, 2013, and L. Bisschop and G. Vande Walle, 'Environmental Victimization and Conflict Resolution: A Case Study of E-waste', in *Debates in Green Criminology: Power, Justice and Environmental Harm*, edited by T. Wyatt, R. Walters and D. Westerhuis, Basingstoke: Palgrave Macmillan, 2013.

5 The governmental actors in this research are national and international government agencies, such as customs, environmental inspectorates, police organizations, prosecution services and administrations.

6 The corporate representatives who were interviewed are producers of computer hardware, e-waste collectors, refurbishers and recyclers, and transport corporations.

7 This includes environmental NGOs, union representatives and research journalists.

materials, instead of being put up for sale on the second-hand market. These 'recycling' practices usually entail manual dismantling of the equipment and the consequent dumping and burning of the remainder, which releases toxic substances such as lead, cadmium, brominated flame retardants, beryllium or mercury (Eidgenössische Materialprüfungs- und Forschungsanstalt 2009). These substances persist in the environment for many years, as they are absorbed into the air, water and soil (Baker et al. 2004; European Environment Agency 2009; Greenpeace 2008a). Illegal transports and the consequent 'treatment' and dumping of e-waste have potential harmful effects for the following 'victims': the natural environment, people living and working in the area, and politics and the economy. Each of these is explained below.

Harmful Effects on the Natural Environment

First, there are harmful effects on the immediate and more distant natural environment. The released toxins pollute the water, air and soil of nearby areas. Through the contaminated water, air and soil, environmental victimization also travels across local and national borders (White 2011). The eventual impact may become apparent only after continued exposure, and can thus be much greater than anticipated (South 1998a). The dismantling and burning of e-waste also influences climate change because it releases greenhouse gases into the atmosphere. Most problematic, however, is the fact that whereas the impact of one device is minimal, it is the mass quantity of monitors, refrigerators and batteries that creates the most harm (Leefmilieu, natuur en energie 2010a).

Harmful Effects on Humans

The consequences of e-waste transports also affect humans. However, the harmful effects are not always immediately noticeable, which brings the risk of this type of environmental crime being considered simply a 'victimless' crime. Hall (2011) argues that it is therefore important to explicitly name these victims. Victims of e-waste dumping often do not know they have been harmed, or they may accept the harms inflicted on them because they need the e-waste business to survive economically. The harmful effects can be further distinguished by reference to those affecting the population living near or working on the dump sites.

One group of human victims consists of those living near the locations where e-waste is dismantled, burned or dumped. Toxins fill the air these people breathe. They grow crops on contaminated soil and irrigate their land with contaminated water. Cathode ray tube monitors, for instance, contain lead and barium, which damages the blood as well as the kidneys and reproductive and nervous systems (Basel Action Network and Silicon Valley Toxics Coalition 2002). Although concentrations are likely to be minimal, such toxins can even have an effect on more distant consumers of vegetables and fruit grown in these areas – think of pineapples, mangos, avocados and many other products exported to Europe.

The informal workers at the dump sites constitute a second group of victims. For those employed in the improper 'recycling' of e-waste, the adverse health effects are most obvious. Several studies have illustrated the precarious working circumstances in Africa and Asia in terms of health, safety and working standards (Sepúlveda et al. 2010; Basel Action Network and Silicon Valley Toxics Coalition 2002; Greenpeace 2008a; Greenpeace 2008b; Basel Action Network 2005). In these regions, adults and children collect waste electrical and electronic equipment (WEEE) and used electrical and electronic equipment (UEEE) on the streets, and rummage through piles of e-waste in search of valuable materials, usually bare-handed and without protective equipment. At Agbogbloshie, many of the e-waste workers are minors and children, who are particularly vulnerable to these conditions (Stephens 2009, p. 232). According to an NGO representative interviewed by the author, many of the e-waste workers work at the dump site for three to five years, after which their declining health forces them to stop. They often return to their families in their northern region of origin with only a few months left to live.

The two groups also experience another level of victimization. Studies show that people working or living near polluting factories or landfills usually lack the necessary knowledge and/or economic capital to stand up against the environmental harm they are faced with (South 1998b; Stretesky and Lynch 1998). This also applies to the Ghanaian case. Importers and sellers of second-hand electronics are an important group of voters. Several Ghanaian respondents explained that this causes politicians to hesitate in drafting more stringent regulations. Furthermore, the informal workers at the Agbogbloshie dump site are members of a minority group who have travelled from the north of Ghana in search of alternative sources of income that their region can no longer provide. They are also a religious minority and do not constitute an important group of voters for politicians in Accra.

Harmful Effects on the Economy and Government Institutions

The illegal trade in e-waste can also harm the economy and government institutions in both the countries of origin and destination. Illegal trade has economic advantages over legitimate trade due to the lower processing costs, and therefore adversely affects trade and competition. Illegal trade disrupts the market of facilities that work in environmentally friendly ways when collecting and recycling e-waste. Moreover, the informal 'recycling' sector has a lower recovery rate of precious and other metals, which has a negative impact on the availability of natural resources. Politically, this illegal trade also undermines the often already weak law enforcement in developing countries through corruption and fraud, and mocks international policy making (Quadri 2010). Finally, there is victimization of Belgian (and other European) consumers, because a fee for recycling is including in the price of new electronic items. For developing countries, the clean-up of dump sites is also a heavy burden.

The social, economic and political characteristics of developing nations thus make them vulnerable to victimization, resulting in e-waste flowing to the poorest nations (Pellow 2007; White 2011). Also, within these regions there is differential victimization, connecting the illegal e-waste trade to social and ecological inequalities. The harm in the trade of UEEE/WEEE is thus not only environmental.

Assessing the Scale

Similar to other environmental crimes, illegal transports of e-waste are difficult to assess (Gibbs and Simpson 2009). Both the Secretariat of the Basel Convention and the European Union keep track of the hazardous waste shipments of their parties. However, the reported data on e-waste of both of these bodies has generally been of poor quality (Fischer et al. 2008). The reasons for this include the lack of harmonization and differences in interpretation of waste codes, which makes inter-country comparisons difficult. Many commodities are also shipped labelled as 'second-hand goods', and thus are not reflected in waste statistics. Generally speaking, these statistics depict the reported movements of hazardous waste and the number of intercepted illegal transports rather than the actual number of illegal transports that occur. The assessment of the scale of illegal trade in e-waste on the global and the European level as well as in the countries included in this study is therefore a 'best guesstimate', and not an incontestable figure. The following data are therefore illustrative rather than hard figures.

Most waste transports stay within the EU or are destined for an OECD country. In the EU, waste constitutes 15 per cent of the total transport volume, and the amount shipped increased from 2.7 to 8.3 million tonnes between 1997 and 2003 (IMPEL-TFS 2006; Fischer et al. 2008). Recent decades have seen a significant increase in the quantity of e-waste – it is one of the fastest-growing waste markets – and the amount of hazardous substances it includes has also increased (Pellow 2007). EU member states provide very limited details on the final destinations of the transports and the amounts shipped to different countries, which makes it difficult to assess trends based on trade and trade control data. Apart from waste statistics, the scale of e-waste streams can be assessed by looking at the amount of electronic products that are being introduced into the market. The amount of e-waste generated is growing due to the increased use of EEE. About 15–20 kilograms of EEE are brought onto the market per EU inhabitant per year (Crem Milieu Onderzoeks- en Adviesbureau 2008). In Belgium, the official take-back system (Recupel) is one of the most effective in Europe, collecting over 10 kilograms of WEEE per habitant per year (Schmidt 2009; Recupel 2012). An estimated 10 per cent of Belgian e-waste is unaccounted for. In comparison, the EU collects about 33 per cent for environmentally sound treatment, while 'part of the other two thirds is potentially still going to landfills and to sub-standard treatment sites in or outside the European Union. Illegal trade of electrical and electronic waste to non-EU countries continues to be identified at EU borders' (European Commission 2011). As discussed below, a large amount of the e-waste generated in the EU travels through Belgium.

WEEE and UEEE flow from industrialized countries to West Africa and South East Asia (Fischer et al. 2008; Crem Milieu Onderzoeks- en Adviesbureau 2008). Analysis of the value of UEEE shipments to Africa indicates that they are often low-quality UEEE (European Environment Agency 2009). There are no details available about the final destination of the retrieved components or scrap metal, but in Ghana complete motherboards of dismantled computers were found being sold for export to Nigeria or China, whereas other recovered metals are used in local industries or sold for export (Prakash and Manhart 2010). One of the Agbogbloshie workers explained that he sold the (burned) copper to Chinese buyers, and the motherboards to 'white men from Europe'.

In Europe, Germany, the Netherlands, Belgium and the United Kingdom are the most important countries for the import, export and transit of e-waste. The harbours of Rotterdam and Antwerp have been labelled hubs for (illegal) waste shipments (IMPEL-TFS 2005; De Rijck 2011). This is partially a result of economic and geographic realities. These ports are economically significant, and function as transit points for inland Europe, also serving shipping routes to Africa and China. Moreover, these ports register waste transports, and it is a law enforcement priority to control illegal transports of waste. The bad reputations of the ports of Antwerp and Rotterdam may thus be a consequence of their own law enforcement success: ports in Spain, Italy and France hardly ever exercise any control over illegal e-waste transports, thereby reducing their likelihood of having high statistics (Van Erp and Huisman 2010). According to the respondents interviewed for this study, waste traffickers are flexible in shifting trade between Rotterdam, Antwerp, Hamburg, Felixstowe, Le Havre and Bilbao.

Antwerp is an economically significant trade and waste hub (Baker et al. 2004), but mainly as a port of transit: 80 per cent of all the waste it handles is in transit, whereas only 20 per cent of waste is imported into or exported from Belgium. A lot of the waste in Antwerp is in transit from Germany, Austria, Switzerland, France and to a lesser extent the Netherlands. The most frequent countries of destination in West Africa are Nigeria, Ghana, Cameroon, Togo and Senegal, partially due to Antwerp's trade connections with this region. As an illustration, Ghana, Benin, Ivory Coast, Liberia and Nigeria illegally import about 250,000 tonnes of waste per annum (Schluep et al. 2011). The Flemish and Federal Environmental Inspectorates maintain that up to 35 per cent of controlled export and transit shipments are in breach of legislation (Leefmilieu, natuur en energie 2010b; Pensaert 2011). These shipments often wrongly declare WEEE as second-hand or scrap metal.

Now that the nature of the victimization and scale have been assessed, the chapter will continue with a discussion of the social organization of the illegal trade in e-waste.

Social Organization

In assessing the social organization of the illegal trade in e-waste, this study found inspiration in the theory on legal/illegal interfaces in transnational crimes (Passas 2003; Tijhuis 2006). This allowed for an open perspective on both the legal and illegal actors who shape e-waste flows. Moreover, it also allows the assessment of whether and how they interact, particularly with regard to either co-operative (symbiotic) or competitive (antithetical) interfaces between them.

Various actors contribute to the illegal trade in e-waste (Bisschop 2012). Both in exporting and importing countries and in supply and demand, there are motivations and opportunities. The nature and scope of this illegal e-waste trade is impossible to grasp unless the economic, political, cultural and social context is taken into account (Van Erp and Huisman 2010). The profit motive is often deemed the most important cause of the illegal e-waste trade, but this requires further contextualization (Gibbs et al. 2010b). The following section explores the diversity of motivations and opportunities that apply to illegal e-waste flows.

E-waste flows originate in production and consumption. Producers regularly launch improved versions of their products with capabilities unachievable through updates. The rate at which we dispose of our electronic products is thus not likely to decrease (Pellow 2007). In this way, producers influence e-waste quantities, and by choosing whether or not to phase out toxic components, they impact the quality and toxicity. Once produced, consumers play a role at the initial phase of the e-waste flow. Corporate, government and individual consumers sometimes sell their e-waste to actors who offer to treat it for (too) low prices. The reasons include a lack of awareness and due diligence, or a conscious choice of cheaper illegal disposal and the externalization of harm. Corporate or government consumers often realize that the collection of e-waste is important, but are not conscious of where the collected materials flow to. The search for cheaper disposal is motivated by the increase in waste management prices as a consequence of more stringent regulation (particularly in the EU). Nowadays, waste is a global market commodity and a sector with criminogenic vulnerabilities (Vander Beken 2007). Corporations that treat e-waste legally and have environmentally sound management systems are few in number, and their prices can be high. This makes it attractive to look for cheaper – less environmentally sound – alternatives. E-waste includes devices for which exportation as second-hand products saves the cost of treatment. Other products incorporate enough valuable components (such as precious metals) to make recycling or treatment profitable, creating a motivation to dismantle the goods as cheaply as possible (Sander and Schilling 2010).

The above sketches the context in which potential interfaces between legal and illegal actors emerge in the phase of waste collection. WEEE/UEEE collection involves scrap metal dealers, urban recycling centres, refurbishers, official take-back systems, registered metal collectors (for example, picking up disposal skips from electronic hardware stores) and informal actors (for example, waste tourists, the Internet or charities). Many of these e-waste collectors and recyclers live up to their proclaimed environmental and ethical standards. As mentioned above, for them, e-waste traffickers are competitors. Other organizations that claim to recycle EEE are less trustworthy, and engage in direct or indirect export – often through brokers – to developing countries. Waste tourists and collection of waste for charity and via the Internet are illegal sources of e-waste that compete with the legal market. E-waste brokers are on an even more complex legal/illegal nexus. On the one hand, they have a role as legal intermediaries in transactions, and therefore promote interests similar to those of the other actors collecting e-waste. On the other hand, through waste storage and handling, these brokers function as intermediaries for illegal transports. Other legal actors in e-waste collection include scrap metal dealers and refurbishers. However, some of those also feed into illegal transports, whether intentionally or unintentionally.

In the transport phase, different actors may simply be shaping the structural context for illegal flows. Some may also be interpreted as facilitating illegal activities. Shipping lines, terminal operators, expeditors and shipping agents – and by extension, banks and insurance firms – each have e-waste smugglers as clients, and can therefore at least be accused of a lack of due diligence, or may even play a more deliberate role in facilitating crime (Kramer et al. 2002).

At the end of the e-waste flows – in countries of destination – the line between legal and illegal may be even more difficult to draw. It involves informal collectors and dismantlers, organized crime, formal recyclers and state actors that tolerate the importation of e-waste in contravention of national or international regulations. Not all actors are necessarily knowingly involved in transnational crime or deliberately crossing the line from legal to illegal. Informal collectors and dismantlers compete on the same market as formal actors and organized crime, and co-operate with legal actors by selling them the extracted secondary raw materials. Moreover, informal dismantlers and sellers of second-hand e-goods in countries like Ghana co-operate with both illegal (e-waste) and legal (used goods) transporters. Governments in countries of destination that tolerate the import of e-waste – contrary to national or international regulations – are competing with the legal actors in countries of origin. These could be categorized as facilitating and perhaps even initiating crime (Kramer et al. 2002).

To complicate this further, illegal WEEE/UEEE transports provide many inhabitants with a stable source of income or access to the digital age. In countries like Ghana, the import, sale, repairing and dismantling of UEEE employs many in the informal economy. Regardless of whether this concerns illegally traded e-waste or legally traded second-hand electronics, both are likely to end up on the dump sites, because there are no adequate recycling facilities in the region. This results in harm to the environment and human health, but may also have positive effects locally (by securing a livelihood, and bridging the digital divide). These informal e-waste collectors and 'recyclers' feed into the legal e-waste industry through the increased demand for secondary raw materials.

In sum, it is difficult to distinguish clearly between legality, illegality and informality. Although profit is major explanatory factor, a broader range of economic, cultural, political and social motives and opportunities also determine the e-waste flows (Heiss et al. 2011; Michalowski 2009). Understanding these flows entails contextualizing them within the reality of origin, transit and destination locations, and thus paying attention to both local and global characteristics.

Against this backdrop of legal/illegal interfaces and this complexity of motivations and opportunities, we will now proceed to the analysis of the illegal trade in e-waste by examining the governance framework.

Governance

Governance refers to the initiatives by government, corporate and civil society actors to prevent and control behaviour – in this case, the illegal trade in e-waste. Individual nation states are principal actors in criminal policy making and implementation, but this is increasingly challenged by the global dimensions of crime (Aas 2007). Indeed, the scale of global trade makes it very challenging to base the governance framework on solely national terms (Sassen 1996), let alone narrow it down to a penal law perspective. In the face of this complexity, national policy making has had to shift to governance arrangements that involve multiple actors (Loader and Sparks 2002). This evolution in governance arrangements has occurred for environmental issues because corporations, NGOs and supranational institutions are increasingly taking up responsibilities formerly reserved for the nation state (Bartley 2007; Gunningham et al. 2003; Holley et al. 2012). The prevention and control of (transnational) environmental crime then comes down to public, corporate and civil society regulators working together in regulatory hybrids. These governance networks and responsive regulatory models are often considered to be a good fit for transnational (environmental) issues (Crawford 2006; Van Erp and Huisman 2010). Theoretically and normatively, these models indeed provide good foundations for addressing environmentally threatening activities of corporate actors. For e-waste, this would then involve initiatives to heighten awareness about e-waste throughout the flows – from production and over-consumption to collection, transport and recycling. Combined with national and international governmental control and self-regulation, these could be ingredients of an 'ideal' governance mix (Gibbs et al. 2010b).

Within the reality of governance, however, the prevention and control of illegal transports of e-waste is challenged to find an answer to the complexity of its social organization. The discussion above illustrated how the e-waste case involves a thin line between legal and illegal. To provide an empirical background to the governance discussion, the empirical reality of governing illegal transports of e-waste was analysed (Bisschop 2013). More particularly, the actual governance of illegal e-waste trade flowing through the port of Antwerp was examined. A nodal-networked governance analysis (Shearing and Johnston 2010) was carried out, which implies an examination of the separate governance actors (nodal governance analysis) and their characteristics,[8] before examining

8 This includes questions about how the nodes problematize the topic (mentalities), what they set as objectives (finalities) and what strategies they use to reach that goal.

their interactions (networked governance analysis).[9] The analysis included both local and global characteristics.

Government actors play a primary governance role. Environmental inspectorates, environmental administrations, customs, maritime and environmental police, and public prosecutors are crucial for definitional guidance, for inducing corporate actors to participate through both positive and negative incentives, and for using their enforcement capacities (see also Holley et al. 2012). Despite waste fraud being a policing priority, each of these government actors suffers from a lack of funding which has a negative effect on the number of personnel and training resources available. This has an impact on the potential for tracing detected illegal transports to their sources. Consequently, law enforcement is deemed too slow to respond and the fines imposed are considered low compared to the potential profits. There are efforts at co-operation between these government actors, but this can be challenging because of differences in methods, objectives and working realities. Especially in countries of destination like Ghana, law enforcement initiatives are lacking, because the international conventions have not (yet) been transposed into national legislation. Even in Belgium, where waste fraud is a priority, law enforcement efforts are often beset by practical limitations. For example, despite the best efforts of many individual government staff, much of the implementation currently remains local and fragmented. This contrasts with one of the prerequisites of responsive regulation: the possibility to escalate to punitive reactions in cases of (continued) non-compliance (Braithwaite 2008).

It is impossible to analyse government initiatives in this field within only one country. An analysis of the governance reality in the port of Antwerp needs to be connected to the European and global context that shapes it. Due to the interdependencies within trade flows, governance is affected by initiatives elsewhere in the flow (Urry 2003). Governance actions by one country are necessarily limited in their effectiveness. Within the EU, the legislative framework on (e-)waste provides a good basis for policy making on environmental issues. However, as is evident from this case study of the port of Antwerp, this has mainly fostered the harmonization of policy, not implementation. Corporate actors referred to this as the absence of a level playing field.

From a governance perspective, non-government actors have a valuable role to play, although this is currently not exploited to its full potential. Both corporations and civil society stakeholders come to mind. When taking the supply chain of electronics into account, producers, recyclers, transport actors and consumers become part of the governance framework. Not all producers, recyclers and transport actors are currently proactive in self-regulating their sector, despite the governance potential they may have. For instance, transport actors could be encouraged to be more diligent and transparent. By phasing out hazardous components, producers can ensure that the recycling of e-waste is less harmful. Through eco-design, they can increase the lifecycles of products. Economic and environmental interests indeed do not always coincide. Consequently, the involvement of producers and recyclers is largely determined by the potential gains from being environmentally responsible, either financially or in terms of their corporate image. An important governance potential, however, lies in linking the illegal transports of e-waste to the EU's lack of raw materials. This is an important incentive for European industry, especially since it is often more energy-efficient to extract precious metals from e-waste than from mines. Protecting the secondary raw materials and keeping

9 This examines whether the interaction is co-operative, competitive or non-existent, whether someone is taking a leading role, and whether there are individuals or groups currently not mobilized despite their governance potential (Braithwaite 2008; Crawford 2006).

these within Europe is increasingly going hand in hand with the objective of avoiding further environmental degradation in countries of destination of e-waste transports. Despite these self-regulatory efforts, corporate actors could play a more significant role, for instance through self-regulation in the governance of illegal e-waste trade. This will, of course, require carefully designed incentives – both positive and negative (Gunningham et al. 1998; Holley et al. 2012).

Apart from the role of corporations, civil society representatives like NGOs play a role in governance by raising consumer awareness and keeping governments and corporations on their toes about environmental topics. During the field visits, it also became clear that NGOs play an important role in engaging local actors in Ghana. By setting up capacity-building projects, they are reaching out to actors who are currently not always involved in governance. Many of these initiatives are small-scale and ad hoc, but have the potential to address the structural causes of the illegal trade in e-waste. They can, for instance, aim to reduce the demand for WEEE/UEEE by highlighting the fact that dismantling e-waste and second-hand electronics in search of precious metals is the sole source of a secure livelihood for many people in countries of destination. More importantly, they can avoid the immediate harm by teaching informal workers about more environmentally and health-friendly dismantling techniques. This addresses both the illegal trade in e-waste and the domestic consumption of electronics.

Conclusion

This study of illegal transports of e-waste illustrated that the line between legal and illegal activities and actors is often thin. As with other environmental issues, it is not always easy to determine what is right and wrong because these definitions change, along with the perspectives taken in different times and places (White 2011). It is nevertheless important to continue discussing environmental issues within the field of criminology precisely because of this thin line between environmental crimes and harmful effects that are not (yet) criminalized. Empirical research from a victim perspective could help to broaden our view beyond the mere legal definitions to include 'less visible' harms, whether they affect humans, animals or ecosystems. Apart from making the victims more visible, it is important to engage them and see them as local stakeholders with a potential role to play in environmental governance. Empirical analyses make clear which elements shape environmental harm and crime, and provide valuable input for the further development of environmental governance.

It is evident from this case study of the port of Antwerp and its illegal e-waste flows to Ghana that a merely reactive governance approach is likely to be inadequate. In dealing with the enormous amount of goods and the complex social organization of waste trafficking, governance frameworks face the complex reality of balancing environmental and economic concerns, and matching these with the goals of crime-fighting and capacity-building.

References

Aas, K.F. 2007. 'Analysing a World in Motion', *Theoretical Criminology* 11(2), 283–303.

Baker, E., Bournay, E., Harayama, A. and Rekacewics, P. 2004. *Vital Waste Graphics*, Basel Convention, GRID, UNEP and DEWA Europe: www.grida.no/publications/vg/waste/ (accessed 1 November 2013).

Bartley, T. 2007. 'Institutional Emergence in an Era of Globalization: The Rise of Transnational Private Regulation of Labor and Environmental Conditions', *American Journal of Sociology* 113(2), 297–351.

Basel Action Network. 2005. *The Digital Dump: Exporting Re-use and Abuse to Africa.* Seattle, WA: Basel Action Network.

Basel Action Network and Silicon Valley Toxics Coalition. 2002. *Exporting Harm: The High-tech Trashing of Asia.* Seattle, WA and San Jose, CA: Basel Action Network and Silicon Valley Toxics Coalition.

Beirne, P. and South, N., eds. 2007. *Issues in Green Criminology: Confronting Harms against Environments, Humanity and Other Animals.* Portland, OR: Willan Publishing.

Bisschop, L. 2011. 'Transnational Environmental Crime: Exploring (Un)charted Territory', in *EU Criminal Justice, Financial and Economic Crime: New Perspectives, Governance of Security Research Papers*, edited by M. Cools, B. De Ruyver, M. Easton, L. Pauwels, P. Ponsaers, T. Vander Beken, F. Vander Laenen, G. Vande Walle, A. Verhage, G. Vermeulen and G. Vynckier. Antwerp: Maklu, 155–83.

Bisschop, L. 2012. 'Is it All Going to Waste? Illegal Transports of E-waste in a European Trade Hub', *Crime, Law and Social Change* 58(3), 221–49.

Bisschop, L. 2013. 'Go with the E-waste Flows: The Governance Reality of Illegal Transports of E-waste in a European Trade Hub', in *Human Dimensions in Organised Crime, Money Laundering and Corruption*, edited by P. van Duyne, J. Harvey, G. Antonopoulos, K. von Lampe, A. Maljević and J. Spencer. Nijmegen: Wolf Legal Publishers, 393–424.

Braithwaite, J. 2008. *Regulatory Capitalism: How it Works, Ideas for Making it Work Better.* Cheltenham: Edward Elgar.

Crawford, A. 2006. 'Networked Governance and the Post-regulatory State?', *Theoretical Criminology* 10(4), 449–79.

Crem Milieu Onderzoeks- en Adviesbureau. 2008. *Een Analyse van Stromen Electronica-afval in Nederland* ['Analysis of E-waste Flows in the Netherlands']. Amsterdam: Crem Milieu Onderzoeks- en Adviesbureau.

De Rijck, R. 2011. 'A Flaw in the Criminal Approach of International Waste Transport in Europe'. Paper presented at the INECE 9th International Conference, Whistler, Canada, 20-24 June.

Eidgenössische Materialprüfungs- und Forschungsanstalt. 2009. 'Hazardous Substances in e-Waste', *ewasteguide.info*: http://ewasteguide.info/node/219 (accessed 23 August 2011).

European Commission. 2011. 'Recast of the WEEE Directive': http://ec.europa.eu/environment/waste/weee/index_en.htm (accessed December 12, 2011).

European Environment Agency. 2009. *Waste without Borders in the EU? Transboundary Shipments of Waste.* Copenhagen: European Environment Agency.

Fischer, C., Hedal, N., Carlsen, R., Doujak, K., Legg, D., Oliva, J., Lüdeking Sparvath, S., Viisimaa, M., Weissenbach, T. and Werge, M. 2008. *Transboundary Shipments of Waste in the EU: Developments 1995–2005 and Possible Drivers.* Copenhagen: European Environment Agency – European Topic Centre on Resource and Waste Management.

Gibbs, C. and Simpson, S.S. 2009. 'Measuring Corporate Environmental Crime Rates: Progress and Problems', *Crime, Law and Social Change* 51(1), 87–107.

Gibbs, C., Gore, M.L., McGarrell, E.F. and Rivers, L. 2010a. 'Introducing Conservation Criminology: Towards Interdisciplinary Scholarship on Environmental Crimes and Risks', *British Journal of Criminology* 50(1), 124–44.

Gibbs, C., McGarrell, E.F. and Axelrod, M. 2010b. 'Transnational White-collar Crime and Risk: Lessons from the Global Trade in Electronic Waste', *Criminology and Public Policy* 9(3), 543–60.

Goodey, J. 2005. *Victims and Victimology: Research, Policy and Practice*. Harrow: Pearson Longman.

Greenpeace. 2008a. *Chemical Contamination at E-waste Recycling and Disposal Sites in Accra and Korforida, Ghana*. Exeter: Greenpeace Research Laboratories.

Greenpeace. 2008b. *Poisoning the Poor: Electronic Waste in Ghana*. Amsterdam: Greenpeace International.

Gunningham, N., Grabosky, P. and Sinclair, D. 1998. *Smart Regulation: Designing Environmental Policy*. Oxford: Clarendon Press.

Gunningham, N., Kagan, R. and Thornton, D. 2003. *Shades of Green: Business, Regulation and Environment*. Redwood City, CA: Stanford University Press.

Hall, M. 2011. 'Environmental Victims: Challenges for Criminology and Victimology in the 21st Century', *Varstvoslovje/Journal of Criminal Justice and Security*, 13(4), 371–91.

Halsey, M. 2004. 'Against "Green" Criminology', *British Journal of Criminology* 44(4), 833–53.

Heiss, R., Ruessink, H., Isarin, N., Koparova, M. and Grabiel, D. 2011. 'International Hazardous Waste Inspection Project at Seaports: Results and Recommendations', paper presented at the INECE 9th International Conference, Whistler, Canada, 20–24 June.

Hillyard, P., Pantazis, C., Tombs, S. and Gordon, D., eds. 2004. *Beyond Criminology: Taking Harm Seriously*. Manitoba: Fernwood Publishing.

Holley, C., Gunningham, N. and Shearing, C. 2012. *The New Environmental Governance*, Abingdon: Routledge.

IMPEL-TFS. 2005. *IMPEL-TFS Threat Assessment Project: The Illegal Shipments of Waste among IMPEL Member States, Project Report*: http://impel.eu/wp-content/uploads/2010/02/2006-x-Threat-Assessment-Final-Report.pdf (accessed 6 March 2014).

IMPEL-TFS. 2006. *Is What You See, What You Get?*: https://zoek.officielebekendmakingen.nl/kst-22343-140-b1.pdf (accessed 1 November 2013).

Kramer, R., Michalowski, R. and Kauzlarich, D. 2002. 'The Origins and Development of the Concept and Theory of State-corporate Crime', *Crime and Delinquency* 48(2), 263–82.

Leefmilieu, natuur en energie. 2010a. *Afvalstromen in Vlaanderen: Risicoprofiel*. Brussels: Leefmilieu, natuur en energie.

Leefmilieu, natuur en energie. 2010b. *Milieuhandhavingsrapport 2009*. Brussels: Vlaamse Overheid – Departement Leefmilieu, Natuur en Energie – Afdeling Milieu-inspectie.

Loader, I. and Sparks, R. 2002. 'Contemporary Landscapes of Crime, Order and Control: Governance, Risk and Globalization', in *The Oxford Handbook of Criminology*, edited by M. Maguire, M. Morgan and R. Reiner. Oxford: Oxford University Press, 78–101.

Michalowski, R. 2009. 'Power, Crime and Criminology in the New Imperial Age', *Crime, Law and Social Change* 51(3–4), 303–25.

Passas, N. 2003. 'Cross-border Crime and the Interface between Legal and Illegal Actors', *Security Journal* 16(1), 19–38.

Pellow, D. 2007. *Resisting Global Toxics: Transnational Movements for Environmental Justice*. Cambridge, MA: MIT Press.

Pensaert, J. 2011. 'Waste Controls in Belgian Ports: A Matter of Cooperation'. Paper presented at the International Workshop on Counteracting Illegal Waste Shipments, Rotterdam, 14–15 November.

Prakash, S. and Manhart, A. 2010. *Socio-economic Assessment and Feasibility Study on Sustainable E-waste Management in Ghana.* Freiburg: Öko-Institut e.V./Inspectorate of the Ministry of Housing, Spatial Planning and the Environment of the Netherlands (VROM-Inspectorate)/Dutch Association for the Disposal of Metal and Electrical Products (NVMP).

Quadri, S. 2010. 'An Analysis of the Effects and Reasons for Hazardous Waste Importation in India and its Implementation of the Basel Convention', *Florida Journal of International Law* 22(3), 467.

Recupel. 2012. *Recupel Jaarverslag: Kerncijfers 2012*: http://recupel2012jaarverslag.devsite.be/#kerncijfers (accessed 30 October 2013).

Sander, K. and Schilling, S. 2010. *Transboundary Shipment of Waste Electrical and Electronic Equipment/Electronic Scrap: Optimization of Material Flows and Control.* Dessau-Roßlau, Germany: Umweltbundesamt.

Sassen, S. 1996. *Losing Control? Sovereignty in an Age of Globalization.* New York: Colombia University Press.

Schluep, M., Manhart, A., Osibanjo, O., Rochat, D., Isarin, N. and Mueller, E. 2011. *Where are WEEE in Africa? Findings from the Basel Convention E-waste Africa Programme.* Berlin: Secretariat of the Basel Convention/UNEP/EU/EMPA/Öko-Institut/IMPEL.

Schmidt, M. 2009. *Evaluatie Milieubeleidsovereenkomst Afgedankte Elektrische en Elektronische Apparatuur (AEEA): Rapportering over 2008.* Mechelen: OVAM.

Sepúlveda, A., Schluep, M., Renaud, F.G., Streicher, M., Kuehr, R., Hagelüken, C. and Gerecke, A.C. 2010. 'A Review of the Environmental Fate and Effects of Hazardous Substances Released from Electrical and Electronic Equipment during Recycling: Examples from China and India', *Environmental Impact Assessment Review* 30(1), 28–41.

Shearing, C. and Johnston, L. 2010. 'Nodal Wars and Network Fallacies: A Genealogical Analysis of Global Insecurities', *Theoretical Criminology* 14(4), 495–514.

South, N. 1998a. 'A Green Field for Criminology: A Proposal for a Perspective', *Theoretical Criminology* 2(2), 211–33.

South, N. 1998b. 'Corporate and State Crimes against the Environment: Foundations for a Green Perspective in European Criminology', in *The New European Criminology: Crime and Social Order in Europe*, edited by V. Ruggiero, N. South and I. Taylor. London and New York: Routledge.

Stephens, S. 2009. 'Reflections on Environmental Justice: Children as Victims and Actors', *Social Justice* 23(4), 62–86.

Stretesky, P. and Lynch, M. 1998. 'Corporate Environmental Violence and Racism', *Crime, Law and Social Change* 30(2), 163–84.

Stretesky, P. and Lynch, M. 2009. 'Does Self-policing Reduce Chemical Emissions?', *Social Science Journal* 46(3), 459–73.

Tijhuis, A. 2006. *Transnational Crime and the Interface between Legal and Illegal Actors: The Case of the Illicit Art and Antiquities Trade.* Leiden: Netherlands Institute for the Study of Crime and Law Enforcement.

Urry, J. 2003. *Global Complexity.* Cambridge: Polity Press.

Van Erp, J. and Huisman, W. 2010. 'Smart Regulation and Enforcement of Illegal Disposal of Electronic Waste', *Criminology and Public Policy* 9(3), 579–90.

Vander Beken, T., ed. 2007. *The European Waste Industry and Crime Vulnerabilities.* Antwerp: Maklu.

Vig, N.J. and Faure, M.G., eds. 2004. *Green Giants? Environmental Policies of the United States and the European Union.* Cambridge MA: MIT Press.

Walters, R. 2007. 'Crime, Regulation and Radioactive Waste in the United Kingdom', in *Issues in Green Criminology: Confronting Harms against Environments, Humanity and Other Animals*, edited by P. Beirne and N. South. Portland, OR: Willan Publishing, 186–205.

White, R. 2003. 'Environmental Issues and the Criminological Imagination', *Theoretical Criminology* 7(4), 483–506.

White, R. 2011. *Transnational Environmental Crime: Towards an Eco-global Criminology*. New York: Routledge.

Chapter 11
Camouflage-collar Crime: An Examination of Wildlife Crime and Characteristics of Offenders in Florida

Matthew Crow, Tara O'Connor Shelley and Paul Stretesky

Introduction[1]

Crimes committed in rural environments are relatively understudied in criminology (Bachman 1992; Weisheit and Wells 1996). Various wildlife crimes, for instance, have been particularly overlooked by mainstream criminology, and include a variety of infractions committed against terrestrial, aquatic, and amphibian animals. The lack of attention devoted to wildlife crime is somewhat puzzling, as research suggests there is significant public concern about environmental crime (O'Connor Shelley et al. 2011). Moreover, nearly three decades ago, Hummell pointed out that 'significant amounts of deviant behavior and crime occur in the forms of poaching and illegal trade in wildlife products' (Hummell 1983, p. 256; see also South and Bierne 2006; Forsyth et al. 1998; Muth 1998). Instead, the discipline of criminology has been, and continues to be, preoccupied by violent crime even though it is an infrequent occurrence relative to other crimes (Burns et al. 2008; Gibbons 1972; Lynch 1990; Ross 1961). A central explanation for this scholarly inattention is the belief that wildlife crime is 'folk crime' (Forsyth et al. 1998). Folk crime is viewed as harmless or an unimportant deviant activity that does not rise to the construct of street crime (Eliason 2003; Eliason 2006; Forsyth 1993; Forsyth et al. 1998; McSkimming and Berg 2008; Muth 1998; Muth and Bowe 1998; Payne et al. 2005; Ross 1961; O'Connor Shelley and Crow 2009). And yet, despite the historical lack of attention to the topic from most criminologists, Eliason (2008) argues there is an increased interest in wildlife crime with the emergence of 'green criminology' (see also Beirne 1999; Granfield and Colomy 2005; Zilney et al. 2006).

Of those studies that do examine poaching and wildlife crime, most rely on small samples of offenders (150 or less) or small samples of conservation officers (70 or less)[2] to collect information about their nature and extent. Most of these studies have been conducted in Colorado (Eliason and Dodder 1999), Kentucky (Eliason 2003; Eliason 2005), Louisiana (Forsyth 1993; Forsyth 1994; Forsyth 2008), Maine (Sherblom et al. 2002), Missouri (Glover and Baskett 1984), Pennsylvania (Lawson 2003; Walsh and Donovan 1984), Utah (Howard and Koehl 1996), Virginia (Carter 2004; Carter 2006; Green 2002; Palmer and Bryant 1985), and Washington state (Patten 2010). These groundbreaking studies indicate that crimes against wildlife are a serious problem, and that additional research is crucial

1 This chapter was previously published as M.S. Crow, T. O'Connor Shelley, and P.B. Stretesky, 'Camouflage-collar Crime: An Examination of Wildlife Crime and Characteristics of Offenders in Florida,' *Deviant Behavior* 34(8) (August 2013), 635–52.

2 Conservation officers are also known by a number of titles, as fish and wildlife officers, wildlife management officers, game wardens, rangers, or nature resource police (see Falcone 2004).

to better understand the nature and extent of wildlife crime. Research using advanced methodologies is also needed in this area (Eliason 1999; O'Connor Shelley and Crow 2009). More specifically, 'studies addressing the sociology of poaching need to move beyond in-depth interviews and small samples to other designs which will enhance our understanding of the phenomenon' (Eliason 1999, p. 35).

The present study contributes to the existing literature through quantitative analysis of 15,657 incidents of wildlife crime (and other related incidents) in Florida. The research questions guiding the current study include:

- What is the nature and extent of wildlife[3] crimes? More specifically, what is the range of wildlife crime and deviance? What are the most and least common types of wildlife crime? Is it possible to develop a categorization scheme of wildlife offenses? Does wildlife crime vary geographically in a diverse ecosystem like Florida?
- What is the demographic profile of wildlife offenders in Florida? Is it possible to develop a profile, and if so, does the profile vary by offense type (for example, fishing offenses versus hunting offenses, or permit versus illegal taking-related offenses)?
- How do offender characteristics and geography influence the type of wildlife offending?

This research makes several important contributions to the existing literature. The present study represents the largest sample of wildlife crimes and offenders to date, and does so quantitatively. It is also one of the few studies to examine wildlife crime as the unit of analysis,[4] and unlike most studies, it includes fishing-related offenses as part of wildlife crime. This is an important development, for while others have provided descriptions and categorizations of types of poachers (Forsyth et al. 1998; Muth and Bowe 1998), issues related to conservation officers (Eliason 2006; Eliason 2011; Forsyth and Forsyth 2009; Patten 2010), and even historical assessments of conservation law (Eliason 2012a), the present study is unique in that it empirically examines and categorizes the nature and extent of cited wildlife-related crime and factors associated with this phenomenon. Thus, while the wildlife crime and conservation policing literature is developing, it still lacks empirical analysis of wildlife offenses. This study provides one of the first such analyses. Finally, the study's setting is Florida—a state with one of the nation's most diverse ecosystems not yet studied in this context.[5]

Defining Wildlife Crime

Wildlife crime has often been conceptualized as 'poaching' or 'camouflage-collar crime' (see Bryant 1979; Eliason 2008; Hummel 1983), while offenders engaged in this type of activity are often viewed as 'camouflage criminals' or 'folk outlaws.' While some scholars define wildlife crime generally as 'the illegal taking of wildlife in various forms, (Eliason and Dodder 1999, p. 239), others provide more specific definitions. For example, Muth and

3 This includes terrestrial, aquatic, and amphibian species of wildlife.

4 Most studies of wildlife crime study the poacher or the game warden/conservation officer as the unit of analysis.

5 One notable exception is the work of Shelley and Crow (2009); however, they examined the work of the FWC officers and their work tasks rather than the nature and extent of wildlife crime.

Bowe describe poaching as: 'Any act that intentionally contravenes the laws and regulations established to protect wild, renewable resources, such as plants, mammal, birds, insects, reptiles, amphibians, fish and shell fish' (Muth and Bowe 1998, p. 9). Regardless of whether one chooses to define wildlife crime generally or specifically, common conceptualizations view it as emerging from activity related to hunting, fishing, and other pursuits associated with engaging with regulated wildlife or land.

Common wildlife offenses include spotlighting, hunting or fishing without a license, illegal baiting, trespassing on private property or in protected areas to hunt or fish, hunting from roadways, failure to tag properly, keeping undersized fish, hunting or fishing off-season or not following other seasonal restrictions, and exceeding posted limits for fish (see Curcione 1992; Eliason 2003; Eliason 2004; Musgrave et al. 1993). Although the literature documents a wide variety of wildlife crimes, systematic typologies or categories of wildlife crime are lacking. Nevertheless, most wildlife offenses can be divided into the following four areas:

- **Improper permitting**—This category refers to failure to own or possess hunting or fishing licenses, or not possessing the proper safety equipment to engage in hunting and fishing as required by law.
- **Illegal taking or methods**—These refer to the methods associated with hunting and fishing, and not the possession of wildlife. For example, hunting off-season, hunting animals with a spotlight, or fishing using dynamite would constitute illegal taking.
- **Illegal possession of wildlife and byproducts**—This refers to the possession of protected wildlife that is endangered or threatened, possessing wildlife out of season, possessing wildlife that is undersized, possessing an exotic species that is not legal, and possessing an amount of wildlife that is deemed excessive by law.
- **Conservation-related offenses**—This refers to offenses in violation of laws designed to protect natural habitats, operating vehicles in protected areas, disturbing protected marine areas and wildlife, and trespassing on wildlife management areas (WMAs).

The Nature and Extent of Wildlife Crime

Understanding the nature and extent of wildlife crime is difficult, as there are no national statistics available to thoroughly document the problem. Despite the lack of reliable statistics, several authors have claimed that there has been increased poaching activity over the past two decades (Associated Press 2009; Musgrave et al. 1993; Muth and Bowe 1998). For example, in California, officials called 2008 the 'year of the extreme poacher,' with arrests for illegal killing of game, birds, and fish rising considerably since 2005 (Associated Press 2009). Academics also believe the problem is serious and widespread (Eliason 2008; Gavitt 1989; Tobias 1998; Warchol et al. 2003), to the point where the number of illegal takings equals or exceeds the number of animals taken legally (Musgrave et al. 1993). There is also concern that species classified as 'trophy game' are increasingly under attack: 'I don't think there was anywhere near the waste or the abuse of the resource that there is today ... poachers are attacking our trophy gene pool' (Lawson 2003, citing Curtis 1998).

Without a consistent and national database to track the problem, it may be premature to make claims that wildlife crime is on the rise or on the decline. What is certain is that given the small ratio of conservation officers to hunters and anglers (Falcone 2004), it is likely that most wildlife offenses go undetected (Eliason 2003; Eliason 2008; Tobias 1998). In fact, estimates of the ratio of discovered offenses to actual offenses range from 1:30 to 1:83 (see Eliason 2003; Green et al. 1998; Kaminsky 1974). Thus, it is important to point out that the current study analyzes official Fish and Wildlife Conservation Commission Law Enforcement data, which is a measure of discovered offenses for which a citation was issued.

Wildlife Offenders

McSkimming and Berg (2008) argue that researchers know more about *why* people poach in terms of motivations and justifications, and less about the *socio-demographic characteristics* of wildlife offenders. This is somewhat surprising, as the need to develop 'a holistic understanding of the wildlife violator' has long been argued, for without such an understanding it is difficult for enforcement agents to develop effective educational and/or enforcement campaigns (Bessey 1985, p. 10). Similarly, Forsyth argued that research into the characteristics of poachers is essential, because 'determining what kinds of crime are committed by local residents is crucial for theoretical understanding of the criminogenic characteristics of rural social structures and for effective prevention efforts' (Forsyth 1994, p. 6; see also Eliason and Dodder 1999).

Unfortunately, only a small handful of studies, employing limited samples, have provided information about the characteristics of wildlife offenders. The limited studies provide two competing profiles of wildlife offenders. First, Bessey (1985) and Eliason (2005; 2008) argue that offenders can come from any social demographic group, as hunters and anglers can be young or old, male or female, rich or poor, employed or unemployed, blue-collar or white-collar professionals, urbanites or rural residents (Bessey 1985; Eliason 2005; Eliason 2008). For example, Eliason quoted a game warden who observed: 'Ten years ago it was your typical redneck now it is everyone' (Eliason 2005, p. 108). Similarly, Carter reported the assessment of another wildlife enforcement officer, who claimed: 'I've caught doctors, lawyers, college professors, teachers, and preachers for just about everything from killing a deer with the aid of a light to not having a license to fish. You would be surprised who some of these people are' (Carter 2006, p. 616). Given these findings and his own research, Eliason (2005; 2008) suggests that no single profile of the poacher can be developed, given the wide range of wildlife offenses (and targets) and the motivations behind their commission (see also Muth and Bowe 1998; Warchol 2004). Similarly, while some research suggests that wildlife crime is disproportionately committed by poor, blue-collar, or unemployed individuals and those from rural areas (Forsyth and Marckese 1993b; Forsyth et al. 1998; Glover and Baskett 1984), one study found no support for the idea that low socio-economic status influences poaching behavior (or at least as reported by wardens) (Carter 2006). Eliason (2005) argues that the role of social class should be understood in the context of offense type (for example, upper-class professionals actively engage in certain types of offenses, like waterfowl offenses).

Yet evidence suggests that a second profile is feasible, particularly with regard to trends involving age, gender, and race/ethnicity. Most wildlife offenders are predominately White, although racial and ethnic minorities tend to be cited overwhelmingly for fishing-related offenses (Carter 2006). Wildlife offenders are most often male (Bissell et al. 1998; Carter 2006; Dizard 2003; Glover and Baskett 1984; Green 2002), and when women are cited, it is most often for fishing violations (Carter 2006). Most poachers are young and in their twenties (Carter 2006; Glover and Baskett 1984), which may also explain why inexperienced poachers are most likely to be detected by conservation officers (Forsyth 1994). It is also argued that most poachers are from rural areas (Forsyth and Marckese 1993b; Forsyth et al. 1998; Glover and Basket 1984) and lack formal education (Forsyth et al. 1998; Glover and Baskett 1984).

Very few researchers have examined the origin of poachers relative to where they committed their wildlife offenses. In other words, do wildlife offenders offend in their own backyard or county (Canter and Larkin's conception of 'marauders'[6]), or do they commute to the location of the offense and travel out of their county (Canter and Larkin's conception of 'commuters'[7])? Depending on the state under examination, the answer may vary based on the proportion of urban and rural populations. Glover and Baskett (1984) examined this issue and discovered that a slight majority (56.7 percent) of deer poachers were lifetime residents of the county in which they committed the offense (they were 'marauders').

Theoretical Explanations of Wildlife Crime

Scholars have offered various explanations for wildlife crime, and several theoretical approaches have been employed to explain the phenomenon. Economic justifications are commonly cited throughout the literature (Forsyth and Marckese 1993a; Muth and Bowe 1998), as poaching and other types of wildlife offending can be lucrative, and also can serve as a means of subsistence for economically disadvantaged individuals. Rebellion or defiance of government authority and the regulation of natural resources are also cited by others as the motivations for some wildlife offenders (Musgrave et al. 1993). Among the theories of offending that have been offered to explain wildlife crime, differential association (Curcione 1992), neutralization (Eliason 2004; Eliason and Dodder 1999; Forsyth and Marckese 1993a), rational choice (Sellar 2007), routine activities (Eliason 2012b), and conflict perspectives (Eliason 2012a) are the primary examples. Routine activities theory and the conflict perspective are most pertinent to the present study's focus on categorizing wildlife offenses and examining the factors associated with the various types of wildlife crime. While the present study is largely exploratory, and did not set out to explicitly test hypotheses derived from routine activities and conflict theories, we are in a position to consider their viability for future research and briefly address each of them.

Routine activities theory posits that crime is more likely to occur with the convergence of motivated offenders, suitable targets, and the lack of capable guardians (Cohen and Felson 1979). Wildlife crime can be conceptualized in this manner. Specifically, motivated offenders are likely to be engaged in legitimate hunting, fishing, and wildlife recreational activities when they encounter opportunities to violate hunting, fishing, and conservation laws. For example, hunters may encounter prohibited species while hunting for other in-season game, or kill certain animals to gain kudos based on their trophy status (Eliason 2012b); fishers may be motivated to exceed catch limits by a particularly fruitful fishing outing, and boaters or other outdoor enthusiasts may be motivated to enter protected

6 A marauder is theorized by Canter and Larkin (1993) as typically young and committing crime close to home.

7 A commuter is theorized by Canter and Larkin (1993) as an offender who travels or commutes to offend.

areas to experience pristine environments. There are countless suitable targets in the wild. In some locations, terrestrial wildlife or marine life is abundant, and these areas are often vast and not amenable to guardianship in the form of police patrol, particularly when one considers the relatively small amount of resources devoted to wildlife law enforcement. Furthermore, the type of wildlife offenses that are committed and/or detected are often influenced by factors associated with routine activities theory. For example, the types of targets (fish species, game, waterways, wildlife management areas) available are often determined by geography and habitat, which in turn attracts motivated offenders.

Eliason (2012a) recently proposed that anti-poaching laws reflect class inequality. His position on poaching laws draws heavily from Karl Marx, and suggests that poaching laws are created and applied in ways that reflect inequality inherent in the relations of production. If Eliason is correct, then social inequality is historically imbedded in anti-poaching laws. In short, Eliason's conflict perspective suggests that poaching laws (and how they are enforced) have helped to produce and maintain class inequality. This proposition can be extended to focus on racial inequality, a topic that is largely neglected in environmental and wildlife scholarship (Stretesky 2008). For instance, Giltner carefully documents racial discrimination in the development of hunting and fishing laws after emancipation, and reports:

> White Southerners recognized that hunting and fishing provided avenues for liberated African Americans to work toward, and sometimes achieve, a life away from the oversight and control of exclusive agricultural labor. These activities posed a serious and continuing problem for Southern landowners [and the] independence provided by fish and game became an increasing point of conflict decades after emancipation. (Giltner 2008)

Clearly, Jim Crow laws that intentionally restricted access to hunting and fishing by race are an example of direct discrimination, and can be considered an environmental injustice.[8] Today, however, these laws no longer exist, but their effects may linger. Giltner concludes his research by noting: 'fish and wildlife researchers might want to consider whether present day disparity [in fishing and hunting] represents exactly what beleaguered elite White sportsman fought over for so many decades' (Giltner 2008, p. 174). While direct discrimination may or may not exist in modern times, participation in hunting and fishing is still disproportionately unequal, and reflects what Feagin (1977) calls 'past in present' discrimination that is 'indirect' in form and occurs even when there is no specific and intentional plan to harm minorities. In short, past discrimination, the historical development of hunting and fishing laws, racial inequality, and behavioral differences rooted in race and class may have produced unintentional variations in hunting and fishing and enforcement practices today.

While years of ethnographic studies have provided a rich understanding of conservation officers and wildlife offenders, we still have very little knowledge concerning the extent and array of offenses that come to the attention of law enforcement officers or the factors that influence this type of crime and its enforcement. Unfortunately, most prior research speaks broadly of poaching, without providing a full understanding of the range of behavior

8 For example, Giltner (2008) notes that even in 1915, hunting without a license could earn a fine of $15–100 in South Carolina under the Zigler Bill. When a Black offender could not pay the fine, the law provided for a lengthy sentence to a chain gang. As Giltner notes, advocates of hunting license laws 'made it clear that farmers and hard-working poor Whites had not been targeted' by the Zigler license law (Giltner 2008, p. 153).

that falls under that general term. Using data collected from the Florida Fish and Wildlife Conservation Commission, Division of Law Enforcement (hereafter FWC), this research examines 15,657 incidents of wildlife crime (and other related incidents) to learn more about the nature and extent of cited wildlife crimes, the demographic profile of cited wildlife offenders in Florida, and factors associated with various types of wildlife offenses.

Research Setting

This chapter examines the nature and extent of wildlife crime and the offenders who are cited for these offenses in Florida—a state relatively understudied in the literature on wildlife crime and conservation policing. This is somewhat surprising given that Florida is home to a diverse ecosystem, ranging from the varied aquatic species in the Florida Keys to an abundance of wildlife in the rural areas of the Florida panhandle (O'Connor Shelley and Crow 2009). This diversity is exemplified by the wildlife found throughout the state: Florida possesses some 672 species of wildlife, 208 species of freshwater fish, 500 species of saltwater fish, 20 species of migratory water fowl, and 500 endangered/threatened species.[9] The participation in wildlife-related activities in Florida also points to the importance of this research setting. Florida Fish and Wildlife officials estimate that Florida has approximately 2.7 million anglers, 200,000 hunters, and 4.2 million watchers of wildlife, which generated some 8.1 billion dollars in recreational expenditures related to these activities in 2006—the year in which data were collected for this study.[10] Therefore, Florida represents an ideal setting to learn more about wildlife crime, as 'Most trends in the fish and wildlife world seem to start in Florida and California' (Lt. Brown, FWC, quoted in Associated Press 2009).

The agency tasked with protection of natural resources and wildlife in Florida is the Florida Fish and Wildlife Conservation Commission, Division of Law Enforcement, which in 2006 had 722 FWC officers to safeguard approximately 37 million acres of public and private land, 8,247 miles of tidal coastline, 12,000 miles of rivers and streams, 3 million acres of lakes and ponds, and 11,000 miles of canals.[11] The FWC divides the state into five regions—Northwest, North Central, Northeast, Southwest, and South. As shown in Table 11.1, the panhandle portion of the state (Northeast, North Central and Northwest regions) has more wildlife management areas than the Southwest and South regions of the state. A wildlife management area represents those locations managed by the FWC to sustain wildlife in their natural habitats. The Southwest and Northeast regions have more fish management areas—water bodies established for the management of freshwater fish. According to the Environmental Protection Agency (EPA), in terms of ecological or eco-region[12] diversity, the FWC regions share some strong similarities while also maintaining some unique features of their own. With respect to fauna (animals), most regions have numerous species of fish, white-tailed deer, black bear, bobcat, raccoons, wild turkey, and resident and migratory birds. The southern regions of Florida are unique in that they are home to the Everglades as well as the Florida manatee, loggerhead turtles, and blue crabs.

9 http://myfwc.com/ (2006); Shelley and Crow (2009).

10 http://myfwc.com/; Shelley and Crow (2009).

11 http://myfwc.com/; Shelley and Crow (2009).

12 Eco-regions are areas with general similarities in the quality and quantity of environmental resources (Environmental Protection Agency 2012).

Table 11.1 Florida regions: wildlife and fish management areas

	Florida	Northwest	North Central	Northeast	Southwest	South
Wildlife management areas	125	25	36	36	15	13
Fish management areas	72	7	14	29	22	None listed

Indeed, the large array of natural resources and wildlife in Florida exemplify the presence of suitable targets that inevitably attract anglers and hunters to the state who engage in their sport legally. However, under a routine activities theory approach, Florida's diverse ecosystem is also likely to attract motivated offenders—particularly given the small number of FWC officers (guardians) who are responsible for a large geographical area containing a plethora of fish and wildlife to protect.

The racial and ethnic makeup of Florida is also diverse (US Census Bureau 2010), with the percentage of a county's population identified as Black ranging from 2.8 to 56.0. The percentage of a county's population identified as Hispanic ranges from 1.9 to 65.1. Regionally, the North Central, South, and Northwest regions have the greatest racial diversity, with 21.1, 19.5, and 19 percent, respectively, of the residents identified as Black compared with 13.4 percent in the Northeast and 10.7 percent in the Southwest. The regional percent of the population identified as Hispanic is highest in the South (38.7 percent), followed by the Northeast (17.6 percent) and Southwest (15.9 percent) regions. The North Central (6.9 percent) and Northwest (5.2 percent) have the lowest proportions of their residents identified as Hispanic.

Methods and Analysis

Data for the present study consist of official wildlife offense citation and arrest data from the FWC. The data are based on FWC incident records on all law enforcement actions engaged in by the FWC in 2006. The original database included 40,370 actions recorded by the FWC. Cases involving non-wildlife offenses,[13] warnings, duplicate cases, and multiple citations involving the same offenders and incidents[14] were eliminated for this analysis. Thus, the data included 17,388 wildlife offenses; 15,770 of these offenses were unique incidents. After eliminating cases containing missing data on key variables, 15,657 cases comprise the data for this analysis.

In an effort to determine the nature and extent of wildlife crime in Florida, a categorization scheme was developed using the categories derived from the literature previously discussed,

13 FWC officers have general law enforcement authority, therefore much of their enforcement activities involve traffic, boating safety, and traditional crime incidents.

14 In an effort to address the research questions regarding wildlife offenders, the authors eliminated cases in which an individual was cited for multiple offenses during the same incident. For example, if an offender was cited for multiple counts of illegal possession of fish, only one case was included in the analysis. In addition, if an offender was cited for one count of illegal taking and one or more counts of illegal possession, only the illegal taking offense was included.

the Florida Statutes, the Florida Administrative Code, and the Code of Federal Regulations to classify the cases into essentially five distinct types of wildlife offenses:

1. permitting violations;
2. illegal taking or methods;
3. illegal possession;
4. land and marine conservation offenses;
5. miscellaneous.

With the exception of permitting issues,[15] these offense types were analyzed separately by fishing-related offenses and hunting-related violations for a total of eight variations of offending across the original four categories discussed earlier:

1. improper permitting;
2. fishing-related illegal taking or methods;
3. hunting-related illegal taking or methods;
4. fishing-related illegal possession;
5. hunting-related illegal possession;
6. marine conservation offenses;
7. land conservation offenses;
8. miscellaneous offenses.

As discussed above, the FWC divides the state into five regions: Northwest, North Central, Northeast, Southwest, and South. We utilized the same regional categorization scheme for this study. The South region served as the reference category in the multivariate analysis. Demographic information for each offender (age, race/ethnicity, and gender) was derived from the arrest and citation data. We also compared offenders' places of residence (county) to the places of their offenses (county) and coded them into categories: commuters or marauders. Cases in which the offender was cited for an offense in a county other than the county within which he or she resided were coded as commuters (code = 1). Offenders who resided outside of the county in which the offense occurred (including those residing out of state) were coded as marauders (code = 0).

The next section will discuss each of these wildlife crime categories, followed by the analysis of the distribution of offenses across region and the characteristics of wildlife offenders in Florida. Finally, we will discuss logistic regression models for each of the offense types.

Findings

Table 11.2 displays the eight wildlife offense categories. The improper permitting category includes violations involving offenders without hunting or fishing permits and those with the wrong kinds of permit for their wildlife activity. Nearly half (49.5 percent) of all wildlife offenders statewide were cited for improper permitting offenses. The vast majority of these

15 Unfortunately, the authors were unable to distinguish reliably between hunting- and fishing-related improper permitting because Florida Statute 372.57 includes both hunting and fishing permit violations and no other indication of offense type was available in the data provided by the FWC.

cases involved the general Florida statute requiring a permit for hunting, fishing, or trapping. Other cases in this category were for more specific permit violations involving particular species (blue crab, crawfish, deer, turkey, and so on) or areas (no wildlife management area hunting permit). Improper permitting violations appear to be most common in the Northwest region, and least common in the South.

The second category of wildlife offenses includes cases related to using illegal methods or taking techniques in the hunting of game. Approximately 7 percent of offenders statewide were cited for some type of illegal hunting method. Offenses in this category include hunting over a baited field, hunting from roadways, hunting with a light, hunting dog violations, hunting out of season, taking protected species, or taking game in protected areas. These violations comprise the greatest percentage of offenses in the North Central region (14.4 percent), while being relatively uncommon in the South (4.3 percent).

Table 11.2 Offense category by Florida region

	Florida	Northwest	North Central	Northeast	Southwest	South
Improper permitting	49.5%	62.5%	44.7%	54.2%	56.0%	36.8%
Illegal taking/ methods – hunting	6.9%	9.9%	14.4%	5.8%	4.6%	4.3%
Illegal taking/ methods – fishing	5.4%	3.6%	1.4%	3.4%	5.0%	9.9%
Illegal possession – fish	13.1%	15.8%	12.6%	8.0%	9.5%	18.5%
Illegal possession – wildlife	1.3%	1.0%	1.3%	1.6%	1.0%	1.4%
Marine life conservation offenses	16.5%	2.4%	16.9%	18.4%	17.3%	21.7%
Land conservation offenses	6.8%	4.7%	8.1%	8.0%	6.3%	6.7%
Miscellaneous offenses	0.5%	0.1%	0.5%	0.6%	0.3%	0.8%
Totals	100% N = 15,657	14.8% N = 2,323	13.8% N = 2,168	21.1% N = 3,296	21.8% N = 3,409	28.5% N = 4,461

The third category of wildlife offenses is similar to the previous category, but involves illegal fishing methods or takings related to prohibited marine wildlife. Just over 5 percent of offenders statewide were cited for offenses in this category. These offenses include illegal means of harvesting oysters, spearfishing, using illegal crab, crawfish, or lobster traps, and illegal trolling. Nearly 10 percent of all violations in the South region fall into this category of offenses, whereas in the North Central region only 1.4 percent of offenses involve illegal fishing methods or illegal taking of fish.

The next two categories of wildlife offenses are illegal possession of marine life or wildlife. Thirteen percent of offenders statewide were cited for illegal possession of marine life, while only 1.3 percent were cited for illegal possession of wildlife. The most common illegal possession of marine life violations involved possession of undersized crawfish, oysters, and various fish species, possession of fish species over the bag limit, or possession of fish species out of season. Illegal possession of wildlife cases include possessing prohibited species (alligators, tortoises) and possession of game (turkey, duck, and so on) over the bag limit. Illegal possession of fish violations comprises the largest percentage of offenses in the South region (18.5 percent), while constituting 8 percent of offenses in the Northeast. Illegal possession of non-fish wildlife is a rare offense, and is relatively consistent across regions (1–1.6 percent).

Two categories of wildlife offenses were also included to account for types of violations that threaten marine and wildlife resources. During their activities, hunters and fishers are often in locations or engaged in behavior that could threaten conservation areas. Therefore, the marine life conservation offense and land conservation offense categories were created to capture those cases in which a specific hunting- or fishing-related offense was not indicated, but in which the offender's behavior violated a law attempting to protect wildlife areas and resources. Over 16 percent of offenders in this dataset were cited for a marine life conservation offense (primarily manatee zone violations and protection of marine animals), and almost 7 percent of offenders were cited for land conservation offenses (illegal entry into a WMA; littering or damaging WMA property). Marine life conservation offenses were relatively rare in the Northwest region (2.4 percent), but comprised 21.7 percent of the offenses in the South region. Land conservation offenses were also rare in the Northwest region (4.7 percent of violations).

In an effort to gain a better understanding of wildlife offenders and the context in which offending occurs, we examined demographic characteristics of offenders by region. Table 11.3 displays the results of this analysis. Across Florida, the typical wildlife offender is White (81.2 percent), Male (95.2 percent), with a mean age of 36 years. While the racial/ethnic[16] composition of offenders was relatively consistent across regions, the North Central region had the greatest percentage of Black offenders (10.4 percent) and the lowest percentage of Hispanic offenders (2.2 percent). Conversely, the Southwest region had the lowest percentage of Black offenders (6.2 percent) and highest percentage of Hispanic offenders (13.5 percent).

16 The FWC data included the following categories for race/ethnicity: Asian (0.5%), Black (8.3%), Hispanic (9.1%), Indian (0.3%), Other (0.5%), and White (81.2%). Due to the low number of cited offenders identified as Asian or Indian, these categories were combined with 'other' for the analysis of demographic characteristics.

Table 11.3 Offender demographics by region

	Florida	Northwest	North Central	Northeast	Southwest	South
White	81.2%	83.8%	86.8%	79.6%	79.3%	80.0%
Black	8.3%	8.0%	10.4%	8.6%	6.2%	8.8%
Hispanic	9.1%	6.2%	2.2%	9.3%	13.5%	10.5%
Other	1.3%	2.0%	0.6%	2.5%	1.0%	0.6%
Male	95.2%	94.6%	94.3%	95.5%	94.3%	96.5%
Age (mean)	36.0	35.5	36.0	36.0	35.7	36.6
Commuter	49.6%	52.3%	47.9%	64.6%	39.0%	46.2%

Table 11.4 examines offense type by race/ethnicity and sex of the offender. The findings indicate several differences in offense type across race and sex. For example, a greater percentage of Blacks and Hispanics were cited for improper permitting compared to Whites. Likewise, a greater percentage of females were cited for improper permitting compared to males. Blacks were also more likely to be cited for illegal possession of fish, whereas Whites were more likely to be cited for illegal hunting methods and marine life conservation offenses.

Table 11.4 Offense category by offender race/ethnicity and sex

	White	Black	Hispanic	Other	Male	Female
Improper permitting	47.4%	60.4%	58.7%	48.3%	49.2%	56.2%
Illegal taking/ methods – hunting	7.9%	1.2%	3.7%	1.9%	7.1%	2.7%
Illegal taking/ methods – fishing	5.0%	1.7%	9.8%	20.3%	5.5%	2.2%
Illegal possession – fish	11.7%	26.7%	12.5%	22.7%	13.3%	10.3%
Illegal possession – wildlife	1.3%	0.7%	1.0%	3.4%	1.2%	1.9%
Marine life conservation offenses	19.0%	7.1%	7.1%	1.9%	16.6%	13.8%
Land conservation offenses	7.1%	6.8%	6.8%	0.5%	6.6%	10.9%

In an effort to better understand the impact of demographic characteristics and region on wildlife offending, we examined logistic regression models for each offense type (excluding the miscellaneous category). The results are presented in Table 11.5. The logistic regression models provide evidence that race/ethnicity, sex, and region significantly influence the type of wildlife offense committed and/or detected. With regard to race and ethnicity, Blacks and Hispanics are significantly more likely to be cited for improper permitting and illegal possession of fish compared to Whites, and Hispanics are more likely to be cited for illegal fishing methods. Specifically, the odds for Blacks of being cited for improper permitting are nearly twice those of Whites being cited for those offenses, and Blacks are two and a half times more likely to be cited for illegal possession of fish compared to Whites. The odds of Hispanics being involved in improper permitting, illegal fishing methods, and illegal possession of fish are 49 percent, 81 percent, and 27 percent greater, respectively, than the odds for Whites. Males are more likely to be cited for illegal hunting methods, illegal fishing methods, and illegal possession of fish compared to females, whereas females are significantly more likely to be cited for improper permitting and land conservation offenses.

Table 11.5 Logistic regression models for offense type (odds ratios displayed)

	Improper permitting	Illegal taking/ methods – hunting	Illegal taking/ methods – fishing	Illegal possession – fishing	Illegal possession – wildlife	Marine life conservation	Land conservation
Black	1.963[3]	0.15[3]	0.32[3]	2.55[3]	0.45	0.17[3]	0.68[2]
Hispanic	1.49[3]	0.56[3]	1.81[3]	1.27[2]	0.75	0.31[3]	0.91
Other	1.34	0.18	8.52[3]	1.10	0.91	0.11[2]	0.00
Male	0.78[3]	2.85[3]	2.28[3]	1.48[2]	0.63	1.16	0.55[3]
Northwest	2.92[3]	2.43[3]	0.34[3]	0.88	0.71	0.09	0.65[3]
North Central	1.41[3]	3.76[3]	0.14[3]	0.64[3]	0.95	0.70[3]	1.17
Northeast	2.02[3]	1.35[2]	0.30[3]	0.38[3]	1.22	0.85[2]	1.18
Southwest	2.21[3]	1.10	0.47[3]	0.48[3]	0.67	0.75[3]	0.89
Age	0.98[3]	0.99	1.00	1.04[3]	1.01[1]	1.02[3]	0.97[3]
Commuter	1.09[2]	1.17[1]	1.18[1]	0.96	0.74[1]	0.79[3]	1.05
Psuedo R^2	0.09	0.07	0.08	0.10	0.01	0.12	0.03

Notes: White and South region serve as reference categories.
[1] $p < 0.05$; [2] $p < 0.01$; [3] $p < 0.001$.

Region also significantly impacts offense type in Florida. For example, offenses involving improper permitting are significantly more likely to occur in all regions other than the South, with the Northwest region having the greatest odds of these offenses. Similarly, illegal methods of hunting are significantly more likely to occur in the Northwest, North Central, and Northeast regions compared to the South. Fishing and marine conservation offenses are most likely to occur in the South.

There are also significant differences in the likelihood of offenders being identified as commuters (those who travel to offend) across offense type. Specifically, commuters are more likely to be involved in offenses related to improper permitting, illegal hunting methods, and illegal fishing methods, but less likely to be cited for illegal possession of wildlife and marine conservation offenses. Thus, wildlife offenders are more likely to travel outside of their home areas for some offenses, while committing other offenses closer to home.

Discussion

In the late 1990s, Muth and Bowe (1998) called for additional research on wildlife crime, while Eliason (1999) argued that research on this topic needed to be more methodologically and analytically advanced. Indeed, Muth and Bowe argued: 'a significant body of literature that constitutes a cumulative and critical mass of scientific findings is yet to be forthcoming. The profession has yet to develop much of a learning curve, in which scientific investigations build on previous foundations to extend what is known about poaching' (Muth and Bowe 1998, p. 10). This chapter aimed to answer this call to help provide more information so that both academia and practitioners alike can apply the results of this study in meaningful ways.

First, we examined the nature and extent of wildlife crimes. The results indicated that there was a wide array of wildlife crime, ranging from fishing without a permit to the unlawful sale of alligator parts. By far the most common type of wildlife crime involved permit violations, and the least common was illegal possession of wildlife (setting aside miscellaneous offenses). Even with the large number of offenses examined in this study—over 15,000—most wildlife offenses fit into the four central categories: improper permitting, illegal taking or methods, illegal possession, and land or marine conservation offenses.

Given that wildlife crime and wildlife offenders may vary geographically, we also examined the nature and extent of wildlife crime across Florida—one of the most diverse ecosystems in the nation. A geographical analysis is also important to further explore the robustness of the proposed typology of wildlife offenses across diverse areas of the state. It is also important to conduct such an analysis for routine activities theory, as targets and guardianship may vary geographically, which could impact the type of motivated offender drawn to any given area (commuter or marauder). The analyses presented here lead to two conclusions regarding region. First, it is clear that with relatively few exceptions, the nature and extent of cited wildlife offenses was relatively consistent across the five regions. For example, improper permitting was by far the most common type of cited offense across all geographic regions, while illegal possession of wildlife was the least common. This consistency lends support to the typology of wildlife offending developed through the analysis presented here. While there are some relatively modest observed differences across regions, the proposed wildlife crime typology appears to be salient, with cases falling into all four broad categories, regardless of the region within the state. Even so, without additional replication, it is not yet possible to suggest that this typology should serve as 'the model' for future studies on wildlife offenses, but it does represent an important first step in establishing such a model, given the large number of offenses examined in this study from a diverse ecosystem. In addition, while important differences in offender profiles and regional characteristics are apparent in these data, it will be important to examine these issues in other jurisdictions.

While relative consistency in the frequencies with which different categories of wildlife offenses are cited is evident, multivariate analyses reveal that region does play an important role in influencing the likelihood of each offense category being cited by law enforcement. For example, the analyses demonstrate that, when controlling for demographic characteristics of cited offenders, individuals are much more likely to be cited for improper permitting and illegal hunting methods in the Northwest region, whereas they face greater odds of being cited for illegal fishing methods and marine conservation offenses in the South region. This regional influence is likely the result of several factors. First, there are geographic and habitat differences across the regions that probably affect the likelihood of certain offenses being committed, and therefore cited. The Northwest region is more rural compared to the South, comprising relatively larger hunting areas and greater populations of commonly sought-after game. Likewise, the South region is home to more marine-based recreational opportunities, resulting in an increased likelihood of fishing and marine conservation offenses being committed, and thus cited. Therefore, the influence of region on cited offense type may be, at least partially, related to differences in lifestyles and recreational opportunities across regions. In other words, the routine activities of individuals and the targets available to them differ based on habitat (region). Another possible explanation, while not empirically verifiable using the current data, is that the enforcement priorities of FWC law enforcement officers differ across regions. These enforcement priorities, in turn, could be impacted by a number of different factors, including funding, number of personnel, and social (class and race) and political influences (Eliason 2011; Stretesky et al. 2010).

This research also sought to address the need identified by Forsyth (1994) and Eliason and Dodder (1999) for a better understanding of who commits what kinds of wildlife crime. Generally speaking, our descriptive results confirm the profile articulated by Carter (2006): that most wildlife offenders are White and male (regardless of region), though the multivariate findings indicate notable differences across specific wildlife offense types that support the argument articulated by Bessey (1985) and Eliason (2005; 2008) that no single profile of wildlife offenders is possible. Thus, it appears that a profile of the wildlife offender is indeed one that varies by offense type; however, these differences merit additional discussion.

The multivariate results indicate that Blacks and Hispanics are significantly more likely to be cited for improper permitting and illegal possession of fish than Whites, and Hispanics are more likely to be cited for illegal fishing methods. As shown in Table 11.5, these differences were substantial. Some of this variation is likely explained by both routine activities theory and the conflict perspective. Under these perspectives, one would argue that minorities and Whites are *not* equally likely to violate all natural resource and wildlife laws. Thus, any observed differences across wildlife offending are likely related to larger social forces that have race and class implications that lead offenders to commit different types of wildlife crimes. It is possible that these findings reflect the fact that Blacks and Hispanics are more likely to be ticketed for fishing violations because they are more likely to fish without a license. However, at the same time, Blacks and Hispanics are *less likely* to be ticketed for hunting violations because Whites are more likely hunt without a license. In short, we argue that the nature of the offense is important in the enforcement outcome, but is complicated by issues of race and class inequality.

This argument is informed by the environmental justice literature and the literature on race. First, Bullard and Johnson observe: 'not everyone buys the fish they consume at the supermarket. There are many people who are subsistence fishers, who fish for protein, who basically subsidize their budgets, and their diets, by fishing from rivers, streams, and lakes' (Bullard and Johnson 2000, p. 561). Therefore, it is feasible that the racial variation observed in wildlife offending could be the result of economic circumstances. For example, in the case of fishing violations, qualitative research suggests that Blacks are more likely than Whites to fish to subsidize their budgets and diets (Brown and Toth 2001). Whites, on the other hand, may be more likely to engage in wildlife crimes that require a higher level of financial resources, such as fishing from boats and hunting, which require more money for equipment to support such endeavors.[17] When racial differences in wildlife offending are examined in this light, it makes sense that Whites are more likely to be cited for violating laws that are associated with greater economic resources, while Blacks are more likely to be cited for violating laws that are associated with subsistence behavior. This is what the results indicate, and seemingly aligns with the work of Carter (2006), who argued that patterns of enforcement are largely due to behavioral differences in offenders. Even so, we argue that behaviors do not operate independently from the social structure. Thus, these racial patterns in wildlife violations are likely to represent an *indirect* form of discrimination based on larger social and economic forces and inequality that shape the types of wildlife crime in which Blacks and Whites are likely to engage (see Stretesky and Hogan 1998). More specifically, it appears that one reason minorities are more frequently cited is not because they are more likely to *engage* in the behavior, but because they are more likely to be *targeted* for doing so. It may also be the case that, as suggested by Eliason (2012a), the historical development of wildlife laws may result in the criminalization of behavior that is more common among minorities and/or more commonly detected by law enforcement among minorities. Future research should examine the role of race and ethnicity in enforcement patterns of fish and wildlife laws.

This study is not without limitations. The research is cross-sectional, and is not generalizable to other states. As discussed above, Florida is a diverse ecosystem that provides opportunities for a wide range of fish and wildlife offending. Less diverse jurisdictions are likely to experience less varied offending patterns. Even with these stated weaknesses, this is the largest study on wildlife offending conducted to date, and it is the first to use multivariate statistical analysis. Given the lack of previous research that is quantitative in nature, it is difficult to produce a model that fully explains the variable of interest in an exploratory study like this. The analysis presented here provides a step forward in understanding the types of wildlife offenses commonly committed in Florida, and the types of offender typically associated with these different types of offenses. By establishing a viable typology for wildlife offenses, the results reveal that not all wildlife offenses are committed or enforced equally. As wildlife laws become more specific and focused, identifying differences across offense types takes on additional importance in understanding the phenomenon of wildlife offending. As such, it is imperative that future research work to identify the specific nature of these differences and a better understanding of the motivations behind wildlife offending.

17 For example, owning a boat to support fishing requires significant financial resources, which are intensified due to maintenance and storage costs. Hunting is also an expensive sport due to the cost of hunting equipment and the cost of taxidermy for trophy hunters.

References

Associated Press. 2009. 'Poaching Ramps Up: Officials See Numbers Jump as Economic Gain Tempts Criminals,' *Reporter Herald* (February 19).

Bachman, R. 1992. 'Crime in Nonmetropolitan America: A National Accounting of Trends, Incidence Rates, and Idiosyncratic Vulnerabilities,' *Rural Sociology* 57(4), 546–60.

Beirne, P. 1999. 'For a Nonspeciesist Criminology: Animal Abuse as an Object of Study,' *Criminology* 37(1), 117–48.

Bessey, M.K. 1985. 'Wildlife Law Revised: Violator Profiles and Their Implications for Management,' *Human Dimensions in Wildlife Newsletter* 4(3), 10–16.

Bissell, S.J., Duda, M., and Young, K. 1998. 'Recent Studies on Hunting and Fishing Participation in the United States,' *Human Dimensions of Wildlife* 3(1),75–80.

Brown, R. and Toth, J. 2001. 'Natural Resource Access and Interracial Associations: Black and White Subsistence Fishing in the Mississippi Delta,' *Southern Rural Sociology* 17(1), 81–110.

Bryant, C.D. 1979. 'The Zoological Connection: Animal-related Human Behavior,' *Social Forces* 58(2), 399–421.

Bullard, R.D. and Johnson, G. 2000. 'Environmental Justice: Grassroots Activism and Its Impact on Public Policy Decision Making,' *Journal of Social Issues* 56(3), 555–78.

Burns, R.G., Lynch, M.J., and Stretesky, P. 2008. *Environmental Law, Crime, and Justice*. New York: LFB Scholarly Publishing.

Canter, D. and Larkin, P. 1993. 'The Environmental Range of Serial Rapists,' *Journal of Environmental Psychology* 13, 63–9.

Carter, T.J. 2004. 'Force Against and By Game Wardens in Citizen Encounters,' *Police Quarterly* 7, 489–508.

Carter, T.J. 2006. 'Police Use of Discretion: A Participant Observation Study of Game Wardens,' *Deviant Behavior* 27, 591–627.

Catlin, R. 1997. *Land Use Planning, Environmental Protection, and Growth Management: The Florida Experience*. Chelsea, MI: Ann Arbor Press.

Cohen, LE. and Felson, M. 1979. 'Social Change and Crime Rate Trends: A Routine Activity Approach,' *American Sociological Review* 44, 588–608.

Curcione, N.R. 1992. 'Deviance as Delight: Party-boat Poaching in Southern California,' *Deviant Behavior* 13, 33–57.

Curtis, S. 1998. 'Change is the Name of the Game Warden,' *Field and Stream* (June), 53–6.

Dizard, J.E. 2003. *Mortal Stakes: Hunters and Hunting in Contemporary America*. Boston, MA: University of Massachusetts Press.

Eliason, S.L. 1999. 'The Illegal Taking of Wildlife: Toward a Theoretical Understanding of Poaching,' *Human Dimensions of Wildlife* 4(2), 27–39.

Eliason, S.L. 2003. 'Throwing the Book Versus Cutting Some Slack: Factors Influencing the Use of Discretion by Game Wardens in Kentucky,' *Deviant Behavior* 24, 129–52.

Eliason, S.L. 2004. 'Accounts of Wildlife Law Violators: Motivations and Rationalizations,' *Human Dimensions of Wildlife* 9(2), 119–31.

Eliason, S.L. 2005. 'Who Poaches? Conservation Officers' Perceptions of the Social Class of Poachers,' *Sociological Imagination* 41, 105–18.

Eliason, S.L. 2006. 'Factors Influencing Job Satisfaction Among State Conservation Officers,' *Policing: An International Journal of Police Strategies and Management* 29, 6–18.

Eliason, S.L. 2008. 'Wildlife Crime: Conservation Officers' Perceptions of Elusive Poachers,' *Deviant Behavior* 29, 111–28.

Eliason, S.L. 2011. 'Death in the Line of Duty: Game Warden Mortality in the United States, 1886–2009,' *American Journal of Criminal Justice* 36, 319–26.

Eliason, S.L. 2012a. 'From the King's Deer to a Capitalist Commodity: A Social Historical Analysis of the Poaching Law,' *International Journal of Comparative and Applied Criminal Justice* 36, 133–48.

Eliason, S.L. 2012b. 'Trophy Poaching: A Routine Activities Perspective,' *Deviant Behavior* 33, 72–87.

Eliason, S.L. and Dodder, R.A. 1999. 'Techniques of Neutralization Used by Deer Poachers in the Western United Sates: A Research Note,' *Deviant Behavior* 20(3), 233–52.

Environmental Protection Agency. 2012. 'Ecoregions of Florida': www.epa.gov/wed/pages/ecoregions/fl_eco.htm (accessed September 9, 2012).

Falcone, D. 2004. 'America's Conservation Police: Agencies in Transition,' *Policing: An International Journal of Police Strategies and Management* 27, 56–66.

Feagin, J.R. 1977. 'Indirect Institutionalized Discrimination: A Typological and Policy Analysis,' *American Politics Quarterly* 5, 177–200.

Forsyth, C.J. 1993. 'Chasing and Catching "Bad Guys": The Game Warden's Prey,' *Deviant Behavior* 14, 209–26.

Forsyth, C.J. 1994. 'Bookers and Peacemakers: Types of Game Wardens,' *Sociological Spectrum* 14, 47–63.

Forsyth, C.J. 2008. 'The Game of Wardens and Poachers,' *Southern Rural Sociology* 23(2), 43–53.

Forsyth, C.J. and Forsyth, Y.A. 2009. 'Dire and Sequestered Meetings: The Work of Game Wardens,' *American Journal of Criminal Justice* 34, 213–23.

Forsyth, C.J. and Marckese, T.A. 1993a. 'Folk Outlaws: Vocabularies of Motives,' *International Review of Modern Society* 23, 17–31.

Forsyth, C.J and Marckese, T.A. 1993b. 'Thrills and Skills: A Sociological Analysis of Poaching,' *Deviant Behavior* 14, 157–72.

Forsyth, C.J, Gramling, R., and Wooddell, G. 1998. 'The Game of Poaching: Folk Crimes in Southwest Louisiana,' in *Society and Natural Resources* 11, 25–38.

Gavitt, J.D. 1989. 'Unlawful Commercialization of Wildlife Parts,' *Transactions of the North American Wildlife and Natural Resources Conference* 54, 314–23.

Gibbons, D.C. 1972. 'Crime in the Hinterland,' *Criminology* 10, 177–91.

Giltner, S.E. 2008. *Hunting and Fishing in the New South: Black Labor and White Leisure after the Civil War*. Baltimore, MD: Johns Hopkins University Press.

Glover, R.L. and Baskett, T.S. 1984. 'Socioeconomic Profiles of Missouri Deer Poachers: Management Applications,' *Transactions of the North American Wildlife and Natural Resources Conference* 49, 104–11.

Granfield, R. and Colomy, P. 2005. 'Paradise Lost: The Transformation of Wildlife Law in the Vanishing Wilderness,' in *Mad About Wildlife*, edited by A. Herda-Rapp and T.L. Goedeke. Leiden: Brill, 147–69.

Green, G.S. 2002. 'The Other Criminalities of Animal Freeze-killers: Support for a Generality of Deviance,' *Society and Animals* 10, 5–30.

Green, G.S., Phillips, H.J., and Black, S.K. 1988. 'The Georgia Deer Jacker,' *Proceedings of the Annual Conference of the Southeastern Association of Fish and Wildlife Agencies* 42, 558–65.

Howard, L. and Koehl, C. 1996. 'Bait 'n' Switch, *Newsweek* (July), 6.

Hummel, R.L. 1983. 'Hunting and Fishing—but Not in Sociology,' *The Rural Sociologist* 3, 255–8.

Kaminsky, M.A. 1974. 'Analysis of the Spatial and Temporal Occurrence of Deer Spotlighting Violations in Virginia', thesis, Blacksburg, VA: Virginia Polytechnic Institute and State University.

Lawson, H.M. 2003. 'Controlling the Wilderness: The Work of Wilderness Officers,' *Society and Animals* 11(4), 329–51.

Lynch, M.J. 1990. 'The Greening of Criminology: A Perspective for the 1990s,' *The Critical Criminologist* 2(3–4), 11–12.

McSkimming, M.J. and Berg, B.L. 2008. 'Motivations for Citizen Improvement in a Community Crime Prevention Initiative: Pennsylvania's TIP (Turn In a Poacher) Program,' *Human Dimensions of Wildlife* 13, 234–42.

Musgrave, R.S., Parker, S., and Wolok, M. 1993. 'The Status of Poaching in the United States: Are We Protecting our Wildlife?', *Natural Resources Journal* 33, 977–1,014.

Muth, R.M. 1998. 'The Persistence of Poaching in Advanced Industrial Society: Meanings and Motivations—an Introductory Comment,' *Society and Natural Resources* 11, 5–7.

Muth, R.M. and Bowe, J.F. 1998. 'Illegal Harvest of Renewable Natural Resources in North America: Toward a Typology of the Motivations for Poaching,' *Society and Natural Resources* 11, 9–24.

O'Connor Shelley, T., and Crow, M.S. 2009. 'The Nature and Extent of Conservation Policing: Law Enforcement Generalists or Conservation Specialists,' *American Journal of Criminal Justice* 34, 9–27.

O'Connor Shelley, T., Chiricos, T., and Gertz, M. 2011. 'What About the Environment? Assessing the Perceived Seriousness of Environmental Crime,' *International Journal of Comparative and Applied Criminal Justice* 35, 307–25.

Palmer, E.C. and Bryant, C.D. 1985. 'Keepers of the King's Deer,' in *The Rural Workforce*, edited by C.D. Bryant, D.J. Shoemaker, J.K. Skipper, and W.E. Snizek. South Hadley, MA: Bergin and Garvey, 111–37.

Patten, R. 2010. 'Policing in the Wild: The Game Wardens' Perspective,' *Policing: An International Journal of Police Strategies and Management* 33(1), 132–51.

Payne, B.K., Berg, B.L., and Sun, I.Y. 2005. 'Policing in Small Town America: Dogs, Drunks, Disorder and Dysfunction,' *Journal of Criminal Justice* 33, 31–41.

Ross, H.L. 1961. 'Traffic Law Violation: A Folk Crime,' *Social Problems* 9, 231–41.

Sellar, J.M. 2007. 'International Illicit Trafficking in Wildlife,' *The Police Chief* (June), 26–32.

Sherblom, J.C., Keränen, L., and Withers, L.A. 2002. 'Tradition, Tension, and Transformation: A Structuration Analysis of Game Warden Service in Transition,' *Journal of Applied Communication Research* 30(2), 143–62.

South, N. and Beirne, P., eds. 2006. *The International Library of Criminology, Criminal Justice, and Penology: Green Criminology*. Farnham: Ashgate.

Stretesky, P.B. 2008. 'The Neglect of Race and Class in Environmental Crime Research,' in *Racial Divide: Racial and Ethnic Bias in the Criminal Justice System*, edited by M.J. Lynch, E.B. Patterson, and K.K. Childs. Monsey, NY: Criminal Justice Press, 241–59.

Stretesky, P.B. and Hogan, M.J. 1998. 'Environmental Justice: An Analysis of Superfund Sites in Florida,' *Social Problems* 45(2), 268–87.

Tobias, M. 1998. *Nature's Keepers: On the Front Lines of the Fight to Save Wildlife in America*. New York: John Wiley and Sons.

US Census Bureau. 2010. 'USA Counties': http://censtats.census.gov/cgi-bin/usac/usatable.pl?State=&County=12000 (accessed September 20, 2012).

Walsh, W.F. and Donovan, E.J. 1984. 'Job Stress in Game Conservation Officers,' *Journal of Police Science and Administration* 12, 333–8.

Warchol, G.L. 2004. 'The Transnational Illegal Wildlife Trade,' *Criminal Justice Studies* 17(1), 57–73.

Warchol, G.L., Zupan, L.L., and Clack, W. 2003. 'Transnational Criminality: An Analysis of the Illegal Wildlife Market in Southern Africa,' *International Criminal Justice Review* 13, 1–27.

Warren, P., Tomaskovic-Devey, D., Smith, W., Zingraff, Z., and Marcinda Mason, M. 2006. 'Driving While Black: Bias Process and Racial Disparity in Police Stops,' *Criminology* 44(3), 709–38.

Weisheit, R.A. and Wells, L.E. 1996. 'Rural Crime and Justice: Implications for Theory and Research,' *Crime and Delinquency* 42, 379–97.

Zilney, L.A., McGurrin, D., and Zahran, S. 2006. 'Environmental Justice and the Role of Criminology,' *Criminal Justice Review* 31(1), 47–62.

Chapter 12
On the Relationship between Animal Victimization and Stigmatization of Ethnic Groups: The Case of Ritual Slaughter

Janine Janssen

Introduction

European Union Directives 93/119/EC and109/2009/EC require animals[1] to be spared avoidable pain, stress and other suffering and therefore to be stunned before slaughter. Directive 109/2009 allows member states to permit slaughter without prior stunning by religious groups. Article 44 of the Dutch Health and Welfare Act for Animals (Gezondheids- en welzijnswet voor dieren) allows Jews and Muslims to slaughter ritually within the Dutch legislative framework. However, in 2008 the Party for the Animals (Partij voor de Dieren; PvdD)[2] proposed a bill to amend the law and remove the exemption that allows animals to be slaughtered without prior stunning in religious communities.[3] The proposition received a great deal of media attention and led to heated debates on the relationship – or more appropriately, the clash – between animal welfare and the religious rights of Jews and Muslims. This chapter aims to contribute to this discussion, and addresses the following central question: Is there a relationship between commitment to animal welfare and the stigmatization of religious minority groups?

In order to deal with this question, the chapter is divided into three sections. The first focuses on some theoretical thoughts with regard to animals. It looks specifically at criminological ideas that regard animals as metaphors for human delinquency, also briefly considering victimological thought on animals. It then turns to the practice and background of ritual slaughter in the Netherlands: what does it mean, how often is it practised, and what are the main issues in the debate on this practice? It will then discuss the central question and relate this to the debate on ritual slaughter in the Netherlands.

Some Criminological Notes on Animals

Animals and Metaphors for Human Delinquency

The great anthropologist Lévi-Strauss describes in his work on totemism (Lévi-Strauss 1962a; Lévi-Strauss 1962b) how humans look at the animal world and think of it in

1 In this chapter, 'animal(s)' refers strictly to other than human animals; where referring to people, I will use the terms 'humans'.

2 The PvdD was established in 2002, and occupies two of the 150 seats in the Dutch House of Representatives.

3 Initially this bill was formulated as a ban of slaughter without stunning. But then an amendment was included with the clause that this form of slaughter was allowed, provided it can be proven that animal welfare is not more affected than in regular slaughter. This would result in a de facto prohibition (Janssen, 2014).

terms of the social world. The huge variety of behaviours within the animal world provides an enormous associative potential for symbolizing variety within the human social context. Criminologists often use animals as a metaphor for delinquency.[4] Here, I will briefly explain how delinquents are presented as animal-like creatures and how ill treatment of animals is seen as a moral flaw in humans (Janssen 2011).[5] Later in the chapter, I will consider the question of whether or not this metaphorical (ab)use of animals plays a role in the Dutch debate on ritual slaughter.

Since the origins of criminology, offenders have been portrayed as beasts. In the nineteenth century, celebrated criminologist Cesare Lombroso studied tattoos on convicts and came to the conclusion that their alleged propensity to get multiple tattoos and place them on sensitive parts of the body was a need they had in common with 'savages' who are less sensitive to pain (Caplan 2000). In that day and age, when social Darwinism was *en vogue*, savages was more or less considered to be a kind of animal, which meant that they were considered wild and beneath contempt. Savages as well as crooks were atavisms that simply had not kept up with the evolutionary progress of modern man. They were closer to beasts than humans.

Conversely, a different strategy for stigmatizing fellow humans as frightening or dangerous was to accuse them of bad conduct towards defenceless and innocent animals. A well-known historical example is Immanuel Kant's opposition to the participation of butchers in the English jury system simply because butchers were, due to their profession, alleged to be cruel to animals, therefore the entire occupational group would lack compassion.[6] Another great thinker, John Locke, who had similar doubts and suspicions about butchers, was also worried about children who abused animals at a young age and consequently would later encounter problems in their relationships with other people in adult life (Janssen 2012a). During the 2008 and 2012 US Presidential campaign, critical observers could not possibly have missed the discussion about Mitt Romney's dog Seamus. During a 1983 holiday, Romney drove twelve hours with Seamus on top of his car in a windshield-equipped carrier. This incident drew negative media attention to Romney and damaged him politically in both the 2008 and 2012 presidential elections.[7] The Democrats,

4 It also works both ways: the vocabulary used in the debate on multiculturalism and the integration of human migrant groups into Western societies has over the years been applied to the migration of other than human animals. For an elaboration of the use of this metaphor in the Dutch language, see Janssen (2009); for a discussion of its use in French, see Rémy and Beck (2008), and for an examination of it use in English, see Davis (2011).

5 Another form of this is associating dangerous animals with people: Arluke and Sanders (1996) mention how in the 1980s the incidence of pit bull dog bites in American cities was reaching 'epidemic' proportions. Although vets agreed that these dogs could be dangerous in certain circumstances, there was no statistical evidence to substantiate their bloodthirsty reputation. Further investigation showed that the reports about aggressive behaviour of pit bulls were often based on wild anecdotes about their macho owners. Furthermore, many of the incidents related to African Americans and Latinos, who were at the bottom of the social ladder. This controversy did not end in the 1980s (Cohen and Richardson 2002), and there are still people who tend to think that the possession of a certain type of dog functions as kind of a marker for future deviant behaviour (Barnes et al. 2006). Ironically, one could argue that the trouble with these dogs is that they tend to surround themselves with the wrong types of humans (Janssen 2011; Janssen 2012b).

6 See Cazaux (2002).

7 See, for example, 'Dog Carrier', Snopes, 21 January 2008 (www.snopes.com/politics/romney/dog.asp; accessed 6 March 2014), and 'Polling on Romney's 'Dog Problem', Public Policy Polling, 20 March 2012 (www.publicpolicypolling.com/main/2012/03/polling-on-romneys-dog-problem.html; accessed 6 March 2014).

however, had their own 'dog-gate' during the 2012 campaign. Barack Obama had written in his autobiography *Dreams from My Father: A Story of Race and Inheritance* that he had eaten dog while growing up in Indonesia.[8] This gave Republicans ample ammunition for a counter-attack on the Democratic candidate: 'Say what you want about Romney. At least he only put a dog on the roof of his car, not the roof of his mouth.'[9]

Animals as (Ideal) Victims

I began this section by mentioning the connection between animals and offenders. The question is whether there is also a (metaphorical) relationship between animals and the processes of victimization. Fitzgerald (2010) states that although increasing attention is devoted to harm inflicted on the environment and on other than human animals within (green) criminology, there is hardly any research and theory on these forms of victimization in the victimology literature. Nevertheless, she herself tried to bridge this gap by using the concept of the 'ideal victim' developed by Christie (1986). Christie sought to identify those who were most readily granted the status of legitimate victim. He came up with six features: the victim is weak; when victimized, the victim is engaged in respectable behaviours; the victim is where he or she cannot be blamed for being; the offender is 'big and bad'; the offender is unknown to the victim (the two parties do not have a previous relationship), and finally, the victim is powerful enough to claim the status of victimhood, or the victim is not opposed by powers strong enough to silence him or her.

Although Fitzgerald studied an entirely different issue, namely a pet food recall, some of her main findings give rise to very important questions. A major issue with regard to the application of Christie's six features other than human victims is that they cannot claim their status as victims. Another important conclusion is that an 'ideal victim' needs an 'ideal offender'. Fitzgerald found that a malicious, predatory individual is the epitome of such an offender. With this example in the back of our minds, we must ask ourselves the question: to what extent are ritually slaughtered animals ideal victims?

Small Country, Big Debate

What to Eat and How to Slaughter

Before discussing the main issues of the debate, we should answer the question, 'What is "ritual slaughter"?' It simply means that livestock is slaughtered for meat in a ritual context.[10] Here, I will address kosher and halal slaughtering practices performed by Jews and Muslims, respectively. Both religious dietary laws classify in detail foods and substances that are

8 For relevant extracts from Obama's biography, see L. Jacobson, 'In Context: Obama's Comments on Eating Dog in Indonesia', Politifact Truth-O-Meter, 20 April 2012: www.politifact.com/truth-o-meter/article/2012/apr/20/context-obama-dog-eating-indonesia/ (accessed 6 March 2014).

9 See B. Montipoli, 'The Doggy Wars: GOP Hits Obama for Eating Dog as a Child', CBS News, 18 April 2012: www.cbsnews.com/8301-503544_162-57415790-503544/the-doggy-wars-gop-hits-obama-for-eating-dog-as-a-child/ (accessed 6 March 2014).

10 Animals can also be slaughtered in a ritual context as a sacrifice instead of for meat production. Those sacrifices are made in order to influence fate and/or God or gods.

either allowed or forbidden for consumption, and define how Jews[11] and Muslims[12] must prepare and eat these foods. Apart from laying down what food is allowed to be eaten, the dietary laws also prescribe how the slaughter of animals is to be performed. In Jewish law, the slaughter of mammals and birds is called *sjechita*, and Muslims refer to it as *dhabiha*. Generally, the animal should be conscious when slaughtered, thus stunning of the animal is not allowed. However, some Muslim authorities accept reversible stunning prior to the cut, such as electro-stunning.[13] The slaughter takes place by means of a cut across the throat. Cutting of the spinal cord should be avoided, although drainage of the blood is necessary.[14] Different religious groups apply different slaughter practices, concerning aspects such as the fixation of the animal, the kinds of knives that are used and how the throat is to be cut (KNMvD 2010). The Dutch Israelite Religious Community (Nederlands-Israelitisch Kerkgenootschap; NIK) has argued specifically against the notion that kosher and halal slaughtering procedures are similar, as is mentioned in the explanatory memorandum of the proposed government bill (Memorie van Toelichting – text with additional background information and clarification that accompanies a bill). Among other things, the NIK referred to the high level of training of Jewish butchers, and to the monitoring by religious authorities and peer reviews by international colleagues and experts (NIK 2011). However, although Jews and Muslims must comply with several rules according to their faith while slaughtering animals, it is important to note that the debate on ritual slaughter focuses particularly on the killing of animals without prior stunning. Although it is often referred to as the 'debate on ritual slaughter', it is in fact a debate about one particular aspect of these methods for slaughter: the prohibition of stunning.

11 Jews are allowed to eat 'beasts of the earth', meaning mammals with the exception of swarming rodents. But these land mammals must have cloven hooves and they must chew their cud, otherwise they are forbidden (like, for example, the camel and the pig). Animals living in the water that have fins and scales can be eaten (therefore oysters and clams are forbidden). The criteria for birds are more obscure, but the Torah provides a list of forbidden birds, including birds of prey and scavengers. Some winged insects are allowed to be eaten, but rodents, reptiles and amphibians are off limits. For a more elaborate explanation of kosher dietary law, see 'Kashrut: Jewish Dietary Laws', Judaism 101: www.jewfaq.org/kashrut.htm (accessed 6 March 2014).

12 Muslims distinguish different categories of animals: there are water and land creatures. Water creatures are divided into fish-like creatures that do not live on land, and creatures that do not resemble fish. In general, fish are considered to be halal. With regard to other creatures, all dead water creatures are regarded as halal, except the frog. Fanged creatures, such as alligators, are forbidden. There are two types of land creatures: animals with or without flowing blood. Except for the locust, all animals without flowing blood are forbidden to be eaten. Animals with flowing blood are divided in two groups: domestic and wild animals. Of the domestic animals, cattle, horses and birds can be consumed, while it is forbidden to eat donkeys, mules, dogs and cats. As far as animals in the wild are concerned, all beasts with fangs and all birds with claws are forbidden for consumption ('Azzām 1981 [2009]; Qardawi 1984).

13 New Zealand is often mentioned as an example. For a description of this procedure in New Zealand, see Pleiter (2005).

14 See 'Is It Kosher?', KosherQuest: www.kosherquest.org/bookhtml/SHECHITA_THROUGH_BUTCHER.htm (accessed 6 March 2014); Mufti Muhammad ibn Adam, 'Islamic Guidelines to Slaughtering Animals', ShariahProgram: www.shariahprogram.ca/eat-halal-foods/islamic-guidelines-slaughtering-animals.shtml (accessed 6 March 2014); 'Azzām (1981 [2009]); Qardawi (1984).

Ritual Slaughter in the Dutch Political Debate

As described above, in 2008 Marianne Thieme of the PvdD submitted a bill (TK 2007–8 31 571) to ban the slaughter of animals without stunning.[15] The Dutch House of Representatives (Tweede Kamer) voted overwhelmingly in favour of this ban in 2011. The right-wing Freedom Party (Partij voor de Vrijheid; PVV), led by Geert Wilders, even demanded a ban on the import of meat of animals slaughtered without stunning. The Christian Democrats, together with other Christian parties, voted against banning this slaughter practice. Their main argument was that such a ban would be a breach of freedom of religion under Article 6 of the Dutch Constitution. Representatives of Jewish and Muslim organizations also spoke out against the proposal.[16]

The bill was passed on to the Senate (Eerste Kamer) in 2012, where it was rejected, much to the relief of the Jewish and Muslim communities. However, the matter did not end there. The Senate's rejection was regarded as an unusual interference by a parliamentary body whose members are not directly elected by the people: some saw the Senate decision as contrary to the public will, since the bill had passed through the House of Representatives with a huge majority.[17] In 2012, Secretary of State for Economic Affairs, Agriculture and Innovation Henk Bleker came up with a covenant appeasing religious organizations and allowing Jews and Muslims to continue ritual slaughter while compelling them to prevent animal suffering. The following measures would apply:

- A veterinarian must be present during the slaughter.
- The animal must die within 40 seconds, otherwise the veterinarian must intervene and kill the animal.
- Animals must be examined before slaughter, and an animal can be rejected for slaughter on the basis of overall weight and the size of the neck.
- A committee of scientists must examine this new protocol.[18]

Although the Dutch are well known for their love of compromise, this covenant was nevertheless subjected to criticism. According to Marianne Thieme of the PvdD, the covenant was not an acceptable alternative to her bill, which aimed at a total ban on ritual slaughter.[19] The Royal Dutch Veterinary Society (Koninklijke Nederlandse Maatschappij voor Diergeneeskunde; KNMvD) regretted the fact that the religious organizations were not receptive to better alternatives such as reversible stunning or stunning immediately after the throat of the animal was cut.[20] Then, the process of formation of the scientific

15 See also Footnote 3.

16 See, for example, Zoethout (2013).

17 For example, Marianne Thieme of the PvdD stated that the Senate was out of touch with the debate over this form of slaughter in Dutch society; see 'Senaat in Debat Rituele Slacht ver van Samenleving', nu.nl, 14 December 2011: www.nu.nl/politiek/2693644/senaat-in-debat-rituele-slacht-ver-van-samenleving.html (accessed 6 March 2014).

18 See 'Convenant Onbedwelmd Slachten Volgens Religieuze Riten', Rijksoverheid, 5 June 2012: www.rijksoverheid.nl/documenten-en-publicaties/convenanten/2012/06/05/convenant-onbedwelmd-slachten-volgens-religieuze-riten.html (accessed 6 March 2014).

19 See W. van der Bles, 'Alleen Thieme Niet Blij met Convenant Ritueel Slachten', *Trouw*, 6 June 2012: www.trouw.nl/tr/nl/4500/Politiek/article/detail/3266852/2012/06/06/Alleen-Thieme-niet-blij-met-convenant-ritueel-slachten.dhtml (accessed 6 March 2014).

20 See 'Convenant Ritueel Slachten Nauwelijks een Verbetering voor Dierenwelzijn', KNMvD, 19 June 2012: http://ggg.knmvd.nl/nieuwsberichten/website/2012/juni/convenant-ritueel-

committee encountered a problem. Ronnie Eisenmann, President of the Jewish Community Amsterdam (Joodse Gemeente Amsterdam; JGA) declared that the Jewish community was opposed to Ludo Hellebrekers's appointment as President of the KNMvD because, according to Eisenmann, Hellebrekers had frequently stated that the key issue in the debate on ritual slaughter was animal welfare, not freedom of religion.[21] Another issue was the fact that the position of the veterinarian who should oversee the slaughter procedure allowed him or her to issue mandatory indications. This caused particular opposition from the Jewish community.

Secretary of State Henk Bleker promised an Order in Council (Algemene Maatregel van Bestuur) and work instructions which would both state that a vet was not allowed to interfere with religious practices. During an interview at the end of his term, Bleker claimed that ritual slaughter was his 'favourite dossier', but he profoundly hoped that the next government would let the issue rest for a while and conduct an evaluation of this covenant in about four years' time.[22]

Frequency

The Netherlands is a relatively small country with almost 17 million inhabitants, of which 850,000 are Muslims[23] and 50,000 follow the Jewish faith.[24] Annually, millions of animals are slaughtered: in 2006, almost 2 million cattle were put down for slaughter, about 14 million pigs, 710,000 sheep and over 400 million poultry.[25] Relatively few animals are slaughtered ritually. According to the KNMvD (2010), in 2006 about 125,000 cattle, 850,000 sheep and goats, 1,170,000 poultry, 25,600 rabbits, 2,000 doves and 500 ducks were allowed to be slaughtered without prior stunning. The actual number of animals slaughtered without stunning is lower, although precise figures are not available. The Secretary of State at the time, Bleker, stated that at least 370,000 but not more than 1,100,000 animals per annum were slaughtered without stunning. The latter figure refers to the number of animals slaughtered in abattoirs with a permit allowing slaughter without stunning. According to the Secretary of State, not all of these animals were slaughtered without stunning.[26] The NIK presented the following figures: less than 0.1 per cent of

slachten-nauwelijks-een-verbetering-voor-dierenwelzijn (accessed 6 March 2014).

21 See I. Weel, 'Convenant Rituele Slacht Wankelt', *Trouwe*, 19 June 2012: www.trouw.nl/tr/nl/4500/Politiek/article/detail/3256155/2012/05/16/Convenant-rituele-slacht-wankelt.dhtml?utm_source=scherm1andutm_medium=buttonandutm_campaign (accessed 6 March 2014).

22 See 'Rituele Slacht was Mijn Mooiste Dossier', nrc.nl, 20 October 2012: www.nrc.nl/handelsblad/van/2012/oktober/20/rituele-slacht-was-mijn-mooiste-dossier-1166855 (accessed 6 March 2014).

23 Most of them are of Turkish or Moroccan decent; see 'Ruim 850 Duizend Islamieten in Nederland', Centraal Bureau voor de Statistiek, 24 October 2007: www.cbs.nl/nl-NL/menu/themas/bevolking/publicaties/artikelen/archief/2007/2007-2278-wm.htm (accessed 6 March 2014).

24 Only 16 per cent of the population are members of a religious community. The majority are unbelievers; see *Bevolkingstrends: Statistisch Kwartaalblad over de Demografie van Nederland, Jaargang 58–4e Kwartaal 2010*, Centraal Bureau voor de Statistiek, 2010: www.cbs.nl/NR/rdonlyres/34B00D52-18DB-4AA3-AEF7-C62573343846/0/2010k4b15pub.pdf (accessed 6 March 2014).

25 See http://statline.cbs.nl (accessed 6 March 2014).

26 In 2010, the Nederlandse Voedsel en Waren Autoriteit (a department of the Ministry of Economic Affairs, Agriculture and Innovation that monitors the health of animals and plants, animal welfare, and the safety of food and consumer products, maintaining legislation on nature and the

the animals that are slaughtered without stunning are slaughtered according to the Jewish rites: 1,000–2,000 animals per year (NIK 2011).

According to the PvdD and KNMvD, there is an imbalance on the market as far as meat obtained from ritual slaughter is concerned. The supply of ritual slaughtered meat in the Netherlands is higher than demand. As the labelling of ritually slaughtered meat is not compulsory, a proportion of it is sold or exported as 'regular' meat, and as a result consumers risk buying ritually slaughtered products without realizing it.

Animal Welfare

The KNMvD (2010) has discussed several issues relating to animal welfare. One of the main ones relates to fixation. Before its throat is cut, an animal is fixated in order to restrict its ability to move. For cattle, a special positioning device is used to bring the animal into a lateral or supine position. This process adds stress to the slaughtering procedure, and because the animals resist, it takes longer for them to lose consciousness. According to vets, it is very likely that these animals suffer pain. They may, for example, inhale blood, and breathlessness may occur due to damage to the vagus and phrenic nerves that can result in a cough reflex. Increased stress may also result from the sudden drop in blood pressure. In the case of cattle, the vertebral artery is not cut, and that particular blood vessel plays an important role in blood supply of the brain. As a result, it takes the animals longer to lose consciousness, and according to the KNMvD, this has a serious effect on animal welfare.

In reaction, the NIK claimed that the veterinarians involved were scientifically biased, and that the KNMvD's findings were inaccurate. The NIK particularly disputed the necessity of stunning, the stress the animals suffered before the throat was cut, the pain caused by the cut and the process of losing consciousness. Furthermore, the NIK regretted that their general arguments in favour of the *sjechita* had not been taken into account.[27] The NIK also stated that animal welfare is profoundly anchored in Judaism and its laws, which stipulated that animals should also enjoy rest on the Sabbath (Exodus 20:10), should be allowed to stay with their mothers for the first seven days of their lives (Leviticus 22:27).[28] The Muslims–Government Contact Institution (Contactorgaan Moslims en Overheid; CMO) also expressed doubts about the presentation of scientific facts in this debate and referred to animal welfare rules and ideas embedded in their religion.[29]

---

environment) began a registration procedure for slaughtering without stunning; see 'Bedwelming bij Ritueel slachten: Debat in de Tweede Kamer op 13 April 2011', Publitiek: http://publitiek.nl/debat/bedwelming_bij_ritueel_slachten_13-04-2011/7 (accessed 6 March 2014).

27 Both the KNMvD and the NIK quote a 2004 article, S.D. Rosen, 'Physiological Insights into Shechita', *Veterinary Record* 154(24), 759–65, while interpreting it differently. Furthermore, both organizations have different interpretations of reports published by the Animal Sciences Group of the University and Research Centre Wageningen, a renowned Dutch facility with a strong focus on food, agricultural and environmental issues (see NIK 2011). The NIK took the Animal Sciences Group to court, claiming – among other things – that this academic centre was not scientifically independent. The court ruled that scientific research results must be published freely so that they can be evaluated through scientific debate; see 'Uitspraak Rapporten Ritueel Slachten', De Rechtspraak, 7 July 2011: www.rechtspraak.nl/Organisatie/Rechtbanken/Gelderland/Nieuws/Pages/Uitspraakrapportenritueelslachten.aspx (accessed 6 March 2014).

28 More examples can be found in NIK (2011).

29 See *Position Paper: Bescherming van Dierenwelzijn Vergt geen Inbreuk op de Vrijheid van Godsdienst!*, Werkgroep Islam en Dierenwelzijn/Contactorgaan Moslims en Overheid, October 2011:

Religious Freedom

The NIK was particularly angered by the following statement by the PvdD when they introduced the bill in the House of Representatives:

> Without having to step into the shoes of religious people, it is perfectly possible to enter into a civilized dialogue with them and to try to make them understand the consequences of slaughter without stunning and convince them that even from their religious perspective it is necessary for animals to be reversibly stunned before ritual slaughter. When more facts and information are becoming available that are also of relevance to the significance worshippers attach to certain rituals, one should confront worshippers with these facts, thereby making it more difficult for them to use their right of freedom of religion. Their uncompromising insistence on unstunned slaughter can no longer be regarded as a necessary expression of religion as there are ample alternatives that are beneficial to animal welfare and at the same time square with the animal-friendly intentions of that religion. (NIK 2011)

The NIK felt that the PvdD had crossed the line between the realm of state influence and the private lives of people for whom religion plays an essential role. In the NIK's view, the state should not interfere in private issues, and in justification it referred to the centuries-old principle of separation of Church and state. The NIK furthermore rejected the use of scientific arguments to curtail the fundamental and absolute right of religious freedom. The CMO also felt that the proposed ban and the ensuing discussions affected the religious freedom of Muslims.[30]

Stigmatization in the Debate

Savages and Torturers

Is there indeed a relationship between the commitment to animal welfare and the stigmatization of religious minority groups? If that is the case, how does it manifest itself and to what extent does metaphorical (ab)use of animals play a role? Before dealing with these questions, it is important to address the difference between the Jewish and Muslim minorities in the Netherlands.

Although today there are more Muslims living in the Netherlands then there are Jews, people following the Jewish faith take a more active part in the debate on the ban on ritual slaughter than Muslims do. There are two reasons for this. Jewish people in the Netherlands have been an integral part of the Dutch community for centuries, whereas most Muslim immigrants did not migrate to the country before the late 1960s and early 1970s. The NIK emphasizes this in its factsheet, stating that *sjechita* in the Netherlands has been practised

---

www.republiekallochtonie.nl/userfiles/files/Final%20Position%20Paper%20kopie.pdf (accessed 6 March 2014).

30 See *Reactie Moslim Organisaties op de Memorie van Antwoord van Marianne Thieme, 25 November 2011, Metbetrekking tot Ritueel Slachten (31 571)*, Werkgroep Islam en Dierenwelzijn/ Contactorgaan Moslims en Overheid: www.republiekallochtonie.nl/userfiles/files/Reactie%20 CMO%20op%20de%20MvA%20inzake%20Ritueel%20Slachten.pdf (accessed 6 March 2014).

for 375 years: 'A de facto ban on the sjechita would be a historic mistake in many respects' (NIK 2011). This refers to the persecution of Dutch Jews during the Second World War – it was during the German occupation in 1940–45 that this practice of slaughter was banned. Such references to the horrific events of the Second World War and older patterns of anti-Semitism severely complicate the discussion of ritual slaughter.

There is an interesting body of literature on how propagandists in general, and Nazis in particular, have abused the discussion of animal welfare and ritual. In Nazi Germany, the Jews were characterized as 'others', or even worse, as 'savages' or 'beasts' (see Arluke and Sanders 1996; Sax 2000; Davids 2013). In this context, the practice of ritual slaughter was often presented as a form of animal cruelty: the logic and practicality behind Jewish dietary laws with regard to issues such as food safety and animal welfare were often neglected. Their way of slaughtering was simply portrayed as a form of torture or sadism, and it was even compared to the sacrifice of children. Jews were presented as 'big and bad', and therefore as 'ideal offenders' with 'ideal victims' – namely helpless, defenceless and suffering animals.[31]

In the Netherlands just after the Second World War, animal welfare groups called for the maintenance of the ban that had been imposed by the Germans during the occupation, but the Dutch government did not comply with this. However, ritual slaughter was only permitted in a limited number of slaughterhouses. During 1949–50 a new debate followed after the Dutch government had signed a trade agreement with Israel on the export of kosher meat. Again animal activists voiced their protests, and this time they received support from the Ministry of Health. Officials argued that the Jewish community had agreed to slaughter animals with prior stunning during the German occupation, and that they should not use their 'exaggerated orthodoxy' as an excuse for ritual slaughter.[32] However, Chief Rabbi Justus Tal pointed out that the Jews had no choice during the occupation, and wondered what sort of people would be willing to copy the conduct of the Nazis out of so-called sympathy for animals. Ultimately, the Minister of Agriculture decided that the economic value of the trade agreement with Israel was more important than the issue of ritual slaughter. In the 1980s the debate flared up again, provoked by a report from the chief inspector of the animal protection service in the Dutch town of Hilversum. He pointed out that Jews were allowed to eat non-kosher meat in emergency situations. Since a ban on ritual slaughter would create such an emergency situation, he wondered what the fuss was about – after all, the Jews had not been allowed to eat kosher meat in the concentration camps either.[33] In this context, it is not surprising that people of the Jewish faith are very much alert when there are discussions of ritual slaughter.[34]

31 For more background information on the rationale behind cultural codes related to taboos with food and dietary laws, see Harris (1974; 1985). On the relationship between humans and meat for food, see Herzog (2010).

32 See B. Krumhout, 'Lessen Uit het Verleden: Kritiek op Ritueel Slachten soms Antisemitisch', *Historisch Nieuwsblad* 3/2011: www.historischnieuwsblad.nl/nl/artikel/27337/lessen-uit-het-verleden-kritiek-op-ritueel-slachten-soms-antisemitisch.html (accessed 6 March 2014).

33 Ibid.

34 References to the Second World War are not limited to the practice of ritual slaughter by Jews. The Dutch performer Robert Long stated in 2000 that what Dachau was for the Jews, the meat-industry was for pigs. Cazaux argued: 'Some authors denote the situation of aothas [other than human animals] in modern husbandry as a "holocaust" of aothas .... We would like to stress ... that ... the Holocaust notion is particularly reserved for that specific genocide acted through during the Nazi-regime of the Second World War against Jews. Although we do want to argue that the treatment of aothas in modern husbandry can be denoted as a genocide ..., our comparison is not aimed at

Shadid and Van Koningsveld (1995) state that campaigns by extreme right-wing activists[35] against ritual slaughter by Muslims, portraying it as an example of their cruel nature,[36] are quite similar to the unfounded nineteenth-century accusations of Jews being 'savages' because of their slaughter practices. These accusations were racist, and in the 1980s and 1990s were partially inspired by feelings of economic competition between Jewish and Muslim butchers.

In the present debate on the proposed ban on ritual slaughter, the metaphor of the 'savage' and the accusations of cruelty have cropped up again. In 2011, Ronnie Eisenmann, President of the Jewish Community Amsterdam, stated that Jews were no savages, and maintained that people should focus on the large number of animals slaughtered with prior stunning in general, whose welfare was not discussed. Why only focus on ritual slaughter? Eisenmann received support from the Muslim community.[37] In 2012, a local Jewish group and a number of people of the Roman Catholic faith filed a complaint of anti-Semitism against Dion Graus, a member of the House of Representatives for the PVV. They accused Graus of making anti-Semitic remarks during an interview broadcast by a local TV station in which he stated that Jews were torturing animals using religious freedom as an excuse. In a newspaper article, a spokesperson for the plaintiffs argued that Graus's remark had

---

denying or obliterating the distinctive features and peculiarities of each specific genocidal policy throughout history …, and as such, the term holocaust is to be reserved to that particular genocide, aimed at that specific group of humans, in that specific time frame' (Cazaux 2002, p. 359). Sztybel (2006), a descendant of a Holocaust survivor, holds the opposite view, and claims that comparisons with the Holocaust are valid. Recently, Israeli animal activists have even begun to brand themselves as a means of demonstrating solidarity with animals and paying tribute to the survivors of Nazi concentration camps; see T. Goldenberg, 'Israelis Brand Selves in Solidarity with Animals', Yahoo! News, 27 June 2013: http://news.yahoo.com/israelis-brand-selves-solidarity-animals-061447667.html (accessed 6 March 2014).

35 An analysis by the Dutch Police of radical animal activism in the period 1999–2003 found that these kinds of activists targeted the fur industry, the (intensive) poultry and livestock sectors, the meat processing industry, and institutes working with laboratory animals. Ritual slaughter was not mentioned specifically (KLPD 2004). Nevertheless, ritual slaughter was not let off the hook entirely. On 8 June 2011, the extreme right-wing group With the Animals against the Beasts (Met de Dieren Tegen de Beesten; MDTB) published an open letter on its website addressed to the spokespersons of the political parties in the Dutch House of Representatives, saying: 'Nobody attacks the Jews and the Muslims; animal protectionists like to point out to religious people that they are not following their own morality by following ancient rules without verifying whether more recent scientific insights and techniques are doing more justice to this morality – that is, to avoid harming animals as much as possible.' On the opposing side of the political spectrum, activists accused the extreme right of using animal welfare as a vehicle for attacking Muslims and people from an immigrant background (De Wit 2002; AIVD 2010).

36 For example, Brigitte Bardot stated in France that: 'from year to year we see mosques flourish across France, while our church bells fall silent … tens of thousands of poor beasts whose throats are slit … with blades that are more or less sharpened by clumsy sacrificers who have to repeat their gesture several times, while kids splashed with blood bathe in this magma of terror, of blood spurting from badly-slit jugulars'; quoted in: Elder et al. (1998, p. 72). For British examples, see Klug (1989).

37 See 'Joodse Gemeente: "Wij Zijn Geen Barbaren"', *Trouw*, 16 June 2011: www.trouw.nl/tr/nl/4500/Politiek/article/detail/2445830/2011/06/16/Joodse-Gemeente-Wij-zijn-geen-barbaren.dhtml (accessed 6 March 2014). Ormel, a member of the House of Representatives, wondered what it would mean if the government was convinced that the killing of animals without stunning in all cases led to more suffering: in that case, what should be done about (sport) fishing or hunting? See 'Bedwelming bij Ritueel Slachten: Debat in de Tweede Kamer op 13 April 2011', Publitiek: http://publitiek.nl/debat/bedwelming_bij_ritueel_slachten_13-04-2011/7 (accessed 6 March 2014).

opened up old wounds from the Second World War. It was Hitler's regime that had instigated the ban on ritual slaughter, and in the end millions of Jews died in the gas chambers.[38] However, Hans Knoop, a columnist for the Dutch-Israeli weekly magazine *Nederlands Israelisch Weekblad*, rejected the comparison and called the comments dangerous. The fact that the Nazis were the first to build motorways would give no reason to implicate contemporary motorway users as Nazi sympathizers. Although Graus was not the only Dutch politician supporting a ban on ritual slaughter, others carefully avoided the use of words such as 'ritual torture'.[39] Knoop did raise a very important point: should one regard every form of criticism of ritual slaughter as a form of anti-Semitism or racism?[40]

Food for Thought

The discussion of ritual slaughter provides plenty of food for thought. There have been examples of racism in this discussion, and undoubtedly negative sentiments from the past play a part in the (past and contemporary) debate on ritual slaughter. But discussing animal welfare in an open and constructive way must be seen as a positive challenge for the near future. Naturally, it means that stereotyping and stigmatizing participants in this debate by portraying them as beasts and accusing them of sadism and cruelty is wrong. Equally, animal welfare activists should not immediately be disqualified as ignorant and naive animal lovers who regard animals as superior to human beings and their religions. Only open minds and constructive attitudes among all the participants in the discussion will eventually ensure a 'stunning' debate.

References

AIVD. 2010. *Dierenrechtenactivisme in Nederland: Gefragmenteerd maar Groeiend*. The Hague: AIVD.

Arluke, A. and Sanders, C.R. 1996. *Regarding Animals*. Philadelphia, PA: Temple University Press.

'Azzām, 'Abdullāh. 1981 [2009]. *The Ruling on Meat Slaughtered in the West*, 2nd edn: http://iskandrani.files.wordpress.com/2009/02/meat.pdf.

38 See 'Klacht Tegen PVV'er Graus om Antisemitisme', Volkskrant, 30 October 2012: www.volkskrant.nl/vk/nl/10346/Vertrek-Hero-Brinkman/article/detail/3339829/2012/10/30/Klacht-tegen-PVV-er-Graus-om-antisemitisme.dhtml (accessed 6 March 2014). The bold statements by Graus did not lead to much commotion within his party. However, there was a dispute with a former member of the PVV (see '"PVV legitimeert antisemitisme"', nu.nl, 20 August 2012: www.nu.nl/achtergrond/2889772/pvv-legitimeert-antisemitisme.html; accessed 6 March 2014), and Israeli Chief Rabbi Yona Metzger called on party leader Wilders to intervene (see Reuters, 'Israel's Chief Rabbi Warns Dutch Populist Politician over Kosher Slaughter Ban', *Haaretz*, 30 August 2012: www.haaretz.com/jewish-world/jewish-world-news/israel-s-chief-rabbi-warns-dutch-populist-politician-over-kosher-slaughter-ban-1.461722; accessed 6 March 2014).

39 See H. Knoop, 'Hoeveel Gekker Kan het Worden', NIW, 19 October 2012: www.niw.nl/hoeveel-gekker-kan-het-worden/ (accessed 6 March 2014).

40 See also Snildal (2012), who describes the discussion on kosher slaughter in Norway during 1895–1913 and cautions historians not to interpret every aspect of the discussion as anti-Semitic.

Barnes, J.E., Boat, B.W., Putnam, F.W., Dates, H.F. and Mahlman, A.R. 2006. 'Ownership of High-risk ("Vicious") Dogs as a Marker for Deviant Behaviors: Implications for Risk Assessment', *Journal of Interpersonal Violence* 12, 1,616–34.

Caplan, J. 2000. '"National Tattooing": Traditions of Tattooing in Nineteenth-century Europe', in *Written on the Body: The Tattoo in European and American History*, edited by J. Caplan. London: Reaktion Books, 156–73.

Cazaux, G. 2002. *Anthropocentrism and Speciesism Regarding Animals Other than Human Animals in Contemporary Criminology: Analysing the Concept 'Animal Abuse' in Criminological Science and in Belgian Legislation Regarding the Protection and Welfare of Animals*. Ghent: Faculty of Law, University of Ghent.

Christie, N. 1986. 'The Ideal Victim', in *From Crime Policy to Victim Policy: Reorienting the Justice System*, edited by E.A. Fattah. London: Macmillan, 17–30.

Cohen, J. and Richardson, J. 2002. 'Pit Bull Panic', *Journal of Popular Culture* 2, 285–317.

Davids, K. 2013. 'Barbaarse Praktijken: Dierenbeschermers tegen Ritueel Slachten', *Geschiedenis Magazine* 5, 14–27.

Davis, M.A. 2011. 'Don't Judge Species on Their Origins', *Nature* 474, 153–4.

De Wit, G. 2002. 'Extreem-rechtse Dierenvrienden tegen Moslims', *De Fabel van de Illegaal* 49 (January/February).

Elder, G., Wolch, J. and Emel, J. 1998. 'Le Pratique Sauvage: Race, Place, and the Human–animal Divide', in *Animal Geographies: Place, Politics and Identity in the Nature-culture Borderlands*, edited by J. Wolch and J. Emel. London: Verso, 72–90.

Fitzgerald, A.J. 2010. 'The "Underdog" as "Ideal Victim"? The Attribution of Victimhood in the 2007 Pet Food Recall', *International Review of Victimology* 17, 131–57.

Harris, M. 1974. *Cows, Pigs, Wars and Witches: The Riddles of Culture*. New York: Vintage.

Harris, M. 1985. *Good to Eat: Riddles of Food and Culture*. Long Grove, IL: Waveland Press.

Herzog, H. 2010. *Some We Love, Some We Hate, Some We Eat: Why It's So Hard to Think Straight About Animals*. New York: HarperPerennial.

Janssen, J. 2009. 'Eigen Dieren Eerst! Over de Criminalisering van de Migratie van Dieren', in *Diverse Kwesties: Liber Amicorum Prof. Dr. Frank Bovenkerk*, edited by C. Brants and S. van der Poel. The Hague: Boom Juridische uitgevers, 27–34.

Janssen, J. 2011. 'Eenzame Kooidieren: De Onderbelichte Rol van Dieren bij het Stigmatiseren en Resocialiseren van Delinquenten', in *De Vogel Vrij: Liber Amicorum voor Prof. Dr. Mr. Martin Moerings*, edited by J.P. van der Leun, E.R. Muller, N. van der Schee and M.A.H. van der Woude. The Hague: Boom Lemma Uitgevers, 413–22.

Janssen, J. 2012a. 'Geweld Tegen Mensen en Dieren: Denken over Correlatie, Causatie en de Angst voor Valse Positieven', *Proces* 3, 156–66.

Janssen, J. 2012b. 'Over Mensen en Andere Dieren in de Criminologie, *Justitiële Verkenningen* 2, 29–38.

Janssen, J. 2014. 'Onverdoofd Slachten. Dierenwelzijnsargumenten Tegen En Godsdienstige Argumenten Voor Deze Slachtmethode', *Tijdschrift voor Religie, Recht en Beleid* 1, 34–45.

KLPD. 2004. *Criminaliteitsbeeldanalyse Radicaal Dierenactivisme 1999–2003*. Driebergen: KLPD.

Klug, B. 1989. 'Ritual Murmur: The Undercurrent of Protest against Religious Slaughter of Animals in Britain in the 1980s', *Patterns of Prejudice* 23(2), 16–28.

KNMvD. 2010. *Standpunt KNMvD over het Onbedwelmd Slachten van Dieren*: http://ggg.knmvd.nl/nieuwsberichten/website/2011/februari/standpunt-knmvd-over-onbedwelmd-slachten (accessed 6 March 2014).

Lévi-Strauss, C. 1962a. *La Pensée Sauvage*. Paris: Plon.
Lévi-Strauss, C. 1962b. *Le Totémisme Aujourd'hui*. Paris: Presses Universitaires de France.
NIK. 2011. *Factsheet Joods – Religieus Slachten*: www.nik.nl/wp-content/uploads/2011/03/Factsheet-Joods-religieus-slachten-maart-20111.pdf (accessed 6 March 2014).
Pleiter, H. 2005. 'Elektrobetäubung vor der Rituellen Schlachtung von Rindern un Shafen in Neuseland', in *Tierschutz bei der Rituellen Schlachtung*, edited by J. Luy, K. von Holleben, M. von Wezlawowicz et al. Gießen: Verlag der DVG Service, 72–6.
Qardawi, Y. 1984. *Halal en Haram: Wat Toegestaan en Verboden is in Islam, Deel 1*. Delft: Uitgeverij Noer al-ilm.
Rémy, E. and Beck, C. 2008. 'Allochtone, Autochtone, Invasif: Catégorisations Animales et Perception d'Autrui', *Politix: Revue des sciences sociales et politique* 21(82), 193–209.
Sax, B. 2000. *Animals in the Third Reich: Pets, Scapegoats, and the Holocaust*. New York: Continuum.
Shadid, W. and Van Koningsveld, P.S. 1995. *De Mythe van het Islamitische Gevaar*. Kampen: Kok Pharos.
Snildal, A. 2012. 'Anti-Semitism without Hatred? The Animal Protection Movement and the Semantics of Kosher Slaughter in Norway 1895–1913', paper presented at the international congress *'Being Different without Fear': Antisemitism and Exclusion Then and Now*, Madrid, 7–9 March.
Sztybel, D. 2006. 'Can the Treatment of Animals be Compared to the Holocaust?', *Ethics and the Environment* 1, 97–132.
Zoethout, C. 2013. 'Ritual Slaughter and the Freedom of Religion: Some Reflections on the Stunning Matter', *Human Rights Quarterly* 3, 651–72.

PART III
Combating Environmental Crime

Chapter 13
Invisible Victims: the Problem of Policing Environmental Crime

Toine Spapens

Introduction

This chapter approaches the question of victims of environmental crime from the perspective of law enforcement in general, and the Dutch police in particular. Environmental crimes and criminals display a combination of characteristics that in many respects differs from other types of crime. They encompass a wide range of different behaviors that fall into two broad categories. The first is the pollution of the air, water, and land, for example dumping waste or blending it with other goods, and importing and using illicit pesticides. The second category concerns illegal acts causing direct harm to flora and fauna, for instance illegal deforestation and the poaching of and trading in protected wildlife. Perpetrators include petty criminals, organized crime groups such as the Italian mafia, corporations, and government agencies (Gruppo Abele-Nomos et al. 2003; Kauzlarich and Kramer 1998; Van Geffen 2001). Tackling environmental crime also involves many actors, both governmental and non-governmental. A final point is that environmental crimes are increasingly transnational in scope.

These characteristics create a number of complexities for the police, and this chapter discusses three of them in greater detail. It begins with a brief historical sketch of environmental crime enforcement in the Netherlands from the early 1970s onwards. Then it will focus on the general problems the police force faces when investigating environmental crimes, for example the lack of visible victims, and the complexity of environmental rules and regulations. It continues by addressing the complexities arising from the need for cooperation between law enforcement and administrative authorities—two institutions that each have a very different focus—and then analyzes the complexities of cross-border police cooperation in the field of environmental crime. The final section offers some brief conclusions.

A Brief History of Environmental Crime Enforcement in the Netherlands

In the 1950s and 1960s, the economies and populations of most Western industrialized countries grew rapidly, and welfare increased accordingly. However, growth and technical innovations also led to increases in pollution and environmental nuisances. At the end of the 1960s, for example, flying to far-away holiday destinations became affordable for most of the population, but the consequence for people who lived near airports was more noise pollution. The introduction of washing machines saved households a lot of time and effort, but it also adversely affected water quality, particularly because of the phosphates that were then still widely used in laundry detergent (Constandse 1975).

Environmental pollution evidently produced highly visible, audible, and odor nuisance for many Dutch inhabitants at that time, fueling pressure on the government to respond appropriately. The 1960s produced the 'protest generation,' whose members also addressed environmental issues and formed activist groups. Overall, the public became better informed about the health threats of chemical substances and asbestos, for example, and groups of people stood up against all types of social inequalities in their local communities. In their view, having to live in a polluted environment was an injustice that called for action like any other.

The phrase 'environmental crime' was first heard in the Dutch parliament in November 1973.[1] This illustrates that thinking about environmental damage in terms of crime is a relatively recent phenomenon. Of course, such behavior was punishable by law when it negatively affected human health or economic activity, but legislation concerning crimes against flora and fauna only began to appear during the second half of the 1960s. In the Netherlands, legislators adopted a wide range of environmental laws in the early 1970s. In 1975, more than ten bills had entered into force, and several others were awaiting parliament's approval.[2]

In order to create new legislation quickly, the government chose to introduce sector-specific rather than integrated environmental laws. Due to the technical complexity of the legislation, enforcement proved to be difficult. In particular, law enforcement agencies lacked public prosecutors and police officers with detailed knowledge. Matters were further complicated by the fact that the administrative authorities also held important enforcement responsibilities. There was a lack of coordination in the interventions targeting perpetrators, and a lack of proactive information exchange between the different agencies. Finally, the people who had drawn up the new environmental laws had not given much thought to penalization and enforceability.

These shortcomings were revealed in the early 1980s when several scandals came to light. One of the first concerned a housing project in the village of Lekkerkerk near Rotterdam, which had been built on a former illegal chemical waste dumping site. The authorities had to clean up the entire neighborhood, and found about 1,600 barrels containing chemical waste. The case led to a public outcry when it became clear that the company responsible for the dumping could not be held liable for the damage owing to the short statute of limitations associated with the low maximum sentences laid down in the law. Not surprisingly, members of parliament immediately pressed the government for more severe sentences for violations of environmental law. But the Lekkerkerk case turned out to be merely the tip of the iceberg; further investigation showed there were approximately 3,000 illegal chemical waste dumping sites in the country. Of these, 350 presented a direct danger to human health and the quality of the drinking water and required sanitation.

Another major scandal in the early 1980s concerned Uniser, a company that treated waste oil and chemical waste. Instead of recycling the waste, the company simply discharged most of it into a river. One of its employees stated that the corporation had a simple rule:

1 Parliamentary documents: *Handelingen II*, November 7, 1973, p. 714.

2 This concerned the Hinderwet (Public Nuisance Act), Wet Verontreiniging Oppervlaktewateren (Pollution of Surface Waters Act), Wet inzake de Luchtverontreiniging (Air Pollution Act), Ontgrondingswet (Soil Removal Act), Wet op de Ruimtelijke Ordening (Spatial Planning Act), Wet Gevaarlijke Stoffen (Dangerous Substances Act), Kernenergiewet (Nuclear Energy Act), Natuurbeschermingswet (Nature Protection Act), Wet olieverontreiniging zeewater (Seawater Oil Pollution Act), and Bestrijdingsmiddelenwet 1962 (Pesticides Act 1962). Awaiting adoption were the Wet op de Geluidshinder (Noise Abatement Act), Wet op de Bodembescherming (Soil Protection Act), and Afvalstoffenwet (Waste Products Act).

'waste that would burn was used as fuel, and everything that did not was dumped.'[3] A special government committee evaluated the enforcement activities of the competent administrative and judicial authorities, and concluded that they had failed to coordinate their work properly. Sometimes one authority called for the rigorous enforcement of environmental law whereas another wanted to give the company another chance and wait for the results of measures intended to improve the situation. Logically, Uniser's activities required all sorts of permits, but these were issued by a number of different agencies, none of which had a clear overview.[4] Administrative licensing procedures were usually time-consuming, and the authorities often allowed the corporation to begin new activities in advance of their being granted. This complicated enforcement, because authorities that had first permitted a formally illegal situation and then wanted to change their policy were vulnerable to claims for damage. Not surprisingly, the government committee called for far-reaching improvements in regulation and in organizing the enforcement of environmental laws, more effective sentencing, and last but not least, harmonization between the myriad of licenses that had evolved from sector-specific environmental legislation and a reduction in the number of competent authorities. The latter recommendation led to the Environmental Protection Act, which came into effect in 1993.

A third example also concerns a company, Tanker Cleaning Rotterdam (TCR), which collected and treated waste oil and chemical waste, mainly from ships. TCR operated a harbor reception facility for these types of waste. Such facilities became necessary after the Netherlands implemented the International Convention for the Prevention of Pollution from Ships (MARPOL) in 1982. TCR collected the waste, but dumped most of it in Rotterdam harbor. It also received a large government subsidy to develop and build a new type of waste treatment facility. The facility never materialized, and it remained unclear how the company owners had used the money. One important detail was that Neelie Kroes (later a European Union commissioner), who had been responsible for awarding TCR the subsidy, was at that time allegedly a close personal friend of one of the company's managing directors. However, corruption could not be proven. TCR and its management finally became the subject of criminal investigation in 1993, leading to its bankruptcy and substantial prison sentences.

The Dutch General Accounting Office investigated the case and concluded that the authorities had known about the violations of environmental law since 1984. Instead of closing down the company's activities, however, for years the administrative authorities chose to give TCR the benefit of the doubt and accept successive promises and plans to improve the situation. They had relatively little room to maneuver because closing TCR's harbor reception facility would have meant that the Netherlands would no longer comply with its obligations under the MARPOL Convention. It was almost ten years before the authorities had had enough of TCR's failure to comply with the different environmental rules and regulations and launched a criminal investigation.

In the mid-1990s, the TCR affair resulted in growing political awareness of severe environmental crimes, and led to the establishment of a special criminal investigation squad. A few years earlier, in 1989, the police and the public prosecution service began to receive extra funding from the Ministry of Housing, Spatial Planning and the Environment to employ specialist personnel and pay more attention to environmental crimes. At the end of the 1990s, however, the sense of urgency slowly ebbed away, particularly among the police.

---

3 Parliamentary Documents: *Kamerstukken II* 1994/95, 22 343, nr. 17: 9–10.

4 Parliamentary Documents: *Kamerstukken II* 1981/82, 17 100 XVII, nr. 89: 3.

The main reason for this is that the budget that had been earmarked specifically for environmental enforcement became part of the overall police budget in 1998. The immediate result was a sharp decline in the number of hours devoted to environmental crimes. In 2003, the police force met only half its targets. The number of specialist detectives decreased further in 2004 after a reorganization of the serious and organized crime squads.

This development clearly annoyed the Environment Minister, who insisted that the law enforcement agencies use the budget he provided to fund environmental investigation squads. This led to the formation in 2005 of 25 regional environmental investigation squads and six inter-regional squads to tackle the most serious cases of environmental crime, with 480 personnel in total. One of the members of the Board of Chief Commissioners was tasked with drawing up a police policy plan on environmental crime. In 2008, additional criticism regarding the quality of the environmental investigation squads resulted in a four-year program to further boost law enforcement efforts. Finally, 2013 saw another major reorganization of the Dutch police, leading to the formation of a unified national police force. This reduced the number of environmental investigation squads to 11, although the total number of personnel was larger because 412 'labeled' detectives remained.

The Dutch national police force (comprising about 65,000 staff in total) has several hundred specialist detectives, and one in 60 of its uniformed officers is tasked specifically with environmental crimes, which puts it in a more privileged position than the police forces in many other countries. However, this has also led to new complexities, such as how to find and investigate the most damaging environmental crimes.

The Complexity of Investigating Environmental Crime

This section addresses specific problems police forces face in investigating environmental crime. The first is that flora and fauna do not report crimes. The same is often true for humans, so the police must actively gather information and intelligence. The second difficulty is that environmental rules and regulations are technically complex; violations and cause and effect in terms of victimization are difficult to prove. The third problem is that the perpetrators are in many cases well-respected and well-connected members of society, such as the managing directors of large corporations. Finally, the investigation of environmental crimes competes with other, usually economic, interests.

The Need for Intelligence-led Policing

The first problem confronting the police is that many types of environmental crime do not produce immediate human victims or other visible damage, and therefore do not land automatically on a police officer's desk. Detecting these crimes requires active information- and intelligence-gathering, either by the police or by other government institutions—in other words, intelligence-led policing. This section will focus on the detection of crimes by the police, and the next one will address the difficulties associated with cooperation and information exchange with other governmental institutions, such as inspection agencies.

Detection of Environmental Crimes

Environmental crimes encompass a wide range of behavior, from visible to invisible violations. For example, a pile of rubbish dumped illegally in a field is easy to detect.

However, police officers may not always define such an action as a crime. During one of my lectures at the Police Academy of the Netherlands, students stated that they would have responded by calling the municipality to have it cleaned up, and did not immediately think of informing a specialist colleague to look for evidence or leads to a possible perpetrator. Other environmental crimes may not be framed as such. One good example is a major fire that occurred in 2011 at a Dutch company that stored and traded in all sorts of chemicals. The fire resulted in air, water, and soil pollution near the plant. Many people overlooked the fact that the disaster was the result of systematic noncompliance with the terms set out in the company's environmental license.

In other situations, it may be more difficult to establish that environmental laws are in fact being violated. For example, is red smoke coming out of a smokestack an environmental crime? You may not know what is causing the smoke, and if you were able to analyze it—and there are forensic methods for doing so—you would still need to find out whether the company is allowed to release certain quantities of particular components into the air. Furthermore, it is the administrative authorities in the Netherlands that are primarily responsible for inspecting facilities issued environmental licenses. The police can only act after the public prosecution service has opened a criminal investigation with regard to the license holder.

Finally, there may be environmental crimes that are mostly invisible. One example is the blending of bunker fuel for ships with chemical waste, which is a serious problem in the Netherlands (Spapens et al. 2013). This mostly leads to pollution that is not directly visible, such as increased levels of particulate matter in the atmosphere.

Proactive Gathering of Information and Intelligence

'Invisible' environmental crimes require the police to gather information and intelligence proactively. Signs of such crimes must also be adequately stored, compiled and analyzed to provide a starting point for further investigation. In the Netherlands, intelligence-led policing in the field of environmental crime is still a developing discipline. Traditionally, the police respond to reported and visible crimes, public order disturbances, and accidents. When such incidents occur, officers leap into action to apprehend the perpetrators, restore order, and provide assistance. This type of work calls for 'doers' who possess the physical and mental abilities to act efficiently in situations that call for immediate intervention. The police force naturally selects and trains its personnel accordingly.

In contrast, intelligence-led policing requires other, more academic, qualities. Although the Dutch police force is increasingly recruiting personnel who match this description, the once-dominant culture of responding to events—and waiting for something to happen in between—is only slowly being replaced by more systematic approaches to less visible crimes (Vis 2012). This is certainly true when it comes to environmental crimes: here, the police force still lacks its own information sources. Below, we will explore three ways it could be improved.

In normal circumstances, the 'eyes and ears' of uniformed police officers working on the street often offer a starting point for criminal investigations. As explained above, many officers on the street fail to recognize environmental crimes even if they are visible. Furthermore, many have little affinity for environmental issues because they associate them with activism. The fact that the Dutch police force employs a relatively large number of specialist detectives prompts other officers to leave things to the 'experts,' partly because regular uniformed police officers usually perceive environmental crimes as complex.

A few years ago, the Police Academy began to pay more attention to training general police officers to recognize environmental crimes.

The second important source of police information is planned checks and inspections. These usually require close cooperation with the administrative authorities responsible for enforcement under environmental legislation. One successful example concerns the integrated checks of the quality of ship fuel carried out four times in 2011 and 2012. These initiatives, codenamed 'Operation Watchful,' included the Water Police, the Human Environment and Transport Inspectorate, Customs, and the Netherlands Forensic Institute. The information gathered during these operations led to several criminal investigations of corporations suspected of causing pollution in ship oil, for instance by blending chemical waste with it. However, such inspections are demanding in terms of preparation and personnel, and cannot be mounted continuously.

Thirdly, the Dutch police force has specialist units tasked with gathering intelligence about ongoing criminal activities, such as drug trafficking. These units receive most of their information from criminal informers. However, environmental criminals are often not part of the urban underworld where the police recruit their informers. Instead of in shady bars, detectives are more likely to find useful informers on the golf course. The running of 'upperworld' informers is something the Dutch police force needs to develop further. Recently, the newly formed national police force decided to establish a small intelligence unit specifically for gathering information on serious environmental crimes.

Finally, if information and intelligence from different sources are to suffice as a starting point for criminal investigation, then they need to be handled and assessed effectively. Until fairly recently, individual police officers who took a personal interest in specific types of environmental crime largely built their own databases, sometimes partly in their own time because their managers did not show much appreciation for their 'hobby.' Currently, however, a specific information unit consisting of about twenty police officers is in the process of being established at the national level.

Complex Rules and Regulations

Environmental rules and regulations are often complex, and the same is true for investigations. The perpetrators usually set up complex international paper trails to mask their activities, and criminal investigation often involves painstaking analyses of corporations' administrative and financial records. Delivering proof requires high levels of expertise and prior experience with specific types of environmental crime, both within the police force and the public prosecution service. However, analysis shows that the police have great difficulty in keeping specialist and experienced officers 'on board.' There are at least three explanations for this, though my list is far from exhaustive.

The first explanation is that the Dutch police force emphasizes generalism rather than specialization. It is not deemed good for one's career to keep working in the same field for too long and management urges most police officers, particularly young professionals, to switch to a different field every four to six years. The same problem occurs within the public prosecution service, where staff switch from one specialist area to another even more frequently than in the police force. One consequence is that public prosecutors choose not to prosecute violations of environmental laws, but to focus instead on general provisions of the penal code, such as forgery of documents and money laundering, with which they are more at ease. Furthermore, these are often easier to prove and result in higher sentences than environmental crimes. The downside, of course, is that this approach contributes to the 'invisibility' of such crimes, for instance in statistics.

Secondly, even when police officers and public prosecutors with the necessary knowledge and experience are available, environmental crimes are still difficult to prove, for example because victimization of human beings and other species cannot be related directly to the crime. A good illustration is the *Probo Koala* case. The *Probo Koala* was a ship chartered in 2006 by a company named Trafigura. *Probo Koala*'s cargo consisted of low-grade oil, and the crew received orders to upgrade it at sea by treating it with caustic soda, a process which rendered a substantial amount of toxic waste. The ship docked at the port of Amsterdam intending to dispose of the waste at the reception facility for waste oil. When the slops were unloaded, it became clear that these were different from the waste that results from the normal operation of a seagoing vessel. The reception facility informed Trafigura that treatment of the slops would cost them more, so the company decided to take the waste elsewhere in the hope of finding a cheaper solution. The ship had already begun unloading the waste, so that process now had to be reversed. The transfer of the waste back and forth caused a considerable stench, and after complaints by people working and living near the reception facility, the police came to investigate. They considered pumping the waste from the reception facility back to the ship to be unlawful, and ordered the operation to cease. However, the management of the reception facility argued that its company had not yet legally accepted the waste. The management convinced the city's inspectors that transferring the waste back to the ship was not illegal, so they allowed the reception facility to continue this process.[5]

The *Probo Koala* left for the Ivory Coast, where Trafigura had found a company to treat the waste. This treatment, however, consisted of dumping it in the countryside. Ivorians who came into contact with the waste allegedly suffered all sorts of physical complaints. There were claims that people had died after being exposed to the chemical waste. However, Trafigura vehemently denied responsibility for dumping the waste, and also denied that people had actually suffered after coming into contact with it. Trafigura spent millions on 'damage control,' for example by hiring legal advisers to sue any journalist who held the company responsible for the disaster. It also paid what it claimed to be independent experts to draw up reports that questioned whether the dumped waste had caused the injuries reported by people who said they had come in contact with it.

Despite all of this, the company was convicted in the Netherlands of failing to inform the port of Amsterdam reception facility of the true nature of the waste. It received the maximum penalty, a fine of €1 million. Although Trafigura's annual turnover is US$74 billion, its managers were very annoyed by this—but clearly not enough to change the name of the company, even though its reputation is totally ruined.

The actual sentences imposed on environmental criminals are a third reason why police officers may lose interest in the topic over time. Police officers usually regard the sentences as lenient and hardly likely to contribute to a change in the perpetrators' behavior. In the Netherlands, many cases are settled outside the courtroom. Corporations in particular tend to settle or receive only a fine, and the management and personnel who actually ordered and committed the crimes are rarely sent to prison or even sentenced to community service. An old but still relevant example is the Booy Clean company, responsible for causing extensive oil pollution in the port of Rotterdam in the 1970s. In 1982, the company settled

5 Later, the court ruled that transferring the waste back to the *Probo Koala* had in fact been unlawful.

for €228,000, and the public prosecutor promptly dropped all criminal charges. The police openly criticized the decision, stating that this sent a signal to environmental criminals to simply reserve a sum of money to prevent prosecution.[6] The public prosecutor, of course, took a different view. Unfortunately, he also forgot that now that the company had escaped sentencing, the authorities were also unable to reject future applications for environmental licenses.

'Well-connected' Environmental Criminals

There are many types of environmental crimes committed by a broad range of perpetrators, varying from petty criminals to organized crime syndicates. In the Netherlands, petty criminals may collect old refrigerators, hire a container, and ship them to West Africa (Mostert et al. 2010, p. 19). Some organized criminals, who tend to be involved in the trafficking and manufacture of narcotic drugs, have poaching as a 'hobby.' In the 1990s, a criminal investigation of a group of wildlife poachers residing in the south of the Netherlands—codenamed 'Operation Bambi'—revealed that almost all of them were also involved in producing the drug ecstasy and other serious crimes (Spapens 2006).

However, in many cases environmental crimes are corporate crimes, and the perpetrators not 'usual suspects,' but the well-respected board members of large companies. Logically enough, people in such positions are often well connected to politicians, mayors, royal commissioners at the provincial level, and sometimes even to central government ministers. This is perfectly understandable because such companies are usually highly important to local economies and employment. Detectives can tell fascinating stories about investigations in which a minister or a mayor was among the regular callers when they ran a telephone surveillance operation on a suspect. None of this implies that such dignitaries actually know about the illegal activities of their 'friends,' but it does cast a different light on the investigations compared to ordinary drugs or murder cases.

When confronted with a criminal investigation, corporations immediately contact the most expensive law firms. They usually send in platoons of lawyers who will use every procedural trick in the book to frustrate the investigation. It is also not uncommon for influential board members of large corporations to try to get the competent authorities to halt an investigation. Public prosecutors and police officers may be put under enormous pressure in this way, without always being sufficiently armed against subtle or not so subtle intimidation. They may also decide to transfer to a department investigating less controversial crimes.

The Complexity of Cooperation between Administrative and Law Enforcement Agencies

As noted above, the administrative authorities in the Netherlands are responsible for enforcing environmental laws involving facilities and transports, sharing this responsibility with the judicial authorities. Consequently, many cases require cooperation and information exchange. However, law enforcement agencies and administrative authorities tend to focus on different issues, often leading to friction between them. This section will first address the problems, and then describe measures for improvement that became effective in early 2013.

6 Parliamentary documents: *Handelingen II*, October 15, 1984, p. 14.

Differences in Focus

When it comes to administrative enforcement, the municipal authorities are, by default, the competent authority for issuing environmental licenses to 'facilities,' and therefore also for checking whether the license holder complies with the rules and regulations and, if applicable, specific conditions set in the license.[7] When the activities of a corporation tend beyond municipal borders or when the company falls into a certain risk category, provincial or even the national authorities take over responsibility, depending on the specific activities. The issuer of the license is also responsible for monitoring the license holder, and consequently performs the inspections. Noncompliance may result in instructions to make improvements, if necessary accompanied by a financial penalty, administrative fines, the closing down of part or all of a corporation's activities for specific periods, and finally, revocation of the license.

Generally, the criminal justice approach is seen as an *ultimum remedium*—a last resort. The administrative authorities thus act first, and if that does not produce the desired outcome, the public prosecution service and the police take over the case. Under Dutch law, coordinated and parallel administrative and penal interventions, for instance to exert pressure on a corporation, are also possible. Although they are jointly responsible for enforcing environmental laws, the administrative authorities and law enforcement agencies have very different DNA, and in practice this can lead to several problems.

The first problem is the differences in focus. The public prosecution service and the police always look backwards. They focus on crimes committed in the past, on proving who was responsible for those crimes, and on punishing the perpetrators accordingly. The administrative authorities, on the other hand, look forward. Their aim is not necessarily retribution, but to end an unlawful situation that is harmful to the environment. Law enforcement agencies tend to complain that the administrative authorities keep them in the dark for as long as they can assume a certain level of goodwill on the part of the perpetrators. Indeed, the administrative authorities are usually inclined to give a corporation that violates environmental laws the benefit of the doubt and the opportunity to make improvements. This may work if the corporation is indeed willing to improve its behavior, but it also allows companies that have no intention of complying with the law and their specific licensing conditions to continue their harmful activities, sometimes for years, before the administrative authorities resort to more drastic interventions.

The Rotterdam-based tank storage terminal belonging to Odfjell is a good example. In 2012, it became clear that inspectors had established a total of 64 violations of environmental and safety regulations during 2003–12. The inspectorate had issued about eighty warnings as well as notices of measures for Odfjell to take, in three cases accompanied by the threat of a financial penalty if the company did not comply with the notice. Odfjell's management announced an improvement program in February 2012 entailing an investment of almost €100 million (Zuidervaart 2012). Nevertheless, the environmental inspectorate decided that safety conditions at the tank terminal were such that all activities had to cease. More recent information revealed that Odfjell had failed to report 451 incidents since 2005,

7 A facility is defined as 'any economic activity taking place in confined space.' All economic activities that may have an effect on the environment, from small shops to large corporations, require a license. A corporation may, for instance, operate more than one facility in different locations, each of which requires a separate license. On the other hand, a single facility may also comprise more than one legal person.

and had probably also destroyed internal reports and other documentation. Local politicians called for a criminal investigation and raised serious doubts about the efficiency of the environmental inspectorate for Rotterdam (Van Kampern 2013).

Secondly, law enforcement personnel are usually 'programmed' to view criminal behavior in terms of 'good and bad.' Instead, the administrative authorities need to find the right balance between different interests, and tend to think more in terms of shades of gray. Inevitably, some economic activities cause pollution and nuisance, which must be weighed against economic interests, for example. A further complication is that the administrative authorities issue environmental licenses while at the same time bearing the primary responsibility for enforcement. In the case of public–private partnerships, for example in waste disposal, a municipality or province may even be a shareholder of a company that violates environmental laws.

It will come as no surprise that police officers are usually suspicious of the methods and motives of administrative authorities with respect to enforcement. In private conversations with detectives, accusations of outright corruption are never far away. Police analysts also raised these issues in a confidential threat analysis completed in 2003. The report pointed out regular breaches of the public administrators' integrity, varying from negligence on the part of civil servants to the issuing of licenses to applicants who should never have been allowed them, and to permitting and even facilitating environmental crimes (Kemperman 2003). When the report was leaked in 2005, it caused considerable commotion and led to a debate in parliament.[8] One of the main questions was how to interpret the statement that the 'integrity of public administrators' was regularly compromised. According to the Minister of Justice, Piet-Hein Donner, this was in no way to be interpreted as 'corruption,' but 'only' as shortcomings in checks and inspections, a lack of clarity in the rules and regulations, and letting economic interests prevail over environmental ones.[9] Of course, members of the opposition criticized this explanation and initially called for a parliamentary inquiry. However, after a 'secret briefing' by the government, they never brought up the subject again.[10] Although claims of corruption are difficult to substantiate, they do make the police force reluctant to share information, even though the squads of environmental police investigators depend heavily on leads provided by the administrative authorities.

Improvement of Administrative Enforcement and Cooperation

It is important to consider how to improve cooperation between the different agencies responsible for enforcing environmental legislation. In 2008, a governmental committee (the Mans Committee) reported substantial shortcomings. The first major problem was the lack of a platform for information exchange between the police and the administrative authorities and for coordinating enforcement activities. The committee observed that it had been 'extremely difficult to forge cooperation agreements between the different enforcement agencies on a voluntary basis.' (Commissie Herziening Handhavingsstelsel VROM-regelgeving 2008, p. 37) The committee also felt that the organization of administrative enforcement was far too complex: 'If this complexity is not reduced, there will be little standing in the way of environmental criminals' (Commissie Herziening Handhavingsstelsel VROM-regelgeving 2008, p. 38).

8 Parliamentary documents: *Handelingen II*, February 2, 2005; *Handelingen II*, February 23, 2005.
9 Parliamentary documents: *Handelingen II*, February 2, 2005, p. 2,891.
10 Parliamentary documents: *Handelingen II*, March 1, 2005, p. 3,447.

At that time, the Netherlands consisted of over 500 municipalities, 12 provinces and a number of national inspectorates that all bore responsibilities for administrative enforcement. It was almost impossible for civil servants in the smaller municipalities to keep up with the complexity and continuous changes in environmental rules and regulations. On top of everything else, the task of issuing licenses and exercising control in small towns was often the remit one person—a highly undesirable situation in terms of both efficiency and the risk of corruption. In addition, local authorities tended to focus on overseeing activities within their territorial jurisdiction, and paid scant attention to environmental crimes that crossed their borders, such as waste trafficking. The problems were even greater in the case of environmental crimes that crossed national borders.

Obviously, this situation called for a substantial reorganization of administrative enforcement and closer cooperation with law enforcement. The Mans Committee recommended concentrating all supervision tasks in 28 separate regional bodies, the Regionale Uitvoeringsdiensten (Regional Executive Services; RUDs). The police force was also to participate in the RUDs, which would thus serve as a platform for information exchange and coordination of interventions. After much discussion, the RUDs began operations in 2013.

The anticipated advantages of these services were threefold. To begin with, they were expected to solve the problem of the lack of expertise in small municipalities and enable civil servants to specialize in specific environmental laws. Secondly, this in turn might enable the administrative authorities to tackle smaller environmental offenses independently, implying that the police would have more time to concentrate on the most serious types of environmental crime.[11] Last but not least, by participating in the RUDs, law enforcement agencies were expected to receive more information, and sooner, about environmental crimes that required criminal investigation. Skeptics within the police, however, argue that the RUDs will have little effect on the inclination of administrative authorities to follow a policy of non-intervention towards corporations they consider economically important. Initial experiences also show that the police are perfectly willing to take part in the RUDs in order to *receive* information, but not to *share* it. Discussing and coordinating interventions remains a bridge too far for the foreseeable future.

The Complexity of Cross-border Cooperation

Environmental crime is in many ways cross-border crime. To begin with, illegal activities may be transnational in their effect, such as the pollution of air and water. Secondly, the 'business process' of environmental criminal acts may be international in scope, such as the trafficking of hazardous waste from an industrialized nation to a Third World country. Another example is the abuse of differences in environmental laws between countries. Soil from a contaminated building site may be considered polluted in one country, whereas it may be considered clean in another, for example. A company hired to clean up the site may therefore decide to simply export the polluted soil illegally, thereby avoiding a costly cleaning operation, and to re-import it for further use once its designation has been changed. Thirdly, members of criminal groups responsible for illegal activity may be operating in two or more countries: for example, the captain of a ship who continuously dumps waste, such as bilge water, instead of taking it to a specialist port facility for processing.

11 Parliamentary documents: *Kamerstukken II* 2008/2009, 22 343, nr. 215: 8.

Finally, cross-border environmental crime may even take place in cyberspace, for example by committing fraud in emission trading schemes. In each of these cases, cross-border police cooperation may be necessary to tackle the problem (Spapens 2013). Effective cooperation, however, is often far from simple. This section will first address the main aspects of cross-border police cooperation, and then consider the specific problems of cooperating on cases of environmental crime with states where government and law enforcement are weak.

Cross-border Police Cooperation

Cross-border police cooperation can be divided into non-operational and operational cooperation. Non-operational cooperation concerns the training of police officers, the exchange of good practices and techniques, and network-building, for example. Operational cooperation is defined as cooperation in an actual criminal investigation.

Non-operational Cooperation

The police maintain a wide range of international contacts in the field of non-operational cooperation. Interpol, for example, has an environmental crime program and regularly organizes seminars. It also has working groups on wildlife crime and pollution crime.[12] During a meeting in Bangkok in early 2012, these groups worked on a handbook for the use of forensic techniques in cases of environmental crime. Dutch police officers have also trained police forces in several African countries in how to tackle environmental crime.

Another important international platform for capacity-building is the International Network for Environmental Compliance and Enforcement (INECE), comprising both administrative and judicial enforcement agencies.[13] In the European Union (EU), its counterpart is the Implementation and Enforcement of Environmental Law (IMPEL) network.

Finally, a relatively recent initiative is Envicrimenet, which was established in 2011. This is an informal network of police officers working in the field of environmental crime in the EU member states. Compared to other police cooperation networks, Europol plays a notable role in supporting Envicrimenet. The agency hosted Envicrimenet meetings in October 2011 and 2012, and opened an online discussion facility within its Europol Platform for Experts (EPE); at present, about 125 police officers are members.[14]

Setting up non-operational police cooperation does not require a specific legal basis. Of course, such initiatives do need adequate funding and secretarial support, for instance to organize meetings. Although the aims of these networks do not include exchanging information about ongoing investigations, the participants do, of course, establish and maintain contacts that are also useful in operational practice.

Operational Cooperation

When it comes to gathering evidence and exchanging information in actual criminal investigations, a more formal approach is necessary. The leading principle in cross-border police cooperation in criminal investigations is the sovereignty of the countries involved

12 See www.interpol.int.

13 See www.inece.org.

14 Envicrimenet also has a publicly accessible website, www.envicrimenet.com, but it was still under construction at the time of writing.

(Michalowski and Bitten 2005). Consequently, there is a well-defined legal framework for mutual legal assistance in criminal matters that guides any operational action, consisting of a patchwork of multilateral and bilateral treaties. The term 'police cooperation' is misleading in some ways, because on many occasions the police need the consent of the competent judicial authorities before they can ask for or provide mutual legal assistance. Which institution is competent depends on the type of assistance required and the country involved.

Within the EU, the Schengen Implementation Convention (1991) allows different police forces to exchange written information already in their possession on their own authority.[15] Such 'police–police' information may only be used for investigative purposes, and cannot be submitted to court without the consent of the competent judicial authorities. Use of a special investigative method—for instance, a request for wiretapping based on the Convention on Mutual Assistance in Criminal Matters between the Member States of the EU (2000)—would require the consent of the public prosecution service or an investigative magistrate.[16] Another instrument is the European Convention on Mutual Assistance in Criminal Matters, drawn up by the Council of Europe in 1959. It remains important because it also encompasses countries outside the EU, such as Russia and Turkey.[17]

On a global scale, the legal framework for police cooperation, which also applies in cases of environmental crime, is less comprehensive. The only global convention is the United Nations Convention against Transnational Organized Crime (2000), now signed by 147 countries.[18] Another example of a multilateral treaty signed by a relatively large number of nations is the aforementioned 1959 Council of Europe Convention, which was signed by 48 states.[19]

The UN Convention may have the most signatory states, but it applies only to serious and transnational crimes involving a criminal group. The UN defines serious crime as conduct constituting an offense punishable by a period of deprivation of liberty of at least four years or a more serious penalty. An organized criminal group is defined as 'a structured group of three or more persons, existing for a period of time and acting in concert with the aim of committing one or more serious crimes or offences established in accordance with this convention, in order to obtain, directly or indirectly, a financial or other material benefit.' Understandably, these requirements limit the UN Convention's applicability in cases of environmental crime, particularly because the penalties imposed on those crimes are often minimal (Elliott 2009, p. 75).

Consequently, in cases of environmental crime, investigative authorities are often forced to fall back on bilateral treaties on mutual assistance in criminal matters, and if these are unavailable, on case-by-case arrangements. The advantage of the latter is that two

---

15 The official title is 'Convention Implementing the Schengen Agreement of 14 June 1985 between the Governments of the States of the Benelux Economic Union, the Federal Republic of Germany and the French Republic on the Gradual Abolition of Checks at their Common Borders.' In 1998, the Schengen Acquis to the Treaty of Amsterdam extended the convention to all EU member states. See *Official Journal of the European Union* L 239, September 22, 2000.

16 *Official Journal of the European Union* C 197, July 12, 2000.

17 See www.coe.int.

18 See www.unodc.org.

19 There is also the Commonwealth Scheme for Mutual Assistance in Criminal Matters (or Harare Scheme), comprising 53 member states: http://secretariat.thecommonwealth.org/shared_asp_files/uploadedfiles/2C167ECF-0FDE-481B-B552-E9BA23857CE3_HARARESCHEMERELATINGTOMUTUALASSISTANCE2005.pdf (accessed March 6, 2014). The Netherlands is, of course, not a member of the Commonwealth.

states may bilaterally agree upon any type of police action as long as it is not in violation of meta-conventions such as the European Convention on Human Rights. The main downside of such arrangements is that the decision-making process is usually slow and the outcomes may differ in otherwise broadly comparable situations.

When it comes to gathering evidence to be used before the court, the main instrument is the request for mutual legal assistance, or rogatory letter. Such letters must include a description of the investigation, the names of the suspects (if known), the applicable provisions in the penal code, and the actions required from the requested state.

Police–police information is shared through organizational frameworks, Interpol being the most important. In the EU, Europol and its liaisons play a similar role, although the mandate of Europol is restricted to serious and organized crime. Interpol's most important asset is its network of national bureaus for the secure exchange of information on a 24/7 basis.[20] In addition, Interpol provides data services, maintains databases of police information, and offers operational support to national and international investigations through its specialist crime units and 24/7 command and coordination center. However, contrary to what the public may think, Interpol itself has no operational investigative powers.

Cooperation with States Where Law Enforcement is Weak

On a global scale, the framework for mutual legal assistance in criminal matters is still limited in scope, particularly when it comes to environmental crime. This is important because the trafficking of waste and endangered species of wild flora and fauna, for example, often involves both industrialized and developing countries. Environmental criminals are usually quick to seize opportunities that become available when effective law enforcement is lacking, which may also be the result of internal disturbances. One example is the offloading of toxic waste in the coastal waters of Somalia, where the state does not have the means to prevent it (Waldo 2009). Another example is the Libyan war of 2011, where Italian and Spanish fishermen immediately took advantage of the lack of supervision in Libyan territorial waters to fish for protected species of tuna (Black 2011).

Developing countries are often not party to the legal framework on mutual assistance in criminal matters, with the possible exception of treaties concluded in the context of the UN. More important than the lack of legal provisions, however, is the reluctance that often exists, at least within the Dutch police, to cooperate with countries known to suffer from corruption issues, for fear that information about the investigation will leak to the suspects, for example. In other cases, perpetrators may walk free even after a conviction.

One example is the case of Anson Wong, a Malaysian national who was a major trafficker in illegal wildlife. He was nicknamed the 'Lizard King' because he specialized in protected lizards, snakes and turtles. An investigation team from the US Fish and Wildlife Service had Wong arrested in 2001 after a sting operation that took five years, and he was subsequently sentenced to 72 months of imprisonment in the United States. This was still quite a modest penalty, but it would have been much lower had Wong not also been successfully charged with money laundering, conspiracy, and fraud (Christy 2010).

Upon his release, Wong returned to Malaysia and basically continued his business. The authorities even let him start his own zoo, which he used as a front for trading in CITES-protected animals. Allegedly, Wong was only able to run his business because he was protected by members of the Malaysian government (Christy 2010). In 2010, Wong

20 See www.interpol.int.

was caught at Penang airport in possession of 100 protected snakes in his carry-on luggage. He was sentenced once more, but apparently he still had friends in high places, because after 17 months in prison he was released again (Christy 2012).

It is a considerable challenge to enhance police cooperation with countries where corruption and weak law enforcement hamper the investigation of environmental crimes. In some countries, non-governmental organizations, such as the Environmental Investigation Agency and Greenpeace, may be the only parties able to collect information and evidence on the ground. In a sense, they fill in the gaps arising from the problems in police cooperation. In Libyan coastal waters, the Sea Shepherd Conservation Society even took on the role of 'enforcer' by trying to chase fishing boats from the territorial waters. The international community should be able to intervene in cases of environmental crimes that are relevant to all humankind, but should this also include establishing an international police force, authorized under the jurisdiction of the UN or a future 'International Environmental Court' to take action in sovereign states that are unable to do so effectively? And if we do not want to go down such a radical road yet, which compromises should we then consider?

Conclusion

This chapter has shown that environmental crime began to appear on the political agenda in the Netherlands in the early 1970s. As a relatively new field for the police—although certain environmental crimes such as poaching were already a police responsibility—there were many difficulties to overcome. Furthermore, many police officers did not view environmental crime as a 'sexy' topic. Some of the problems that first occurred in the 1970s and 1980s are still relevant today, most notably the difficulty of obtaining information that allows detectives to investigate 'meaningful' cases, the complexity of environmental rules and regulations, and the sometimes problematic cooperation with administrative enforcement authorities.

Although the Dutch police force is paying more attention to such concepts as intelligence-led policing, it remains in many respects a reactive force, accustomed to tackling the immediate problems of today, and less capable of devoting systematic attention to less visible problems over longer periods. In the case of environmental crime, the victims are often unable to report transgressions to the police, either because they are non-human or because they are not aware of being adversely affected. The increasingly transnational dimension of environmental crime, often involving developing countries, has made the effects of such crimes less visible in Western industrialized countries such as the Netherlands. Constant external pressure on the enforcement authorities is therefore necessary to ensure that they give environmental crimes the attention they deserve.

References

Black, R. 2011. 'Tuna Fished "Illegally" During Libya Conflict,' BBC News, November 7: www.bbc.co.uk/news/science-environment-15597675 (accessed October 16, 2013).

Christy, B. 2010. 'The Kingpin,' *National Geographic Magazine*, January: http://ngm.nationalgeographic.com/print/2010/01/asian-wildlife/christy-text (accessed October 16, 2013).

Christy, B. 2012. 'Anson Wong Goes Free,' *National Geographic News Watch*, February 28: http://newswatch.nationalgeographic.com/2012/02/28/anson-wong-goes-free/ (accessed October 16, 2013).
Commissie Herziening Handhavingsstelsel VROM-regelgeving. 2008. *De Tijd is Rijp* ['The Time is Now']. The Hague: Commissie Herziening Handhavingsstelsel VROM-regelgeving.
Constandse, A. 1975. 'Welvaart is Ook Niet Alles' ['Welfare isn't Everything'], in *Onze Jaren*, edited by A.F. Manning et al. Amsterdam: Amsterdam Boek, vol. 80, 2,547–52.
Elliott, L. 2009. 'Combating Transnational Environmental Crime: "Joined Up" Thinking about Transnational Networks,' in *Eco-crime and Justice: Essays on Environmental Crime*, edited by K. Kangaspunta and I. Haen Marshall. Turin: Unicri, 55–77.
Gruppo Abele-Nomos, Legambiente, and GEPEC. 2003. *The Illegal Trafficking in Hazardous Waste in Italy and Spain: Final Report*. Rome: Gruppo Abele-Nomos.
Kauzlarich, D. and Kramer, R. 1998. *Crimes of the Nuclear State: At Home and Abroad*. Boston, MA: Northeastern University Press.
Kemperman, J. 2003. *Inventarisatie Milieucriminaliteit. Onderzoek naar Aard, Ernst en Omvang van Zware Milieucriminaliteit 2001–2003* ['Inventarization of Environmental Crime: A Study of the Nature, Seriousness, and Scope of Environmental Crime 2001–2003']. Zoetermeer: Korps landelijke politiediensten.
Michalowski, R. and Bitten, K. 2005. 'Transnational Environmental Crime,' in *Handbook of Transnational Crime and Justice*, edited by P. Reichel. London: Sage Publications, 139–59.
Mostert, M., Raaijmakers, P., and Vreugdenhil, D. 2010. *Witboek Milieucriminaliteit: Wat er goed Gaat in de Opsporing van Milieucriminaliteit* ['White Paper on Environmental Crime: What Works in the Investigation of Environmental Crime']. The Hague: Raad van Korpschefs.
Spapens, T. 2006. *Interactie Tussen Criminaliteit en Opsporing* ['Interaction Between Criminals and Investigative Services']. Antwerp and Oxford: Intersentia.
Spapens, T. 2013. 'Cross-border Police Cooperation in Tackling Environmental Crime,' in *Transnational Environmental Crime*, edited by R. White. Farnham: Ashgate, 505–17.
Spapens, T., Bruinsma, M., Van Hout, L., and De Jong, J. 2013. *Vuile Olie* ['Dirty Oil']. The Hague: Boom Lemma uitgevers.
Van Geffen, S. 2001. *The Court Rules: Modelling and Testing Supreme Court Influence on Policy*. Assen: Van Gorcum.
Van Kampern, A. 2013. 'Onderzoek naar 451 Incidenten bij Odfjell' ['Investigation of 451 Incidents at Odfjell'], nrc.nl, September 17: www.nrc.nl/nieuws/2013/09/17/onderzoek-naar-451-incidenten-bij-odfjell/ (accessed March 6, 2014).
Vis, T. 2012. 'Intelligence, Politie en Veiligheidsdienst: Verenigbare Grootheden?' ['Intelligence, Police, and Security Services: Compatible Entities?']. PhD thesis, Tilburg University.
Waldo, M.A. 2009. *The Two Piracies in Somalia: Why the World Ignores the Other?*: www.imcsnet.org/imcs/docs/somalias_twin_sea_piracies_the_global_aramada.pdf (accessed March 6, 2014).
Zuidervaart, B. 2012. 'Inspecteurs Meden Odfjell' ['Inspection Agencies Neglected Odfjell'], *Trouw*, February 13: www.trouw.nl/tr/nl/5009/Archief/archief/article/detail/3175534/2012/02/13/Inspecteurs-meden-Odfjell.dhtml (accessed March 6, 2014).

Chapter 14
Project LEAF, and Interpol's Work on Illegal Logging and Forest Crime

Davyth Stewart

Introduction

Every two seconds, an area of forest the size of a football field is clear-cut by illegal loggers around the globe (Pereira Goncalves et al. 2012). Illegal logging is estimated to account for 15–30 per cent of the total volume of wood traded globally (although exact figures can be difficult to estimate given its clandestine nature). The majority of the world's illegal logging and illegal land clearing continues to take place in the tropical forests of the Amazon Basin, Central Africa and South East Asia, and still occurs in many formally protected high-conservation value forests. In some key producer tropical countries, illegal logging is estimated to account for 50–90 per cent of the timber volume (Interpol and UNEP 2012).

The International Criminal Police Organization, or Interpol as it is more commonly known, recognizes that illegal logging and organized forest crime are undermining national and international efforts to reform governance of the forestry sector, and that sustainable forest management practices cannot be implemented effectively on the ground unless steps are first taken to improve law enforcement capabilities.

Interpol is the world's largest police organization, providing logistical, technical and analytical support to law enforcement agencies across its 190 member countries. Interpol's mandate is to build the capacity of countries' law enforcement agencies to enforce national and international laws and facilitate co-operation between countries, especially in the conduct of cross-border police operations. Interpol enjoys a strategic global position as the only international police organization with a mandate to work closely with partners in the United Nations, inter-governmental organizations and national law enforcement agencies. Interpol's mandate extends to all government agencies whose mission is to prevent or combat crime. This includes police, customs and non-police law enforcement agencies (agencies whose officers are not police officers, but who nevertheless enforce laws), such as national park services, wildlife enforcement services, forest authorities and financial regulators.

In 2009, Interpol established the Environmental Crime Programme as a dedicated unit targeting natural resource theft and environmental crime. The programme has since established specialized projects focused on the illegal trade and dumping of hazardous wastes, illegal fishing and wildlife crime, including poaching and the illicit trade in key protected species (including rhinoceros, elephants and Asian big cats). On World Environment Day, 5 June 2012, Interpol launched Project LEAF (Law Enforcement Assistance for Forests), an initiative dedicated to combating all aspects of forest crime. Project LEAF was formed as a consortium between Interpol's Environmental Crime Programme and the United Nations Environment Programme (UNEP) centre in Norway (UNEP GRID Arendal), and provides a co-ordinated international response to the growing levels of organized crime involved in illegal logging and the international trafficking of illegal timber. Interpol is well placed to help connect stakeholders and generally promote the improvement of forestry law enforcement, through capacity-building and training, sharing regional and international intelligence, co-ordinating collaborative operations and sharing best-practice techniques.

Through Project LEAF, Interpol will support its member countries to strengthen forest governance and build an effective enforcement framework to address illegal logging and corruption in the forest sector. In this way, Project LEAF supports national and international climate initiatives to reduce greenhouse gas emissions (such as REDD+[1]) through supporting sustainable forest practices and protection of forests.

A recent global assessment of law enforcement capacity needs conducted by Interpol confirmed that not enough resources are currently being invested to ensure an adequate law enforcement response to forest crime. Governments have, for the most part, failed to prioritize tackling this type of crime, resulting in a failure to enact the legislative reforms necessary or provide the financial and technical resources needed. The law enforcement community itself has also failed to adequately prioritize enforcement of forest crime, instead focusing available resources on other crimes perceived to be more serious. This, in turn, creates the perception that since the crime is not serious, the damage it causes must also be minimal. Consequently, the judicial system is discouraged from harshly punishing criminals or deterring illegal logging and forest crimes, further reinforcing that perception. So the cycle continues.

One possible reason for this low priority is that illegal logging and forest crimes are generally seen as victimless crimes that cause minimal harm. This view is reinforced by the fact that in many countries, traditional or customary rights to access forestland are not recognized under the law. Local communities which are being denied access to the forest because of logging operations are not seen as victims, since no 'legal' right was infringed. However, this position fails to acknowledge the significant negative social impact forest crime has on the livelihoods of local communities, and its economic impact on the general population through revenue losses. And of course, the ecological impact causes far-reaching environmental damage in the long term. Raising awareness of the serious and devastating effects of forest crimes at local, national and international levels will be necessary to raise the priority this crime is given by both legislatures and law enforcement.

This chapter outlines some of the harm caused by forest crime to the environment and society at large, and the hurdles facing the law enforcement community that must be addressed and overcome if we wish to bring forest crime under control. Addressing forest crime is necessary not only to protect the forest ecosystem, but also to promote the economic viability of countries, their political stability, and improve public health and national security.

Illegal Logging: Outline of the Problem

Forests Play a Central Role in Safeguarding the World's Environment, Economy and People's Livelihoods

Unfortunately, many governments in highly forested countries have historically shown some reluctance to reform forest laws and regulations for fear this may accidentally hinder

1 REDD+ is the acronym for Reducing Emissions from Deforestation and forest Degradation in developing countries, the international mechanism agreed at the UN Climate Change Conference in Cancun, Mexico in December 2010, to reduce emissions from deforestation and forest degradation, and to address the role of conservation, sustainable management of forests and the enhancement of forest carbon stocks. The Cancun agreements are available at https://unfccc.int/meetings/cancun_nov_2010/meeting/6266.php (accessed 6 March 2014).

the legitimate activities of the timber industry, which after all bring in much-needed revenue to their economies. While these are genuine concerns, they often ignore the significant negative impact the failure to address forest crime has on government revenue and economic stability. Illegal logging costs governments around US$30 billion every year in lost revenue and theft of their natural resources (Interpol and UNEP 2012). As shown by *The Economics of Ecosystems and Biodiversity: An Interim Report*,[2] developing countries are the most affected by the illegal trade in, and over-exploitation of, natural forests, with biodiversity loss and ecosystem degradation damaging their development efforts. Illegal international trade in timber deprives these countries of resources which, when managed sustainably, are key to safeguarding their long-term revenues, particularly for rural communities. Furthermore, illegal logging, and the corruption that supports it, undermines the rule of law and public confidence in government institutions, significantly hampering efforts to implement the governmental reform needed to tackle poverty in what are some of the world's poorest countries.

The vast majority of biodiversity hotspots are located in parts of the world where the levels of illegal logging are perceived to be moderate to high. These are areas with the richest, but at the same time the most endangered, diversity of animals and plants in the world, The impacts of logging in these areas can be particularly severe, as the ecosystems are particularly vulnerable to threat and degradation. Operators engaged in illegal logging will move quickly into and out of forested areas to extract timber, to avoid detection. Such operations pay little regard to implementing best-practice logging techniques to reduce the impact on the surrounding forest, or to take the time to replant or otherwise restore the damage afterwards. Consequently, illegal logging operations are often the most destructive forms of wood extraction, destroying biodiversity and wildlife habitats, causing the pollution of water sources, erosion, landslides and other natural disasters, while facilitating the spread of diseases.

Forests the world over also support people's livelihoods by providing food security and pharmaceutical products. A quarter of the world's population are estimated to depend on forests for their fuel, food, medicine and shelter (UN Food and Agriculture Organization Forest Policy Service 2011; World Bank 2001). Over 90 per cent of those living below the US$1 a day poverty line depend fully or in part on forest products for their livelihoods (Scherr et al. 2003). The devastation of the natural environment through illegal logging and forest crime has increasingly harmful social effects, threatening the local communities reliant on forest resources through loss of income, livelihood and life-threatening environmental damage. In many cases, it is also common for illegal logging gangs to be armed. Such gangs engage in violence and intimidation towards local forest-dependent communities, cutting them off from access to the forest upon which they depend.

---

2 The report, released in 2008, provided evidence for significant global and local economic losses and human welfare impacts due to the ongoing losses of biodiversity and degradation of ecosystems. It focused largely on forests, and looked at the extent of losses of natural capital taking place as a result of deforestation and degradation. The Economics of Ecosystems and Biodiversity organization estimates this at US$2–4.5 trillion per year, every year; see http://www.teebweb.org/publication/the-economics-of-ecosystems-and-biodiversity-an-interim-report/ (accessed 6 March 2014).

Forests are at the Centre of Global Discussions on Mitigating Climate Change

Forests are vital components of the world's ecosystem, and provide important functions such as the supply and filtration of water resources, prevention of soil erosion and mitigation of climate change by absorbing carbon dioxide from the atmosphere and storing that carbon both above ground and in the soil as biomass. Forests are also an important reservoir of biodiversity, providing habitats for more than two-thirds of the world's terrestrial species (Secretariat of the Convention on Biological Diversity 2010).

Deforestation and forest degradation are currently estimated to account for 17 per cent of global carbon emissions – more than from all the world's air, road, rail and shipping traffic combined (Interpol and UNEP 2012). Over the last several years, international climate change negotiations have focused on establishing a financial mechanism to reward countries for implementing policies that promote sustainable management of their forests. This mechanism, known as REDD+, has focused principally on identifying financial incentives to motivate industry and governments to change their policies to favour more sustainable forestry practices. The REDD+ mechanism is supported by a number of national and international frameworks, including United Nations and World Bank initiatives.

Since 2008, approximately US$7 billion has been committed to REDD+, which has been directed predominantly to support forested countries in developing national strategies and policy reforms (Simula 2010). The ultimate objective is to shift government policy and industry practice towards forest protection and sustainable forest management. Providing financial incentives, such as tax breaks, subsidies and the opportunity to generate revenue or carbon credits, will play an important role in encouraging this shift.

Alongside the familiar risks of criminal activity encountered with such large financial flows – for example, theft of REDD+ funds and tax evasion – REDD+ poses some specific and unique risks. The recognition of carbon as a commodity to be measured and paid for creates a number of new criminal opportunities, including the fraudulent manipulation of forest carbon measurements to exaggerate results and increase payments. Measuring forest carbon is difficult given its intangible nature, and relies on complex calculations that can be easily manipulated. Furthermore, until countries reduce the proportion of their timber being harvested illegally, they will be unable to measure the forest carbon performance of their REDD+ activities, as a significant 'missing portion' will remain unaccounted for. Policing the forest sector, including REDD+, will stretch even further the already under-resourced forest law enforcement agencies in many developing countries.

Effective implementation of REDD+ must also necessarily involve stricter regulation of the logging industry to improve existing logging practices and limit the overall amount and scale of logging taking place in natural forests. However, even the best forest management policies will be ineffective unless complemented by enforcement mechanisms that help to ensure compliance. Increased regulation places a correspondingly increased burden on forest law enforcement agencies to enforce those rules. If sufficient resources are not invested in forestry law enforcement, officials will be left over-stretched. Consequently, there is now growing recognition that global efforts to reduce emissions from deforestation and forest degradation must also include strategies to strengthen forest governance, address illegal logging and build the capacity of law enforcement authorities. Without effective law enforcement, even the best government policies will be repeatedly undermined by an industry that simply ignores those policies in favour of quick financial gains. The REDD+ mechanism also includes a number of safeguards that focus on social and environmental risks, addressing governance, maintaining environmental integrity, and ensuring the participation and upholding the rights of indigenous peoples and local communities. Corruption and organized crime in the forest sector will seriously undermine the realization of these safeguards.

Transnational Organized Crime is Becoming Increasingly Involved in the Forest Sector

Due to the increased profitability of wood and its by-products, crime involving the world's forests has become more prominent, increasingly organized, sophisticated and transnational. There are a number of factors that explain why the forest sector is particularly vulnerable to criminal exploitation through corruption and illegality. Many forests, particularly tropical ones, are situated in developing countries with weak governance, poor regulatory regimes or systemic corruption. Forests cover remote and often huge areas, making them difficult to monitor without sufficient resources, and forest laws can be unclear and ambiguous, increasing the opportunities for criminals to exploit legal loopholes.

Illegal logging and the illicit trade in timber are also not restricted by national borders. In fact, they usually involve an international network that extends far beyond the forest in which the logging takes place. The logging companies involved may be registered in another territory, while their workers may be foreign nationals. They may be operating in the forest without proper clearance from immigration. After cutting, the timber may be smuggled across the border and processed elsewhere before shipping to a third country for sale. Meanwhile, the profits are transferred to overseas bank accounts. The transnational nature of illegal logging and related financial crimes raises difficulties for law enforcement and regulators, who are often limited in their ability to work outside their own domestic jurisdictions. To be truly effective, actions against illegal logging must be co-ordinated, collaborative and transnational. Crackdowns in one country must be supported by their neighbouring countries in order to prevent illegal logging operations moving across borders to evade detection.

Interpol has observed over recent years that criminal groups formerly involved in drug trafficking and other serious crimes are beginning to engage more and more in forest crime, driven by perceptions of low risks and high profits. These organized criminal groups bring with them years of experience in using violence, intimidation and extortion to obtain their objectives, as well as expertise in money laundering, financial crime and trafficking in illicit goods, all of which they use to avoid police detection. They also have access to extensive international funding channels in addition to using illicit land, sea and air networks to move from country to country and evade detection.

These criminals are well placed to take advantage of the new funding streams presented by REDD+. Corruption in the forest sector has until now been overwhelmingly linked to bribery, fraud and illegal logging, but the new incentive mechanisms such as REDD+ are beginning to change the nature of organized crime's involvement. Interpol has observed that in recent years, criminals in the forest sector are becoming more sophisticated in their laundering operations to mask their criminal activities, including bribery, fraud and collusion with senior government officials, and computer hacking to obtain fake permits. Greater efforts are being made to launder the criminal proceeds, including creative accounting utilizing international networks of quasi-legitimate businesses and corporate and tax structures. These corporate entities are often located in secrecy jurisdictions, or tax havens, making law enforcement efforts to trace the criminal proceeds difficult.

Forest Laws and the Mandate of Law Enforcement are Often Ambiguous or Unclear

Forest crime often falls within the jurisdiction of a number of agencies – including forestry, agriculture, mining, financial regulators, police, wildlife officers and customs. The lack of a clear legal mandate between these different institutions, and a lack of clear legislation generally, can create confusion among officers involved in forestry law enforcement. Officers may at times overlook crimes, not knowing which laws apply, or how to interpret those laws.

In many countries the laws dealing with forest, land and carbon rights, recognition of customary rights, and the allocation of licences and concessions are ambiguous or inconsistent, making their enforcement difficult. Ambiguous laws can include a variety of issues, ranging from problems with land tenure, where ownership and rights to land are unclear, to the provision of logging permits, where permits are granted without proper guidelines to regulate logging operations. Criminals exploit these as opportunities to successfully carry out their illegal logging operations. Ambiguities regarding unclear land boundaries and the overlapping of forest, farm, protected and unprotected lands continually exacerbate the problems created by a lack of adequate permit systems or databases to regulate logging activities.

Unclear forestry laws also complicate criminal prosecutions and make convictions difficult to obtain. Legislative reform must take place to clarify laws and remove legal obstacles impeding frontline officers. The law enforcement community will benefit significantly from the enactment of clearly defined laws that can be practically enforced. Appropriate law reform to clarify and harmonize forestry laws should be a priority, and will significantly help law enforcement efforts.

The Interpol Response

Interpol recognizes the need to build law enforcement capacity to tackle forest crime. Interpol works with the governments of its member countries and other international organizations to ensure that long-term law enforcement and capacity-building are central components of the actions taken by developing countries to implement forest protection policies, such as REDD+, to address deforestation and forest degradation. Some of the strategies being adopted by Interpol to support member countries are explained below in more detail.

The Need to Focus Law Enforcement Investigations on Those Higher Up the Chain

To dismantle these criminal networks, law enforcement agencies must look beyond those wielding the chainsaws or driving the logging trucks, and instead target the criminals who are at the top of the organized networks. Law enforcement operations that lead only to the arrest of those in the forest operating the machinery do nothing more than delay the logging temporarily. Particularly in poor developing countries where illegal logging is at its worst, these workers are easily replaced by others in desperate need of work.

Law enforcement should target those higher up the chain, including those involved in importing or processing illegal timber, those who facilitate the laundering of illegal timber, or those who are involved in establishing the financial mechanisms that fund and support illegal logging and associated operations. Intelligence-led operations targeting those in managerial positions can stop the illegal activity over the longer term. However, law enforcement operations that target these white-collar criminals are not easy. These people often keep as much distance as possible between themselves and the illegal logging, in an attempt to maintain a façade of legitimacy in their business dealings. Following the money, however, can be an effective way to identify those higher up the criminal networks and link them to the illegal logging. Evidence available to Interpol shows that forest crime often occurs hand in hand with other offences. These same organized criminal gangs involved in illegal logging are also involved in a variety of other crimes, including smuggling weapons and drugs, as well as bribery and corruption of government officials, tax fraud, money laundering and other financial crimes.

Law Enforcement Authorities Lack the Resources to Tackle Forest Crime

Law enforcement officers in many timber-producing countries face severe difficulties, including low wages, little training and poor equipment. In many countries, forest law enforcement officers do not have the resources to do more than administer the logging permit system for those extracting timber from forests. Many forestry officers lack the capacity to undertake proactive police investigations or law enforcement operations. Law enforcement officers must be able to travel and respond to criminal activities swiftly and efficiently in order to enforce laws adequately. In many countries, forest authorities lack even basic equipment, such as motor vehicles and the fuel necessary to conduct site inspections of logging concessions. To effectively tackle forest crime, law enforcement agencies need to be well equipped. In addition to routine equipment such as vehicles, enforcement officers need access to satellite technology, global positioning system (GPS) devices, along with financial surveillance and auditing tools to undertake more advanced investigations, including financial inquiries.

A lack of resources can create stressful working environments due to the workload and responsibilities of staff who are often underpaid. Organized illegal logging operations usually occur in remote areas and are accompanied by armed criminals. Without sufficient personnel to support enforcement operations, officers can find themselves at a severe disadvantage and in extreme danger.

Investing in those resources and building up law enforcement capacity to tackle forest crime must be among governments' highest priorities as part of any national strategy to protect forests. Illegal logging costs governments around US$30 billion every year in lost revenue and theft of their natural resources. Stronger law enforcement efforts can help recover this revenue. For every US$1 invested to build law enforcement capacity to tackle illegal logging, the government can recover additional revenue of US$2–6 (Lawson and MacFaul 2010, p. xviii). That is up to a sixfold return on investment.

Establishing Multi-agency Taskforces to Build the Necessary Law Enforcement Capacity

Forestry crime is multi-disciplinary, involving illegal logging, trespass on private and public land, smuggling timber across borders, tax evasion, fraud and money laundering. An appropriate law enforcement response should therefore be multi-disciplinary, looking into the full gamut of crimes, including financial investigations to trace where the profits go. Law enforcement officers and prosecutors must be educated in all aspects of legislation and investigative techniques relevant to forest crime. Tackling these criminal networks requires highly skilled and experienced enforcement officers with a deep understanding of the forestry industry and how illegal activity takes place and is hidden. Experienced officers are better placed to develop proactive investigative strategies to look for patterns of illegality rather than single events. Not only can the greatest possible number of criminals be arrested in this way, but the weaknesses across the forestry sector (such as legal loopholes) can be addressed to prevent other criminals becoming involved in similar arrangements.

It is important to acknowledge that despite the complexity of forest crime, much of the expertise to tackle it already exists in the law enforcement communities of most countries. Many law enforcement agencies already have anti-corruption units, financial investigation teams and similar specialized crime units. The problem is simply that these experts have little experience of working on forest-related issues. Bringing these experts together with forestry officials is the most effective way to build up the necessary expertise and capacity to tackle forest crime. This allows for a multi-pronged approach to forestry crime that increases the likelihood of apprehension, since illegal logging syndicates can also be successfully targeted and prosecuted for other more commonly recognized crimes, such as tax fraud.

Interpol has developed a programme to support individual countries to establish multi-agency taskforces, which Interpol is calling National Environmental Security Taskforces (NESTs). These taskforces are made up of officers seconded from a number of agencies with a wide range of skills and experience. Their objective is to bring together expertise from various law enforcement agencies such as police, customs, forest authorities, and financial and tax regulators. To improve their effectiveness, Interpol also recommends that such dedicated forestry crime taskforces are supported legislatively to ensure they are given the clear legal mandate necessary to investigate forest crime across multiple government agencies, to avoid problems with conflicting jurisdictions of different government departments (such as mining, agriculture and forestry).

Tackling Corruption

It is also important to acknowledge that corruption in the forestry sector is an endemic problem facing law enforcement. In some cases, it may be one of the reasons responsible for blocking adequate resources being distributed to law enforcement, resulting in weak enforcement capability. Corruption contributes to a lack of awareness of forest crime and its low priority on legislative agendas, weakening support that is important for the creation of a robust, responsible industry sector. Ultimately, corruption both fosters criminal activities and allows criminals to avoid serious penalties for their crimes. Lack of transparency in government, and of independent oversight or auditing tools, are some examples of systemic problems that can foster and encourage corruption. Unfortunately, circumstances occur where those responsible for managing the forestry sector, including law enforcement officers, are provided with criminal opportunities that offer substantially greater benefits than their regular income, with little risk of apprehension.

The first step in any efforts to tackle corruption must be to increase transparency through independent oversight, monitoring and audits. One advantage of the Interpol National Environmental Security Taskforces is that by bringing different law enforcement agencies together to work in a co-ordinated manner, they not only improve enforcement through co-operation, but also increase transparency and oversight between the agencies, and reduce the risk that corrupt officials in one agency may block effective law enforcement efforts. Furthermore, governments should ensure that adequate salaries are made available for enforcement officers, with promotion based on merit, equal opportunities and competitive positions for them, supported by education and training to identify and discourage corruption.

Engaging with Civil Society

Civil society can play an important role in supporting law enforcement efforts to detect and solve forest crime. Interpol recommends the formation of collaborative partnerships between civil society and law enforcement agencies to tackle forest crime, aimed at building trust between law enforcement and local communities while also supporting efforts to source intelligence and information. This engagement could include basic law enforcement training for members of the local community in the use of tools such as mobile phones and GPS devices for collecting evidence of illegal logging, and the establishment of community-based forest law enforcement officers to provide intelligence from remote areas.

Civil society networks often have better access to on-the-ground intelligence concerning illegal logging activities, and can support awareness-raising among local communities to support law enforcement efforts. Because of their independence, civil society organizations are also well placed to address issues that may be politically sensitive, such as government corruption. They also have the ability to operate across national and regional borders.

Looking Ahead

A number of new and innovative forensic techniques which could potentially be game-changers in our response to forest crime are becoming available to law enforcement agencies. The analysis of wood anatomy, as well as DNA and chemical isotope analysis, to identify protected species can provide crucial evidence that timber has been taken from a protected area. At the same time, using satellites to monitor forests can catch illegal loggers in the act, directing frontline officers to a specific suspect location to conduct their operations.

Forensics

Forensic analysis based on wood anatomy, DNA and chemical isotopes is expected to grow in importance as a law enforcement tool, for a number of reasons:

1. **The analysis can be used for species identification purposes** – Many timber species (particularly after processing and treatment) can look and feel very similar. However, forensic techniques can identify the particular timber species, providing clear evidence for the prosecution of illegal trade in protected species.
2. **Collecting timber samples from different locations allows for the creation of genographic maps, which can be used to identify genetic and chemical differences on a location-by-location basis** – Although the DNA make-up of each individual tree is unique, there are common features among the genetic information found in trees of the same species from a particular location. Given limits in the distance tree seeds are distributed naturally, this can create gene pools of low genetic diversity. If these genetic variations can be identified, it may be possible to trace DNA taken from a suspect sample of wood to a particular geographical region.

Considerable research is already being conducted with key high-value protected tree species to identify variations in DNA restricted to specific regions. This is particularly important in cases where a particular species of timber is cut in country A in breach of a total logging ban, transferred to country B and fraudulently re-labelled as originating in country B.

Another important forensic tool is the analysis of the chemical isotope composition of timber. Variations in chemical isotopes occur naturally, and these are often found in proportions and composition unique to each location. Trees that grow in a particular area absorb these chemicals from the air and the soil. An analysis of the chemical isotopes found in a piece of timber can help to identify the location of the original tree from which it was cut.

For DNA and chemical isotope analysis to be effective, however, it is first necessary to create a baseline of data. In time, these data are expected to become precise enough to be used to pinpoint timber to a particular protected area. To achieve this, however, significant further work still needs to be done to collect data from across a range of species and geographical locations.

Satellite Monitoring

Reviewing satellite photographs taken over a period of time can identify areas of deforestation. This provides the local law enforcement taskforces with the intelligence required to guide them to specific suspect areas. These operations can initiate further investigations. As an example, by identifying the likely transit routes (rivers and roads) used to transport the timber, the law enforcement taskforces can audit the sawmills and ports along these routes and gather further intelligence necessary to launch law enforcement investigations.

A wave of new satellite imagery is also being developed for Google Earth, Microsoft's Virtual Earth and other mapping tools. The US Geological Society also makes Earth-observing satellite data available to the public free of charge. Its Landsat 7 satellite covers the entire Earth every 16 days (covering one quarter of the Earth's landmass during that period). As environmental changes occur on the Earth's surface, these can be compared to recent prior data, to detect changes such as deforestation.

A number of projects have already been initiated using this freely available satellite data. Groups of people and non-governmental organizations are assisting in curbing deforestation by following a satellite monitoring platform through social media. When land clearing is identified in areas of protected forest, the law enforcement authorities are notified. Such innovative investigative tools, together with support from and in collaboration with members of the public, are examples of the exciting new developments in the field of international efforts to combat illegal logging and forest crime.[3]

References

Interpol and UNEP. 2012. *Green Carbon, Black Trade: Illegal Logging, Tax Fraud and Laundering in the World's Tropical Forests*, Nairobi: UNEP: www.unep.org/pdf/RRAlogging_english_scr.pdf (accessed 6 March 2014).

3 For further reading, see Interpol and UNEP (2012) and Interpol and The World Bank (2010).

Interpol and The World Bank. 2010. *Chainsaw Project: An INTERPOL Perspective on Law Enforcement in Illegal Logging*: www.illegal-logging.info/sites/default/files/uploads/WorldBankChainsawIllegalLoggingReport.pdf (accessed 6 March 2014)

Lawson, S. and MacFaul, L. 2010. *Illegal Logging and Related Trade: Indicators of the Global Response*. London: Chatham House.

Mackey, B., Keith, H., Berry S.L. and Lindenmayer, D.B. 2008. *Green Carbon: The Role of Natural Forests in Carbon Storage, Part 1: A Green Carbon Account of Australia's South-eastern Eucalypt Forest, and Policy Implications*. Canberra: Australian National University Press.

Pereira Goncalves, M., Panjer, M., Greenberg, T.S. and Magrath, W.B. 2012. *Justice for Forests: Improving Criminal Justice Efforts to Combat Illegal Logging*. Washington, DC: World Bank: http://siteresources.worldbank.org/EXTFINANCIALSECTOR/Resources/Illegal_Logging.pdf (accessed 6 March 2014).

Scherr, S.J., White, A. and Kaimowitz, D. 2003. *A New Agenda for Forest Conservation and Poverty Reduction: Making Markets Work for Low-Income Producers*. Washington, DC: Forest Trends: http://lib.icimod.org/record/11339/files/3107.pdf (accessed 6 March 2014).

Secretariat of the Convention on Biological Diversity. 2010. *Forest Biodiversity: Earth's Living Treasure*. Montreal: Secretariat of the Convention on Biological Diversity: https://www.cbd.int/idb/doc/2011/idb-2011-booklet-en.pdf (accessed 6 March 2014).

Simula, M. 2010. *Analysis of REDD+ Financing Gaps and Overlaps*, Washington, DC: REDD+ Partnership.

UN Food and Agriculture Organization Forest Policy Service. 2011. 'Forests and Poverty Reduction': www.fao.org/forestry/livelihoods/en/ (accessed 6 March 2014).

World Bank. 2001. *Recommended Revisions to OP 4.36: Proposals for Discussion*. Washington, DC: World Bank.

Chapter 15
Communities as Victims of Environmental Crime: Lessons from the Field

Melissa Jarrell and Joshua Ozymy

Introduction

Environmental victimization is a far-reaching and widespread global problem: 'An estimated 40 percent of deaths around the world can now be attributed to various environmental factors, especially organic and chemical pollutants' (Bullard et al. 2009, p. 286). It is well established in the sociological and criminological literature that low-income people of color in the United States are more likely to be exposed to environmental risks than other groups (Bullard 1983; US General Accounting Office 1983; United Church of Christ 1987; Mohai and Bryant 1992; Stretesky and Lynch 1999). While attention to victims of traditional 'street' crimes has increased in recent years, victims' rights advocates have generally ignored victims of corporate and environmental crimes (Moore and Mills 1990; Stretesky and Lynch 1999). Environmental crimes (and harmful behaviors not necessarily identified as crimes) are responsible for a great deal of harm to the environment and human health; yet social scientists are well aware that 'traditionally, harmful environmental practices have not been viewed with the same moral repugnance as crimes against person or property' (Skinnider 2011, p. 19). Green criminologists play an important role in identifying green harms that produce injury and victimization that currently exist beyond the boundaries of the law.

Even though environmental victimization is widespread, the vast majority of environmental victims will never be recognized as victims in a legal context, or receive restitution or redress. Few victims of environmental crimes will ever be given the opportunity to address the courts or their governments about the consequences of their victimization as most environmental crimes will go undetected or escape criminal prosecution (Jarrell and Ozymy 2012). Current scientific and legal standards for establishing environmental harm and victimization are problematic because they often require immediate and definitive 'proof' of victimization, which often is not available in cases involving environmental harm. Researchers engaging in environmental crime research and activists fighting for the environment and public health must take into consideration several challenges inherent in these pursuits. For one, the immediate consequences of an environmental offense may not appear obvious or severe. Political and economic climates often favor corporate interests over community concerns. The media rarely report on environmental crimes (Jarrell 2007). Individuals are often divided on what is best for their community. Industry is a formidable foe, with some companies spending millions on greenwashing to tout their 'green' image (Jarrell 2007; Jarrell 2009). Much of the pollution data are self-reported by industry to regulatory agencies (Jarrell 2007). Regulatory agencies are under-budgeted, under-staffed, and out-gunned, and many state officials leave their positions to work for regulated industries (Simon 2000).

Even though these challenges often seem insurmountable, progress, if measured in small ways, is possible. Among other things, environmental justice communities and victims have effectively challenged industry permits for expansion, undertaken legitimate health and air monitoring studies, brought concerns to the attention of regulatory agencies, teamed with more established environmental organizations to bring litigation against powerful companies that abuse them, and assisted in passing the legislation required to reduce their environmental burdens. Little understood is the important and unique role that social scientists can play in assisting victims of environmental crime and the communities in which we live and work—a path that not only helps some of the most vulnerable members of our society, but can assist in producing interesting, policy-relevant work that is of interest to both an academic audience and the broader public.

The purpose of this chapter is to provide a personal account of how social scientists can play a positive role in helping victims of environmental crime in their communities while engaging in academic research that is scholarly and intrinsically satisfying. It presents a seven-year case study (conducted by Melissa Jarrell) of how working with local grassroots activists in an environmental justice community in Corpus Christi, Texas (including legally recognized victims of environmental crime) has yielded a litany of successes while directly informing published academic work.

The Rise of the Environmental Justice Movement in Corpus Christi, Texas

The Corpus Christi, Texas is a coastal city of approximately 300,000 people about 225 miles south of Houston. Corpus Christi, located in Nueces County, is home to a lengthy corridor of refineries and chemical plants known as 'Refinery Row'—one of the densest concentrations of petroleum refineries in the United States. According to data from the US Environmental Protection Agency's Toxics Release Inventory (TRI) from 2002, as reported in Scorecard (2009), Nueces County is the seventh most polluted county in Texas and the eighty-fourth most polluted county in the nation. Three corporations own and operate six oil refineries in Corpus Christi: Valero, Flint Hills (Koch Industries), and CITGO. According to the Environmental Integrity Project (2007), Corpus Christi is home to two of the most polluting oil refineries in the nation (Flint Hills and Valero). Residents from the predominantly low-income minority communities within close proximity to the refineries in Corpus Christi (several homes within a few blocks) constantly complain of foul chemical odors, and many residents believe their health problems, including respiratory ailments and cancer, are directly associated to toxic air pollution emitted by the refineries (Lerner 2007).

In the early 1990s, community activists began voicing the concerns of two environmental justice communities, Oak Park and Hillcrest, to local politicians. The Oak Park Neighborhood Association met to discuss groundwater concerns in 1993, and began taking up air quality issues as well. In concert with a local Baptist Minister, Reverend Malveaux, residents of Hillcrest united to form People Against Contaminated Environments (PACE). Through pressure from both groups, investigations were undertaken by the Texas Commission on Environmental Quality (TCEQ) the next year to assess the severity of their environmental problems. Regulators found that damaged storage tanks had contaminated the groundwater in the community, also finding lead contamination in the proximate vicinity of the Dona Park neighborhood. Reacting to a series of accidents at the refineries that spring, the city council held a public forum for the communities. The outcome of this meeting and many other discussions and negotiations was an agreement to create a limited buffer zone between Oak Park (and to a much lesser extent Hillcrest) and the oil refineries.

However, residents were frustrated that they were often left out of the discussions and it appeared that industry and city officials were meeting without their input.

These groups began to pursue litigation after three years of back-and-forth negotiations with government officials. With the help of the Lone Star Chapter of the Sierra Club (one of the oldest and largest grassroots environmental organizations in the United States) and Grover Hankins, a law professor at Texas Southern University and director of a well-known environmental justice clinic, community members filed a civil rights lawsuit against the state environmental regulator. The litigation resulted in a buy-out of roughly two hundred homes in Oak Park, while Hillcrest was mostly excluded from the settlement. The vast majority of families were not relocated. For these residents, the city maintained that they should protect themselves from the toxic environment and emissions by simply 'sheltering in place.' The environmental justice movement began deteriorating as PACE dissolved, members were offered jobs by industry, and Reverend Malveaux felt pressured to leave his position (Lerner 2007).

The Reemergence of the Environmental Justice Movement in Corpus Christi

In 2000, a new grassroots environmental justice organization was formed, Citizens for Environmental Justice (CFEJ). Comprised of concerned citizens in Corpus Christi, initially CFEJ focused its attention on old dump sites in another part of Corpus Christi, but in 2002 the group turned its attention to Refinery Row and the Hillcrest community. CFEJ was challenged to provide research and data that supported its claims that people were suffering from exposure to toxic pollution in the Hillcrest community. As a result of CFEJ's efforts, particularly the work of founder Suzie Canales, several studies were undertaken that supported residents' claims of toxic exposure. For example, birth defects studies conducted by the Texas State Department of Health Services found that the rates of severe birth defects in Nueces County were 17 percent higher than the rest of the state, and rates of overall birth defects were 84 percent higher (Langlois 2008).

Suzie never intended to spend her life as an environmental justice activist in her hometown. When her sister was diagnosed with breast cancer, Suzie came home to support her sister and family. On December 29, 1999, Diana Bazan died of breast cancer at the age of 42. Several people at her funeral approached the family to talk about other people who were Diana's age and lived in the Westside community that were suffering from or had died of cancer. The family became concerned that Diana's death and the deaths and illnesses of others was due to the fact that they grew up sandwiched between old pre-regulation dump sites, and decided to investigate; CFEJ was born.

In January of 2000, Suzie and members of her family placed advertisements in *Thrifty Nickel* and *Ad Sack* (two free want ads newspapers), asking for anyone from the Cunningham area who had cancer or knew someone who had cancer to please contact the family. The family went door-to-door in the Cunningham area and conducted an informal health survey. The response to the ads was overwhelming, and hundreds of residents participated in the health surveys. Many residents reported various forms of cancer, hysterectomies (some from young women aged under 20), birth defects, and immune deficiency diseases. Suzie and her sister spent hundreds if not thousands of hours combing through public records, including city council meeting minutes, building permits, and other city and country records. They discovered that their neighborhood was essentially built on old pre-regulation dump sites, waste pits, and pipelines. Race zoning laws from the 1940s restricted people of color from living far away from heavy industry. Not surprisingly, they discovered old city council meeting minutes that included a discussion of 'where do we put the Negroes.'

In March of 2000, Suzie and her family petitioned the Agency for Toxic Substances and Disease Registry (ATSDR) to investigate the landfills on the west side of Corpus Christi. The ATSDR sent an investigator from the Environmental Justice division to conduct an assessment of the community. In September of 2000, the Environmental Protection Agency (EPA) took topsoil samples from a large field next to the elementary school. The Texas Commission on Environmental Quality took air samples by inserting a measurement device into the areas from which the EPA took soil samples. One week later, the TCEQ returned to the site to take more samples because the original samples contained trace levels of volatile organic compounds. According to both the EPA and the TCEQ, although the soil and air samples did contain toxic chemicals, the levels were not a cause for concern. Canales and her family were upset with the results given that the elementary school was located adjacent to the site of concern.

The budding activists initiated a letter-writing campaign to local and state public officials, asking them to reopen the case. Over a year later, the Texas Department of State Health Services responded by providing another cancer study looking at cancer rates by zip code in April 2001. The results of the study showed that the zip code in question had high rates of colon cancer, and that the county had elevated rates of esophageal cancer. In May 2001, CFEJ petitioned the state to conduct another cancer analysis and also examine birth defects in Nueces County; Canales also requested assistance from Congressman Solomon Ortiz's office. The request for additional health studies was granted. The cancer study conducted in October 2001 found several high rates of cancer throughout the county; however, the analysis did not find high cancer rates in any particular zip code. In August 2001, the first birth defects study was complete and the result showed high rates of birth defects in Nueces County. State epidemiologists admitted that all the researchers could really do with their zip code and mortality data was answer the question: 'Do you have high rates of cancer?' They admitted that they could not definitely determine the causes of high rates of cancer.

In 2002, CFEJ began to look into problems in the Hillcrest community along Refinery Row. Through her research, Canales discovered that an air monitor (called the Huisache monitor) was installed by the TCEQ at the corner of Huisache and Buddy Lawrence roads in October of 1997. Instantly, the monitor began reporting very high levels and spikes of benzene, a toxic chemical known to cause cancer. In 2002 and 2004, the Huisache air monitor ranked first in the state of Texas for benzene levels. Canales noted that the TCEQ, industry, and members of an industry-funded community group were aware of the benzene spikes, but no one had told the community about the high levels. In 1999, while Oak Park went through a buy-out for two years (from the time the monitor went up to the time the community was relocated), the site was a school bus stop.

In 2003, CFEJ launched a bucket brigade program with the help of Denny Larson of Global Community Monitor, a non-government environmental group formed to help communities monitor their air for themselves to avoid having to rely on regulators and industry for data. The program enabled the group to take samples of the air using a simple bucket equipped with a standard Tedlar air sampling bag. In 2005, Suzie and her sister Cindy first used the Cerex Hound (a real-time chemical monitor) to test for levels of chemicals in the air near the fenceline of the oil refineries. Members of CFEJ felt empowered by the buckets and the Cerex Hound. Even though the group members documented chemicals in the air leaving the fenceline via the buckets, Cerex Hound, video, and photos, the TCEQ did not respond to their concerns. Members of CFEJ began to experience harassment because of their efforts. Canales was accused of terrorist activity by the CITGO refinery for collecting air samples and filming explosions at the refineries, prompting an FBI investigation.

In addition to conducting air monitoring, CFEJ learned how to challenge air permits and expansion permits with assistance from Denny Larson, Neil Carman, Eric Schaeffer (of the Environmental Integrity Project), and Enrique Valdivia (of Texas Rio Grande Legal Aid). The data continued to pile up. In 2007, Steve Lerner, an author, came to Corpus Christi to interview Canales and residents of the Hillcrest community for a book on fenceline communities. After his visit, Lerner wrote to Canales:

> Hillcrest residents live on the frontlines of toxic chemical exposure in the United States. In many of the homes I visited with you, the smell of emissions from the plants was clear to me. It burned my throat, stung my eyes, and gave me a headache. I can only begin to imagine what a hardship it is to live with this kind of contamination on a daily basis 24 hours a day, seven days a week, 365 days a year. My own exposure was brief, I came to visit for a few days and then went home to a community that is located in an area without these kind of intense emissions but I leave behind people who cannot escape these polluted conditions.
>
> The fact that I could smell the fumes from the plant and was affected by the pollution myself, combined with the air monitoring data you showed me which indicates periodic spikes in benzene and other contaminants in the air, suggest to me that it is not safe to live this close to these heavily-polluting facilities.
>
> All the residents of Hillcrest I spoke with also report health problems that they associate with the pollution. This, combined with the studies, which show elevated rates of cancer and birth defects, suggests to me that a more thorough epidemiological study or health study, combined with more comprehensive air monitoring, is warranted in this community.
>
> I take away from my visit to Hillcrest many powerful images of dignified people living in intolerable conditions in which their health is being injured by a source of pollution they can see from their backyards. One individual I spoke with said: 'The fumes from the plant are killing me.' As he spoke he was connected to an oxygen machine that was helping him to breathe. A few minutes after he spoke these words, a woman next door was being carried out to an ambulance to have a dialysis treatment. Occupants of the surrounding homes had either died of cancer or were living with life-threatening diseases. While it may be impossible to prove to the satisfaction of a court that this heavy concentration of health problems are caused by emissions from the neighboring refinery, common sense suggests that there is a strong connection.

On February 22, 2008, an explosion at the CITGO refinery severely injured four workers and spewed hot oil across the community. Initially, the TCEQ refused to investigate, and instead sided with CITGO, suggesting that nothing hazardous had been released and that no violation had occurred. It was only after CFEJ conducted its own investigation and sampled oil specks found on cars over two miles from the explosion that the TCEQ decided to investigate. The TCEQ's sampling results supported CFEJ's results, concluding that hazardous chemicals were released, resulting in an enforcement action against CITGO. CFEJ continues to work diligently to draw attention to environmental problems in the communities along Refinery Row.

Helping Our Communities: The Role of the Social Scientist

I arrived in Corpus Christi in the fall of 2005, fresh out of doctoral school, armed with a great deal of academic knowledge about environmental crime and injustice. Descending upon Corpus Christi via Interstate 37 South from San Antonio, I was surprised to see a brilliant and massive display of bright lights—what appeared to be a major city skyline in the distance. As I came closer, it became overwhelmingly clear that I was not observing a stream of city lights. I was witness to acre upon acre of massive oil refinery operations. Mile after mile, I passed one refinery after another. Although excited about my new position as an Assistant Professor of Criminal Justice, my apprehension about moving to Corpus Christi had less to do with the size of the city and much more to do with my concerns about pollution. As I familiarized myself with the environmental conditions in Corpus Christi, I became more and more concerned. I reasoned that as an environmental criminologist, my presence would be an asset to the community. My field notes from my first week in Corpus Christi in August 2005 reflect my naive enthusiasm:

> I want to help the community. My activism may not make me very popular in the community and even in the academy. You need to worry about publishing, they say. But I am worried about lives. My words will probably only be read by a few, if any, because it is not likely this will even be published. It is not academic enough. It is too passionate. It is too subjective. I'll take that chance because it's my actions that will truly speak louder than my words.

I still have much to learn, but my seven years of working with the fenceline communities in Corpus Christi have taught me many valuable lessons. Within just a few weeks of moving to Corpus Christi, I was introduced to Suzie Canales and members of CFEJ. I had been listening to a morning radio show, and comments from a conservative talkshow host prompted me to call in. I tried to refute claims the host made about environmental pollution in the local community. Another listener contacted Suzie Canales to let her know that she had a potential ally: a new professor at the local university. Soon, I was regularly attending meetings, going on toxic tours, and participating in efforts to plan and implement studies in the community.

As social scientists, we use our knowledge and expertise in traditional ways when we teach our students, publish our research, and engage in university and community service. Many of us want to do more, and we have the skills and expertise to empower activists, residents, students, and our peers. For me, assisting environmental justice communities and their victims has involved a three-stage process: (1) learning about the community and its problems, (2) gaining rapport and providing a voice, and (3) taking the lead in original research and legal advocacy.

Learning

Academics may be the most educated people in the room, but I quickly learned that I was not the most knowledgeable. First, we must learn. I thought I knew a lot about environmental justice. I wrote a dissertation about environmental justice. I had read hundreds of articles and books about environmental justice. I knew all about the efforts of my 'environmental justice heroes,' such as Dr. Bullard and Lois Gibbs. However, in 2005, at my first meeting with activists, members of non-governmental organizations (Sierra Club, Global Community

Monitor, Environmental Integrity Project), Environmental Protection Agency officials, and Texas Commission on Environmental Quality representatives, it become abundantly clear that I while I had a very in-depth academic understanding (from a social scientific perspective), I was the most clueless person in the room. I remember feeling like a fish out of water as they discussed chemical compounds, air monitoring flaws, refining processes, permit totals, and so on. In fact, much of what was discussed went completely over my head. In my field notes from my first meeting in early 2006, I wrote:

> I have a PhD but I was pretty clueless as to the information being exchanged during this meeting. It would take an environmental engineer to understand it all. Very technical information, difficult to comprehend. Obviously, the permitting process is very complicated. I could see how the public would not challenge these permits. You'd need a pretty savvy lawyer.

I quickly learned that many of the people now working for environmental non-profits such as Sierra Club and Environmental Integrity Project had once worked for the EPA or other regulatory agencies. They talked the talk because they had also walked the walk. While most of the community members-turned-activists did not have college degrees, they spoke as if they had extensive educational backgrounds in environmental engineering, chemistry, and environmental law. I remember feeling very frustrated in the beginning. I had just spent that past eleven years of my life immersed in education. I remember feeling a deep sense of frustration that I was starting over in many respects; but I learned a lot very quickly. I read all of the documents and studies CFEJ had collected and compiled over the years. I met with community members, local officials, regulatory representatives, members of NGOs, and anyone else that could tell me about the community, the refining process, air monitoring, studies, and the like.

All disciplines have their own language that can be used to exclusionary effect. I learned, much like the activists around me, that one need not have a background in environmental science to help out. Once you master the jargon and stakes at hand, you find that there are actually more than enough scientists on both sides fighting political battles with data. We have learned from the tobacco companies and every other corporation that produces dangerous products that science is often as much a diversionary tactic as a solution to contentious policy debates. The world is not lacking in chemists, engineers, and other consultants to undertake health impact studies for profit. Environmental victims are often in more need of people of all stripes, but especially those of higher social status and educational status, to help with what is ultimately a fight over power and representation first, and science second.

Gaining Rapport and Providing a Voice

Establishing rapport and building trust between academics and community activists takes time, patience, and mutual understanding. It took over a year before I gained an in-depth understanding of most of the issues in the local community, and twice as long for local community activists to trust me and recognize that I was in this for the long haul. I don't live in the community. I can go to meetings and visit with people in the community, but I don't have to live with the smells, the explosions, and the fear. I get to leave. At first, activists and people in the community were convinced that I was like every other academic they had encountered: I was there to collect data for my research and then go on my merry way.

I did my best to disabuse them of this impression by showing up to meetings, by speaking up on their behalf, by attending media events, by sitting down and listening to their stories. I learned that my credentials lent credibility to their concerns, and the officials from the city and the refineries were more likely to listen with a PhD in the room, even though in the beginning I was an observer rather than a participant. Community members and activists began to trust me because I didn't let them down. I showed up, I expected nothing from them, and I listened.

As I learned more about the community and gained the trust of its people, I began to participate in efforts in the community. I prepared remarks for the record in public hearings. I collected additional data from regulatory agencies to assist the community in compiling data to support its cause. I became a co-principal investigator in the Nueces County Family Health Study with toxicologists from Texas A&M University—College Station who had procured funding from the National Institute of Environmental Health Sciences to examine benzene in the blood and urine of people in the Hillcrest community. In essence, I became an organizer of people and information, and learned that one of my greatest assets was the ability to bring these together, underscoring the 'social' in 'social scientist.'

Because I hold a PhD in criminology, I am often chosen as the default expert on environmental justice issues from the community's perspective. To encourage the media to report on environmental crime, researchers with important information to present to the public need to establish ties with reporters and members of the media in order to provide a voice for victims. I quickly learned that we must be able to explain our findings to reporters in clear and concise terms, and that even if we talk to a reporter for thirty minutes, we will likely only get a two-sentence quote or a ten-second soundbyte. In addition to establishing relationships with media personnel and providing different perspectives for crime news, we can be more than just information sources. We can also *produce* crime information. My research has attracted interest from the Center for Public Integrity, Bloomberg News, National Public Radio, *The Texas Observer*, and other media outlets, which have gone forward to report on these issues. This has led to an appearance on MTV and in the documentaries *Tapped* (Atlas Films, 2009) and *Koch Brothers Exposed* (Brave New Foundation, 2012). More recently, we convinced Lois Gibbs, the mother of Superfund and the Executive Director of the Center for Health, Environment and Justice (CHEJ) to travel to Corpus Christi in winter 2012 to go on a toxic tour and give a press conference that garnered significant press coverage.

Taking the Lead

In addition to assisting with ongoing efforts, social scientists can bring new ideas and take the lead in efforts in the community. I offer two primary examples of ways in which I have taken the lead to help my community: undertaking policy-relevant research, and legal advocacy for victims.

Undertaking and promoting policy-relevant research

In 2006, I attended a community meeting and learned about 'upset events' for the first time. One of the local refineries was sharing environmental data with the community. While most people were more interested in the elaborate buffet provided by industry, I was appalled to learn that in just one month this refinery had 16 upset events. Through my subsequent research, I learned that many states allow companies to exceed their air pollution permit limits through a host of exclusions, including system maintenance and equipment malfunctions. These excess emissions events are known as upset events. Even though many of these excessive emissions may be considered illegal under the Clean Air Act (CAA), in over half of all states companies are able to offer a number of affirmative defenses in order to avoid enforcement action, alleging that these events were unavoidable (Public Citizen 2005). Events can last for just minutes, or possibly for several weeks. In fact, upset events often involve large releases of concentrated toxic chemicals over a brief period (although some may last for weeks), unlike emissions from routine operations, and represent the release of highly concentrated pollutants that can have serious health implications. Teaming up with my colleague in political science Dr. Joshua Ozymy, we conducted our own studies on upset events in Texas and have since published three studies (Jarrell and Ozymy 2010; Ozymy and Jarrell 2011; Ozymy and Jarrell 2012).

Upset events are just one of many examples of behaviors that are harmful to the environment and humans that are not considered criminal behaviors in law, but which produce severe public health consequences. Undertaking policy-relevant research in this context has brought additional academic attention to an under-studied issue while helping to draw attention to the issues in the community and providing good data for original peer-reviewed research—something we have continued to pursue with recent research on similar environmental struggles in the community (Jarrell et al. 2013). Moreover, we have endeavored to help tell the story of CFEJ's efforts and bring it to an academic audience by working with Suzie to produce another peer-reviewed publication (Canales et al. 2012).

Legal advocacy

In 2006, a federal grand jury in Corpus Christi, Texas, returned a 10-count indictment charging CITGO Petroleum Corporation, its subsidiary CITGO Refining and Chemicals Co., and the environmental manager at its Corpus Christi East Plant Refinery with criminal violations of the CAA and the Migratory Bird Treaty Act (MBTA). According to the indictment, CITGO operated two large open-top tanks as oil/water separators between January 1994 and May 2003 without the required emission controls. More than 4.5 million gallons of oil were discovered in the tanks during an unannounced inspection by the Texas Commission on Environmental Quality in March 2002. Residents' complaints of odors were investigated by the TCEQ, and it was determined that tanks 116 and 117 were the source of continuous emissions into the neighboring community. The indictment did not mention that state regulators within the TCEQ had been aware of problems at CITGO for several years (Caputo 2006). Even though the indictment included charges related to excessive benzene emissions in 2001 and 2002, TCEQ records indicated that CITGO had also exceeded regulatory limits in 1998, 1999, and 2000 (Caputo 2006). State regulators had been trying unsuccessfully for years to force CITGO to install lids on tanks 116 and 117. State enforcement actions against CITGO occurred in 1999, 2001, 2002, and 2004, and totaled over $5 million in penalties (Caputo 2006).

On May 17, 2007, a federal jury in Corpus Christi heard opening statements in the case against CITGO. The case represented the first criminal trial for a refinery under the CAA where the corporation did not settle out of court. Witness for the prosecution Jean Salone, a resident of Hillcrest, the predominantly low-income, minority community bordering CITGO, testified for the prosecution that she woke up on the morning of September 23, 2001 because of a 'strong heavy smell from the refinery that was making me sick.' Salone said that she had gotten used to the smell, but noticed when it was much worse than usual. Salone immediately contacted the TCEQ to report the strong odor. 'The smell was so strong, it woke me up. The smell was indescribable,' Salone stated at the trial.

Two years later, Salone was diagnosed with breast cancer. According to Salone, burning throat, watery, irritated eyes, and itchy skin are a common occurrence for residents of Hillcrest and Oak Park.

On June 27, 2007, four and a half weeks after opening statements were heard and numerous witnesses had testified for the United States and for CITGO, a Corpus Christi federal jury unanimously determined that CITGO knowingly operated two large open-top tanks as oil/water separators between January 1994 and May 2003 without the required emission controls that regulate the amount of benzene released into the environment.

Over 400 Hillcrest and Oak Park residents attended townhall meetings held by the Department of Justice in the fall of 2007. More than 300 people signed victim impact statements describing the health problems associated with breathing toxic air. Fifteen residents testified at the pre-sentencing hearings held in 2008 about the odors and health problems associated with CITGO's crimes. In a letter to Judge John Rainey from lead Prosecutor Howard P. Stewart on July 7, 2006, Mr. Stewart stated:

> The emissions from these tanks were uncontrolled for more than ten years and routinely engulfed the Hillcrest community and physically affected the citizens that live there. The government introduced evidence that the emissions from tanks 116 and 117 made people living in the community and at least one TCEQ investigator physically sick.

Three years later (after numerous delays for no apparent reason), Judge Rainey issued an order excluding the community members as 'victims' under the Crime Victims Rights Act (CVRA), based primarily on lack of medical evidence as proof of victimization, even though the evidence presented at the pre-sentence hearings clearly showed that people living in close proximity to the CITGO refinery, including elementary school children, experienced health effects including but not limited to burning eyes, nose, and throat, nausea, and dizziness. A toxicologist and medical doctor testified that the chemical emissions from the tanks were the cause of the health effects exhibited by the people. On one occasion, a state inspector responding to an odor complaint (emissions event) got sick about a mile away from the tanks. Even though the government worked diligently to identify victims and include victims in the case, the court did not believe that the evidence supported victimization under the CVRA.

I am proud to say that I played a major role in providing support for the victims in this case. After the judge denied the government's motion to include the community members as victims, it appeared that we had no recourse. I spoke with the DOJ prosecutor, who told me that the only recourse was to hire an attorney for the victims and make an appeal to a higher court. The community members did not have the money to hire an attorney, and I knew that finding a local attorney to work pro bono would not happen in a refinery town (we had already gone down this road many times). I decided to review the literature pertaining to the CVRA and environmental crime cases. I know this case intimately, as I attended the trial in 2007 and have read every document in the case (over 800 filings as of 2012). In the scholarly and legal literature, I found very little written about the CVRA and environmental crimes, and few previous cases involving the CVRA and environmental crime. The few articles and cases I read in the legal literature had one person in common: a former federal judge and current law school professor at the University of Utah. I decided to give him a call to see if he would help us. He asked me to provide a brief of the case. Over the course of the next year, along with assistance from a legal aid office in Austin, Texas, we worked on motions to file in the district court as well as a petition for writ of mandamus to file with the Fifth Circuit Court of Appeals. Victims' attorneys filed additional motions with Judge Rainey to include the victims. These motions were subsequently denied. One week prior to the sentencing in late 2012, the victims' attorney filed a petition for writ of mandamus with the Fifth Circuit Court of Appeals, asking the appellate courts to overturn the district court's ruling, suggesting that the judge erred when he required medical proof of victimization. The Fifth Circuit quickly ruled that district judge needed to re-examine the victims' previous filing. At the sentencing, after hearing oral arguments from the victims' attorney, the district court judge reversed his previous order, declaring the community members victims of CITGO's crimes—a huge victory for the community.

This case is far from over, and it remains to be seen whether the community members, now designated as victims, will receive any type of restitution or compensation for their victimization. However, this case is extremely important in that it represents the first time in the history of environmental crime cases that members of an environmental justice community have been designated crime victims under the CVRA. While producing academic research has not been the primary reason for working as a legal advocate on the case, the important contributions to case law that are illustrated in the CITGO case should be analyzed and brought to an academic audience. Our work recently culminated in a publication that accomplishes this goal (Jarrell and Ozymy 2012), again highlighting the fact that service to the community can help serve a dual academic purpose.

Conclusion

Universities in refinery towns may find it hard to see past their financial relationship with industry to consider the negative impact of industry actions in the community. I learned that my own credibility would be called into question when I began to speak out on the community's behalf. It did not matter if I was referring to the data and presenting empirical findings, I quickly became persona non grata with industry representatives, city officials, and even at my own institution. At times, I questioned my resolve and worried that I might lose my job. Community groups need us, though—dedicated academics willing to give their time, expertise, and skills. At this same time, it can help us pursue our intellectual interests in a way that embodies the great tradition of civically minded social scientists such as Frances Fox Piven or Robert Bullard, who appreciated the social and academic value of long-term involvement in their communities well before the overarching need to appear scientific and generalizable sapped the life out of countless graduate seminars. We are needed.

References

Bullard, R.D. 1983. 'Solid Waste Sites and the Houston Black Community,' *Social Inquiry* 53, 273–84.

Bullard, R.D., Johnson, G.S., and Torres, A.O. 2009. 'Addressing Global Poverty, Pollution, and Human Rights,' in *The Quest for Environmental Justice: Human Rights and the Politics of Pollution*, edited by R.D. Bullard. San Francisco, CA: Sierra Club Books, 279–97.

Canales, S., Ozymy, J., and Jarrell, M.L. 2012. 'Risk Assessment or Risk Acceptance: Why the EPA's Attempts to Achieve Environmental Justice Have Failed and What They Can Do About It,' *Environmental Justice* 5(1), 59–62.

Caputo, A. 2006. 'Citgo Pollution Charges in Corpus Highlight Problems with Law,' *The San Antonio Express*, September 30.

Environmental Integrity Project. 2007. *Refinery Rankings*. Washington, DC: Environmental Integrity Project.

Jarrell, M.L. 2007. *Environmental Crime and the Media: News Coverage of Petroleum Refining Industry Violations*. New York: LFB Scholarly Publishing.

Jarrell, M.L. 2009. 'Environmental Crime and Injustice: Media Coverage of a Landmark Environmental Crime Case,' *Southwest Journal of Criminal Justice* 6(1), 25–44.

Jarrell, M.L. and Ozymy, J. 2010. 'Excessive Air Pollution and the Oil Industry: Fighting for Our Right to Breathe Clean Air,' *Environmental Justice* 3(3), 111–16.

Jarrell, M.L. and Ozymy, J. 2012. 'Real Crime, Real Victims: Environmental Crime Victims and the Crime Victims' Rights Act (CVRA),' *Crime, Law, and Social Change* 58(4), 373–89.

Jarrell, M.L., Ozymy, J., and McGurrin, D. 2013. 'How to Encourage Conflict in the Environmental Decision-making Process: Imparting Lessons from Civic Environmentalism to Local Policymakers,' *Local Environment* 18(1), 184–200.

Langlois, P. 2008. *A Case-control Study of the Association Between Birth Defects Elevated in Nueces County and Sites of Concern to Citizens for Environmental Justice*. Houston, TX: Texas Department of State Health Services.

Lerner, S. 2007. *Corpus Christi: Hillcrest Residents Exposed to Benzene in Neighborhood Next Door to Refinery Row*. Bolinas, CA: The Collaborative on Health and the Environment.

Mohai, P. and Bryant, B. 1992. 'Environmental Racism: Reviewing the Evidence,' in *Race and the Incidence of Environmental Hazards: A Time for Discourse*, edited by B. Bryant and P. Mohai. Boulder, CO: Westview Press, 163–75.

Moore, E. and Mills, M. 1990. 'The Neglected Victims and Unexamined Costs of White Collar Crime,' *Crime and Delinquency* 36(6), 408–18.

Ozymy, J. and Jarrell, M.L. 2011. 'Upset Over Air Pollution: Analyzing Upset Event Emissions at Petroleum Refineries,' *Review of Policy Research* 28(4), 365–81.

Ozymy, J. and Jarrell, M.L. 2012. 'The Underreported Story of the Year: Upset Events, Regulatory Drift, and the Regulation of Air Emissions at Industrial Facilities in the United States,' *Environmental Politics* 21(3), 451–66.

Public Citizen. 2005. *Industrial Upset Pollution: Who Pays the Price?*: www.citizen.org/documents/08.01.05%20Industrial%20upsets%20report.pdf (accessed February 3, 2013).

Scorecard. 2009. *Nueces County Pollution Report Card 2002*. New York: Environmental Defense Fund.

Simon, D.R. 2000. 'Corporate Environmental Crimes and Social Inequality,' *American Behavioral Scientist* 43, 633–45.

Skinnider, E. 2011. *Victims of Environmental Crime: Mapping the Issues*. Vancouver: International Centre for Criminal Law Reform and Criminal Justice Policy.

Stretesky, P.B. and Lynch, M.J. 1999. 'Corporate Environmental Violence and Racism,' *Crime, Law and Social Change*, 30, 163–84.

United Church of Christ. 1987. *Toxic Wastes and Race: A National Report on the Racial and Socio-economic Characteristics of Communities with Hazardous Waste Sites*. New York: United Church of Christ.

US General Accounting Office. 1983. *Siting of Hazardous Waste Landfills and Their Correlations with Racial and Economic Status of Surrounding Communities*. Washington, DC: US Government Printing Office.

Chapter 16
The Treadmill of Production, Planetary Boundaries and Green Criminology

Michael Long, Paul Stretesky and Michael Lynch

Introduction

Criminologists rarely examine the effects of state enforcement mechanisms on the overall trends in toxic releases. This is surprising because the overall goal of environmental regulation regimes should be to prevent or reduce environmental harm in general. This harm reduction might occur through a variety of mechanisms, including some form of specific or general deterrence where the punishment of environmental violators would help reduce toxic releases in general. Moreover, we would expect that if a regulatory regime were effective, there would be a negative correlation between large penalties and general toxic releases that would limit the global expansion of environmental damage.

While the issue of punishment and toxic releases is neglected within criminology more generally, the development of green criminology has drawn greater attention to issues of environmental enforcement, whether environmental enforcement efforts limit environmental damage, and whether environmental enforcement patterns are equitable or are unevenly distributed across communities in relation to their class, racial and ethnic composition (Stretesky and Lynch 1999; Stretesky and Lynch 2002; Stretesky and Lynch 2009b; Stretesky and Lynch 2011; Lynch et al. 2004a; Lynch et al. 2004b; Stretesky 2006; Stretesky 2008; Long et al. 2012; Stretesky et al. 2013a). While green criminologists have drawn attention to the effects of environmental enforcement and the efficiency of those responses, they have largely drawn on the environmental justice literature and more orthodox criminological studies of the effects of penalties on environmental compliance as a means of situating those studies (Lynch et al. 2004a). In this chapter we break from that tradition and expand upon the kinds of theories that have been employed in green criminology to examine environmental enforcement patterns and results by addressing the treadmill of production (ToP) theory as developed by Schnaiberg (1980).

ToP theory analyzes environmental harm from a political economic perspective. The treadmill disrupts the ecology through ecological withdrawals or the extraction of raw materials used in production, and through ecological additions that are produced in the manufacturing process by pollution that is added to the environment. In this chapter we focus attention on ecological additions associated with manufacturing. We argue that as toxic releases increase, they are more likely to create the potential for harm to humans and non-human species. We also argue that as more toxins are released into the environment, the more likely it is that ecosystems that rely on that environment will be disrupted. Toxic releases may disrupt ecosystems by altering the nature of those systems in a way that negatively impacts biodiversity and species' health by threatening the equilibrium of the ecosystem and its ability to reproduce the conditions for life. An example of the large-scale effects of ecological additions related to carbon dioxide pollution can be seen in the form of ecological disorganization, commonly referred to as 'climate change.'

Due to the tremendous scale of ecological disorganization that is currently occurring, we argue that criminologists must focus on the broad problem of planetary boundaries as opposed to compliance with some particular regulation (see Rockström et al. 2009a; Rockström et al. 2009b). Planetary boundaries can be described as the nine environmental thresholds that if crossed, could have catastrophic repercussions for the planet. Focusing on ecological disorganization and threats to the biosphere in general by referencing planetary boundaries is much more important for green criminologists than observing, for example, whether a company complies with a US governmental environmental regulation such as the Clean Water Act (CWA). We emphasize that it is entirely possible to comply with the CWA even as we destroy the biosphere. This disturbing condition occurs because harm to ecosystems is not synonymous with violations of environmental law.

In our view, we are drawn to the political economic orientation of ToP theory because we see that orientation as compatible with the forms of political economic analysis some green criminologists have taken up in the study of environmental harm and environmental social control (Lynch 1990; Long et al. 2012) and other related harm and theoretical issues (Lynch and Stretesky 2003; Stretesky and Lynch 2009a). At the same time, our interest in ToP theory is related to our observation that political economic explanations of environmental harm have been underdeveloped within green crime, especially in relation to the use of this approach in other disciplines (for example, Boyce 2002). In our view, ToP theory offers one method for extending the use of political economic theory within green criminology.

In the sections that follow, we review ToP theory and its connection to green criminology. We then review the nine planetary boundaries, with particular emphasis on two: climate change and chemical pollution. Next, we present data on indicators of climate change and chemical pollution, and environmental enforcement in the United States. We conclude by situating the data within ToP theory, and argue for a green criminological focus on ecological disorganization.

Treadmill of Production

We begin with the observation that treadmill of production theory has had an important influence on the analysis of environmental harms within the field of environmental sociology, especially within the United States (Buttel 2004). It has also had an impact on various varieties of ecological Marxism, and is consistent with the preference for political economic explanation taken in that approach (O'Connor 1998; Foster 2002; Burkett 2007). As noted, this preference for political economic explanations of green crimes and patterns of justice and injustice sits well with some varieties of green criminology. To make this point and to clarify the content of ToP approaches, we review the core general and specific assumptions of ToP approaches below.

General Assumptions

The basis of ToP theory was proposed by Schnaiberg (1980). ToP theory is based on a political economic understanding of capitalism in which two issues become central to Schnaiberg's depiction of the intersection of capitalism and environmental crisis. The first is the internal mechanism of expansion. Capitalism is driven by constant efforts to expand production, and capitalism must expand to accelerate the generation of profit (for extended discussions of capitalist expansion and the environment see Foster et al. 2010).

That expansionist tendency is the treadmill of production—a process that is constantly in motion, and constantly seeking expansion. Thus, 'treadmill of production' refers to a political economic system characterized by the continued expansion of 'industrial production, economic development as well as increasing consumption' (Gould et al. 1996, p. 5).

The expansionary tendencies of capitalism place it in direct conflict with and opposition to the natural world or the ecological order (Foster 2002; Burkett 2007). In order to expand constantly, capitalism requires raw material inputs. Those inputs must be extracted from nature. Thus, as capitalism expands, its consumption of natural resources also expands, accelerating with its expansion the destruction of nature (Foster 2002; Burkett 2007). Because the world is finite, so are the raw materials in the world, and capitalism's constant expansionary tendencies can be seen as being inherently contradictory to the preservation and health of the ecological system. In ToP theory, the effects of capitalist expansion on the destruction of nature through the consumption of raw material for productive purposes is defined by the term *ecological withdrawals*.

In addition to ecological withdrawals, capitalism produces expanding ecological harm through *ecological additions*. Ecological additions include the waste products of production, and are composed of an array of polluting outcomes that include waste materials, harmful pollutants and toxic waste. Ecological additions have two important impacts. First, these chemicals can disrupt processes in the natural world and affect the health of the ecological system (Balmford and Bond 2005). A widely cited example is climate change, which is an outcome of ecological additions that force warming and change the equilibrium of the entire ecological system (Lovelock 2007). Second, ecological additions cause environmental toxins to accumulate in the environment. Those toxins create biologically disruptive forces that impact the health and morbidity of the various species that inhabit ecosystems.

Taken together, capitalism's continuous expansion of ecological withdrawals and ecological additions challenges the health of the ecosystem, and forces large-scale transformations in the ecosystem. When combined, those large-scale transformations of the ecosystem, which can vary from one geographic location to the next in quality and quantity, cause what ToP refers to as *ecological disorganization*—or the disruption of the natural order and mechanisms of the ecological system. At this point, this general description of capitalism addresses how the capitalist treadmill of production tends to generate ecological disorganization. Schnaiberg's theory, however, is not a general theory of capitalism, but was specifically designed to address the relationship between capitalism and ecological disorganization that occurred following the Second World War, or in the modern era of monopoly capitalism and its association with chemically intensive production practices.

Chemically Assisted Production

According to ToP theorists, ecological disorganization intensified after the Second World War, and was tied directly to the expansion of chemically assisted production technology (Gould et al. 2008). A number of these new technologies were an outgrowth of war-related technological discoveries, and many were based on the manipulation of fossil fuels into new materials for production and that were used in production.

These new chemical technologies of production played a role in both the withdrawal of raw materials and the process of producing commodities. From a capitalist standpoint, these new technologies were highly valued since they promoted economic growth and the escalation of profit by reducing the costs of production. Energy-intensive chemical technology allowed workers to produce considerably more, leading to declining commodity prices, which in turn stimulated demand for commodities and for the natural resources needed to make those products. For these investments in the new methods of production and extraction to pay off, production must increase (for criticisms, see Foster 2005). As a result, both the volume and the toxicity of waste being released into the environment increased (Gould et al. 2008). In this way, the modern ToP tends to increase environmental problems by 'expanding resource consumption and waste emissions' (York 2004, p. 355).

New Dimensions of Conflict

Political economic theories typically address conflict from the perspective of class conflict. ToP theory expands the concept of conflict by focusing attention on the forms of political and social conflict that emerge around efforts to protect and contain the treadmill of production. As a result, ToP theory identifies the state, labor and capital as three groups that impact the treadmill. In addition, some ToP theorists include the public and social movements (Gould et al. 1996; see also Bonds 2007 and Stretesky et al. 2013b).

In theory, the state, labor and capital all assert that economic growth is critical for social well-being (Obach 2004). Capital supports increasing production for the purpose of expanding profit; labor's interests relate to increased wages and job growth assumed to accompany increased levels of manufacturing; for the state, expanded economic development generates additional revenue. Thus, these various actors often work together to adopt policies that advance production. Although conflicts among these actors exist, at some level each subscribes to the economic logic of the expansion of production and to the ideological belief that expanded production will advance public welfare. As ToP theorists note, there is little evidence supporting the connection between public welfare and economic expansion (Gould et al. 2008). Moreover, as ToP theory suggests, increases in production and productivity tend to undermine the interests of labor in the long run, since, consistent with Marx's analysis of capitalism, the acceleration of chemically assisted production reduces the need for human labor and lowers wages (Schnaiberg 1980).

For purposes of the current discussion, we draw attention to the state. ToP theory suggests that the state, though influenced by the ToP, is also relatively autonomous. As an autonomous entity, the state also has an interest in maintaining its legitimacy with the general public. To do so, the state must demonstrate a commitment to protecting the public from large-scale harms such as ecological disorganization. As a result, the state sometimes engages in efforts to control, slow or even reverse the treadmill of production when its effects are clearly detrimental to public and environmental health. We examine this possibility further below.

The Role of Enforcement in the ToP

As noted, in the modern ToP, chemical-intensive production is an important cause of ecological disorganization. Chemically intensive production also expands social disorganization by expanding ecological withdrawals and additions. These effects will often be overlooked, since treadmill actors typically privilege economic expansion over the effects of production on ecological disorganization. Nevertheless, as the ToP expands, its ecologically disorganizing effects become more and more apparent. These effects can be seen in dramatic ecological disasters related to the ToP's ecologically disorganizing effects (for example, Love Canal, deadly smog, Bhopal and the proliferation of toxic waste sites). In such circumstances, the state must act to impose external constraints on production to limit its ecological disorganization impacts. In some cases, the state may only take these actions if pressured by the public (Gould et al. 1996).

Given its public responsibilities and its connection to the ToP, the state plays opposing roles in influencing the treadmill. Sometimes, the state makes environmental concessions to non-corporate actors to maintain the legitimacy of the treadmill and the state (Obach 2004; Bonds 2007). In response to citizens' concerns, the state sometimes slows the speed of the treadmill (Schnaiberg 1980; Gould et al. 2008). When ecologically destructive behaviors of the treadmill become extreme and obvious, the state must make larger concessions to protect the public, such as creating broad environmental regulations. Unfortunately these concessions are as likely to be symbolic as they are to protect the environment. Nevertheless, environmental regulations create a routine means through which the state can potentially influence the speed of the ToP and its impacts on the ecology.

Environmental regulations contain a variety of mechanisms for constraining the ToP. These include enforcement tools such as cease and desist orders, the permitting and monitoring of toxic and polluting emissions, and the use of financial penalties in an effort to enforce compliance with environmental regulations. In theory, financial penalties ought to impact corporate behaviors, since they possess the ability to impact profit-making and, when large and public enough, can send a message that bad environmental behavior will not be tolerated (Stretesky 2006). Again, evidence on the effectiveness of penalties in controlling environmental violations is mixed. In some cases, penalties may not be sufficient to alter the behavior of corporations since they do not affect their bottom line.

On this point, York (2004, p. 358) notes that environmental enforcement is influenced by the interests of the ToP, and consequently fines are 'not a serious counter-force' to the treadmill. For instance, Stretesky et al. (2013a), using a ToP framework, found that monetary penalties levied against corporations by the EPA for various pollution violations had no effect in reducing the level of toxic releases by those companies. In addition, in a study of waste disposal in Germany and the Czech Republic, Vail (2007) discovered that illegal waste simply moves across borders in response to state-imposed regulations when those regulation are not uniform across locations. More generally, Gould et al. (2008) suggest that despite increased state environmental regulations, the treadmill has not contracted. Thus, while ToP theorists support state-centered solutions to ecological disorganization, they simultaneously claim that there is little evidence that the state is effective in reducing environmental disorganization.

Due to the apparent lack of ability or desire by the state in the United States to meaningfully reduce the amount of ecological disorganization that is created, we question whether assessing compliance with state-created, socially influenced environmental regulations is the best framework for studying green crime. Instead we recommend examining the impact of environmental withdrawals and additions on planetary boundaries.

Planetary Boundaries, the ToP and Green Criminology

Rockström et al. have identified nine 'planetary boundaries' which 'define the safe operating space for humanity with respect to the Earth's system and are associated with the planet's biophysical subsystems or processes' (Rockström et al. 2009a, p. 472). Identification of these boundaries comes in response to the Earth moving from the Holocene era, a time of relative stability, to the post-Industrial Revolution Anthropocene era, where humans have become the major force driving environmental change. The boundaries include: (1) climate change, (2) the nitrogen/phosphorus cycle, (3) biodiversity loss, (4) ocean acidification, (5) stratospheric ozone depletion, (6) global freshwater use, (7) changes in land use, (8) atmospheric aerosol loading and (9) chemical pollution. In order to maintain the climate conditions of the Holocene era, roughly the last 10,000–12,000 years, Rockström et al. (2009a) argue that these nine boundaries need to remain under certain levels (see also Magdoff and Bellamy Foster 2011, p. 13), or we at risk of cataclysmic environmental changes that could have horrendous effects on humans, non-human animals and the entire planet.

The planetary boundaries are relevant in this case because, as we argue elsewhere (see Stretesky et al. 2013b), orthodox definitions of environmental crime are social constructions based on politically influenced power relations. A political economy approach, informed by ToP theory, to defining green crime recognizes that powerful actors in society create laws, and these laws do not significantly reduce ecological disorganization. Rather, orthodox approaches to green criminology often rely on whether or not a company violates an EPA statute like the Clean Air Act or Clean Water Act (Winter and May 2001; Stretesky 2006; Burby and Paterson 2007). Studies of this nature are problematic because they may find that companies are complying with EPA statutes but are still releasing environmental additions at alarming rates. A focus on planetary boundary indicators as outcome measures, rather than whether a company adheres to laws subject to manipulation by politicians and corporations, would provide a much more accurate picture of the damage that is being done by the ecological disorganization created by the ToP.

In this chapter we focus on two planetary boundaries: climate change and chemical pollution. We choose these two boundaries because of the presence of both ecological additions and enforcement data, but all planetary boundaries should be examined by green criminologists, because 'protecting the planet requires that we attend to all of these planetary boundaries, and others not yet determined' (Foster et al. 2010, p. 17). According to Rockström et al. (2009a), the planetary boundary for climate change has already been reached. It is measured by two indicators: (1) atmospheric carbon dioxide (CO_2) concentration and (2) change in radiative forcing (Rockström et al. 2009a, p. 473). There are many repercussions of climate change, including loss of polar ice sheets, regional climate disruptions, loss of glacial freshwater supplies, and poleward shift of subtropical regions (Rockström et al. 2009b).

On the other hand, the planetary boundary level of chemical pollution has yet to be determined, primarily because it is impossible to measure the effects of all chemicals that have been released into the environment: 'By current estimates, there are 80,000 to 100,000 chemicals on the global market .... Some toxicity data exist for a few thousand of these chemicals, but there is virtually no knowledge of their combined effects' (Rockström et al. 2009b, p. 32). It is difficult to determine the planetary boundary of chemical pollution because of the sheer magnitude of chemicals released into the atmosphere. The results of chemical pollution on the planet include: (1) 'a global, ubiquitous impact on the physiological development and demography of humans and other organisms with ultimate impacts on ecosystem functioning and structure' (Rockström et al. 2009b, p. 32) and (2) interaction effects with other planetary boundaries, including climate change and biodiversity loss.

We argue that in order to determine whether the state is helping to substantially reduce ecological disorganization created by the expansionary nature of capitalism, a ToP-informed green criminological framework should be employed that focuses on slowing the march toward planetary boundaries. We now present data on environmental additions (CO_2 emissions and Toxic Release Inventory, or TRI) and contrast them with levels of environmental enforcement in the United States.

Trends in Environmental Additions and Environmental Enforcement

Table 16.1 reports data on two measures of environmental additions: first, US and world CO_2 emissions measured in kilotonnes and metric tonnes per capita for the years 2002–11; secondly, we also present the total EPA TRI figures measured in pounds (lbs.) for the same time frame. The TRI contains information on the disposal and release of nearly 650 toxic chemicals in the United States (for further details on the TRI, see Burns et al. 2008). The TRI data represent a measure of total reported chemical releases in metric tonnes per year for each company for air emissions, surface water discharges, underground injections and releases to land by year. These toxic releases measure the overall level of ecological disorganization created by each company annually. The TRI figures reported in Table 16.1 are the sum total of all company-reported toxic releases for that year.

Table 16.1 US and World CO_2 Emissions and TRI values, 2002–11

	CO_2 emissions (US)[1]		CO_2 emissions (world)[1]		Total TRI (lbs.)[2]
Year	Kilotonnes	Metric tonnes per capita	Kilotonnes	Metric tonnes per capita	
2002	5,650,957	19.6	25,661,666	4.1	4,774,130,320
2003	5,681,664	19.6	27,212,807	4.3	4,468,288,838
2004	5,790,761	19.8	28,646,604	4.5	4,231,287,236
2005	5,826,393	19.7	29,724,702	4.6	4,358,983,455
2006	5,737,615	19.2	30,700,124	4.7	4,327,118,860
2007	5,828,696	19.3	31,433,524	4.7	4,123,355,536
2008	5,656,838	18.6	32,155,923	4.8	3,875,380,211
2009	5,299,563	17.3	32,042,246	4.7	3,392,594,741
2010	5,120,926	17.3	32,099,085	4.7	3,785,152,724
2011	5,031,608	17.2	32,127,504	4.8	4,086,529,225

Notes:

1 The values of CO2 emissions for the US and the world in 2010 and 2011 are estimates.

2 Total TRI includes total on- and off-site disposal and other releases for all chemicals and industries.

An examination of the trends in US CO_2 emission is illuminating. The first point that is readily apparent is the difference is overall size of the US CO_2 emissions compared with the figures for the entire world. Over the ten-year span, the average US value was 18.8 metric tonnes per capita, while the average value for the entire world was 4.6 tonnes. During those years, the United States released over four times the amount of CO_2 into the atmosphere compared to the world as a whole. Clearly, environmental additions are not released equally throughout the globe. If we look at the total overall CO_2 releases measured in kilotonnes, emissions in the United States decreased by roughly 10 percent from 2002 to 2011; however, global CO_2 releases increased by 25 percent over the same time frame. These trends are consistent with the ToP. Overall global ecological disorganization is increasing, while a shift in environmental additions from the global North to the South is simultaneously occurring. Table 16.2 reports that civil/administrative penalties for violations of EPA air statutes are generally trending upward, with the exception of 2011. However, as noted earlier, a small reduction in US emissions masks the real problem of moving toward and past the planetary boundary of climate change.

Table 16.2 EPA civil and administrative enforcement of air, water, and hazardous waste violations, 2008–11

	Air		Water		Hazardous waste		Totals[2]	
Year	Total no.	Total penalty	Total no.	Total penalty	Total no.	Total penalty	Total no.	Total penalty
2008[1]	1,211	$46,136,135	1,082	$351,803,943	799	$20,174,602	3,092	$418,114,680
2009	1,241	$125,254,551	1,322	$62,403,017	806	$24,790,511	3,369	$212,448,079
2010	1,911	$172,953,421	1,395	$131,559,343	823	$44,723,902	4,129	$349,236,666
2011	1,536	$147,663,413	2,254	$416,947,457	654	$25,690,945	4,444	$590,301,815

Notes:

1 All 2008 values are actually the average values of the 2007 and 2008 enforcement cycles, due to limitations in the data availability for those years.

2 The values in the totals column are the sums of the air, water and hazardous waste columns.

Trends in TRI data also provide information about environmental additions and the impact of the state's response to chemical pollution. Table 16.1 shows that total TRI values decreased between 2002 and 2009, but they began to increase in 2010 and 2011, so it is unclear in what direction these values will move in the future. It should be noted that TRI data are self-reported by companies, and it is likely that the actual values of toxic releases into the environment are greater than are reported to the EPA.

If we examine the years 2008–11, for which we have data on civil/administrative violations (Table 16.2) and criminal prosecutions (Table 16.3), there was a 5 percent increase in the total TRI value, while there was a 41 percent increase in total civil/administrative penalty amounts (measured in US$), a 44 percent increase in the total number of violations and a 53 percent increase in the number of criminal prosecutions. Over that four-year span, environmental additions measured by TRI increased, while the three measures of environmental enforcement also increased. Although this is a short time frame, it shows that the current US approach to enforcement does not appear to effectively *reduce* chemical pollution in any meaningful way.

Table 16.3 Number of EPA criminal prosecutions, 2002–11[1]

Year	Total prosecutions[2]
2002	51
2003	130
2004	73
2005	85
2006	133
2007	108
2008	57
2009	79
2010	99
2011	121

Notes:

1 Fiscal years, not calendar years.

2 Total prosecutions for violations of all EPA statutes.

To be sure, there are numerous criticisms that can be levied against our brief presentation of the environmental additions and enforcement data, such as the short time frame of the data presented (we were limited by the availability of EPA compliance data), and it is possible that for deterrence to truly work, we would need to examine environmental additions data far into the future to give the deterrent aspect of enforcement time to work. However, in our opinion, these arguments are moot. A brief look at Table 16.1 shows that if environmental additions are decreasing, they are not doing so to a degree that will help reduce the possibility of reaching (in the case of chemical pollution) or returning to (in the case of climate change) the planetary boundaries. Tables 16.2 and 16.3 show that in most cases civil/administrative EPA penalties are increasing, while the number of EPA criminal prosecutions varies a great deal from year to year. In sum, in the case of the United States, the state's approach to reducing ecological disorganization is not working; rather, the ToP continues to treat nature and the planet as an expendable resource, without concern for the future repercussions of its actions.

Discussion and Conclusion

Treadmill of production theory emerged to explain the causes of ecological disorganization. Despite its importance in other disciplines, this explanation of ecological disorganization has not been applied widely within criminology (see Long et al. 2012). We suggest that this is a surprising omission, especially within green criminology, given the origins of that view in political economic theory and the obvious connections between green criminological political economic positions and the political economic origins of ToP.

The orthodox criminological literature has long argued that large penalties should alter the behavior of rational actors. Moreover, that position has been widely adopted as a model for controlling environmental crime by regulatory agencies. In contrast, ToP theory argues that ecological disorganization is driven by the nature of capitalist production and the inherent contradictions and conflict between capitalism and nature (Foster 2002). According to that view, since the systemic properties of the system drive ecological disorganization, it is unlikely that financial penalties will affect the polluting behavior of corporations since fines do not change the basic nature of the capitalist system of production.

The data on environmental additions and enforcement we have presented appear to reject the orthodox criminological position and provide some support for ToP arguments. These data leave open the argument that the efforts of the state to control ecological disorganization are more likely to represent legitimation efforts than real attempts to control social disorganization (Barclay et al. 1980; Marshall and Goldstein 2006; Bonds 2007; Gould et al. 2008). Bonds, for instance, reports that state 'environmental reviews [that are supposed to protect the environment] are typically used in a way that is conducive to the expansion of production' (Bonds 2007, p. 159). Thus, environmental enforcement, including the use of penalties, may be a legitimation tool that increases levels of state trust, reduces state autonomy and expands rather than reduces production and ecological disorganization (York 2004). Because the state can use environmental enforcement as a legitimation tool, we argue that it is better for green criminologists to focus on the effects of environmental withdrawals and additions on planetary boundaries. Planetary boundaries represent a much more valid measure of ecological disorganization than state-level environmental regulations.

Ecological disorganization is a serious issue that should attract greater criminological attention, especially with respect to the process of social control—an issue that has been widely studied in criminology with respect to street crime. However, criminology has often excluded the examination of the problem of controlling corporate and environmental crime, and when it does address this issue, it is typically examined in relation to deterrence theory. Evidence on the deterrent value of penalties is generally mixed at best (Stretesky 2006; Ariel 2012; Prechel and Zheng 2012), and those mixed results indicate that deterrence arguments ought to be rejected (Paternoster 2010).

These findings raise a larger question that is central to ToP approaches. Rather than social control, it is the nature of the system of production that generates ecological disorganization. Thus, the remedy is to reconfigure the system of production to prevent the typical forms of ecological disorganization capitalism creates. Studies conducted outside the United States report similar observations and conclusions (Vail 2007).

Whether these green crimes involve forms of ecological disorganization related to timber crimes, wildlife crimes, mountaintop mining, hydrofracturing or to ecological additions and withdrawals, there is reason to begin to addresses these crimes in relation to broader political economic theories of green harms, and specifically in relation to views such as those offered in ToP approaches.

Consistent with our results and ToP arguments, we suggest that it is not the structure of penalties nor the nature of social control that ought to receive the attention of green criminologists who examine the control of green harms; rather, it is the structure of the system of production and its relationship to ecological disorganization that deserves greater attention from green criminologists. ToP theory presents one way of accomplishing that task.

There is significant evidence of ecological disorganization in a variety of forms in the contemporary world. Green criminologists need to begin to contemplate how the dispersion and occurrence of these forms of ecological disorganization are related to explanations for these behaviors that span the national and situational contexts in which these harms are committed. That animals are abused, that wildlife is trafficked, that deforestation, climate change and pollution occur are all serious issues. Indeed, these outcomes are changing the very world in which we live. The issue is what lies behind the broad scope of these behaviors, and whether green criminology can explain these forms of harm collectively rather than individually. For example, it is one thing to describe environmental atrocities or violence against animals; it is quite another to locate the forces that connect these problems. In our view, a political economic approach to green criminology continues to offer the best method for understanding the widespread appearance and dispersion of green crimes across the nations of the world in an era in which the world's economy and the economies of individual nations are dominated by the capitalist world system.

References

Ariel, B. 2012. 'Deterrence and Moral Persuasion Effects on Corporate Tax Compliance: Findings from a Randomized Control Trial,' *Criminology* 50(1), 27–69.

Balmford, A. and Bond, W. 2005. 'Trends in the State of Nature and Their Implications for Human Well-being,' *Ecological Letters* 8(11), 1,218–34.

Barclay, B., Schmidt, J. and Hill, D. 1980. 'State, Capital and Legitimation Crisis: Land and Water in California's Imperial Valley,' *Contemporary Crises* 4(1), 1–26.

Bonds, E. 2007. 'Environmental Review as Battleground: Corporate Power, Government Collusion, and Citizen Opposition to a Tire-burning Power Plant in Rural Minnesota, U.S.A,' *Organization and Environment* 20(2), 157–76.

Boyce, J.K. 2002. *The Political Economy of the Environment.* Cheltenham: Edward Elgar.

Burby, R.J. and Paterson, R.G. 2007. 'Improving Compliance with State Environmental Regulations,' *Journal of Policy Analysis and Management* 12(4), 753–72.

Burkett, P. 2007. *Marxism and Ecological Economics: Toward a Red and Green Political Economy.* Chicago, IL: Haymarket Books.

Burns, R.G., Lynch, M.J and Stretesky, P.B. 2008. *Environmental Law, Crime and Justice.* El Paso, TX: LFB Scholarly Publishing.

Buttel, F.H. 2004. 'Treadmill of Production: An Appreciation, Assessment, and Agenda for Research,' *Organization and Environment* 17(3), 323–36.

Foster, J.B. 2002. *Ecology Against Capitalism.* New York: Monthly Review Press.

Foster, J.B. 2005. 'The Treadmill of Accumulation: Schnaiberg's Environment and Marxian Political Economy,' *Organization and Environment* 18(1), 7–18.

Foster, J.B., Clark, B. and York, R. 2010. *The Ecological Rift: Capitalism's War on the Earth.* New York: Monthly Review Press.

Gould, K.A., Pellow, D.N. and Schnaiberg, A. 2008. *The Treadmill of Production: Injustice and Unsustainability in the Global Economy.* Boulder, CO: Paradigm.

Gould, K.A, Schnaiberg, A. and Weinberg, A.S. 1996. *Local Environmental Struggles: Citizen Activism in the Treadmill of Production.* Cambridge: Cambridge University Press.

Long, M.A., Stretesky, P.B., Lynch, M.J. and Fenwick, E. 2012. 'Crime in the Coal Industry: Implications for Green Criminology and Treadmill of Production,' *Organization and Environment* 25(3), 299–316.

Lovelock, J. 2007. *The Revenge of Gaia: Earth's Climate Crisis and the Fate of Humanity.* New York: Basic Books.

Lynch, M.J. 1990. 'The Greening of Criminology: A Perspective for the 1990s,' *The Critical Criminologist* 2(3), 3–4, 11–12.

Lynch, M.J. and Stretesky, P.B. 2003. 'The Meaning of Green: Contrasting Criminological Perspectives,' *Theoretical Criminology* 7(2), 217–38.

Lynch, M.J., Stretesky, P.B and Burns, R.G. 2004a. 'Determinants of Environmental Law Violation Fines Against Oil Refineries: Race, Ethnicity, Income and Aggregation Effects,' in *Society and Natural Resources* 17(4), 333–47.

Lynch, M.J., Stretesky, P.B. and Burns, R.G. 2004b. 'Slippery Business: Race, Class and Legal Determinants of Penalties Against Petroleum Refineries,' *Journal of Black Studies* 34(3), 421–40.

Magdoff, F. and Bellamy Foster, J. 2011. *What Every Environmentalist Needs to Know About Capitalism*. New York: Monthly Review Press.

Marshall, B.K. and Goldstein, W.S. 2006. 'Managing the Environmental Legitimation Crisis,' *Organization and Environment* 19(2), 214–32.

Obach, B.K. 2004. 'New Labor: Slowing the Treadmill of Production?', *Organization and Environment* 17(3), 337–54.

O'Connor, J. 1998. *Natural Causes: Essays in Ecological Marxism*. New York: Guilford Press.

Paternoster, R. 2010. 'How Much Do We Really Know About Criminal Deterrence?', *Journal of Criminal Law and Criminology* 100(3), 765–824.

Prechel, H. and Zheng, L. 2012. 'Corporate Characteristics, Political Embeddedness and Environmental Pollution by Large U.S. Corporations,' *Social Forces* 90(3), 947–70.

Rockström J., Steffen, W., Noone, K., Persson, A., Chapin III, F.S., Lambin, E.F, Lenton, T.M., Scheffer, M., Folke, C., Schellnhuber, H.-J., Nykvist, B., De Wit, C.A., Hughes, T., Van der Leeuw, S., Rodhe, H., Sörlin, S., Synder, P.K., Costanza, R., Svedin, U., Falkenmark, M., Karlberg, L., Corell, R.W., Fabry, V.J., Hansen, J., Walker, B., Liverman D., Richardson, K., Crutzen, P. and Foley, J.A. 2009a. 'A Safe Operating Space for Humanity,' *Nature* 461(24), 472–75.

Rockström J., Steffen, W., Noone, K., Persson, A., Chapin III, F.S., Lambin, E.F, Lenton, T.M., Scheffer, M., Folke, C., Schellnhuber, H.-J., Nykvist, B., De Wit, C.A., Hughes, T., Van der Leeuw, S., Rodhe, H., Sörlin, S., Synder, P.K., Costanza, R., Svedin, U., Falkenmark, M., Karlberg, L., Corell, R.W., Fabry, V.J., Hansen, J., Walker, B., Liverman D., Richardson, K., Crutzen, P. and Foley, J.A. 2009b. 'Planetary Boundaries: Exploring the Safe Operating Space for Humanity,' *Ecology and Society* 14(2), 32.

Schnaiberg, A. 1980. *The Environment: From Surplus to Scarcity*. New York, NY: Oxford University Press.

Stretesky, P.B. 2006. 'Corporate Self–Policing and the Environment,' *Criminology* 44(3), 671–708.

Stretesky, P.B. 2008. 'The Neglect of Race and Class in Environmental Crime Research,' in *Racial and Ethnic Bias in the Criminal Justice System*, edited by M.J. Lynch and R. Paternoster. New York: Criminal Justice Press.

Stretesky, P.B. and Lynch, M.J. 1999. 'Corporate Environmental Violence and Racism,' *Crime, Law and Social Change* 30(2), 163–84.

Stretesky, P.B. and Lynch, M.J. 2002. 'Environmental Hazards and School Segregation in Hillsborough County, Florida, 1987–1999,' *The Sociological Quarterly* 43(4), 553–73.

Stretesky, P.B. and Lynch, M.J. 2009a. 'A Cross-national Study of the Association between Per Capita Carbon Dioxide Emissions and Exports to the United States,' *Social Science Research* 38, 239–50.

Stretesky, P.B. and Lynch, M.J. 2009b. 'Does Self-policing Reduce Chemical Emissions? A Further Test of the EPA Self Audit Policy,' *The Social Science Journal* 46(3), 459–73.

Stretesky, P.B. and Lynch, M.J. 2011. 'Coal Strip Mining, Mountain Top Removal and the Distribution of Environmental Violations Across the United States, 2002–2008,' *Landscape Research* 36(2), 209–30.

Stretesky, P.B., Long, MA. and Lynch, M.J. 2013a. 'Does Environmental Enforcement Slow the Treadmill of Production? The Relationship Between Large Monetary Penalties, Ecological Disorganization and Toxic Releases Within Offending Corporations,' *Journal of Crime and Justice* 36(2), 233–47.

Stretesky, P.B., Long, MA. and Lynch, M.J. 2013b. *The Treadmill of Crime: Political Economy and Green Criminology*. London: Routledge.

Vail, B.J. 2007. 'Illegal Waste Transport and the Czech Republic: An Environmental Sociological Perspective,' *Czech Sociological Review* 43(6), 1,195–211.

Winter, S.C. and May, P.J. 2001. 'Motivation for Compliance with Environmental Regulations,' *Journal of Policy Analysis and Management* 20(4), 675–98.

York, R. 2004. 'The Treadmill of (Diversifying) Production,' *Organization and Environment* 17(3), 355–62.

Chapter 17
Assessing the Partner and Media Engagement with the International Consortium on Combating Wildlife Crime

Tanya Wyatt[1]

Introduction

Wildlife trafficking is a global green crime of growing concern, as is evident by the establishment of several wildlife law enforcement networks, for instance the Association of Southeast Asian Nations – Wildlife Enforcement Network (ASEAN – WEN), and the subject of this chapter: the International Consortium on Combating Wildlife Crime (ICCWC, pronounced 'i-quick'). This initiative is comprised of Interpol (predominantly its Environmental Crime Programme), the Secretariat of the Convention on International Trade in Endangered Species of Wild Fauna and Flora (CITES), the World Customs Organisation (WCO), the United Nations Office of Drugs and Crime (UNODC), and the World Bank. Wildlife crime in this case is defined as the exploitation of fauna and flora, in particular the poaching, trafficking, and possession of illegal wildlife (CITES 2011), which is also referred to as wildlife trafficking. From its official launch in November of 2010, ICCWC was intended to:

> bring coordinated support to national wildlife law enforcement agencies and to the subregional and regional networks that, on a daily basis, act in defence of natural resources. Ensure that perpetrators of serious wildlife crimes will face a more formidable and coordinated response, departing from the present situation where the risk of detection and punishment is all too low. It also seeks to deploy modern techniques and technologies that are applied in different areas to tackling wildlife crime, such as controlled deliveries and the use of wildlife forensics. It aims to address international cooperation, money laundering and corruption. (CITES 2012a)

In short, then, ICCWC was designed to support, expand, and enhance ongoing wildlife law enforcement efforts to combat wildlife trafficking. In the middle to long term, ICCWC is well placed to enhance awareness of wildlife crime and make wildlife crime mainstream within national law enforcement agencies. This chapter analyses whether, after two-plus years, ICCWC is managing to work towards these goals. First, the methodology used to gauge ICCWC's progress towards these aims is detailed.

1 My sincere thanks to Interpol's Environmental Crime Programme for allowing me to spend a week with them conducting interviews and observing operations. Thanks, too, to Edward van Asch at CITES.

Methods

In order to assess whether ICCWC is making progress in the intended direction, a mixed-methods approach was employed. This first included analysis of world news coverage of wildlife trafficking, to search for evidence of increased reporting by the media about this green crime, which may also indicate enhanced awareness by the public. In turn, this is related to the question of whether wildlife trafficking is becoming a more mainstream rather than marginalised topic. Using LexisNexis, *all* available newspapers in *all* languages were searched using the terms 'wildlife trafficking' and 'illegal wildlife trade' from July 2002 to July 2012. This was done in order to gauge the historical trends of the coverage of this topic. As seen below, the countries discussed in this chapter are a selection of those with the most coverage. The use of the term 'wildlife crime' was also explored, but as this can be used as a generic term to refer to a variety of crimes in addition to wildlife trafficking, such as badger baiting and hare coursing, this term was not included in the analysis. In addition, a search was conducted for the 'International Consortium on Combating Wildlife Crime' from July 2008 to July 2012, to be sure to capture all references made to it as it was being created, once it was launched, and during its active period. Each newspaper article was entered into the computer program Nvivo, and queries were formulated around month and year, species, and countries to gain an understanding of the nature and extent of the media coverage of wildlife trafficking.

The second part of the methodology consisted of eight semi-structured interviews with staff of the Interpol Environmental Crime Programme and one with a member of the Interpol Environmental Crime Committee. A representative of CITES answered a questionnaire on behalf of CITES and the WCO. No responses were received from the other partners. Interpol was the main focus as it is the focal point for the sharing of wildlife law enforcement information and intelligence, and therefore was judged to have the most complete picture of countries' engagement with wildlife trafficking. All respondents were guaranteed anonymity, and are not referred to by name or position in this chapter in order to maintain this. Interviews and questionnaires focused on whether staff felt that wildlife law enforcement engagement with the partners or with wildlife crime had changed since the launch of ICCWC, whether ICCWC's activities were successful in raising awareness and increasing engagement, and what the next actions of the consortium would be to continue the progress towards the objectives. This was followed up by a search of the partners' websites for documents and press releases related to ICCWC, in order to gauge the levels of partner engagement with the consortium.

In order to undertake a complete analysis of the data that was obtained and the institutional factors that affect the formation and effectiveness of such a collaboration, the chapter will begin by giving the background and history of the creation of ICCWC. This will be followed by an exploration of the partners that are involved in ICCWC, including their missions and objectives as agencies. Next, an analysis of partner engagement with ICCWC will take place through examination of each agency's online ICCWC profile and the activities that have been organised through ICCWC, then the results from the interviews will be shared. This will lead to dissemination of the results of the newspaper searches. Finally, an analysis in the discussion section will assess ICCWC and its future.

Background and History of ICCWC

The use and trade of wildlife has always been taking place. Coinciding with that has been the overuse and exploitation of non-human animals and plants, which continues in the modern era, but has begun to receive more attention, including in some cases the criminalisation of such over-exploitation (Lyster 1985; De Klemm 1993). This is evident from the creation of a variety of international conventions designed to limit and/or stop the overexploitation and degradation of the world's wildlife. These include, but are not limited to; the Convention on Biological Diversity, the Convention on the Conservation of Migratory Species of Wild Animals, the Ramsar Convention on Wetlands of International Importance, and of particular importance to this discussion, the Convention on the International Trade in Endangered Species of Wild Fauna and Flora. The latter was specifically created as a safeguard against trade threatening wild non-human animals and plants (CITES 2011). Since 1975, CITES and its member states having been working around the globe to combat the illegal trade in wildlife, which is a contributing factor to the extinction faced by many of the planet's species. Annually, hundreds of millions of non-human animals and plants are traded within the legal international trade (CITES 2012b), and woven into this fabric is the illegal trade estimated to be worth around US$10 billion for non-human animals (Fison 2011) and US$30 billion–100 billion for timber (Nelleman and Interpol Environmental Crime Programme 2012). This does not include the illegal trade in fish, which is a large and highly profitable black market.

Despite these focused national and international efforts of law enforcement and CITES, wildlife trafficking continues, and it could be argued that it is increasing. This is seen in the news coverage over the last several years. For instance, in 2009 BBC News reported on the 'global surge' in rhinoceros poaching, whereby hundreds of rhinos were poached in several African countries (BBC News 2009). A similar increase has been seen in the poaching of elephants, with hundreds of elephants each year being poached for their ivory (Hamlin 2011): as was reported at the time of writing this chapter, over 11,000 elephants have been killed in Gabon in eight years (Dabany 2013). These disturbing trends and the persistent facts that wildlife crime is not a mainstream crime and that the risks of detection and punishment for wildlife crime remain low (CITES 2011) seemed to have prompted CITES and the four other partners, detailed below, to undertake a targeted effort to decrease the incidents of wildlife crime. As stated in the document introducing and detailing ICCWC, these five partners bring a unique set of complementary skills and expertise that should enable ample support, and hopefully improvement, in the combat against wildlife crime undertaken by wildlife law enforcement agencies around the world (CITES 2011).

The ICCWC Partners

The ICCWC partners are a conglomeration of different types of organisations that inevitably have different missions and different objectives. As with any collaboration, particularly those that are large-scale and international, the dynamics between the organisations involved have a bearing on the project created. This is true of ICCWC as well, so it is important to establish the type and purpose of each organisation before exploring in more detail how ICCWC is working. The Environmental Crime Programme of Interpol aims to 'assist member countries in the effective enforcement of national and international environmental laws and treaties. Through this we can contribute to the on-going conservation of the world's environment, biodiversity and natural resources' (Environmental Crime Programme 2011, p. 2). To do this, the programme has set itself four strategic goals: (1) enhance and develop capacity, capability, and co-operation for effective enforcement of environmental laws; (2) encourage and assist in the exchange of environmental information and intelligence; (3) provide operational support in enforcing environmental laws, and (4) encourage and provide opportunities to network, communicate, and exchange skills related to environmental crime enforcement (Environmental Crime Programme 2011). Though not strictly a law enforcement agency, as it does not have arrest powers and so forth, Interpol's information exchange facilitates the sharing of intelligence, often confidential, about crimes and suspects. Gathering criminal intelligence and developing crime prevention programmes is a very particular mission that differs from some of the other partners of ICCWC.

The WCO's organisational purpose is similar to Interpol's, including a focus on law enforcement and compliance:

> the development of global standards, the simplification and harmonisation of Customs procedures, trade supply chain security, the facilitation of international trade, the enhancement of Customs enforcement and compliance activities, anti-counterfeiting and piracy initiatives, public-private partnerships, integrity promotion, and sustainable global Customs capacity building programmes. The WCO also maintains the international Harmonized System goods nomenclature, and administers the technical aspects of the WTO Agreements on Customs Valuation and Rules of Origin. (WCO 2014a)

So there is common ground between the WCO and Interpol in terms of illegal activities that take place at borders and violate criminal laws and customs regulations. This is certainly applicable with regard to ICCWC, as wildlife trafficking involves the smuggling of wildlife across borders or through customs. Yet, in addition to this, the WCO also works to facilitate trade and oversee implementation of the World Trade Organisation agreement, which again is about streamlining trade. Furthermore, the WCO's 'Customs enforcement is concerned with the protection of society and fighting trans-national organized crime based on the principles of risk management' (WCO 2014b). In order to do this, like Interpol's Environmental Crime Programme, the WCO facilitates the exchange and use of information and intelligence in relation to smuggling of wildlife, but also in relation to other black markets, such as cigarettes, drugs, and so on, which would fall into the remit of other divisions of Interpol. Much of the information the WCO is seeking is related to compliance with various trade conventions in addition to criminal violations.

The United Nations Office of Drugs and Crime's title might make it appear that it has much in common with Interpol and the WCO regarding its purpose and information gathering, but this is not the case. In essence, the UNODC is a research organisation that aims to improve the capacity and knowledge of UN member states to combat drugs, crime and terrorism. A particular emphasis of its work is the ratification and implementation of relevant international treaties and national legislation targeted at these areas, for instance the United Nations Convention against Transnational Organised Crime. This includes projects to expand the evidence base for policy and operations (UNODC 2012a). Primarily, it gathers data on an array of crimes, but focuses on drugs, terrorism, and organised crime.

The World Bank has a purpose that is again different to the partners previously described. It serves as a source of technical and financial support for developing nations, and creates and implements strategies to reduce poverty.[2] Its involvement in ICCWC is connected to the overlap between development, poverty, and poaching. This type of wildlife crime can be associated with inadequately designed or implemented environmental protection regimes in transitional or developing nations, which may then fail to protect wildlife. In addition, wildlife crime may be committed by impoverished people poaching or over-exploiting wildlife as a source of income and/or subsistence. The information the World Bank obtains from its projects therefore pertains to very different elements of society then the other partners. It tends to focus on the success of poverty reduction projects as well as information on grant recipients and financial services. There is an element of research to these activities as they relate to poverty and then knowledge transfer.

Finally, CITES aims 'to ensure that international trade in specimens of wild animals and plants does not threaten their survival' (CITES 2012b). Its approach to wildlife trafficking regards wildlife as a resource. As it is an international convention, the 178 member signatories adhere voluntarily to its regulations, such as the protection afforded to different species by listing them in one of the three Appendices, which limit trade depending upon whether the species are endangered or threatened. The information CITES gathers is not typically intelligence data related to crime. In fact, it predominantly covers population numbers of wildlife, scientific estimates of the amount of certain species that can be 'harvested', trade data, including quantities, units, import and export countries, and the purpose of transactions. As is evident, this differs substantially from a law enforcement-orientated mission, a research mission, and/or one that aims to reduce poverty. These differences translate into different expectations and objectives which may clash within a co-operative project such as ICCWC. With these differing missions in mind, the next section explores the online profile of ICCWC at each of the partners' websites, as well as detailing data from Interpol's Environmental Crime Programme that may give some indication of member states' engagement with wildlife trafficking and ICCWC.

ICCWC in Action

Information that reveals aspects of the various partners' engagement with ICCWC can be gathered by searching their websites to ascertain the number of press releases and other documents they have generated or posted about ICCWC. At the time of writing, CITES had the most coverage, with 239 separate entries mentioning ICCWC, ranging from documents from Standing Committee meetings to press coverage of major events like the Tiger Summits and the ICCWC launch, from film clips of the events to a job announcement for a post specifically created to co-ordinate ICCWC activities. The UNODC had 192 Web pages, which were quite similar to those of CITES in terms of content, which consisted of coverage of the ICCWC launch, the Tiger Summit that took place in February 2012, and the release of the UNODC's Wildlife and Forest Crime Analytic Toolkit, intended to provide a framework assisting government officials, customs, police officers, and others engaged in combating these crimes to analyse, prevent, and detect wildlife and forest offences (UNODC 2012b). In contrast, Interpol's Environmental Crime Programme had six Web pages, the WCO five, and the World Bank three. While the content again was similar – the ICCWC launch, the Tiger Summit in February 2012, and the UNODC toolkit, there was an evident difference in the level of engagement with ICCWC.

2 See www.worldbank.org/en/about (accessed 6 March 2014).

It is possible that this stems from the differing organisational missions of the partners discussed above. Wildlife crime is not the main focus of either the World Bank, the WCO, nor the UNODC. Yet, perhaps because the UNODC is a research organisation that seeks to increase the knowledge of its member states, it engaged in more outreach through its website, in this case resulting in more coverage of ICCWC. The World Bank has a multitude of other programmes to both manage and disseminate information from, so the fact that ICCWC falls outside its main priority areas may explain its limited coverage. The WCO and Interpol's Environmental Crime Programme websites focused on events that had taken place under the ICCWC banner – again, the ICCWC launch, the Tiger Summit, the UNODC toolkit – but also covered workshops on how law enforcement officers can conduct controlled deliveries of wildlife products to catch wildlife criminals. The fact that there have been very few events actually labelled with ICCWC's involvement may explain the apparently low engagement by the WCO and Interpol's Environmental Crime Programme, as their coverage is a direct reflection of the activities undertaken. In addition, their law enforcement orientation may explain their different approaches to public presence and outreach, resulting in websites that are concerned with raising awareness among the general public. More dissemination of ICCWC information may occur more directly with members of the WCO, though this is not the case with Interpol's Environmental Crime Programme (personal communication). CITES is unique in this partnership, as its focus is solely on wildlife, and this inevitably leads to a pronounced concern with wildlife crime. This may explain why CITES is the most vocal, at least on its website, about ICCWC.

As mentioned above, up to February 2013, when data collection stopped for this chapter, only a few activities had taken place in connection with ICCWC. In fact, just four notable events had occurred in the two years of ICCWC's existence: the aforementioned Tiger Summit in February 2012; the creation and dissemination of UNODC's toolkit; the controlled delivery workshop, and CITES also hosted a workshop discussing rhinoceros poaching. It is difficult to say whether four events in two years is a sufficient or effective number of activities to raise awareness of wildlife crime. Almost certainly, member nations of these different partners are hearing about wildlife crime in other capacities. Yet to make an impact on increasing awareness and promoting the importance of wildlife crime, it could be argued that ICCWC needs to increase its efforts beyond reaching out only twice a year. This may possibly come about in the future with changes to ICCWC's funding. While ICCWC has drawn interest in terms of possible funders from the US Fish and Wildlife Service, the US State Department, the Environmental Investigation Agency, the World Bank, the International Fund for Animal Welfare, TRAFFIC, the World Wide Fund for Nature, and the UK's Department of Environment, Food and Rural Affairs (personal communication), the European Commission has allocated €1.73 million to Interpol over the three years from 2012 onwards to support ICCWC (European Commission 2012). In addition, ICCWC was on the agenda multiple times at the March 2013 CITES Conference of the Parties meeting, and several other events are currently in the planning stages (personal communication from CITES), which indicates an increase in future activity.

Findings

Interview and Questionnaire Responses

As Interpol is the main focus of centralised communication for law enforcement worldwide, especially its Environmental Crime Programme in terms of wildlife crime, staff from Interpol's Environmental Crime Programme were interviewed to gauge the possibility that law enforcement agencies were growing increasingly aware of wildlife crime, so it might be becoming a more mainstream crime. They were asked whether, after the launch of ICCWC, they witnessed an increase of engagement with wildlife crime from member countries. This would be in the form of direct contact with their unit or through what are called 'Ecomessages' directed through the members' in-country Interpol National Central Bureaux to Interpol headquarters and then to the Environment Crime Programme (Interpol 2013). Initially, their impression was that Ecomessages had not increased in relation to ICCWC (personal communication). The number of Ecomessages did increase during 2006–10 by approximately 20 per cent, then rose again during 2010–11 by about 25 per cent (personal communication). From 2011 to July 2012, the number of Ecomessages declined, which is probably attributable to a change in the way the intelligence is managed rather than a decrease in engagement with law enforcement members (personal communication). However, while the number of Ecomessages had increased, staff felt this was not specifically or directly connected to ICCWC. Member countries also contact Interpol about wildlife and other green crimes through standard intelligence channels rather than via Ecomessages. It was estimated that around 100 information reports were received by the Environmental Crime Programme in 2010, and the number had risen to over 300 at time of writing (personal communication). Although this increase coincided with ICCWC's launch, again there was no indication that the two were directly related.

There are a number of factors that limit the conclusions that can be drawn from this information. First, it is standard practice for Interpol not to give specific statistics on this sort of information in terms of the number of messages per month, the country contacting it, or more specific details of incidents. This is because Interpol is not technically the 'owner' of the information (personal communication). It has not obtained permission from the source of the information to share it with third parties (personal communication). There are also presumably security and confidentiality concerns regarding ongoing investigations. In order to obtain more specific data about the level of contact between countries and Interpol about wildlife crime, or any crime, it would be necessary to contact each country individually. Secondly, there is no way to link ICCWC activities to the increase in the number of Ecomessages or reports, as the Environmental Crime Programme and all the other ICCWC partners engage in projects that are not related to ICCWC, but may deal with wildlife crime. Thirdly, member countries are also involved with non-governmental organisations and inter-governmental programmes to combat wildlife trafficking, so those may also be increasing their awareness.

In general, interviewees tended to think that ICCWC had been limited in its effectiveness so far as it had not undertaken very many activities (personal communications). This could be attributed to the growing pains of a new project and partners learning to work with one another at the more senior levels within the organisations (personal communication). It could also be that other similar co-operative efforts have taken up partners' time or have not achieved their intended aims, such as the Green Customs Initiative (personal communication). This initiative began in 2004, and was designed as 'an unprecedented partnership of international organisations cooperating to prevent the illegal trade in environmentally-sensitive commodities and the facilitation of trade in these' (Green Customs n.d.). It, too, seeks to improve the capacity of customs and related enforcement agencies to detect and prevent illegal trading of wildlife, but also other environmental black markets (Green Customs n.d.). All partners in ICCWC except for the World Bank are involved, so it could be argued that the organisations have spread themselves too thinly and have been duplicating efforts. If these attempts at co-operation are repeatedly unsuccessful or undertaken half-heartedly, this will affect the enthusiasm and level of engagement of the partners involved because of distrust and concerns about the other agencies' level of commitment. At the operational level for the partners involved, ICCWC is not particularly relevant (personal communication). Individuals from each of the partner agencies have always worked together and will continue to do so regardless of programmes like ICCWC when assisting each other with seizures, for instance, and sharing intelligence (personal communication).

While ICCWC as yet may have had limited impact on member country engagement with wildlife trafficking, CITES indicated that there is evidence of more high-level international awareness of this green crime (personal communication). This is seen in discussions at UN Security Council Meetings and other UN bodies such as the Commission on Crime Prevention and Criminal Justice, where wildlife trafficking has been recognised as a serious organised crime and ICCWC has been encouraged to continue its efforts to combat it (personal communication from CITES).

ICCWC is designed in the medium and long term to increase awareness of wildlife trafficking and bring it more into the mainstream. The discussion above shows that the actions undertaken under the ICCWC banner so far have been limited, but are showing clear signs of progress and commitment to continue the efforts. There is awareness on the part of Interpol's Environmental Crime Programme of ICCWC's potential to improve and a willingness to make this happen (personal communication). There is some indication that wildlife crime awareness among law enforcement organisations may be growing, evidenced by the increase in the number of Ecomessages and reports received by the Environmental Crime Programme. While this cannot be directly correlated to ICCWC, it is a small piece of evidence that the aims of ICCWC are being realised. Part of making wildlife crime more mainstream involves making it part of the global consciousness, and there are indications of this in the discussions taking place at the UN.

Another way to gauge increased global consciousness of wildlife trafficking is to assess the issue's newsworthiness by examining media coverage. The next section outlines the findings from the content analysis of the newspaper articles collected for this study.

ICCWC and Wildlife Trafficking in the Media

The Media Coverage

The LexisNexis newspaper archive searches identified nearly 1,400 articles of interest between July 2002 and July 2012. When looking at full calendar years during 2003–11, the level of news media coverage was consistently around 100 articles during 2003–8, with a noticeable dip in 2009, then a doubling in coverage in 2010, followed by an increase of nearly 50 per cent in 2011 (see Figure 17.1). Again, we should bear in mind that ICCWC was launched in November 2010.

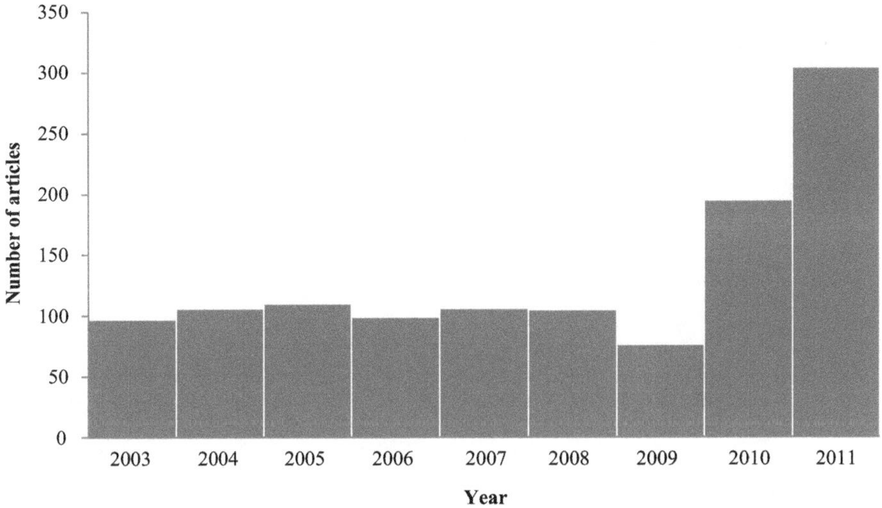

Figure 17.1 Illegal wildlife trade in the world news, 2003–11

Looking more closely at the period around when ICCWC came into being, it can be seen that news coverage in 2009, the year with the least frequent coverage in this sample, consisted of less than 15 articles per month, with both March and October having only one article in the global media about wildlife trafficking (see Figure 17.2). The year 2010 also started off with low coverage, but this was not repeated to the same degree after February 2010. The lowest numbers of articles were in December 2010 (seven articles), and April and May 2010 (nine articles). The average number of articles per month from

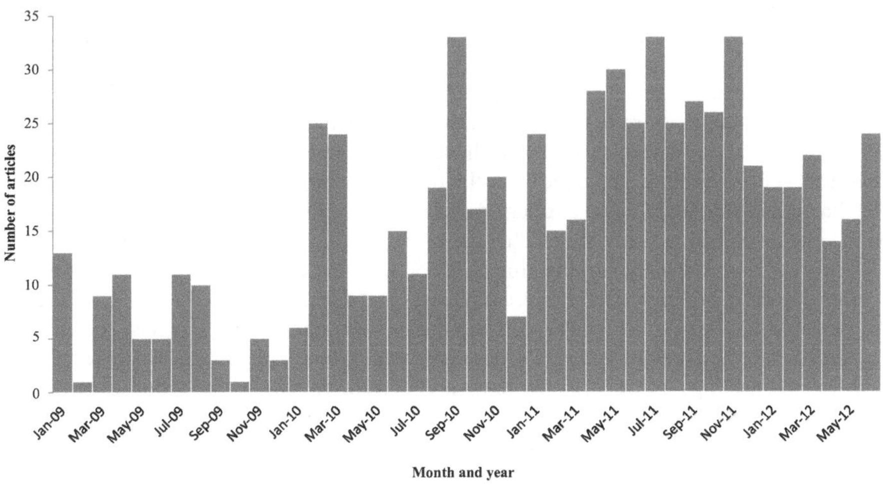

Figure 17.2 Illegal wildlife trade in the world news, January 2009–June 2012

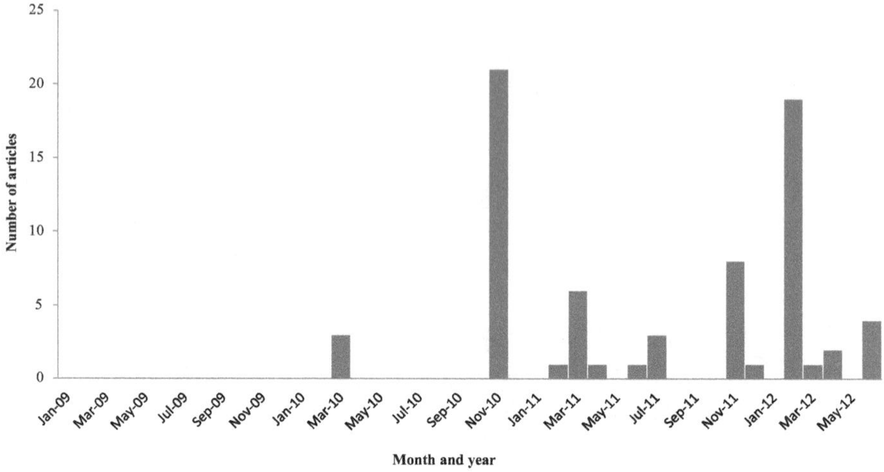

Figure 17.3 ICCWC in the world news, January 2009–June 2012

January 2009 to June 2012 (the last complete month of data) was 16.4. The year preceding the introduction of ICCWC (November 2009–October 2010) had an average of 14.7 articles per month. After the introduction of ICCWC (December 2010–November 2011), the monthly average was 24.1. This might indicate that ICCWC may have had some initial impact on the increase in coverage.

Also of interest is how much press coverage ICCWC itself received, and the search results show that this was limited (see Figure 17.3). The earliest mentions of ICCWC are a few articles in March 2010 announcing that a co-operative project to combat wildlife crime would be launched later in the year. Most of the reporting then coincided with its launch (21 articles) and the Tiger Summit in Bangkok in February 2012 (19 articles). In other months, there were occasional mentions of it. The reports on ICCWC were in addition to those on the illegal wildlife trade.

Further content analysis of the sample of articles reveals connections between the news coverage and the press releases at the partners' websites. In particular, the coverage of ICCWC by the news media appears to have been prompted by press releases from the partner agencies. This is apparent from the date of reporting and the quotes in the news media taken from the ICCWC partners' press releases. That is not to say that this was not impactful or influential, only to note that there was a clear engagement by the partners with the media. This is mostly coming from CITES, then the UNODC, which, as mentioned earlier, are more prolific in terms of press releases and documentation of ICCWC according to the websites survey. Press releases from the partners about other projects, such as law enforcement operations by Interpol's Environmental Crime Programme or Conference of the Parties meetings by CITES, also feature within the sample. Other wildlife trafficking news media coverage appeared to be self-generated: researched by a journalist rather than the journalist being given material to report on. These often stemmed from a particularly dramatic poaching incident or a major seizure by a police agency.

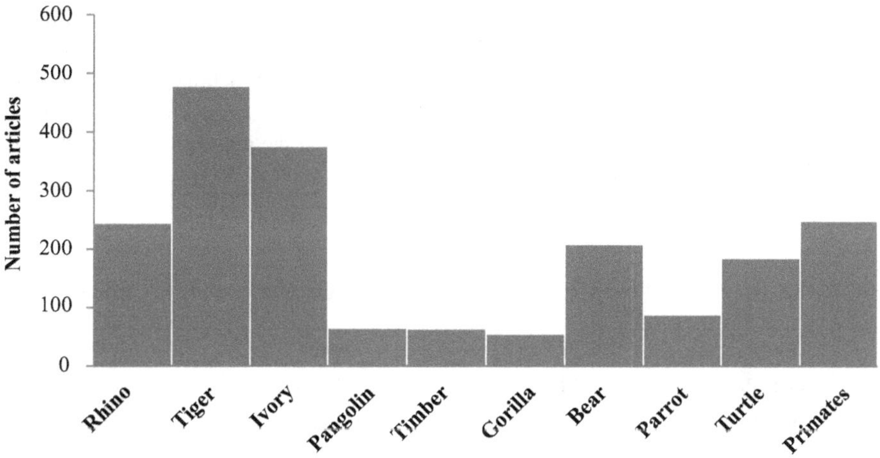

Figure 17.4 Trafficked wildlife in the world news, July 2002–July 2012

The Species and the Countries in the Media

Now that the trends of wildlife trafficking coverage in the media and the type of reporting have been discussed, it is interesting to note the species that receive media coverage as well as the location of the reporting and the places that are being reported on. As would be expected, the so-called 'charismatic' mega-fauna receive the most newspaper coverage.

The majority of articles (24 per cent) concerning wildlife trafficking or wildlife trade discussed the tiger. These queries were run through Nvivo using only frequency. This means that one article may be counted more than once if it refers to multiple species (that is, the same article may be counted under 'tiger' and 'elephant'). This explains why the number of articles in Figure 17.4 exceeds the total sample number. In addition, this is not a comprehensive list of the species mentioned, but merely an indication of those discussed most frequently. Tigers were followed by elephants, primates, rhinoceros, and bears, in descending order of frequency. Turtles also received some coverage, as did parrots, pangolins, and to a lesser degree gorillas, though the latter might also feature in the articles concerning primates. Timber was reported on the least of those species queried (see Figure 17.4).

Of further interest is where is the news media coverage was coming from and which countries or regions of the world were being discussed in the context of wildlife trafficking. Not every country was queried, and with the global profile of many media organisations, it was not always possible to link a particular country with a specific article. That being said, some indications can be gleaned as to which countries were reporting on wildlife trafficking, which means there is also information on those who were not. The country with the most coverage was the United States, which is most likely connected to its population size of over 300 million people and to the nearly 1,400 daily newspapers that exist there (Newspaper Association of America 2012). The total number of US articles over the ten-year period of this study was 289 (see Table 17.1). This was followed by the United Kingdom with 204 articles. Proportionally, it would seem this indicates greater coverage, considering the UK's population is smaller at around 63 million, although the UK has more newspapers. Media UK has a database of 1,592 newspapers in the UK.[3] Australian newspapers carried 113 articles about wildlife trafficking, and Canadian newspapers 104. The next country ranked by the number of articles was Malaysia (75), followed by Singapore (54), and Thailand (50). There was also coverage in Africa, as South African newspapers ran 49 articles. Therefore, although the West may have had the most coverage of wildlife trafficking, other regions of the world were also reporting on it. Missing from the list of more substantial coverage, though, was China, which had only 17 articles.

Table 17.1 Selected countries' newspapers reporting about wildlife trafficking

Country	No. of articles	Country	No. of articles
Australia	113	**Malaysia**	75
Botswana	0	**Mexico**	4
Brazil	0	**Nepal**	15
Cambodia	2	**New Zealand**	15
Cameroon	1	**Singapore**	54
Canada	104	**South Africa**	49
China	17	**Tanzania**	0
France	16	**Thailand**	50
Germany	2	**UAE**	13
India	27	**UK**	204
Indonesia	0	**US**	289
Ireland	4	**Vietnam**	0
Kenya	0		

However, it is possible that even though LexisNexis was searching all languages, the concepts of wildlife trafficking and wildlife trade may not translate readily, so it is possible that it was being covered in different contexts in those countries in this sample that appear not to engage with the topic. What is apparent, however, is that in the sample generated here, China was mentioned in 395 articles as being connected to wildlife trafficking (see Table 17.2). This is significantly more than any other country, the next being Thailand (275), followed by India (224). In reviewing the articles where these countries are mentioned, it is clear that these three countries are referred to in the context of being the drivers of wildlife crime in the case of China, and the origins of the wildlife in the case of Thailand and India, though Thailand is a driver to a lesser degree. Queries were not undertaken for the US or the EU simply because there would be too many search variables (countries and major cities) to capture a complete picture of those particular areas' connection to wildlife trafficking in this context. It is interesting, though, that Australia was mentioned fairly often (190 articles). While this may be partly because Australia is an origin country of trafficked species such as birds, it is more that the coverage discusses the measures taken to protect its wildlife and Australia's involvement in international efforts to curb global wildlife trafficking.

3 See www.mediauk.com/.

Table 17.2 Selected countries correlated to wildlife trafficking in the world news

Country	No. of articles	Country	No. of articles
Australia	190	**Malaysia**	207
Botswana	17	**Mexico**	49
Brazil	58	**Nepal**	104
Cambodia	88	**New Zealand**	38
Cameroon	46	**Singapore**	119
China	395	**South Africa**	133
Congo	52	**Tanzania**	35
India	224	**Thailand**	275
Indonesia	187	**Vietnam**	170
Kenya	69		

Having outlined all the data, the next section will discuss what this means for ICCWC and the increase in awareness of wildlife crime.

Discussion and Conclusion

It could be argued that only four events over the course of two years is not enough to make a difference or meet the goals ICCWC has set itself. Of concern as well as is the apparently skewed nature of partner engagement with ICCWC, where CITES and the UNODC generate substantial documentation which reveals discussions with ICCWC at regular meetings, while the other partners have limited coverage of the same project, only discussing a few events. As indicated above, this may be due to the organisations coming to terms with how ICCWC would work in reality, so it could simply be an indication of a slow start. There is evidence to support this in the numerous ICCWC events in the planning stages and others that have since taken place, such as the March 2013 CITES meeting (personal communication from CITES). In addition, a substantial €1.73 million influx of funding for the three years from 2012 onwards may increase activities. Despite this possible negative first impression, data from Interpol's Environmental Crime Programme, while scant, shows that the numbers of Ecomessages and reports have increased, which could indicate an increase in awareness and therefore the possibility that wildlife crime is becoming more mainstream in members' law enforcement agencies. Of some concern is the fact that on certain levels ICCWC seems to be replicating other activities, such as the Green Customs Initiative. Hopefully, though, with a clear source of funding, ICCWC can organise events in addition to those its partners take part in through other collaborative efforts. From the interviewee responses, it seems that ICCWC's best avenue to generate impact is for its senior managers to overcome their reservations and develop more joint operations that draw on the many strengths of its various partners.

The prospects of success in increasing awareness are further supported by an exploration of the media coverage of wildlife crime around the time of ICCWC's launch. While, as acknowledged above, there are limitations to this study, the analysis has value since as is known that the media play a crucial role in how environmental crimes – in this case, wildlife trafficking – are perceived (Jarrell 2009) and whether they receive attention. Exploring the media connections to ICCWC has given us some indications of how wildlife trafficking is being conceptualised on a global scale as well as the apparent importance of this type of crime to the public. In turn, this allowed exploration of whether efforts such as ICCWC's are making the difference they intended. There is a possibility that ICCWC is helping to raise awareness of wildlife crime. The content analysis of the sample of world news coverage shows that wildlife crime articles were reported upon with more regularity than before the launch of ICCWC. Admittedly, there is no way to definitively connect the two, but this provides a basis for further examination. The mega-fauna receive the most coverage, and this may be useful to know, as efforts can be made to increase the awareness and concern over the exploitation of other species that are threatened but currently overlooked. The media coverage was shown to be centred in certain regions of the world, and this too may be helpful in revealing where to target campaigns to increase awareness. This seemed to particularly be the case in parts of Africa and South America. The lack of coverage may not only indicate a lack of awareness, but also a need to improve or create the media apparatus itself. This is important, as a majority of the regions outside the West, where coverage is highest, are victimised by this wildlife crime as they are the centres for biodiversity. Therefore, in addition to uncovering concern over wildlife trafficking, assessing the media coverage in certain areas also exposes the possible need to develop media, not only to help to combat green crimes, but other crimes and human rights violations as well.

Wildlife trafficking is a multi-billion-euro black market that involves hundreds of millions of plants and non-human animals annually (Fison 2011; CITES 2012b). This has finally begun to gain the attention of academics and law enforcement communities, who are collaborating with environmental and conservation non-governmental organisations to develop strategies to reduce this violent, environmentally destructive green crime. Key to this is raising global awareness of the prevalence and impact of wildlife trafficking, and co-ordinating law enforcement operations, which is the aim of the International Consortium on Combating Wildlife Crime discussed in this chapter. While there is no concrete evidence to suggest that in the brief term of its existence ICCWC has succeeded in increasing the awareness of wildlife crime or making it more mainstream, there are indications that these are taking place, albeit on a small scale so far. With increased funding and the commitment of dedicated agencies and people, ICCWC is a collaboration worthy of continued observation and exploration, as it may yet prove to have significant impact.

References

BBC News. 2009. '"Global Surge" in Rhino Poaching', 1 December: http://news.bbc.co.uk/2/hi/science/nature/8388606.stm (accessed 16 October 2013).

CITES. 2011. 'Information Note: The International Consortium on Combating Wildlife Crime': www.cites.org/eng/prog/iccwc.php (accessed 6 March 2014).

CITES. 2012a. 'ICCWC Launches Wildlife and Forest Crime Toolkit': www.cites.org/eng/news/pr/2012/20120725_ICCWC_toolkit.php (accessed 6 March 2014).

CITES. 2012b. 'What is CITES?': www.cites.org/eng/disc/what.php (accessed 6 March 2014).

Dabany, J.R. 2013. 'Gabon Elephant Poaching: More than 11,000 Animals Killed in Minkebe National Park since 2004', *Huffington Post*, 2 June: www.huffingtonpost.com/2013/02/06/gabon-elephant-poaching_n_2629267.html (accessed 16 October 2013).

De Klemm, C. 1993. *Biological Diversity Conservation and the Law: Legal Mechanisms for Conserving Species and Ecosystems*. Cambridge: International Union for Conservation of Nature and Natural Resources.

Environmental Crime Programme. 2011. *Strategic Plan 2011–2013*. Lyon: Interpol.

European Commission. 2012. 'Environment: Funding to Boost INTERPOL Fight Against Wildlife Crime', 21 December: http://europa.eu/rapid/press-release_IP-12-1428_en.htm?locale=en (accessed 16 October 2013).

Fison, M. 2011. 'The £6bn Trade in Animal Smuggling', *The Independent*, 6 March: www.independent.co.uk/environment/nature/the-1636bn-trade-in-animal-smuggling-2233608.html (accessed 16 October 2013).

Green Customs. n.d. 'About Green Customs': www.greencustoms.org/background (accessed 6 March 2014).

Hamlin, D. 2011. 'Elephant Pictures: Killed Female Highlights Poaching Rise', *National Geographic Daily News*: http://news.nationalgeographic.com/news/2011/08/pictures/110817-elephant-poaching-samburu-reserve-khadija-kenya/ (accessed 6 March 2014).

Interpol. 2013. 'Ecomessage': www.interpol.int/Crime-areas/Environmental-crime/Ecomessage (accessed 6 March 2014).

Jarrell, M.L. 2009. 'Environmental Crime and Injustice: Media Coverage of a Landmark Environmental Crime', *Southwest Journal of Criminal Justice* 6(1), 25–44.

Lyster, S. 1985. *International Wildlife Law: An Analysis of International Treaties Concerned with the Conservation of Wildlife*. Llandysul: Gomer Press.

Nellemann, C. and Interpol Environmental Crime Programme, eds. 2012. *Green Carbon, Black Trade: Illegal Logging, Tax Fraud and Laundering in the Worlds Tropical Forests. A Rapid Response Assessment*. Arendal, Norway: United Nations Environment Programme, GRID-Arendal.

Newspaper Association of America. 2012. 'Newspaper Circulation Volume': www.naa.org/Trends-and-Numbers/Circulation-Volume/Newspaper-Circulation-Volume.aspx (accessed 6 March 2014).

UNODC. 2012a. 'About UNODC': www.unodc.org/unodc/en/about-unodc/index.html?ref=menutop (accessed 6 March 2014).

UNODC. 2012b. 'ICCWC Launches Wildlife and Forest Crime Toolkit': www.unodc.org/unodc/en/frontpage/2012/July/iccwc-launches-wildlife-and-forest-crime-toolkit.html?ref=fs4 (accessed 6 March 2014).

WCO. 2014a. 'About Us': www3.wcoomd.org/home_about_us.htm (accessed 6 March 2014)

WCO. 2014b, 'Overview': www.wcoomd.org/en/topics/enforcement-and-compliance/overview.aspx (accessed 6 March 2014).

Index

Page numbers in **bold** refer to figures and tables. EC in subentries means Environmental Crime.

FSC
www.fsc.org
MIX
Papier | Fördert gute Waldnutzung
FSC® C083411

Kolibri 360 GmbH
Ferdinand-Jühlke-Straße 7
99095 Erfurt, Deutschland
produktsicherheit@kolibri360.de